Archaeology yesterday and today

Archaeology yesterday and today

The development of archaeology in the
sciences and humanities

JAROSLAV MALINA & ZDENĚK VAŠÍČEK

Translated and edited by Marek Zvelebil

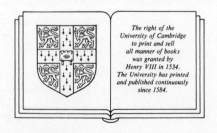

The right of the
University of Cambridge
to print and sell
all manner of books
was granted by
Henry VIII in 1534.
The University has printed
and published continuously
since 1584.

CAMBRIDGE UNIVERSITY PRESS
Cambridge
New York   Port Chester   Melbourne   Sydney

Published by the Press Syndicate of the University of Cambridge
The Pitt Building, Trumpington Street, Cambridge CB2 1RP
40 West 20th Street, New York, NY 10011, USA
10 Stamford Street Road, Oakleigh, Melbourne 3166, Australia

First published in English by Cambridge University Press 1990 as *Archaeology
yesterday and today. The development of archaeology in the sciences and humanities*

Printed in Great Britain by Redwood Press Limited, Melksham, Wiltshire

British Library cataloguing in publication data

Vašíček, Zdeněk
Archaeology yesterday and today: the development of archaeology in the sciences
and humanities.
1. Archaeology, history
I. Title II. Malina, Jaroslav
III. Zvelebil, Marek
IV. Archeologie včera a dnes. *English*
930.1'09

Library of Congress cataloguing in publication data

Vašíček, Zdeněk
[Archeologie včera a dnes aneb Mají archeologové šedé hmoty více za nehty než za
ušima? English]
Archaeology yesterday and today: the development of archaeology in the sciences
and humanities / Zdeněk Vašíček and Jaroslav Malina; translated and edited by
Marek Zvelebil.
    p.   cm.
Translation of: Archeologie včera a dnes aneb Mají archeologové šedé hmoty více za
nehty než za ušima?
Includes index.
ISBN 0–521–26621–1. – ISBN 0–521–31977–3 (paperback)
1. Archaeology – History. I. Malina. Jaroslav. II. Zvelebil, Marek. III. Title.
CC100.V3313 1990
930.1–dc20   89–35776
                                                                              CIP

ISBN 0 521 26621 1 hard covers
ISBN 0 521 31977 3 paperback

CE

To Judith

Zdeněk Vašíček wishes to thank R. Derricourt, M. Edgeworth, A. Harding, I. Hodder and R. Sharman for valuable advice and words of encouragement, as well as King's College, Cambridge, for its hospitality.

Contents

Foreword

by A. F. Harding

The appearance of a book on archaeological history and theory is today nothing unusual. Every year brings a considerable crop of these works, which the leading archaeological publishers in Britain and the United States have been promoting vigorously for some twenty years. It is a notable fact, however, that the vast majority of these works have been written by Americans, a few by British authors and other Anglophones (mainly edited conference volumes), and a few by those scholars from other countries who feel at home in the Anglo-Saxon world, notably the Scandinavians and the Dutch. There have been a few theoretical volumes in French (Gardin 1979, Courbin 1982, Gallay 1986), but apart from a long article by Manfred Eggert (1978) virtually nothing of book length in the main archaeological language of Central Europe, German. The socialist countries, especially Poland, have been more active in this field than is commonly realised in the West, but little of this has found a readership outside its homeland, a state of affairs for which problems of language are naturally much to blame. It comes as a great change, then, to see a theoretical book on archaeology by two Czech scholars, and in an English translation, though it would be wrong to imagine that this is the only theoretical work recently emanating from that country (see Neustupný 1983). *Archaeology Yesterday and Today* is, however, in many ways an unusual creation, even for its homeland, and a few words of explanation are in order.

The book falls into three quite distinct parts: the first, chapters 1 to 4, is a critical account of the development of the subject that we call archaeology from its perceived earliest beginnings in the works of the Greek philosophers up to the middle of the twentieth century. Chapter 5 is a discussion of more recent developments, from the last war up to the present, including trends of the sixties and seventies as represented by the work of 'New Archaeologists'. The third part, chapters 6–7, is a theoretical discussion of

the intellectual and conceptual framework of archaeology, and though it
draws on the work of many previous writers, is different in form and tone
from most discussions of such matters that one can find today emanating
from the Anglo-American sphere.

The authors' aim has been to write a new history of archaeology, and to
combine it with an overview of the subject with which the baffled student
can orientate himself. They believe this to be especially important at a time
when 'Anglo-Saxon' (i.e. Anglo-American) and 'Continental' (i.e. European) archaeology know little about each other. They believe the work will
point to a wider range of possibilities than most archaeologists currently
recognise; will promote understanding between the various schools and
factions of the subject; and set archaeology in the context of the wider scene
of human intellectual endeavour.

Malina and Vašíček believe that archaeology's area of interest is represented by the gradual changes in human behaviour that arise unintentionally, unconsciously, even by chance when behaviour is reproduced.
These are the changes typically seen in the development of artefacts and
technological operations when they are tending towards a particular
functional optimum; or changes typical for human behaviour over long
spans of time (see the longue durée approach of the French Annalistes).

This concern with hypotheses stems from a desire to seek the specific
forms of prehistoric development that influence the form and content of
hypotheses: those of communication and organisation. They are also
dependent on the form and nature of our picture of the past, i.e. they will
differ according to whether we emphasise continuity or synchronicity,
large or small spans of time, large or small spatial areas, and so on. In the
authors' opinion, archaeology tries to create synthetic pictures of the past
events, just as a description of artefacts is not a copy of them. An
archaeological synthesis supposes a certain pattern to the whole, the
description of which has its own rules that the archaeologist must be aware
of, just as he must know the rules for describing artefacts.

Unlike many previous writers, Malina and Vašíček draw on a quite
exceptionally wide field of human endeavour to support their discussion.
The range of literature cited is enormous, and it comes from philosophy,
history and historiography, sociology, anthropology, and the history of
science. This makes the discussion quite different from that provided by
most previous historians of archaeology, for example Karel Sklenář, a
fellow Czech, who has provided us with a useful book (1983) summarising
the main developments in the history of archaeology in Central Europe.
The works of Glyn Daniel, which are more familiar to a British readership,

point to many intellectual predecessors for the nineteenth-century scientists and investigators whom we now regard as the originators of the modern discipline of archaeology, but they are concerned with that ancestry as a matter of fact, of genealogy, of chronology. Malina and Vašíček, on the other hand, are concerned to point to broad trends of thought at particular periods of the past, not merely to detect the 'backward-looking curiosity' but to analyse it, to determine its cultural and intellectual milieu and its implications for the study of the past. This they have been able to achieve by encyclopedic reading, seemingly in all fields of the humanities and social sciences, in all the main European languages including Russian, and over a long period – the more remarkable when one considers the difficulties of obtaining access to books in the circumstances in which both Malina and Vašíček have found themselves over the last twenty years.

This means that the view of archaeology presented here is not the same as, or even very similar to, the prevailing perspective in the West. It is true that one would be hard put to tie a common label on all Western archaeologists, in an era of structural, processual, post-processual, neo-functionalist, and many other kinds of archaeologists. But the attitude to the raw data of archaeology tends to be similar between archaeologists of widely differing conceptual persuasions, so that a common concern with the potential of the data, of manipulation by various means, statistical or other, links us all, in the belief that while archaeological facts are artefacts, higher-order statements can only be made by the drawing of inferences. Many people do not realise that these perceptions are not widely shared in Central Europe. Let us leave aside the implications of practising archae-ology in a Marxist state, where on the one hand archaeology is expected to be relevant to the daily concerns of the masses, and on the other it is expected to take into account those few indications that the founders of the Marxist canon provided for the proper orientation of the discipline. It is rather the widespread feeling that the aim of archaeology is to write a kind of history that is so striking, the belief that only differences of scale, or period, or detail separate archaeology from history, and that no worthwhile reconstruction of the past is possible unless it attempts to be history. Some of the main differences in these national schools of archaeology have been examined in a recent volume of *World Archaeology* (vol. 13, Nos. 2–3, 1981; see Trigger 1984b).

There have, of course, been criticisms of many aspects of the 'New Archaeology', some constructive, or at any rate formulated because the author's perspective was different (e.g. those by Ian Hodder); and some entirely destructive, reactionary and showing a complete lack of understanding that archaeology even has a problem to overcome (e.g. Courbin 1982). The present account is critical in many respects, but it is written in such a disarmingly modest and readable way, free from jargon yet addressing itself to central theoretical problems of the discipline, that it hardly seems like criticism. Although the dramatic language utilised to describe the birth of New Archaeology, that of confrontation and war, is unaccustomed, one can appreciate how it might have seemed to dispassionate observers on the outside looking in. Would that more New Archaeologists were as self-critical, as frank in assessing their own intellectual leanings.

This book, however, does not pretend to comprise a complete résumé of all that New Archaeology has striven for. It draws on the work of New Archaeology only as far as is thought to be necessary to provide a picture of where it falls in intellectual terms. Its main areas of originality lie rather in its detailed work on classification and description, and in its assessment of the intellectual ancestry and present-day place of archaeology. It aims to treat all types of archaeology and archaeologist even-handedly; the contrasting pictures of archaeology in the USSR and the United States provide a striking example, and one which few, except perhaps Leo S. Klejn, could have adequately discussed. If it brings about a greater international understanding of and agreement on the nature of our discipline through this one thing alone, its authors will be happy; but it has the potential to strike chords in all sorts and conditions of archaeological practitioners.

1   The search for *arche*

The same I am, ere ancient'st order was,
Or what is now received: I witness to
The times that brought them in, so shall I do
To th' freshest things now reigning, and make stale
The glistering of this present, as my tale
Now seems to it ... Your patience this allowing,
I turn my glass.

Shakespeare, *The Winter's Tale*

To us human beings the passage of winter into spring is imperceptible. But for nature it is a time of rebirth: she comes alive. A similar air of anticipation must have pervaded the world two and a half thousand years ago. Separated by enormous distances and independent of one another, the great men of the Old World – Lao Zi and Confucius in the loess plains of China, Buddha under the burning sun of India, Zarathustra in the endless mountain ranges of Iran and the prophets of the Old Testament on the shores of the Dead Sea – all initiated a new epoch in the development of mankind. The Greek miracle, whose offspring was one day to be the European and Atlantic civilisation, was beginning to take shape in the eastern Mediterranean.

Until that time, the world had the likeness of a myth, the activities of men were subordinated to mythical patterns and mythology represented almost the entire body of human knowledge.

But these men brought changes. Even though their thinking was influenced by myths, these myths could no longer encompass new thoughts. Thus, theoretical thinking, which could comprehend society and nature in an entirely new way, and which was capable of examining its own assumptions, came into existence. The teaching of each of the thinkers became a cognitive basis which attracted at first isolated followers, then an entire nation. Supplemented later by Christianity and Islam, these systems of thought became the foundations for the principal social systems of the world. Societies still in existence keep returning time and again to their fundamental sources, which issued forth during that remarkable period two and a half thousand years ago. In this way, the fifth century BC marks the end of the mythical era and the beginning of the history of mankind; it marks the beginning of a whole range of cultures and traditions of which we are the heirs. Appropriately, Karl Jaspers has called this period the 'Achsenzeit' (Jaspers 1966).

It was during this time in ancient Greece that concepts such as archaeology, history and philosophy originated within the context of the new pattern of thought which was then forming. Originally, these terms had a different meaning from those of today.

Let us begin with the notion of history. As every schoolchild knows, it was used for the first time by the 'father of history', Herodotus, in the title of his book *Historias Apodeixis*, in the sense of investigation and research in general. Subsequently, Aristotle defined the term more precisely as the investigation of all empirical events which can be observed through personal experience or traced through reports. Such a definition still manages to include all past events experienced or reported and, further, most of biology and geography. As the ancient Greeks gathered information about these subjects, mostly in the form of reports about distant lands, foreign peoples and curious natural events, the need arose for a more discrete categorisation.

Pliny's *Naturalis Historia* does not describe the history of nature, but talks about the curiosities of nature, and this approach persisted well into the modern age. For Francis Bacon, *historia naturalis* remained a descriptive account, the investigation of causes of natural events being left to the realm of theoretical sciences: physics. It was only in 1575 that J. Lipsius drew a distinction between *historia naturalis* and *historia narrativa*. Gottfried Leibnitz, writing around 1694, still included universal history, geography, antiquities, philology and history of literature all as a part of 'histoire humaine'.

In the past, therefore, history did not cover the same range of phenomena as today. Aristotle considered history in its chronological sense merely as a chain of political and military events. It did not occur to him that history could have a value of its own. Nevertheless, historical processes were becoming a part of political life among the Greeks just at this time (Meier 1973). The public administration of the Greek *polis* included contacts, through commerce, with other Greek settlements, as well as with barbarians abroad, and this made the compilation and organisation of historical and geographical facts an indispensable condition for responsible government. Furthermore, the development of abstract social relations liberated the arts from the constraints of religious activity and isolated beauty as a special, independent value. Similarly, the concept of good was divorced from its immediate societal context. In this way, Greek democracy became the basic condition of Greek history. Consequently all empirical knowledge was quite naturally recorded as history.

Theoretical knowledge, on the other hand, was delineated as philosophy, which was held to encompass all theory. This left one remaining class of phenomena: empirical events which are inaccessible to our immediate experience and which did not leave any personal records. This gap was filled by archaeology. In *Hippias Major*, Plato described archaeology as a science concerned with the most remote past, referring to it as 'pleasant fairy tales of old grandmothers' (285d).

In the view of the ancients, archaeology, if it was to have any value, constituted a chronological extension of history. As a result, early writers considered the more remote historical events as archaeology. This was the case, for instance, in *Biblioteke Historike* of the Greek historian Diodorus of Siculus, writing in the first century BC, or in the work *Romaike Archaiologia of Dionysius of Halicarnassus*, describing the origins of Rome. Archaeology remained a somewhat questionable extension of the historical past until the end of the eighteenth century, when Immanuel Kant described his nebular hypothesis about the origin of the solar system as the 'archaeology of nature'. According to Kant, the 'archaeology of nature' included statements about the past which lack convincing evidence and therefore have to remain hypotheses, rather than becoming theories. It is evident that in terms of recognition as a serious, empirical discipline, archaeology has not made much progress in the intervening two thousand years.

Let us return to the meaning of archaeology. Originally, it was perceived as the knowledge about *arche*: beginnings, sources, origins. These left no record, save for their consequences. Origins preoccupied Greek thinkers ever after. According to Simplicius, it was Anaximander (611–547 BC) who first introduced the term *arche*. Aristotle characterised the water of Thales as the *arche* – the primeval matter, the original state of things. The intention of Empedocles was to explain 'the oldest beginnings of everything'. Plato noted that 'it is very important to begin from the very beginning'. And Aristotle judged that 'probably the best way to proceed would be to follow things from the beginning and observe how they come into existence and how they develop'.

Beginnings are taken for granted, for they must always have been. It is recognised that knowledge about beginnings is of great importance, for everything has its beginning, which predetermines further evolution. The enormous importance accorded to beginnings among past societies and cultures stemmed from their intimate relationship with the world of mythology – a connection from which we have not freed ourselves entirely even today. In the mythical world, the majority of human actions merely imitated the actions of a mythical hero, prescribed by fate. The past and the present merged, and when they were later separated, it was the connecting link – genealogy – which was accorded a special importance. Ancestry and descent defined one's very existence, one's position in society and the quality of one's life, all of which could have been legitimately inherited only by descent.

At the very beginning of history, the distance in time between origins, for which there was no record, and the more recent past, which was preserved and recorded, did not appear so great. Origins, therefore, were rightly seen as having a decisive influence on contemporary life. Descent provided the link between the two spheres.

Cosmogonic myths aimed to explain the very beginning: how the world and man came to be created and how they reached their contemporary state. Religious ideas about predestination reduced everything to beginnings, the subsequent development being merely the growth of the original form, thus precluding any idea of evolution.

In antiquity and during the Middle Ages, the term 'archaeology' was used only rarely, for knowledge was developing in other directions. Rather than being viewed as the origin of all things, *arche* was considered as a beginning of something. The more specialised the knowledge became, the more *arche* itself became specialised as a part of the process. Correspondingly, the amount of effort spent on explaining the beginnings decreased, as each individual discipline defined its field of interest. The importance of origins began to be perceived as formal, rather than real.

European civilisation accepted history not only as a science but above all as a way of understanding society. Although historical knowledge in the genealogical sense still survived, a different function of history became prominent: one which examined its own assumptions. So from this point it evolved with history as a discipline concerned simultaneously with understanding and influencing society itself.

In the Middle Ages the beginnings of our civilisation were specified through the Old Testament. There was no need, therefore, to study the origins of mankind independently, indeed, to do so would have been blasphemous. The only problem which was felt to merit a legitimate enquiry was that of connecting biblical events with the recorded history of the ancient world, and of seeking descent for specific feudal polities from noble families or nations of antiquity. Moreover, according to the Jewish calendar only five thousand years had passed since Creation, leaving no time for more ancient, prehistoric beginnings. Hence no need was felt, nor was there a chronological or philosophical framework, to accommodate even isolated discoveries about the world beyond the biblical paradigm.

Given this situation, the emergence of archaeological evidence capable of being examined and analysed was the decisive factor in the establishment of the discipline. The process of enquiry then formed the basis of methodology, which installed archaeology at a level above mere speculation. In this, archaeology followed other disciplines which had established their data base earlier, such as botany or geology. Thus, for instance, the whole system of classification of Montelius, which rendered scientific archaeology possible, amounts to no more than a modification of the approach through which palaeography qualified as a science.

The examination of the cathedral library in Verona, where a continuous library of manuscripts has been preserved since the fifth century, enabled S. Maffei in 1713 to establish palaeography as the science of the development of writing. Writing was an artefact of human culture and its changes created an evolutionary chain. One hundred and fifty years later, in establishing the evolution of prehistoric artefacts on the basis of their shape, O. A. Montelius applied a similar method to archaeology. In contrast to the former case, however, he was not guided by the comparative method, but by the Darwinian theory of evolution.

Stratigraphy and typological classification formed the means by which archaeological artefacts could be ordered in time. The interpretation of the chronological sequence, however, was the subject of ideas about evolution which have been carefully monitored by nearly all disciplines since the eighteenth century. Rather than developing their own concepts of evolution, scholars concerned with the remote past depended on, and provided supporting material for, approaches developed by other disciplines.

Within archaeology itself, remarkable regional differences developed in the application of concepts and theories. There were, and still are, entire national schools of archaeology which excelled in their collection of artefacts and compilation of data, but failed in theoretical applications. The theoretical and methodological advances in archaeology were achieved to a greater extent by prehistoric rather than protohistoric or historic archaeology. Similarly, it was the archaeologically impoverished North, rather than the richer South, which stimulated advances in archaeological method and theory. Flinders-Petrie, compelled to excavate difficult sites in the Egyptian Fayum, was forced to develop original and delicate methods, which those with rich and easily excavated sites at their disposal failed to attain.

Today archaeology is understood as a science investigating the past on the basis of material culture, such as artefacts, monuments and other remains. The emphasis is placed, therefore, on the nature of the material finds. From the beginning, the methodology of the discipline was built up by the selective adoption of methods and experiences from other disciplines. The conceptual framework of archaeology has developed in a similar way. Only today do we witness a deliberate and extensive methodological and theoretical reorganisation, the aim of which is to maintain pace with the general progress of science. Nevertheless, the investigation and retrospective assessment of the *arche* itself remains neglected.

Just as the history of individual nations would be incomprehensible without noting the historical events in the world at large, the history of archaeology cannot be understood without the history of science and knowledge. For the study of the discipline, therefore, the relations with other subjects and the general philosophical climate are as important as its specific methods and theories.

The fact that archaeology came into existence in the nineteenth century does not mean that the old approaches can be written off, or that they can be regarded as naive or worthless. On the contrary, reflective contemplation of the *arche* did not vanish, it merely received a new direction. In fact, it remains a constituent element of archaeology, in the same way as the investigation of finds. This is especially the case for the contemplation of the *arche* within different subjects (with implications for archaeology and for the investigation of past remains), and the examination of scientific methodology and theory in general; in other words, the analysis of one's own discipline's assumptions. Prehistory remains open not only for archaeology, but also for the *arche* of all other subjects and for scientific knowledge in general.

In focusing on the material phenomena, archaeology provides a general ground for the investigation of the *arche* not only by organising prehistoric events in time and space, but also by the continuous examination of artefacts, thus creating opportunities for their use in the testing of hypotheses. But where do the hypotheses come from?

The assumption that hypotheses depend solely on induction has long been discredited. Moreover, the difference between the formulation of a hypothesis and the deduction and testing of the results has often not been fully appreciated in archaeology, where the usual procedure is to adopt hypotheses from other disciplines, modify them to suit archaeological problems, and only then attempt solution. Once the structure of such hypotheses is accepted in archaeology, they soon come to be regarded as routine procedures. Another approach, common in archaeology, consists of the classification and seriation of finds. Here the rules defining types and typological series are given, albeit intuitively, and each concrete typology constitutes, in fact, a test of their validity. Today when we use cluster or factor analysis, we are in fact testing the assumptions of the analyses themselves; for instance, the suitability of the coefficients of similarity employed.

Finally, hypotheses from such different sciences as sociology, social and cultural anthropology, folkloristic studies or psychology enter into archaeology because of their chronological dimension. For these disciplines, or, rather, their aspects related to the *arche*, archaeology remains a subject concerned with events for which there is no real evidence. This will probably never be otherwise. Of course, this in no way disqualifies them; it is a mere fact. After all, these sciences cannot do without their extrapolations into the past and in fact they play an important, active role in the development of their other aspects. Neither palaeopsychological hypotheses, nor hypotheses about primeval languages, have within their disciplines any testable indicators, but are verified only by their implications for the contemporary state of science and by logical consistency. As hypotheses, they are not developed on the basis of concrete knowledge of the past, but are constructed within the particular framework of their discipline's theory and methodology. They can, however, profit from the artefacts and the knowledge accumulated through archaeology, and, at the same time, provide tests for archaeological reconstructions of the past.

Contemplation of the *arche* as beginnings for which there is no evidence is in fact a sort of prediction backwards, the 'foretelling' of the past. When we consider the future of mankind, we usually begin with the contemporary state of affairs and with historical knowledge. From this information we then attempt to define the range of probabilities. The *arche* is explored in the same way. We can begin with the same assumptions, but proceed in the opposite direction. From this it is evident that our contemporary state and our understanding of it is the determining factor in our interpretation of the *arche*. Even if we managed to get rid of all contemporary views, we would still be left with the present-day methods of research. In this sense archaeology has always been and remains an extrapolation of the present into the past. The history of ideas about the *arche* is therefore the history of methods and ideas about the whole world.

2   The earliest history

Sed fugit, interea fugit irreparrbile tempus.
Ovid

A resolution

The purpose of the following summary is to illustrate how the individual disciplines formed their ideas about the *arche*, what results they achieved, and what methods they used. Only with this background in mind will it be possible to comprehend the position, the significance, as well as the evolution, of archaeology as an independent science, for archaeology is but one among several disciplines which deal with prehistory.

Examples from language, and folkloric expressions in particular, when they are taken to be the remnants of the past, can be used to illustrate the methodological similarities between these approaches and archaeology. Unless we wish to postulate, as in biology, some 'preformistic' theory of archaeological development, we must accept that these similarities stem from the general state of knowledge and from mutual influences.

The picture we may get will certainly not be comprehensive, if only because our task is complicated by the existence of many schools of thought, subjects and disciplines concerned with *arche* which interconnect and mutually influence each other. Moreover, the articulation of problems and research tasks does not always correspond with the accumulation of knowledge. Our account aims, therefore, at overall clarity of exposition rather than at reconstructing the strict chronological order of events. It is not by chance that we emphasise the initial phases in the exploration of the past, when archaeology as we comprehend it today did not exist. In so doing we can discuss the state of society which served as a model for the development of the discipline. It is during this formative period that we can isolate certain basic tenets of archaeology, which were subsequently obscured, yet remained influential. In a nutshell, we shall investigate how the theory and methodology of archaeology absorbed the changes in our ideas about prehistory, about society and about knowledge in general, how it evolved under the influence of the broader social and philosophical context, and how it was modified by its own discoveries, and, in turn, how it functioned, itself, as a paradigm in social evolution.

The earliest forms of archaeology

Although the description of archaeology as 'speculation about empirical events for which there is no evidence' defined the scope of the discipline in antiquity, archaeology in fact became a marginal field of philosophy. Philosophy was intimately connected with myths, towards which it has adopted a critical approach: mythology came to be viewed as a model and as an opportunity for comparative investigation.

Initially, philosophy concentrated on the study of the origins of the universe, a subject which it shared with mythology. The origins, the formation and the working of the universe were at first only in part, but later in their entirety, explained as arising from their own existence. Consequently, the philosophers of antiquity aimed at describing the form and the rules of operation of the forces within the universe. Although explanation remained enveloped in the form of a tale, the emphasis shifted from mere narration to the definition of causalities.

As with myths, no need was felt to verify philosophical reasoning. No clear distinction was made between the possible and the real, nor was it necessary to demonstrate an immediate correspondence between reality and thought. Every proposition which was logical and was not contradictory, and which did not violate common sense, was held to be valid: words about that which persists, that which is constant and that which is elucidated by mind are persistent and ineradicable, states Plato. There was no mechanism for bringing hypotheses to test, however, nor was there an adequate amount of specific observations, supporting hypotheses or theories at a specific, rather than general, level. This meant that a gap emerged between general statements about the origin and the nature of the universe and empirical observations, a gap bridged only much later by specific scientific disciplines (the existence of which would not have been possible, of course, without the generalised hypotheses which render the universe a rational and harmonious phenomenon. This process is paralleled today in the development of new approaches, such as evolutionary theory or functionalism, which also create a gap, a void, which has to be filled.)

Myths were gradually being replaced by a whole range of ideas about the origins of the universe, man and society. Plato's philosophy, the philosophy of the new, detribalised human being, serves as a good example of the new approach. Plato examined the development of conceptual thinking, erecting at the same time a hierarchical framework of abstract concepts. The essential validity of the mythological and concrete, cosmogonic model was not questioned by Plato. Consequently, towards the end of his life, he accepted the mythical view as the real aim of his investigations in the *Timaeus* and *Kritias*, dialogues which in fact constitute not only perfect archaeology but also perfect cosmogony.

Plato was searching for the natural, the eternal, the abstract and the general, which would form, at the same time, a certain basic substance, a substratum. These concepts are contrasted against the individual, the concrete, the diachronic and the derived. The whole scheme is brought into the present through generalisation, and it is also through synchrony that the differences between the general and the particular are emphasised. Change is consequently perceived as a progression from the general to the particular, and is thus endowed with meaning and direction. This is the first concrete philosophy of evolution. At the same time, however, it was felt that every particular time in the past could only have been composed of concrete events – this is the subject of *Timaeus*. This dialogue traces the rise of the original human society from primeval chaos, from the beginnings, through the development and actions of elements, 'demiurgy', heavenly bodies, plants and animals. In this it represents the earliest archaeology.

In antiquity, the general starting point of philosophical considerations was speculation about the natural. The natural and the *arche* were held to be similar and often overlapping. But the idea of what is natural can be meaningful only in relation to the unnatural. It can exist, therefore, only from the time when something is felt to be unnatural and usually also negative. These concepts, in turn, can be defined only at the level of society as a whole, especially if we are dealing with early societies.

The concept of the natural in antiquity was, however, very different from our own today. It was identified with the ideal, the norm, the state of accomplished perfection, which had existed in the past. Thus Hesiod speaks of the Golden Age at the beginning of human society, Diogenes of Sinope considers as unnatural everything except the existence of beasts and barbarians. The unnatural, being identified with evil, is then seen as a deviation from the natural state. Because of its presumed existence in the past, the natural state is connected with the *arche* or *principium*.

In considering the human condition and society in general, we can distinguish several interpretations of the natural, some of which are contradictory. In particular, the interpretation of the natural, based on some innate understanding of what is natural human behaviour, can be contrasted with the view stressing the existence of society and social control as being inherently natural. The third position is to regard only nature as natural and life in harmony with it as the human objective.

For Plato, the emergence of the state takes place because, without it, humans cannot satisfy their needs; but its constitution is given to the people by the gods. Naturality, originality, sensibility and the ideal merge in the model of the perfect state.

For Aristotle, the human being is *zoon politikon*, a creature of society, which is accorded control over men as a superior, natural formation, comparable to an organism. Society is based on the natural form of management, the division of labour and the dichotomies man/woman, master/slave being comprehended as the natural state of things.

Lucretius reconstructed the entire evolution of society, ranging from earliest existence, which was comparable to the life of wild beasts, to the formation of the family, clan and the tribe. The state developed by agreement and the evolution of society followed the course of technological change.

According to Herodotus, the gods were aiming at a constant balance in the world, maintaining it through punishments for sins. Pragmatic historiography subsequently excluded the interference of supernatural forces, but in considering the causes of historical development, historiographers have nevertheless constrained the range of choice to human will and motives, and to independently operating fate. For Thucydides, for instance, history repeats itself because of unchanging human nature. Even fate is regarded as a natural necessity, outside human control, while according to Polybius, human actions can be analysed for patterns because similar cases will produce similar results. The influence of the environment is only occasionally recognised. The idea of change never matures to one of evolution. Cyclical evolution, marked by the eternal return, remains unknown outside the philosophy of history.

It follows, therefore, that reflection about the nature of society during ancient times was based on the *arche* and on the natural order of things, which had been established speculatively. Further evolution of these concepts was restrained by the existing conceptual framework and by the lack of independent means of verification, in other words, such means as could apply outside the anthropomorphic categories of *arche*, natural order, and teleological purpose.

Artefact-collecting also began in antiquity. In the sixth century BC, the Babylonian King Nabonidus carried out excavations in the ruins of earlier temples and palaces in his kingdom. King Assurbanipal (seventh century BC) founded a library of ancient Sumerian and Akkadian texts as well as a collection of antiquities for the third millennium BC. A sign at the entrance to his library proclaimed: 'I understand the words on the stones originating in the times before the flood.' To begin with, collections primarily served a religious purpose; later, especially in ancient Rome, they were an expression of status and prestige.

The first test of a hypothesis by reference to archaeological indicators was also carried out in the ancient world. At the end of the fifth century BC, Thucydides affirmed that the Carians had earlier inhabited the island of Delos. On the basis of similarities in the burial rites between the archaeological context and the contemporary Carians, he decided that his assertion was correct. But his discussion of the other problem has an oddly familiar ring:

Let us assume that the capital of the Lakedaimonians [Sparta] would become deserted and nothing would be left save for the temples and the foundation of buildings; from these our descendants could hardly believe that the power of the city could equal its famous reputation . . . Compare this with Athens, the buildings of which would lead one to believe that its power was twice as great as it is in reality.

Burckhardt did not exaggerate when we wrote about the first chapters of Thucydides' Archaeology: 'In these chapters, the Hellenic Age turns its attention on to the past with brilliant foresight – even though all these observations could be in error, they shall forever hold an enormous significance for general historical thinking' (Burckhardt 1977:414, translated from the original German).

The concept of the past during the Middle Ages

Christianity introduced biblical realities as the framework for the understanding of the universe and the entire history of mankind. The biblical interpretation, held to be divine in origin, was considered unquestionable and compulsory. In such a philosophical climate, early medieval historiography did no more than reflect the contemporary system of values and the perception of reality.

The medieval mind was firmly oriented towards the past, rather than the present. Human beings were held incapable of adding anything new, except evil, to the model of human existence as outlined in the Bible. Good, on the other hand, was merely an imitation of the model. Only those things which persisted were real, while things which changed were imperfect, evil and human, and therefore without value. The present, therefore, was without any value of its own, it could only gain in value by becoming the past, unchanged. Since the past was an ideal, transcending the present and the future, it was the chronology of the days in the year (still preserved in our calendar in the form of holidays), rather than the linear succession of years, that was held to be important.

Since God does not deceive, understanding was identified with vision. The past itself was therefore outside the reach of knowledge and was the subject of faith; hence the medieval reliance on authority, which can be attained through social standing and virtue.

For Thomas Aquinas, the world operated as part of a perfect hierarchy, where the individual was controlled by higher formations. These ideas were further developed by the Continental thinkers in particular, such as Rousseau and Comte, who postulated the precedence of society over the individual.

The second school of thought developed in the medieval period, has its roots in antiquity as well. For the nominalists, the state was a nominal unit of individuals bound by an agreement (Marsilius of Padua, 1324) and as such it had a profane, as opposed to sacred, nature (the latter was held to be the case by the realists).

Judaism and Christianity did introduce one original thought: namely the idea of linear evolution (as opposed to the cyclical evolution of ancient times). During the medieval period, however, this idea was confined to the history of the Church (*tempus aevum*), the history of the profane world being regarded as an accidental course of events. From this it follows that the observation of patterns, similarities and evolutionary links were beyond the scope of the contemporary description of human affairs. The arts, for example, were perceived as a trade, the purpose of which was to carry out specific tasks, especially ritual, commemorative and monumental ones, by the application of a range of techniques. Until the Renaissance, we do not have a single text which would consider art as having a value of its own: the medieval period lacked even the appropriate terminology. There is a close relationship between the description of artistic work and the feelings which it provokes – but the people of the medieval period were not, in general, accustomed to introspection.

There was no place for prehistory in such a cognitive framework. The tradition of collecting curiosities, which had begun in antiquity, carried on among the nobility as a symbol of power and wealth. For ideological reasons, the Church too was piling up old artefacts and other remains. Owing to shallow ploughing and limited building activity, the number of incidentally collected finds were small. As a result, the finds were not comparable, each appearing as a unique object, more or less held to be a result of divine intervention. Intentional excavations were rare and, when they did occur, they were intended to illustrate some event from Church history. Thus in 861 Methodius and Constantine, during their mission to Khazaria, searched for the remains of St Clement on the Crimean coast. Similarly, the Abbot of St Albans made an attempt to discover the grave of St Alban, the first English martyr. In 1390, Louis, the Duke of Brzeg, carried out excavations of a Slavonic hillfort in Silesia, in search of the ancient seat of the Bishops of Breslau. All these excavations were guided by religious motives; in addition, excavations were carried out for more bizarre reasons. A Polish chronicle, compiled by Dlugosz, notes that in 1416 the King of Poland, Ladislaus II, commissioned an excavation in central Poland in order to convince a friend that earthenware pots can grow underground. John Lackland excavated the Roman camp at Corbridge in search of treasure: in this activity he had many predecessors and successors.

Archaeological finds, collected either incidentally or deliberately, attracted many ingenious explanations. They occurred through the creative force of nature (*vis plastica*), or were made by underground gnomes; stone tools specifically were seen as a message directly from the heavens (Isidore of Seville, seventh century; Albertus Magnus, thirteenth century). Other interpretations invoke both God and Devil as forces responsible for the existence of lithic instruments.

Despite the keen interest in curiosities of all kinds, anomalies and fantastic beings, the medieval view of the world was not threatened. This was because the idea of the harmoniously organised universe allowed for the existence of abnormalities, as prehistoric artefacts were thought to be. When attempts were made to identify some old monuments, especially the megalithic tombs and barrows, as a human creation, they were usually ascribed to undifferentiated 'old heathens' or Huns. An alternative explanation for the megalithic architecture was recorded by the Danish chronicler Saxo Grammaticus around 1200: the fact that in remote antiquity Denmark was cultivated by giants is illustrated by enormous stones in old tombs. If anyone would wish to doubt this, all they have to do is to look at hilltops and explain what sort of people could carry up such heavy loads. An anonymous writer in a fourteenth-century manuscript at Cambridge explained the construction of Stonehenge in a similar way: the huge structure stood originally in Ireland and it was not until 483 that it was brought over to England by the powerful magician Merlin. To the same author we are indebted for the contemporary drawing of Stonehenge – one of the earliest of the monument.

To summarise, the biblical interpretation of history left little room for elaboration. Although the medieval world was aware of the heathen past, it was irrelevant to the medieval perception of the world and therefore beyond the concern of medieval Europe.

For humanism, the past is a source of nourishment as well as adornment

Great social changes, the discovery of the unknown world of stars, of other lands and cultures, and the past of antiquity, are reflected in Renaissance thought and in the Reformation. 'Sailors of our time gave us a new world', said J. Fernel in 1530. To Leonardo da Vinci, 'knowledge of the past and of the situation of the earth is the source of adornment and nourishment for the human spirit'.

The decentralisation of feudal power to individual landlords, city states and the Church, the development of national states, the territorial expansion of European civilisation, as well as a rapidly developing technology and new industrial relations, divided the Christian world. The generally shared understanding of the universe as a harmonious whole disintegrated and was replaced by a set of mutually contrasting ideas. In their own way, both the Renaissance and the Reformation led to the displacement of the biblical model as irrelevant to profane matters. The Protestant faith internalised the relationship between God and man, thereby rendering human society as a unit independent of God. The separation of the profane and the sacred also meant the end of authority as the means of verification, opening doors to new information. At the same time the scope of teleological explanation became limited.

Renaissance society

Facts acquired their own value, and their collection, examination and explanation grew rapidly in all branches of the humanities. This was already anticipated by St. Thomas, for whom each thing was of irreplaceable value in its relation to God. For Peter Damian, a scholastic philosopher in the thirteenth century, eternal truths were monsters which had to be killed to enable man to survive. With the Renaissance and the Reformation, a space was opened in the existing structure which could accommodate new facts and observations. In painting, for example, we can see how reality, originally expressed according to the literary models (icons), was now transformed by the formation of perspective as the impersonal, orientational, ordering scheme of space.

European traders and colonists, in order to organise the conquered territories, needed some knowledge of the foreign lands and people they colonised. As a result, tales about foreign lands became increasingly popular. Usually, they are composed of an ad hoc mixture of geographical, historic, ethnographic and biological information, first resurrected from antiquity by Marco Polo in his *Million*.

The new geographical space opened the mind to the value of the time perspective and led to a reappraisal of the European past. Even though the speculative approach lacked any methodology, it helped to create a social, evaluative and notional space which enabled things from the past to be noted and recorded as having some, as yet obscure, significance.

Already in antiquity, the method of describing foreign lands concentrated on things which in the observer's view seemed unusual, different and peculiar. A similar approach was applied towards unusual and curious things at home, with the difference that native curiosities often consisted of antiquities. In this way, the silent sphere of the obvious came into existence, posing the problem of its description. A conceptual framework had to be found which would permit the description and explanation of mundane, unexceptional matters. This could be done only by concentrating on the least obvious aspects of commonplace phenomena: the countability of the data. Taking a census of the population, an ancient practice already enshrined in the Roman constitution of Servius Tullius, can serve as a good example of this approach.

The necessity to gather and systematise information led F. Sansovius to the formulation of descriptive politology in 1562: the collection of data which gave us the original meaning of the term statistics. Subsequently, J. Graunt in 1662 and W. Petty in 1687 developed so-called political arithmetics. The description of these mundane matters was bound to be different from the qualitative account of the curious.

Comparative studies, such as that of Johannes de Bry, who in 1592 resolved to 'showe how that the inhabitants of the Britainne have been in time past as sauvage as those of Virginai', led to the articulation not only of differences, but also of similarities. Human nature was futher examined through quite specific discourses, which today could be characterised as ethnographic (B. de las Casas 1562, A. Thévet 1545, F. de Avila 1553, G. de la Vega 1609, B. Ayala 1613). It was no accident that the authors of such texts were mostly missionaries, convinced that the different races of man could be traced to Adam and Eve. This was more than an academic exercise, since the unified, biblical origin of all mankind would legitimise the status of 'savages' as human beings and consequently protect them, at least to some extent, from genocide.

Comparisons were also being made between the heathen inhabitants of the Christian lands and the 'savage'. The writings of J. Lafiteau (1724) are particularly inspiring. Lafiteau compared the contemporary American Indians to the prehistoric groups and to the 'barbarians' mentioned in the texts of antiquity and concluded that they appear to be on the same level of development. He then went on to postulate qualitatively the same, but chronologically staggered the course of social evolution for all of the groups.

The perception of society and of human nature underwent profound changes as well. Social phenomena were now seen to develop as a result of human nature, rather than divine intervention. Man became endowed with *appetitus socialis* and with natural rights. Moreover, the concept of natural law and of the natural exchange of social and economic values, determined internally by the individual (the psychic force of man, the dexterity of the human hand), and externally by the environment (social and natural), gained ground at the expense of the earlier concepts inspired by Strabo, Hippocrates, Ibn Khaldun, Bodin, Grotius and Montesquieu.

Historiography

Historiography reflects these changes in the perception of society. Ibn Khaldun, an Arabian historian of the fourteenth century (1332–1406), emphasised the influence of social, anthropological, geographic and climatic influences in his observations. Among the first historians who examined the impact of natural influence on historical events were F. Guicciardini (1483–1540) and L. V. de la Popelinière (1599) and J. Bodin (1566). Bodin also argued for the expansion of the data base and for the application of criticism, aspects which were later developed by G. J. Voss (1623), the Bollandists (1643) and J. Mabillon (1681). Through these developments, a distinction was made between the primary data and the secondary sources.

A historian of the humanistic period gained enormously from the rediscovery of antiquity during the Renaissance: for the first time he was able to study and describe a world markedly different from his own – a situation which could not have occurred in antiquity or the Middle Ages. As a result, he acquired a feeling for anachronisms, and consequently had to devote greater attention to methodology and the organisation of research itself.

What had so far been authoritative had been based on evidence held to be reliable. A long period of seemingly nonsensical scholastic disputations, however, bore its fruit in undermining the concept of personal authority. The epistemological theory of abstraction enabled scholars to move beyond the mere reproduction of observations and assertions by authoritative sources; the rationalisation and systematisation of philosophy led to the appearance of criticism. Abelard, in his twelfth-century manuscript *Sic et Non*, had already laid down five procedures for the criticism of philosophical texts:

1 Question the authenticity of the text and the credibility of the authority.
2 Differentiate between the original and secondary sources.
3 Establish what the author said, what he wanted to say and what he possibly might have said but did not.
4 Revise the meaning of the concepts employed.
5 In case of differences between authors, select the best-reasoned theory as the one that is most probably correct.

Even though this criticism was originally valid only for philosophical texts, it gradually extended to historiography (i.e. the work of Flavio Biondo in the fifteenth century) as did the referencing of texts, bibliography and the use of notes. These new conventions, in turn, brought to the foreground the authorship and the personality of scholars.

History of art

We can speak about the history of art only after its monumental and ceremonial function had been eclipsed by autonomous artistic and aesthetic considerations. Such a shift in emphasis occurred during the Renaissance, thanks to the contrasts produced by the recently discovered art of antiquity, and also as a result of the new understanding of the role of the individual, especially the personality of the artist. Nevertheless, for a long time, the painters in Florence, for instance, belonged to the guild of the herbalists, while the sculptors were adjoined to the masons and tilers.

Gradually, artists and their works gained in respect and appreciation. In 1381–2, F. Villani wrote a book about the history of Florence which included a number of sculptors and painters, such as Giotto, Gaddi and Daddi. This marks the beginning of a close relationship between art and literature. It can be said without exaggeration that this marriage formed the backbone of artistic existence in European civilisation. Not only did this mutual relationship lead to the development of the history of art, aesthetics and criticism, and to the application of these subjects in philosophy, but above all it galvanised the world of the artists themselves and offered possibilities for expanding the scope of emotion and self-reflection to both artists and audience alike. Only after these developments had taken place was it possible to understand more fully the art of antiquity and, by extension, other monuments, including the prehistoric ones.

In order to discuss art and its qualities, a new language, terminology and system of values had to be created, a process which involved a shift in the perception of the world as a whole. Advancing from the description of the personality to that of the individuality of the artist, the development of the language of art was slow; only later did the shift to the description of different traditions, schools and styles take place. Leaving apart global periodisations (the earliest of these was created by Ghiberti before 1450, dividing the evolution of art into the golden age of antiquity, the barbarian Middle Ages and the contemporary regeneration), art was introduced as a series of biographies by Vasari in 1550, and by his successor Balducci whose extensive six-volume work was published between 1672 and 1728. The biographic method of presentation extended north of the Alps with the work of van Mander (1604), von Sandrart (1675–9) and Houbraken (1718–21).

Archaeology before archaeology

By this process, works of art became a part of history. The notion of archaeology was reintroduced, this time as a discipline concerned with monuments and antiquities of mainly artistic nature. Thus the first journal about art in England was named *Archaeologia*. The artistic orientation of Renaissance archaeology provided the basis for the subsequent work of one of the founding figures of modern classical archaeology – J. J. Winckelmann.

Interest in the monuments of antiquity, generated during the Renaissance, became the mainstay of new collecting activity. Petrarch's dictum 'preserve the monuments of the glory of Rome and become famous' illustrates the emotional and aesthetic appeal of such activity. The notion of archaeology was broadened to include almost any information about the past. During the Renaissance, archaeology encompassed numismatics, epigraphy and the history of art. Cyriacus of Ancona, for example, is regarded not only as a 'father of archaeology', but also as a father of epigraphy. Similarly, J. Spon interpreted archaeology as a discipline concerned with past material remains, subdividing it into epigraphy, iconography, glyptography, the study of ancient architecture, the study of reliefs and of manuscripts. As late as the middle of the eighteenth century, J. F. Christ understood archaeology as the combination of the history of art, epigraphy, diplomatics, etc.

Such catholic interests were reflected in the organisation of the discipline, first formalised through the foundation of societies. In 1478, the earliest antiquarian society in Italy was founded; in 1717, the Society of Antiquaries was founded in Britain, receiving the Royal Charter from

George II in 1751; and in 1630, Gustavus II Adolphus, the Swedish monarch, founded the Royal Society of Antiquaries of Sweden. Both private individuals and societies which were interested in archaeology concerned themselves also with literature, history, philology, geography and biology. Antiquarian archaeology formed merely a part of their far broader interests.

Despite the increase in the volume of archaeological activitity, archaeology remained at the level of ad hoc collections of 'curiosities' for most of the Renaissance period. Prehistoric artefacts continued to be collected by chance, rather than intentionally; finds and monuments continued to be seen as individual remains of the past, and no attempts were made to achieve a more comprehensive interpretation. Such 'Kunstkammer' archaeology continued well into the eighteenth, even the nineteenth century. As the collections grew larger, however, tentative attempts began at their sorting and systematisation. Because the prehistoric artefacts were the last to be discovered, they reflected the latest trends in Renaissance perspective, first applied in Italy.

By the middle of the sixteenth century, the Italian Renaissance scholars succeeded in making most of the basic works of the great authors of antiquity accessible. These classical works preserved Homer's and Hesiod's observations, mirroring Greek life in the ninth century BC, and in the case of Homer, also the oral traditions of the post-Mycenaean period. These and other works preserved contemporary records from the period transitional between the Bronze and Iron Ages, together with ethnographic speculations about the earlier existence of the era of stone weapons and tools, such as those the Greeks saw in the hands of their barbarian neighbours. So far as we know, however, the ancient Greeks made no attempt to apply these philosophical speculations to the archaeological context, or to arrange in their correct chronological order the stone, bronze or iron tools found in the ground. We can observe, in this lack of practical application of ideas, the basic difference between the Renaissance and the classical approach to the past.

Italian scholars read with interest the classical works about the succession of different periods, where the use of stone preceded the use of bronze and iron. These were ideas based on ancient traditions and observations, yet without any connection to prehistoric artefacts. The farmer, who dug up and preserved prehistoric objects, continued to believe that they were thunderbolts from the heavens, endowed with magical powers. The heavenly origin of these objects crept even into the 'learned' literature, such as the texts of Marbodius and Paracelsus.

The Renaissance brought about a direct conflict between the classical interpretation of artefacts as prehistoric remains and the popular medieval belief that these objects had supernatural origins. In contrast to the philosophical approach to antiquity, the Renaissance scholars were quick to search for ancient objects in the fields, sorting them together with other interesting curiosa. Within this context, several scholars ventured to suggest the human origin of the finds. G. Agricola, for instance, rejected the idea of heavenly origin in 1546, and the famous anatomist and biologist U. Aldrovandi (1522–1605) asserted that stone tools were used by prehistoric men before they knew the use of metals, supporting his argument with quotations from Pliny. Finally, M. Mercati united in his work the practical observations of the farmers, the knowledge of classical authors and the fresh discoveries and ideas of his own time. Nevertheless, this did not eradicate the old beliefs about the supernatural origin of stone tools, or, in the case of pottery, the creative force of nature, which continued to be held by some scholars in the seventeenth century (e.g. Balbín 1679).

Mercati (1541–93) was above all a natural scientist, and as the chief caretaker of the Vatican's botanical gardens, he maintained a collection of minerals and fossils. At the same time, he was active as the medical adviser to Pope Clement VIII. As a field biologist, he also turned his attention to the problem of stone implements. Renaissance education gave him a good knowledge of the works of Pliny, Lucretius and Festus. He was, therefore, aware of the classical theories about the successive periods of stone, bronze and iron instruments. As a devout Vatican cleric he was also inspired by another great compilation of ancient oral traditions: the Old Testament, which matched Homer as a source of references to stone and bronze instruments. It was also a valuable account of the introduction of iron metallurgy by the Philistines. The third element in Mercati's process of thought, and finally understanding, was the increasing collection of Asian and American artefacts brought to the Vatican by the Italian, Portuguese and Spanish scholars, missionaries and travellers. These three constituents were the starting points of Mercati's interpretation. Together with Aldrovandi and other scholars, Mercati maintained that artefacts found in the field were of human origin and prehistoric in age. For the first time, he related them directly to the classical scheme postulating the existence of the stone, bronze and iron ages.

Mercati's manuscript forms only a part of his great work on minerals and fossils called *Metallotheca*, which lay in the Vatican library until 1717, when Pope Clement XI had it published. Even as an unpublished manuscript, Mercati's work influenced generations of natural scientists. Although he could not be regarded as an archaeologist, his work contained elements which were independently rediscovered by Thomsen three hundred years later, and which form the basis of modern archaeology.

The Age of Enlightenment: knowledge about the past accumulates

During the sixteenth century, the natural laws of human life began to be discussed in philosophical writings concerned with man and society, political science and economics and also in subjects which today can be identified as the dawn of anthropology and sociology.

The comparative method reached the level of a standard methodological procedure during the Enlightenment, and in the form which was further elaborated in the nineteenth century, remained so into the twentieth: to Malinowski, the comparative method was the basis of any generalisation, of any theoretical approach.

Since the Renaissance, nature and things natural formed the basic reference point for philosophical and scientific speculation. The concept was, however, invested with several meanings: it symbolised the ideal, Utopia, justice (T. Campanella, Thomas More), it provided the foundations of rationality (Grotius), as well as the common basis of all separate manifestations (different constructs of natural religion, Hume 1757). The natural was also identified with necessity, as Montesquieu intimated: 'in the broadest sense of the word, laws are necessary relationships, arising from the nature of things'.

Political economy

The concept of the natural also penetrated the field of political economics, where E. Petty (1623–87) began the search for 'natural explanations' and for 'natural values'. It is in this field of the humanities that the systematic approach was applied for the first time. Quesnay's *Tableau économique* divided society for the first time into groups according to economic conditions, and attempted to define the relationships between these groups in a systemic way. In the English classical school of economics (Smith 1776, Ricardo 1817), the systemic approach was applied in the only way which was then possible: as a deductive abstraction. Finally, in a development which later became significant for economic anthropology and archaeology, the notion of *Homo oeconomicus* emerged, based on the behavioural assumption of the inherent egoism of human nature. Under the conditions of a free market, individual egoism would ensure the mutual balance of interests, resulting in 'happiness maximisation'.

Philosophy

Philosophers of the Enlightenment also emphasised the notion of progress. By this they understood social and ethical progress, rather than an advance in production and material well-being. For example, Voltaire (1754) believed that society progresses from the barbaric stage to civilisation by way of suffering and deception, through a struggle between knowledge and ignorance. Similarly, the idea of predictability of social evolution found favour with the philosophers of the Enlightenment. Thus Turgot maintained that agriculture leads to population increase, which in turn promotes the accumulation of knowledge and consequently greater progress. Condorcet in 1795 divided social evolution into ten stages, the first three of which were prehistoric: (1) hunting and, (2) pastoralism and farming, (3) farming and the beginning of writing. The idea of natural selection and adaptation to the natural environment is mentioned by Diderot, but only in passing. The prevailing belief was that contemporary natural peoples can serve as a model for the reconstruction of historical developments. The comparative method reigned supreme.

Historiography

Meanwhile, historians were busy defining the scope of their subject. In dividing the course of history into repetitive cycles of epochs of gods, heroes and people, Vico was merely following the classical scheme; at the same time it is significant that people alone were held to be responsible for the historical world, which can therefore be understood by them. Vico recognised the existence of history as such (*una storia ideale eterna*) as an independent discipline, rather than a history of some subject. These ideas were further elaborated by Rousseau (1751), Kant (1784) and Novalis (1799). The history of art was no longer presented as histories of individual artists (*à la* Vasari) but as the history of art (Winckelmann). The concept of history as the source of moral instruction came to an end forever.

As a human creation, and as a subject in its own right with universal application, history was able to provide a framework which was capable of accommodating prehistory in more than just a formal sense. A space was created for prehistory. This space remained as yet empty, because the historical method of the presentation of events was not suited to the exposition of prehistory, the period without ethnographic or literary sources. Meanwhile historians, in a learned and erudite fashion, were busy filling thousands upon thousands of pages with concrete historical facts, principally concerning political and ecclesiastical events.

Developments in philology mirror those in history. In the sixteenth century, Tolomei began research into relationships between languages. In 1559, Scaliger defined eleven languages of the European family. Subsequent research enabled Pallas to issue a dictionary of 272 languages between 1786 and 1791. The continuously increasing pool of information, especially lexicographic data, led to the first hypotheses about the common origin of Indo-European languages (Lomonosov 1755, Jones 1786). The grammatical connection, as opposed to a mere lexicographic one, between Sanskrit, Latin, Greek, Germanic and Slavonic languages was demonstrated by Schlegel in 1808.

One of the founders of the modern history of art, and at the same time of classical archaeology, was J. J. Winckelmann (1717–68). In his work he moved from evaluating the personality of the artist to the artwork itself. Such a move required the development of a new literary form – the aesthetic description of the actual works of art. Winckelmann also introduced the notion of styles and recorded their history. The history of art, expressed within such a framework, can then be included in the general historical development, provided that style is perceived as a chronological period. As well as being subject to the same natural and cultural influences, historical periods and styles, Winckelmann argued, classical archaeblogy and the history of art shared common chronological characteristics, namely their beginnings, development and disintegration.

As in earlier times, prehistory remains a relatively poorly investigated subject during this period. The only subject which was related to prehistory, and which was researched extensively, did not concern material culture, but mythology. The investigation of myths as sources reporting about the past could take place only after they had ceased to be regarded merely as allegorical tales, or even as deception (Voltaire). It was not until 1725 that Vico came to regard myths as the initial phases of history. He can be credited with the first analysis of myths according to their form, rather than their content. In so doing he was preparing the ground for a new perception of the past, and for the development of a new discipline.

Antiquarian archaeology

Archaeology was introduced not as a subject in its own right, but as a part of antiquarianism, which varied in character from one country to another. In France and Italy, local prehistory was neglected in favour of ancient and oriental civilisations. In England, northern Germany and Scandinavia, on the other hand, antiquarians developed a strong interest in the local pre-Roman antiquities. These interests reflect the national and political trends already detectable in the historical works of antiquity and the Middle Ages. From that time on, archaeology has been stalked by nationalism and by the threat of political exploitation. Although this influence has added some stimulus for its development, it has also led the discipline astray.

It cannot be denied that during times of intensified patriotic sentiments, respect for archaeologists and their discipline increased. Thus, in 1628, the Swedish Royal Chancellery empowered J. Bure to examine ancient remains and publish their description 'for the respect and glory of our nation'. Two years later, Gustavus II Adolfus instructed the Royal Antiquary to ensure that his work 'glorifies the fatherland'. During the *stormakstiden* (the imperial period between 1611 and 1718), the fatherland expanded into an empire. Correspondingly, in 1661 we come across the exhortation to work 'for the respect and glory of the empire', and in 1693 Rudbeck states that his work has no other end than 'the glory of Sweden' (Moberg 1969: 36–7). Moberg has also demonstrated by historical arguments how this generated a greater interest in local antiquities.

Subsequent generations of archaeologists and antiquarians have similarly succumbed to nationalism, which became a major stimulus for the archaeologists of the Romantic period. From the end of the nineteenth century, Kossinna's 'settlement archaeology', advocating the ethnic interpretation of settlement patterns, became a powerful tool of nationalist aspirations. The lack of research methodology, inherent in this approach, made it possible to put forward conflicting explanations for the same set of data. Nevertheless, it was applied extensively after the First World War, when the ruins of the large multinational empires – Germany, Austria, Russia and Turkey – served as the basis for the emergence of small national states, which employed archaeology to justify their existence and the extent of their territories. During this time, archaeologists were given resources which in other times they could only dream of. The new states, such as Czechoslovakia, Poland and the Baltic Republics, were attempting to show that the roots of their history lay deep in the prehistoric age, while Germany, which had lost territory as a result of the war, was aiming to demonstrate how the Germanic peoples introduced civilisation into lands of Eastern Europe long before Christ. The Polish–German border was a particularly disputed territory in this respect, causing an archaeological war between Kossinna's and Kostrzewski's supporters, both equally oblivious to explanations other than ethnic ones for the distribution of archaeological patterns. The abuse of 'nationalistic archaeology' reached its climax during the Nazi period in Germany, when notions about the glorious Germanic prehistory dreamed up by archaeologists and alleged to cover enormous areas of Europe became part of the official Nazi ideology and of the political propaganda, intended to justify the conquests of the Wehrmacht. The response of the Slavonic archaeologists, whose countries were the principal recipients of German expansion, was based on similar methods, but was aimed at countering the German claims.

The earliest works on prehistory began to appear in print by the sixteenth century. The earliest basic work on Danish prehistory consists of a six-volume text, *Danicorum Monumentorum Libri Sex*, compiled in 1643 by the antiquarian and collector O. Worm. This work illustrates well the antiquarian approach of the time. Worm cultivated contacts with travellers, captains of seagoing ships, and farmers, requesting that they contribute to his 'curiosity cabinet' at every opportunity. In this way, his collection assumed the proportions of a museum and became one of the most popular places to visit in Copenhagen. Its organisation is known to us from the book *Museum Wormianum*, an illustrated catalogue of the collections, published shortly after Worm's death in 1655 (Klindt-Jensen 1975: 22–3). The position of the exhibits reflects the cognitive framework of antiquarian archaeology: artefacts of nature (bizarre skeletons, stuffed animals) and those of culture (especially classical remains) appear mixed together, with cheerful disregard for anything else but the value of the object, which was determined by its relative rarity.

The description of Olearius' collection by von Mellen, published in 1679, is probably the first serious archaeological work. Apart from the descriptions of individual collections, attempts were made at a more comprehensive treatment: in the survey of C. Patin, dated 1695, some of the Western European and Central European collections are described.

In 1724, J. Lafiteau published an important four-volume account of Indian customs and material culture, which he studied during his stay in America as a missionary. The title of the work alone, *Mœurs des sauvages américains comparées aux mœurs des premiers temps*, indicates that the author was well aware of the early evolutionary stages of European society, and that he attained his convictions as a result of the application of the comparative method. In 1730, Mahudel quoted Mercati and supported the idea of three successive stages of cultural evolution. In 1734, B. de Montfaucon, in an illustrated publication, postulated the existence of the stone, bronze and iron ages. This is further elaborated by Goguet, who in 1758 argued that the use of bronze was preceded by that of iron, and that in even more remote times, objects produced in metal today were made in stone, bone and other non-metallic materials. From this we can make two observations: Mercati's work was not forgotten, his ideas continued to pose a subject for discussion; and the idea of three ages is specifically elaborated by authors such as Montfaucon and Mahudel, and complemented by illustrations of prehistoric artefacts for each of these periods. The stratigraphic and practical implications of these ideas continued to be elaborated in France during the subsequent period.

Archaeology also came to be delineated in a passive way, by the emergence of the related disciplines and subjects in their own right. Thus Mabillon helped to establish scientific palaeography in 1708, while Eckel can be credited with the establishment of numismatics. Winckelmann, by focusing on the potential information contained in the artefacts of material culture (on this basis he created the notion of style and described its evolution), was responsible for the birth of modern classical archaeology. Even so, the objects of material culture were not initially considered as independent sources for the reconstruction of the classical period, but were merely seen as supporting evidence for the knowledge gained from the study of classical authors. This practice, however, helped to establish the status of material culture as a valuable and effective form of evidence, which can be used not only to support written records, but in its own right. New respect for the material remains of the past was extended to prehistoric artefacts, and became one of the main factors contributing to the establishment of prehistoric archaeology. Fieldwork, carried out at Herculaneum (from 1738 onwards) and, above all, at Pompeii (from 1743), helped to consolidate this attitude. By the end of the eighteenth century, large expeditions into Egypt (1798), followed by those to Mesopotamia (French expedition in 1842, British in 1845), opened a new phase in the development of fieldwork and in the approach towards archaeological finds.

Throughout this time, prehistoric artefacts were often thought of as artistic objects, and understanding of them depended on the attitudes and approaches adopted towards works of art during the formative period for the history of art. Prehistoric artefacts, however, lacked the associated data, such as the identity of the artist, circumstances of the find, or written reports, which commonly accompanied the artefacts of antiquity, the Middle Ages and contemporary artwork. For these reasons, prehistoric artefacts could be comprehended only in terms of general categories and ideas. While classical archaeology was developing under the umbrella of classical philology, prehistoric archaeology lacked parental models and paradigms, with the possible exception of the biblical and classical accounts of the past. Consequently, artefacts were interpreted within the antiquarian range of interest and knowledge; this meant that most of them were regarded as objects of cult and ceremony after the more recent models, which were medieval or classical in date. In this way many objects ended up with the wrong identification, a situation criticised by Kant, who in 1781 argued emphatically against the religious interpretation of artefacts in his *Anthropologie in pragmatischer Hinsicht*.

The notion that stone artefacts were made by man, rather than by nature, became generally accepted only in the eighteenth century. Moreover, with the exception of the large chipped spearheads and axes, only the polished tools were recognised as artefacts. It is therefore surprising to find that in his dissertation entitled *De Cultris Veterum Lapideis* and completed in 1735, J. Engeström, professor of oriental studies and theology and later Bishop of Lund, devoted considerable attention to chipped flint artefacts of the Lapp people of northern Scandinavia. In the section concerned with the description of chipped flint knives used specifically for circumcision, he argued that heathens of old may well have used similarly inconspicuous, but specialised instruments. (One wonders whether this may provide some inspiration for those specialising in the functional analysis of stone tools through trace wear analysis and experimental archaeology.)

In a similar manner, the idea of the great antiquity of ceramics was slow to find favour. The problem was that the contemporary pottery was not much different from the prehistoric. Thus Agricola in 1546 argued that prehistoric pottery is Germanic in date, a view shared by Albinus, who nevertheless put it to the test in 1587 by carrying out excavations at Marzahn.

The antiquarian approach also affected the selection of monuments in the field for investigation. Megalithic structures, burials and extensive cemeteries such as urnfields were the kind of remains selected for investigation. Settlements were neglected, while the cave and rockshelter sites were not discovered until the beginning of the nineteenth century. Regardless of their true function, the antiquarian orientation attributed to almost all sites ceremonial or funerary-ritual significance.

Because the principal aim of antiquarian archaeology was to obtain unique and valuable artefacts, early excavators paid little attention to the context of archaeological finds, or to their exact location. The earliest attempts at organisation and standardisation of archaeological excavations include instructions by Treuer in 1688 on how to excavate funerary urn burials, and a treatise by Rhode at the beginning of the eighteenth century against the careless excavation of burials, with instructions for proper procedures. In Russia in 1730, Tatiščev published instructions for archaeological excavations; a similar text was published in Germany in 1754 (*Hannoverische gelehrte Anzeigen*) and six years later Mushard wrote a textbook for archaeological excavations. Aubrey (1626–97), and later Stukeley (1687–1765), can both be credited with discovering that prehistoric pits, ditches and walls can be detected from surface vegetation. Less than a hundred years later, R. Colt Hoare went on to develop the archaeological method by providing meticulous drawings of his excavations, and also by applying the principles of seismology: in the search for sub-surface features, he systematically pounded the ground with a mallet.

In the course of the eighteenth century, archaeological finds came to be regarded as independent sources, different from, but equal in importance to, the written records. The antiquarian approach, however, restricted the range of their interpretation to objects of cult and ceremony; consequently, their evaluation to the level of historical sources had only a formal significance (F. Bacon 1605, J. Spon 1673, A. A. Rhode 1719, B. de Montfaucon 1724, J. Dobrovský 1786). Rhode, however, went a step further by declaring that archaeological finds make up the only non-falsified sources capable of greater revelations about the prehistory of Germany than the entire *Germania* of Tacitus. He went on to investigate prehistoric cemeteries, dividing the burials chronologically into those without metals, those of transition and those belonging to the age of bronze. He also noted the difference in the material wealth of the burials, while the funerary equipment led him to postulate fifteen categories of craftsmen.

The most common method of sorting collections is typological classification. The classification of archaeological artefacts, however, did not extend beyond individuals who developed their own system of classification. One of the earliest schemes was applied by N. M. Thurius (*c.* 1470–1525) to megalithic tombs; this was followed by Treuer's division of ceramics into pots, jars, bowls, etc., in the following century. At the beginning of the nineteenth century a number of schemes, such as those of R. Colt Hoare and M. G. Bruzelius, were introduced; for the interpretation of finds, however, they were of little or no value. At the same time, the possibility of comparative studies was precluded by the small size of the individual collections, the paucity of publications and the lack of continuity in research (which was restricted by the interest and capabilities of each individual).

It was only after the basic chronological and functional framework for the classification of artefacts had been established, and after the initial ideas about the character of individual epochs were articulated, that it was possible to recognise the age of the individual finds as belonging to the time 'before the flood' and 'after the flood', 'before the Romans' and 'after the Romans', and before or after the introduction of Christianity. The time range of any of these slots was not long by today's standards, since the estimates for the age of the earth, and therefore of human history, did not reach beyond seven thousand years. In the middle of the seventeenth century, Archbishop Ussher placed the date of Creation at the year 4004 BC. French encyclopedists calculated the beginnings of human history as two thousand years earlier. These chronologically narrow limits were imposed not only on the history of mankind but also on the evolution of nature. W. Buckland, as late as 1823, divided the geological history of the earth into diluvial and alluvial epochs. In the series of catastrophic events which were thought to have accompanied the creation of the earth (see chapter 3), the latest catastrophe had taken place, according to G. L. de Cuvier, only a few thousand years ago. Very slowly, the time perspective was extending, demolishing the notion of history as a sequence of isolated historical events, and introducing the idea of process. The newly discovered ocean of time extended beyond the reach of the conventional histori-ographical methods. The ensuing need for more suitable approaches encouraged the development of archaeology and of those forms of research which were later to become sociology, anthropology and ethnology. Thus the extension of the time perspective became the principal condition for the development of prehistoric archaeology.

General ideas about the nature of change and progress were developing very gradually, slowly replacing the old ideas about the unchanging, fixed condition of the universe. It was only as a part of the rationalist thinking of the Enlightenment that these vague ideas about change were applied more concretely to technology and to social and economic relations. Such considerations were also inspired by, and in turn encouraged further, ethnographic studies, which supported the idea of technological progress. As a result, the notion that stone implements, being the most primitive, are also the oldest, was beginning to find general acceptance during the eighteenth century (J. de Laert 1646, B. de Montfaucon 1734, P. Mahudel 1734, A.-Y. Goguet 1756, J. G. Eccard 1750, C. Lyttelton 1766). It is worth noting, however, that the Chinese already divided human existence into the ages of stone, bronze and iron in 52 BC.

Were we to consider this period in its entirety, we would find that the humanistic and antiquarian perception of archaeology did not allow the prehistoric past an independent role. It was fully subordinated to the ideas about the past drawn from classical sources and from the contemporary ethnographic and geographic literature, later supplemented by the general notions about change and progress. Artefacts as such were appreciated above all for their aesthetic, ritual potential as a source of information about the past was only superficially recognised. In this way, prehistoric archaeology failed to adopt Winckel-mann's initiative, which was based on artefacts themselves and on the reconstruction of their development.

During this period, a professional scientist was *rara avis*. On the contrary, this was the heyday of the dilettante. Just as a new perception of nature preceded the work of a natural scientist, a new interest in and enthusiasm about antiquity, generated by the Renaissance, constituted a decisive element in the development of archaeology. It was the dilettante who carved the cradle of archaeology out of the general interest in the past. The first antiquarian society, founded by J. P. Laetus in 1478, became the focus of the dilettante activity in Rome. Other societies were founded in the sixteenth and seventeenth centuries. In England, the Society for the Preservation of National Antiquities was founded in 1572, the Society of Antiquaries of London in 1717 and the Society of Dilettanti in 1732.

The discovery of the printing press facilitated the speed and the extent of production of books. Printing was cheap, democratic and nationally oriented; with its introduction, national languages began to replace Latin. It created its own market, which required a constant flow of new manuscripts. It also changed the relationship between the author and his work: the book now took on an independent identity with its own separate existence. Medieval disputations were now replaced by scholars writing books. Scholarly positions were now available in schools, univer-sities and, as earlier, in monasteries. There were few public offices so far available.

Professor Morhoff's lectures about antiquities at the University of Kiel in the 1650s and 1660s remained for a long time the only example of teaching on the subject. Restricted by their long-established and traditional defi-nition of scientific disciplines, the universities had little understanding for such a 'trendy' subject as archaeology. The first signs of a break-through came in 1662 when a Chair of Antiquities was created at the University of Uppsala in Sweden.

The first publications concerned with antiquities appeared in the six-teenth century. By 1700 they could be counted in the hundreds, and by the end of the eighteenth century they reached the figure of about three thousand. The earliest illustration of ancient ceramics was discovered in a compendium of Roman inscriptions, published in Erfurt in 1502. The first illustration of prehistoric pottery to be published in a learned magazine (a Lusatian amphora) appeared in 1678 in *Miscellanea Curiosa Medico-Physica*, published in Leipzig. The earliest accounts of past cultural remains, such as

those of Olaus Magnus (1555), J. J. Chiflet (1655) and C. Patin (1696), were
restricted in content and appeared in volumes dedicated to more general
topics. The works published subsequently by von Mellen in Germany
(1679), Borlas in England (1754) and Biener in Bohemia (1778–85) were
more extensive. Archaeology received full treatment in the fifteen-volume
work of B. de Montfaucon, entitled *L'Antiquité expliquée et représentée en
figures* and published between 1719 and 1724, as well as in the seven volumes
by P. Caylus, published between 1752 and 1756. Both works cover, in
addition to the classical antiquities, the prehistoric and post-classical
monuments in Western and Southern Europe. In addition, Montfaucon
embellished his work with an astonishing 40,000 beautiful engravings. The
steady rise of popular interest in archaeology finally resulted in 1719 in the
first popular journal devoted to prehistoric archaeology, published and
edited by A. A. Rhode in Germany (*Cimbrisch-Hollsteinische Antiquitaeten
Remarques*, Hamburg).

The birth of modern archaeology

In the course of the nineteenth century, the isolated figures of clergymen
and of scholars which characterised the previous period were gradually
replaced by the continuously expanding number of professional men, who
emerged as a new social group, even though their independence was
restricted by obligations to the social classes which they were supposed to
represent. Nevertheless, it is at least partly possible to view the development of the social sciences in the nineteenth century in terms of the
opposition of the intelligentsia to the existing social order.

Rather than continuing in the philosophical traditions of the Enlightenment, the Romantic period elaborated, in fact, on far older notions. While
the scholars of the Enlightenment found no purpose or laws in history,
during the Romantic period thinkers such as Herder looked for a harmonic
interpretation of organic evolution, while Hegel sought the demonstration
of the universal 'Weltgeist'. These were more than non-functional speculations: such contemplation managed to broaden the idea of evolution, to
specify it and to popularise it.

The particularisation of science into separate disciplines constituted
another important trend during the nineteenth century. General, abstract
notions, which had hitherto prevailed in the humanities, began to be
surrounded by empirical observations, theories were becoming more
specific, and separate social sciences began to emerge. Even so, the path
towards the establishment of a social science was not always straight-
forward. Attitudes towards folklore can serve as a good example. During

the Enlightenment, folklore had to be recorded in writing in order to have any value, and even then it was evaluated solely on its literary and aesthetic merits. In Germany, a pedantic Aristotelian view of time excluded the understanding of specific aspects of folklore until it became incorporated into national histories and their peculiarities. The neo-Platonic idea of the single origin of the creation myth, which gave birth to the great religions of the world (Hermes Trismegistus, Zarathustra, Moses), also contributed to the more serious evaluation of folklore, especially myths and fairy tales. Interest in myths was further stimulated by the work of Wolf and Niebuhr (1811–12), who regarded all classical records which were not substantiated by other sources as mere folklore. Creuzer compiled an impressive collection of myths (1810–12), indirectly laying the foundation for comparative mythology. F. G. Welcker initiated research into the origin and the evolution of myths, while K. O. Müller began the investigation of historical myths. During the same period, the study of religion also took shape (C. Meiners 1806–7).

Influenced by the emerging study of the Indo-European languages, the brothers J. and W. Grimm (1812–14) came to regard fairy tales as the remains of the original Indo-European myths (the Aryan theory). According to their view, fairy tales constituted a historical source, representing an era which witnessed a contemporaneous development of language and epic traditions. Moreover, they saw in the language of myths and fairy tales 'the highest and the most valuable speech of man'.

Historiography

Comparable developments could be observed in historiography. As stated earlier, the belief in principles – or, more precisely, in the inherent naturalness and reason of man – formed the basis of 'enlightenment'. Reason itself could, in turn, be reduced to several principles, which follow the laws of nature. Therefore, the Enlightenment adhered to an ahistorical philosophy, interested not in concrete situations, but in the broader notion of progress. In historiography, this was reflected in the tendency to elevate abstract criteria above empirical facts. It is quite clear that the historiography of the Enlightenment saturated the limits of the then prevailing abstract paradigm. Further development which later became known as historicism could only have taken place through the emphasis on the individual nature of events, the role of individual nations, ethnic groups and movements, and on the relative independence of individual eras. The important point is that this shift in emphasis changed the goals of the discipline: the creation of abstract historical constructs was replaced by the reconstruction of the historical past within a dynamic, dramatic and multi-dimensional narrative framework.

Such a framework required a strong personal commitment to the past. Despite the emphasis on objectivity (e.g. Ranke's insistence on relating history 'wie es eigentlich gewesen'), an intuitive understanding of the course of history as a dynamic encounter between different forces began to take shape. At the end of the eighteenth century we also see the emergence of hermeneutics, a science concerned with the explanation of texts (Schleiermacher 1768–1834), which was later developed as a discipline of interpreting systems of signs.

Historicism brings the historical-philological criticism and the critical analysis of source material to the state of near perfection. In the sixteenth and seventeenth centuries, these approaches were the domain of classical philology. Now, a distinction was perceived between internal and external criticism. External criticism was concerned mainly with archaeography (knowledge of source materials), epigraphy (analysis of inscriptions), diplomatics (analysis of documents), palaeography (evolution of writing) and sphragistics (investigations of seals).

Textual criticism and editorial techniques emerged at first within the framework of, and in response to, the needs of historiography and historical philology (K. Lachmann 1816). Changes in formal aspects of literary texts (lexicon, grammar, scribal errors, calligraphy, anachronisms, typesetting conventions, etc.) served as the basis for the development of the comparative method, which in turn was used to construct the history of the text in question, identify and reconstruct the original text, separate the palimpsest into its constituent parts and construct the succession of mutually interdependent manuscripts (*schema*).

Screening of texts through the interpretation of their contents facilitated the development of auxiliary historical disciplines, such as heraldry, historical geography, metrology and genealogy. Internal criticism, on the other hand, focused on the content of the information. Already in 1808 G. A. F. Fast noted that spiritual understanding is a form of knowledge superior to historical grammatical understanding.

Historicism can claim the membership of most of the great historians and authors of national histories in the nineteenth century: A. Thierry, J. Michelet, F. A. Mignet, F. Guizot, T. B. Macaulay, T. Carlyle, B. G. Niebuhr, L. Ranke, J. G. Droysen, N. M. Karamzin, J. Lelewel, F. Palacký. In the field of fine arts, K. F. Rumohr (1827–31) emphasised the role of history through the development of historical criticism and the elaboration of methods of evaluation. K. Schnasse (1843–6) represents the historical approach rooted in Hegelian philosophy and Romanticism. For him, the arts symbolised the expression of national conscience: consequently, he went on to emphasise their national and religious aspects. Methodologically, however, Rumohr and Schnasse remain captive within the chronological framework of epochs and biographies.

Historical linguistics

The first truly historical theory of language was offered in 1772 by J. G. Herder. In his work, Herder related the development of language to thought and emotion, and suggested a contemporaneous development of language and thinking. These notions were further elaborated by J. Priestly and, later, J. Grimm.

The development of linguistics as a scientific discipline in the early nineteenth century was at first confined to Germany. This occurred through the integration of the comparative method with historical analysis and reconstruction of language. Although the comparative method found application in almost any discipline, it was in linguistics and zoology that it produced the most spectacular results.

Modern linguistics and the philosophy of language were established by W. von Humboldt, whose complex conceptions encompass all the approaches to the analysis of language extant in the nineteenth and even the twentieth century. In these he contrasted language and thought, conventionality of signs and 'inner forms' of language elements, the notions of the objective and the subjective, language as an activity and as a product, totality and individuality, the individual and the collective, language and speech, and finally understanding and incomprehension.

F. Bopp (1816) is generally considered to be the actual founder of comparative linguistics, credited with the deployment of the historical-comparative method to isolate common elements in words of different languages. Both word supply (lexicon) and grammar were subjected to analysis (R. Rask 1818, Grimm–Rask phonetic law). Extant languages were studied as they evolved, while the search for the 'original language' (*Ursprache*) led Bopp to focus attention on Sanskrit.

Archaeology

The idea of development and the comparative method, as well as historical criticism, also found application in archaeology. The methods used, in fact, were very similar. Against this background, archaeology too underwent profound changes during the first half of the nineteenth century. It is clear that the foundations for these changes were laid earlier, and, in many cases, the traditional forms of antiquarian archaeology continued to flourish alongside its prehistoric counterpart. If we compare, however, the archaeology of the 1820s with that of the 1850s, we are comparing two qualitatively different disciplines.

As different approaches which originally defined the antiquarian science began emerging as disciplines in their own right, prehistoric archaeology was left to define its own scope and methods. As a result, it emerged as a discipline with its own identity. Thomsen's technological framework liberated the prehistoric artefact from its antiquarian constraints. C. J. Thomsen divided artefacts into those made of stone, bronze and iron. He then invested his scheme with chronological significance, artefacts of stone being the oldest, those of iron the youngest. Thomsen's Three Age System has, of course, notable antecedents. Apart from the models extant in antiquity and during the Renaissance mentioned earlier, several scholars of the Enlightenment postulated similar schemes. Later, in 1813, the Danish historian L. S. Vedel Simonsen contemplated the existence of ages of stone, copper, bronze and iron. M. Bruzelius in Sweden supported the same idea in his book *Specimen Antiquitatum Borealium*, published between 1816 and 1818. The French archaeologist F. Jouannet also noted the existence of three ages in 1814, as did J. G. G. Büsching in Breslau ten years later. They failed to elaborate their ideas in greater depth, however, and only some of these scholars related these notions specifically to archaeological materials. This was done explicitly only by Thomsen. The remarkable increase in the size of prehistoric collections as well as their classification are an integral part of Thomsen's contribution to the understanding of prehistoric artefacts.

With exceptional diligence and enthusiasm, archaeologists of the Romantic period searched for and discovered more and more antiquities, which accumulated in private collections and, later, in public museums. They even handed out questionnaires to the public, obtaining, in this way, valuable information about the artefacts themselves. This activity was widespread across Europe: one only has to mention Father V. Krolmus in Bohemia or Abbé J. B. D. Cochet in France as two outstanding figures among ecclesiastics active in the investigation of antiquities at that time.

Thomsen combined a strong interest in antiquities and a profound knowledge of French philosophical thought with practical experience derived from the family merchant business and the classification of goods bought in bulk. These qualifications served him in good stead in 1816, when, at the age of twenty-seven, he was appointed by the Royal Commission for the Preservation and Collection of National Antiquities as its unpaid secretary. On that occasion, Bishop Münter made the following far-sighted remark:

[Mr Thomsen is an] amateur with a great range of accomplishments ... It is true that although he has learnt Latin he is not a university student. I must insist, however, that in my opinion, given the present state of archaeological science, that is a point of minor significance. It matters not at all where a man gets his knowledge from, the important thing is whether he has it.

Between 1816 and 1819 Thomsen began reorganising the Royal Commission's growing collection of antiquities. In 1819 the collection was made accessible to the public in a former monastery of the Holy Trinity in Copenhagen, which now became the Museum of Northern Antiquities. At first it would appear that Thomsen simply applied his experience, gained in the classification of merchandise, to prehistoric artefacts. It is worth noting, however, that formal and consistent division of objects into those made of stone, bronze and iron was applied right from the beginning of Thomsen's work. His critics, therefore, are wrong in asserting that Thomsen created his framework without forethought of an ad hoc basis. From the beginning, Thomsen believed in the Three Age System, at first perhaps as a useful frame of reference, later as a conceptual model of great predictive significance.

The first stage of Thomsen's elaboration of the Three Age System became evident with the opening of his museum in 1819, later to become the National Museum. Initially, the three ages were illustrated in three cabinets. Further elaboration of the model led to its full description in 1836 in Thomsen's *Ledetradd til Nordisk Oldkyndighed* (published in English in 1848 as *A Guide to Northern Antiquities*). Apart from the main study by Thomsen, a number of others, members of the Royal Society for Scandinavian Antiquities, contributed to this book. The translations of the volume into German (1837) and English (1848), as well as Thomsen's correspondence and personal contact with other scholars, led to a rapid dissemination of the Three Age System throughout Europe.

In more recent times, it has become fashionable to denigrate the significance of the Three Age System. Naturally, it would be odd if the subsequent evolution of archaeology had failed to modify some of Thomsen's ideas. It would be equally unusual if Thomsen's work did not have antecedents: most great discoveries do. If we wish to assess Thomsen's work honestly, we have to compare the information value of artefact collections prior to Thomsen on the one hand, and following his work, on the other. Before Thomsen demonstrated his scheme with the extensive collections housed in his museum, all an archaeologist had at his disposal was an array of unrelated bits of information. Thomsen organised this information into a clear chronological scheme, based on the idea of technological evolution. Subsequently, he verified the validity of his scheme stratigraphically. However coarse the Three Age System remained, it implicitly engendered the beginnings of the technological, functionalist and economic approach to prehistory, the notion of cultural taxonomy and the elements of comparative and typological method. With the help of these conceptual tools, prehistoric artefacts suddenly became rich sources of information. Thomsen can be credited with advancing archaeology to the level of a scientific discipline.

Technological and morphological criteria, such as the distinction between flaked and polished industries, or Schreiber's classification of bronze axes (1842), introduced a further dimension into the original scheme. In 1834, F. Jouannet made an observation in a regional journal which heralded the subsequent recognition of the Palaeolithic and Neolithic periods. On the basis of finds of flaked and polished stone artefacts from two southern French localities, he suggested that the period of polished stone artefacts was preceded by one when the polishing of stone was unknown. Functional comparative studies were emphasised by S. O. Müller (1846–1934). J. J. A. Worsaae (1821–85) can be credited with the development of the comparative method, which, he believed, was the only way to trace the great historical events in antiquity. Its application was enhanced by the increasing accuracy of archaeological excavations, now aimed at the retrieval of information, and not just of valuable curiosities. Already in the 1840s, Worsaae recommended the drawing and the description of artefacts, with reference to their spatial and stratigraphical location within a site, and urged the preservation of such apparently worthless objects as human and animal bones. Most importantly, he elevated the importance of whole artefactual assemblages above those of individual finds. His own investigations meticulously followed these principles.

The concept of the assemblage, and of its relationship to the surrounding environment, gradually replaced the antiquarian attitude to finds. K. von Lewezov (1825), G. C. F. Lisch (1837) and R. Virchow (1874), all emphasised the importance of assemblages, but it was O. A. Montelius who elaborated these ideas into a clear methodological procedure. Stratigraphic method, used in isolated cases as early as the seventeenth (O. Rudbeck) and eighteenth centuries (Thomas Jefferson, A. A. Rhode), became more widespread from the beginning of the nineteenth century. Thus, in 1797, John Frere estimated the age of flint artefacts from the depth of their deposition. In 1814, L.-J. Traullé dated finds in peatbogs according to their stratigraphy. Some years later, C. Picard and J. Boucher de Perthes followed Traullé's lead and investigated the terraces of the river Somme. Boucher de Perthes, on finding his first flint artefact in 1828, remarked: 'I am not a scientist, only a scientific bohemian. Stone tools were there for everyone to see. But I was the first to recognise them.' He went on to argue that the crudely shaped tools (later to be recognised as hand axes), found in undisturbed geological layers, which were clearly Quaternary in age, were fashioned by 'ante-diluvian' man. In 1837, E. Lartet used stratigraphy of cave deposits to estimate their age and the age of artefacts found therein. In the 1850s, Worsaae applied the principles of stratigraphy to check the validity of the Three Age System.

In this process of the development of the stratigraphic method, the verification of the age of finds by reference to geological strata played a critical role.

In earlier times, archaeological finds were placed within an altogether different chronological perspective. In England, for instance, fossils found together with artefacts were interpreted as the remains of elephants brought by Claudius to Britain, and the artefacts were classified accordingly. W. Buckland in England and G. L. de Cuvier in France led the debate against the existence of antediluvian man, refusing to recognise the accumulating evidence offered by bones of extinct animals, stone artefacts and in some cases human bones found together under the sealed floors of caves in France, Britain and Germany. It was not until the end of the 1850s that the uniformitarian view, promoting the great antiquity of man, prevailed over the views of Cuvier and Buckland – but this is a story which will be told in chapter 3.

The use of the stratigraphic method resulted in the detailed and accurate division of strata. This was not confined to only a few sites but, thanks to analogous geological layers, could be effected at most stratified sites. For the first time there was a reliable and clear procedure for the establishment of relative chronology. This was especially the case for earlier prehistory.

During the same period we can also observe the gradual emergence of the typological perspective. Its roots can be detected in observations such as those made in 1812 by P. Knight, who noted that some polished axes served as prototypes for the manufacture of axes in bronze. In 1835, C. Picard identified flaked stone axes as predecessors of the later polished types. In 1836, Thomsen considered the possibilities of typological dating on the basis of shape and decoration, and in the same year, G. Klemm attempted to produce an evolutionary typological sequence of bronze axes. H. Schreiber, in 1842, proceeded along the same lines. In the second half of the nineteenth century, General Pitt Rivers, probably inspired by Fergusson's *True Principles of Beauty in Art* (1849), which placed much emphasis on progress in art through the perfecting of style, reconstructed technological evolutionary sequences of individual tool types and weapons. The two men who laid the true foundations of the typological method, however, came from Sweden: these were H. O. Hildebrand and O. A. Montelius. They both began by applying to archaeology the knowledge gained by Hildebrand's father, B. E. Hildebrand, who in 1846 developed the typological method in numismatics.

The ascendancy of evolutionism
The idea of evolution

One natural source of inspiration for the idea of evolution is the development of an individual. This is the basis of all organic theories, which perceive the evolution of an individual as a process determined solely by its original or internal conditions. Such conditions control the process mechanistically, through growth, and culminate with the development of all embryonic characteristics into the achievement of the optimal state. Goethe's notion of evolution as an expression of ideal design and Winckelmann's view of it as an approximation of an ideal form are merely an elaboration of this pattern of thought.

A real change took place only in the nineteenth century, when notions such as the evolution of species, phylogeny and general evolution were introduced. Although the Hegelian system as a whole considered everything as a qualitative evolution of a single 'super-organism', it nevertheless categorised constituent 'organisms' into an evolutionary sequence, albeit through the notions of theses, antitheses, and syntheses. At this juncture, the idea of evolution represented an organising principle, rather than an explanation, because it was not capable of explaining itself. It was only with the work of Marx in political economy and that of Darwin in biology that qualitative change took place. Their thoughts about the mechanisms of social and biological change became new premises which could not be ignored by any subsequent scientific concepts. As far as the general characteristics of evolution were concerned, it was characterised as a progression from simple to complex, from smaller entities to larger ones (Spencer), or, alternatively, as a tendency to equilibrium, symmetry and simplicity (Mach); or, even, towards increased perfection and independence from the environment.

The composition and development of the social sciences were closely connected with evolutionary theory, which represented a theoretical framework sufficiently broad to allow for a synthesis of an enormous range of observations without discarding the knowledge attained during the Enlightenment. Human naturalness, the essential nature of human society, and certain organisational frameworks, such as gradualism and stadialism, remained as basic points of reference. The fundamental assumption that knowledge can be gained above all by understanding the origin of things found general acceptance. This view increased the importance of the comparative method, which can be used to observe events which are recurring, general and natural. With the establishment of the evolutionary framework and the comparative method, occurrences which contradicted these approaches could not but be regarded as anachronisms, which merely lent further support to the general scheme. This is why evolutionism was inherently ahistorical: history was used only to the extent of illustrating evolutionary notions. Such evolution then, was unidirectional, unilinear, and deviations, when not perceived as relics, were regarded as side branches in the evolutionary process, which were, sooner or later, bound to merge with the mainstream of evolution.

Evolution in sociology

A. Fergusson (1792), the inventor of the celebrated stages of savagery, barbarism, and civilisation, can be regarded according to H. E. Barnes, the historiographer of sociology, as 'the first truly historical sociologist'. The first truly great sociological theory, however, is represented by the work of A. Comte, completed between 1830 and 1842, in which he defined for the first time the role and the methodology of the new discipline. Society is perceived here as an organism governed by the universal law of progress, which can be described through sociology. Sociology is composed of statics (morphology of a society) and dynamics (evolutionary theory). Evolution is unilinear and consists of progress towards greater perfection. It can be divided into a teleological (fetishism, militarism), metaphysical (polytheism, law) and positive (monotheism, industry) stage. Individual phases are perceived as internally organised, structured units, especially those of religion, law, economy, philosophy and social relations. As was the case with Hegel and his followers, Comte believed in the culmination of the historical process, represented by the Great Being – Mankind. Naturalness is consequently relegated towards the end of the historical process and represents its conclusion. Emphasis is placed on a non-speculative and objective approach to phenomena, on empirical observation, experiment and the comparative method. The objective of this approach remains, however, the construction of evolutionary sequences, above all of the 'Grand Etre!'

The system worked out by Herbert Spencer between 1862 and 1896 can be seen as the true Bible of positivist evolutionism. Spencer regarded society as analogous to a biological organism. For him evolution meant a progressive differentiation from uniformity to variation, from undefined to specialised structure and function. It is understood as a process without sudden changes, marked by the increase in the differentiation and complexity of structures and by the increase in the number of links between the constituent parts of societies. His approach demands the investigation of individual cases, of facts. Only research which is broad-based and comprehensive can isolate common and typical occurrences from accidental variability. These are the reasons which led Spencer to promote ethnographic research and concrete investigation of the evolution of social institutions.

Evolution in ethnology

Ethnology, too, was transformed by evolutionism, at first by the pre-Darwinian variety. In 1836, zoologist and ethnologist S. Nilsson divided the prehistoric period into the ages of savagery, pastoralism, agriculture, and civilisation. J. K. Bachoven (1861), concerned with kinship, proposed the stages of promiscuity, matriarchy and patriarchy in the evolution of mankind. H. J. S. Maine (1861), J. F. McLennan (1866) and J. Lippert (1884) adopted a similar approach. Myths often served as points of departure in such investigations, for they were often regarded as vestiges of the prehistoric period. Myths and ethnographic observations enabled Sir John Lubbock (later Lord Avebury) to carry out a reconstruction of animism, fetishism, totemism and shamanism (1865).

Henry Morgan placed special emphasis on technical discoveries, innovations and production (1877). The evolution of social institutions, on the other hand, was reduced to the emulation of a few basic ideas. Morgan's attempt to understand society through technology and economy is summarised in his highly specialised evolutionary scheme, with each stage corresponding to certain types of technology and subsistence. Thus the main stages of savagery, barbarism and civilisation correspond to hunting, agriculture (from middle barbarism) and literacy.

The 'anthropological school' (E. B. Tylor 1865, A. Lang 1884) assumed that the physical and psychological nature of man are identical and that human beings at the same level of evolution will react in a similar way to the same events: the so-called doctrine of the psychic unity of mankind. Psychological explanations were emphasised. In 1871, E. B. Tylor was the first to formulate the theory of animism and to define the concept of culture, including material culture.

Evolutionism in mythology and folklore

Similar trends were discernible in the study of folklore. M. Müller attempted, on the basis of comparative Indo-European linguistics, to reconstruct Indo-European mythology assuming the common evolution of languages and myths. Epic literature was viewed as a continuation of myths, while folklore was perceived as their relic. Müller was the first to note the connections (relationships) between culture and individual language groups. He explained myths symbolically: gods, for example, symbolise natural forces; Little Red Riding Hood symbolises the morning star, and the Wolf symbolises the night. This approach was adopted by the 'naturalist school', which Müller founded. While Müller preferred solar symbols, however, others favoured meteorological occurrences (A. Kuhn 1859, W. Schwartz 1860).

In contrast to the naturalist school, T. Benfey chose a diffusionist path, long before diffusionism became fashionable. Comparisons with Indian folk tales led Benfey to formulate his 'Indian theory', based on the conviction that some tales originated in India and diffused from there via Islam, Buddhism and Mongolian intrusions, while others, such as those with animal motifs, spread from Greece to India with the armies of Alexander the Great. Thus folk tales are regarded here as a creation of the historical period. In their analysis of myths, W. Schwartz, W. Mannhardt and E. H. Meyer, as well as the anthropological school of Benfey, came close to the evolutionary theory when they suggested a link between myths and specific stages in social evolution. While in the Anglo-Saxon world the investigation of myths was dominated by ethnology, in Germany, the interpretation of myths was closely related to philology.

Culmination of evolutionary thought

Evolutionism – bounded by its declared belief in unilinear evolution – is time-conscious, rather than space-conscious. Time is not comprehended chronologically, however; rather, it is perceived as a sequence of successive steps. Similarly, human beings are viewed as an entity – as Human Beings. One can then understand the identification of individuals, of mankind, humanity and society with that mythical Great Being of Comte, the youthful Marx, and others. At first, evolutionism made do with data that were available at the time: indiscriminately accumulated heaps of facts, which precluded comparison and quantification. It was only with the periodisation which occurred as a consequence of evolutionary thinking, that data, old and new, could be categorised according to the organising principle of evolution. Thanks to the evolutionary hypothesis, facts could now be classified and compared and finally accepted or discarded as evidence in support of the evolutionary view. Endowed with such a perspective, and fed with the growing store of data supplied by the second generation of fieldwork-conscious investigators, the only further route open to evolutionism was further specification and periodisation. This development duly took place, but the pigeon-holing of data into various phases and cultures turned out to be fruitless, inadequate and bereft of practical application. In ethnology, for instance, the celebrated work of J. G. Frazer, can be seen as an apex of the evolutionary approach. (The first edition of *The Golden Bough* appeared in print in 1900.) Frazer, a gentleman scholar, *homme de lettres*, constructed a grand universal scheme concerning the use of ritual and its relationship to myth, where ritual is regarded as a primary source. He did this by applying the comparative method to an enormous number of data, which were, nevertheless, fragmentary and inconsistent. He never came face to face with a primitive man, and he rejected with horror the mere thought of such an encounter.

In the second half of the nineteenth century, evolutionary successes in biology (Darwin, Haeckel, Huxley) and physiology (C. Bernard) acted as sources of inspiration, which penetrated beyond the scholarly world. Thus Honoré de Balzac wrote *The Physiology of a Tie and a Cigar*, and evolutionary influences can be found in his other works. The influence of physiology was due to the early successes of its experiments, revealing functional properties of the human organism with measured precision, and to the creation of a scientific vocabulary applicable to other disciplines (terms such as function, homeostasis, pathology, etc.).

Advances in biology provoked the adoption of biological parallels in the humanities. This is demonstrated by the growing acceptance of biological terminology, and by the adoption of entire biological theories. Thus, A. Schleicher, the linguist and botanist, proposed a biological explanation in linguistics. Following the Hegelian triad, he divided languages into three groups: mineral, vegetable, animal; and into two evolutionary levels. Language was analogous to a natural organism with its own laws (1850). Later, in 1863, Schleicher adopted a thoroughly Darwinian approach, including such concepts as the struggle for existence. Language was equated with genus, dialect with subgenus, root of a word with a cell. *Ursprache* (parent language) formed the basis of the subsequent evolution of languages; these genetic relationships were illustrated using dendrograms, again following the dendrograms of the biological evolution. Reacting against such biological determinism, W. D. Whitney (1871) and many others argued that language is a cultural, not a biological, phenomenon.

During the second half of the nineteenth century, biological evolutionism served also as a model in history (H. Taine), literary history (Bruntière 1890), sociology (Gumplowitz 1909), and prehistory (J. A. de Gobineau 1853–5, Montelius 1855). In the second half of the nineteenth century, the intuitive ideas of historicism were often countered by positivist historiography. On the one hand, emphasis was placed on complete objectivity and an impersonal approach which would preclude any value judgements (T. Mommsen, 1854–5; G. Monod, 1876); on the other, sociological theories of positivism which perceived historical processes as analogous to biological ones were modified to suit the requirements of historical disciplines (H. T. Buckle 1857–61, E. Renan 1864).

The great, dynamic, all-embracing schemes of historicism, although providing a good description of political history at different times, failed to analyse the sources of their development. Such achievement also eluded the naturalist-positivist school of thought. As a consequence, historiography divided the unified concept of history into separate constituent structures: social, economic, cultural, etc., reflecting, perhaps not accidentally, the divisions which were beginning to emerge in contemporary nineteenth-century society (J. Burckhardt, Fustel de Coulanges, M. M. Kovalevskij).

History depersonified, history without singular events, history that is processual, and reflected by general and repeated events, forms the core of K. Lamprecht's work (1912). Lamprecht regarded history as a kaleidoscope with a whole range of possible combinations. This led him to introduce statistics and quantification, and apply them in the analysis of variability, sequences and trends.

The works of Marx and Engels, so influential in our own time, form a part of this general picture, marked by the fragmentation of history. They introduced the notions of economic base and superstructure and brought to light the importance of forces of production, the relations of production, and the role of class struggle. To both of these scholars, the history of mankind is a natural-historical process. They present general laws of social evolution as well as a detailed analysis of its various forms, above all, the capitalist society. Their teaching is based on the assumption that social existence determines social consciousness, social existence consisting mainly of forces and relations of production. Historical materialism divides the evolution of mankind into socio-economic formations. With the exception of the earliest formation, the original classless society, the operational mechanism of the historical process consists of class struggle.

The main significance of Marx's teaching rests in his historicism (the absence of universal economic laws). Inspired by the works of Bachofen and Morgan, Engels gives special consideration to the evolution of man and to the origins of human society. For him, the human hand is not only 'an organ of work, but also its product'.

Linguistics as a cultural-historical discipline

In linguistics, the period of positivist historiography was represented by neogrammarians of the second half of the nineteenth century (the 1878 manifesto, G. Ascoli, M. Bréal, B. Delbrück, H. Paul, W. Whitney, and others). It was marked by empirical orientation and by apprehension towards philosophical concepts. The general theory of language and the perception of language as the 'soul of the nation' was sometimes replaced by individual psychological approaches, rooted in the notion that the only real language is that of an individual, and reflected in speech rather than literary record. Even syntax was explained in psychological terms. Linguistics was considered a cultural-historical discipline; the focus of attention shifted from the search for *Ursprache* to the study of extant languages and their dialects. A search was initiated for phonetic laws which would apply without exceptions. The problem of the origin of language was set aside, or explicitly discarded: in 1866 the Linguistic Society of Paris resolved to reject any work concerned with the origins of language. Working within this perspective, H. Paul drew an analogy between the origins of language and the condition of a child learning one: both processes were seen as marked by a lack of conscious selection and by incidental and irrational circumstances.

Typological developments in archaeology

In archaeology, the application of the typological method constituted the most important theoretical development of the second half of the nineteenth century. Following the earlier application of the method in palaeography, history of art, classical archaeology and numismatics, H. O. Hildebrand introduced the method in archaeology in 1866. His use of the approach was purely practical, however, and did not lead to its theoretical rationalisation or methodological elaboration. This task was performed by Montelius, who can therefore be regarded with justification as the real creator of the typological method in archaeology. In developing his methodology, Montelius made use of not only ethnographic parallels, but also contemporary technological evolution, illustrated, for example, by the development of railway carriages. He took the simple functional form as a point of departure, which evolved further to create a series; in other words, genetically related groups. In the course of such evolution, attributes which were functional originally but had since lost their significance were retained, much as is the case in biological evolution. Such traits could then serve as features diagnostic of the age of artefacts: artefacts with characteristics which had lost their function being more recent than those which had fully functional characteristics.

Later, S. O. Müller introduced typological investigation of whole complexes, as opposed to individual artefacts.

In his work, Montelius reveals influences of the Darwinian evolutionary theory. His pupil, N. Åberg wrote in 1930 that the typological method represents the application of Darwinism to the products of human labour. It is based on the assumption that human will is bound by certain laws, which are close to those governing the evolution of the biological world. Artefacts evolve as if they were living organisms, single objects are treated as individuals, typological series represent evolution at a generic level, and groups of typological series are akin to the branching of genera which together comprise a family.

Typological methodology not only helped in the recognition of the development of individual artefacts, but also became a significant aid to relative dating. Typological sequences reconstructed by O. A. Montelius, S. O. Müller, P. Reinecke, O. Tischler, O. Almgren and others conferred upon European prehistory, especially its later part, a more accurate chronological framework. Further advances, made with the discovery that individual typological sequences of different types of artefacts can occur relatively independent of one another, led to the investigation of entire assemblages, as opposed to single artefacts. The investigation of the relationship between distances in space and the occurrence of different typological sequences of artefacts resulted in 1874 in the development of so-called horizontal stratigraphy.

The emergence of field archaeology

With the increasing recognition of the variety and scope of prehistoric material culture, attention turned to the morphology of archaeological sites: their size, nature, and variability. In the 1840s, the first prehistoric workshops and kitchen-middens came to light; in 1854 the first lake dwellings were discovered. Spurred by the debate over evolution and the existence of ante-diluvian man, the exploration of cave deposits took off in the 1850s and 1860s. From 1866, J. J. A. Worsaae began an investigation of cache finds and fortified hilltop settlements.

Objets d'art, dating to later prehistoric times, were not uncommon; on the contrary, they had traditionally taken up most of the space in collections. Now other forms of art were beginning to catch up: rock pictures or engravings. Although first described in Sweden by P. F. Suhm in 1784, the earliest monographs concerned with rock engravings did not appear until 1846 (L. C. Wiede). Two years later, a book by A. E. Holmberg accorded a more extensive treatment to the same subject.

Prehistoric art, belonging to the earlier periods, remained neglected for a long time, however. The first examples of Palaeolithic art were discovered in 1840, but they were not recognised as such. Only twenty years later, further discoveries by E. Lartet led to the reconsideration of these finds and to their correct chronological classification. Satuola discovered cave paintings at Altamira in 1875. In 1878, L. Chiron argued for their acceptance as authentic Palaeolithic remains, but the idea of prehistoric cave paintings at such an early date was rejected in learned journals. It was only at the turn of the century that the full extent of Palaeolithic art was finally acknowledged. Since then prehistoric art has been subjected to systematic analysis, especially at the instigation of the art historians G. Semper and A. Riegel, and the ethnographer J. G. Frazer.

Comparative and typological methods also led to the reappraisal of the hitherto neglected value of pottery, including sherds. A. Conze, in 1872, declared ceramics to be the leading archaeological source (*Leitfossil*). F. Klopfleisch, an art historian, turned his attention to the analysis of the decoration of Neolithic pottery, defining, in 1874, linear and corded wares (*Bandkeramik, Schnurkeramik*). Ceramics were also used by classical archaeologists as objects undergoing rapid morphological changes, and offering, therefore, significant chronological insights (A. Furtwängler 1879, Sir Flinders Petrie 1890).

Prehistoric and classical archaeology developed a grudge against one another at this time. Prehistory, especially in Germany, was more attached to physical anthropology than ever before; in 1880, R. Virchow, the well-known anthropologist, declared: 'We can be credited with breathing new life into prehistory and palaeontology', and, 'in such a way we, the lowly anthropologists, penetrated the polished corridors of classical archaeology: as intruders' (Virchow 1886). They were not welcomed: T. Mommsen commented at the time that prehistory was 'a discipline of illiterates, its research a matter for provincial clerics and retired army officers'.

Above all, more attention was now accorded to settlement archaeology. Archaeologists were beginning to gain more profound knowledge about the prehistoric way of life, which in turn generated improvements in the organisation and reporting of archaeological excavations. Original excavation reports and reporting of finds began to occur with greater frequency. In this aspect of archaeology, General A. H. Pitt Rivers became a leading figure. His fieldwork, marked by excellent field research, especially of settlements, by meticulous documentation, consistent use of stratigraphy and recording of spatial relationships, and by his attention to small finds, set standards not only for his own generation, but also for future ones. Exceptionally for his time, he recorded the location of such apparently 'worthless' objects as animal bones. He employed experiments and concrete models in the reconstruction of sites; as, for instance, in his replication of the formation and destruction of ditches, or experimental flint mining. He built a comparative bone collection for his bioarchaeological finds, procured from his own livestock and supplied with all the necessary statistics, such as age, sex, size and stature.

Field archaeology benefited further from photography. In 1875, classical archaeologist A. Conze used a photograph for the first time in an excavation report. From the 1890s, aerial photography entered the scene: in 1891, a British officer, C. F. Close, took photographs of ruins at Agra from a balloon; in 1906, P. H. Sharpe photographed Stonehenge by the same means; in 1911, Italian soldiers again used a balloon to photograph the Roman Forum and the ancient port at Ostia. The practical application of aerial photography to archaeological prospecting did not occur until after the First World War, however.

Another significant contribution to field archaeology occurred in the 1870s when German archaeologists, in particular C. Schuchhardt, realised in the course of settlement investigations that dark stains so frequently occurring in a horizontal profile were the remains of decomposed posts and other uprights. At last a way was found for the reconstruction of ground plans of dwellings, the layout of fortifications, palisades and other wooden buildings.

The investigations at Pompeii, especially after 1860 under the leadership of G. Fiorelli, also contributed to the advances in field archaeology. In contrast to his predecessors, who had been in the habit of excavating by the 'telephone box' method (by sinking narrow, vertical shafts into the ground), Fiorelli excavated in wide horizontal layers, uncovering house floors and entire blocks of houses which until then had been destroyed. He also came up with the idea of plastering over the potholes in which workers were losing their tools. In this way, he stumbled across casts of the victims of the catastrophe, often capturing the expressions of agony at death on the faces of the deceased.

In the last decades of the nineteenth century, fieldwork and field documentation reached such a level of complexity that methodological textbooks and instruction manuals became necessary. These early publications, written some seventy to a hundred years ago, remained in use until recently.

Advances in field research were matched by developments in the analysis of artefacts, using methods often borrowed from the natural sciences. Chemical analysis of bronze objects and of glass was commonly applied, especially among German and Scandinavian researchers, in the 1820s, although isolated cases of such applications existed even earlier. In the 1860s, A. Damour introduced the use of petrographic analysis. Between 1878 and 1910, G. de Geer developed his varve chronology. At the beginning of the twentieth century, L. von Post laid the basis of pollen analysis.

In a broader perspective, the use of experimentation, applied in archaeology to test the production and function of stone implements, or to find out the range of ancient musical instruments, was inspired by the natural sciences. Hardly out of its nappies, experimental archaeology found celebrated supporters and benefactors, such as the Danish King Frederick VII, captivated by the problems of megalith construction, or Napoleon III, who tested the capability of Roman siege machines using replicas based on finds made at Alesia. Finally, the botanical and zoological context of archaeological finds helped to maintain links between archaeology and the natural sciences, a fact evident in the contemporary palaeontological or palaeobotanical (i.e. Steenstrup 1842) work.

Developments in chronology

Relative chronology attained significant successes which were due in no small measure to stratigraphical dating, checked by reference to geological layers. Although Thomsen's Three Age System served as the original point of departure for the construction of relative chronology, the Montelian typological method supplied the meat on the bones. It offered a way of ordering the European prehistoric past and of tying it with the familiar evolution to the world of antiquity (O. A. Montelius 1898–1900, S. O. Müller 1912). While O. A. Montelius and S. O. Müller used it to order the European prehistoric past and to tie it with the by then familiar evolution of ancient Greece and Rome, Flinders Petrie synchronised the events of classical antiquity with those of ancient Egypt.

The lack of an adequate methodology continued in absolute dating, however, especially for the earlier periods, or in areas removed from the literate ancient civilisations. Boucher de Perthes estimated the age of the

Lower Palaeolithic at 16,000–20,000 years ago on the basis of the accumulation of peat layers, but G. de Mortillet increased this estimate tenfold. At the beginning of the twentieth century, A. Penck and E. Bruckner used the sedimentary processes associated with glaciations to estimate the beginning of the first glacial epoch at 600,000 years: an estimate which remained unchallenged until recently.

The age of later periods could be assessed by reference to historical civilisations; as a consequence, in the last decades of the nineteenth century, chronological estimates began to be based on firmer ground. With the general acceptance of the Montelian system, the advent of the Neolithic in Europe was dated into the third millennium – five hundred years earlier in the south-east of Europe than in the north – with the following five periods dated between 1800 and 750 BC. This chronological framework remained in force until the radiocarbon revolution.

The eclipse of evolutionism

With these developments, the original Three Age System soon underwent fragmentation. Already in 1834, F. Jouannet divided the Stone Age into that of polished stone preceded by chipped flint tools. Boucher de Perthes placed the age of chipped stone tools in ante-diluvian times. In 1865, J. Lubbock formalised this distinction in terms of the Old Stone Age, marked by the chipped stone industries, and the New Stone Age, characterised by polished stone tools. A year later, the Palaeolithic and Neolithic periods were separated by the Mesolithic or Middle Stone Age. The term was first suggested by H. Westropp (1866), and then again in 1892 by J. A. Brown, but it remained ill defined and was not generally accepted until the 1920s and 1930s. Arguing from stratigraphically verified palaeontological data, E. Lartet (1865) divided the Stone Age into four periods according to the dominant fauna: the age of cave bear, that of mammoth, that of rhinoceros, and finally the age of aurochs or bison.

Inspired by evolutionary theory, G. de Mortillet specified two laws of human cultural evolution in 1869: the law of human progress and the law of analogous development. He then proceeded to divide the Palaeolithic accordingly into *chelléen*, *moustérien*, *solutréen* and *magdalénien*. *Acheuléen* was added later between the Chellean and Mousterian stages, as were two initial Eolithic stages. Abbé H. Breuil expanded the sequence by adding a further three periods: Clactonian, Levalloisian and Aurignacian. In the field of later prehistory, the concept of the Eneolithic, or, rather, Copper Age, was discussed in the 1870s and 1880s (F. Pulszky 1876, P. Berthelot 1889). In 1874, H. O. Hildebrand divided the Iron Age into Halstatt and La Tène periods. Finer divisions of the Bronze Age, the Hallstatt, la Tène and Roman periods, were carried out by Montelius, Müller, Reinecke, Tischler and Almgren. Montelius, for instance, distinguished four Neolithic phases, six Bronze Age periods and eight phases of the Iron Age in Northern Europe. This periodisation was challenged by Müller, who worked out an alternative scheme marked by a different number of periods and different divisions among them. To give a further example, the dating system developed by Arthur Evans for the Bronze Age of Crete is based on the recognition of the Early, Middle and Late Minoan periods. Each of these periods is divided into three further phases. Such units of time, staked out by scholars, also serve as components of the relative chronology.

Contemporary with this process of classification, or ethnological evolutionism, the categorisation of the social, economic and cultural evolution occurred. The archaeological and ethnographic division was subjected to mutual influences, and, in some cases, integration. H. M. Westropp in 1872, for example, identified the Palaeolithic with hunting and gathering, the Neolithic with pastoralism and the Bronze Age with agriculture.

In the course of the nineteenth century archaeologists succeeded in accumulating so many material remains of the past that discrete breaks in time, marked by material culture, appeared well established. Thomsen's framework is built on solid foundations. Its simple structure, consisting of three basic components, did not initially provoke much disagreement. With increasing elaboration, however, the sharp divisions between individual periods and phases, often exaggerated for the sake of definition, emerged as a problem in its own right. The fundamental question – why and how certain archaeological units, whether ages, periods, phases, industries or cultures, persist for some time, undergoing, perhaps, a gradual change, and then are all of a sudden replaced by qualitatively alien forms – became the focal point of archaeological explanation. This is important because hidden inside this problem is the understanding of the dynamics of cultural evolution, which underpins the reconstruction of the past.

During the years of evolutionary rule, gaps, breaks and sharp changes in the evolutionary sequences were taken to reflect the fragmented nature of the archaeological record – as indeed was the case in many instances – and not the true nature of the cultural-historical process. The evolutionists expected that future fieldwork would close these gaps in empirical knowledge, evening out the sharp boundaries, and that, in the end, the whole process would reveal itself as a smooth evolutionary continuum. That is why it was characteristic for this period to search for missing links, which were expected, in more than one sense, to join and reconcile all the major differences between periods and cultures of a given evolutionary sequence. This expectation was borne out at first, because most areas outside Western Europe were still poorly researched, with the result that the European sequence of cultural evolution could be exported to other areas of the world without the likelihood of contradiction by the empirical evidence.

Only the primitive societies, surviving in the distant corners of the world, continued to defy the straight and clear pathways of the nineteenth-century evolutionary world. Were these living fossils, as evolutionists maintained? The problem which, it might be expected, would have disrupted the model of continuous parallel evolution was turned on its head and made to fit the prevailing evolutionary notions. Primitive societies were seen as 'backward', they represented the side branches of the evolutionary tree, they were faithful reflections of the Palaeolithic way of life, petrified in time. They were used as blueprints for the reconstruction of prehistoric life, as time capsules in the evolutionary process of the past, preserved into our own time. No one, so far, entertained the thought that these societies, too, might have undergone hundreds and thousands of years of evolution, even though these changes were considerably different from ones experienced by the European cultures.

With the increase in the quantity of archaeological sources, some gaps were filled as expected, but overall the number of sharp breaks failed to diminish. On the contrary, gaps increased. Many discontinuities, unnoticed at first, could no longer be ignored in spite of the evidence; and many ostensibly smooth evolutionary sequences became ruptured with new discoveries – such as Abbé Breuil's Aurignacian period, or Palaeolithic cave art. Evolutionists did not anticipate, for instance, that the Cro-Magnon people of the Upper Palaeolithic had any religious beliefs, and therefore they refused to recognise a whole range of ritual artefacts (Baer 1879, de Mortillet 1883, M. Hoernes 1892). Eventually, evolutionism began to crumble under the weight of these new facts. It was no longer adequate as an explanation.

Archaeology as a profession

The rapid growth of archaeology in the course of the nineteenth century was also aided by the democratisation of society and the development of education. 'Rationalist philosophy is an altogether democratic discipline', noted A. Comte. For a scientist, this observation had a profound practical implication: it broadened the market for books and increased the number of jobs. Greater numbers of academic institutions, the quest for knowledge, the accumulation of knowledge – all these factors of scientific existence were altered by the new factor of time. Although the question of priority and the originality in research had played an important role since the Renaissance, it was now invested with more real, practical significance. The number of scientific journals increased, as did their specialisation; there was a greater need for contributions as feedback. Leibnitz's prophecy, that libraries would grow into cities, almost came true. The nineteenth century saw the publication of thousands of books specifically devoted to pre-history. Single-authored publications gave way to edited volumes, the number of contributions to learned journals increased, and eventually specialised archaeological journals appeared. Published material provided the data for the comparative method. The gentleman scholar was more and more drawn into the situation of a research worker and author as we know him today, increasingly governed by the dictum 'publish or perish'.

Already in 1784, A. L. Schlözer had insisted that historiography should form 'eine grosse unendlich zusammengesetzte Fabrik' (one large, endlessly articulated workshop). The number of scientific workers increased rapidly, repudiating, in some cases, the actual scientists. 'This is not a victory for the sciences,' noted Friedrich Nietzsche, 'it is a victory of methodology over science.'

In 1818, C. J. C. Reuvens was appointed to the first ever chair of archaeology, which combined classical and prehistoric archaeology at the University of Leiden. The first chair of solely classical archaeology was created in 1823 in Berlin. Chairs of prehistoric archaeology were created in two phases: in the middle of the nineteenth and at the turn of the twentieth century. For instance, J. J. A. Worsaae was appointed a professor of archaeology in 1854, while the Disney Professorship of Archaeology at Cambridge was created in 1851, and the Abercromby Chair in Edinburgh was founded in 1927. In summary, the nineteenth century can be seen as the classical period of institutionalisation of learning. The number of new universities, colleges of further education and museums grew rapidly, as did their social significance. As a corollary, archaeology was becoming more professional, at first as a specialised research discipline, later as a vocational profession.

Migrationist and diffusionist intoxication

Further development occurred mainly as a reaction against both the theory and the method of evolutionism. Space replaced time as the main subject of investigation, and a shift in emphasis took place away from abstract concepts such as epochs, periods and stages, towards more particularistic and concrete developments. This meant that individual ethnic identity was stressed at the expense of universal notions of mankind, historical particularism was on the way in and evolutionary generalisations were on the way out; and the idea of independent parallel evolution dissolved in a flood of migrations, contacts and communication.

The extreme diffusionism of W. H. Rivers (1906), W. J. Perry (1926) and G. E. Smith (1925) postulated a single centre of origin for all cultural innovations. Before diffusionism had been brought to such absurd extremes, however, it represented a positive and healthy reaction, enabling a new evaluation of a huge amount of material.

Human geography and spatial anthropology

K. Ritter can be considered the father of anthropogeography. For him, the natural environment was the scene of human evolution, as is obvious from the title of his main work: *Allgemeine vergleichende Erdkunde im Verhältnis zur Natur und zur Geschichte des Menschen* (1822–59). Among his most prominent followers were F. Ratzel in the years 1894–5, and the founder of the morphological method, L. Frobenius (1893). Nevertheless, their study did not go beyond the investigation of a few traits according to which individual cultures were compared. This approach flourished most in the German and Austrian cultural-historical schools (F. Graebner 1904, B. Ankermann 1905, W. Koppers 1906, W. Schmidt 1906, 1907), and also in the United States (R. M. Lowie, A. L. Kroeber). In 1937, Schmidt summarised the theoretical premises and results of the cultural-historical school in a normative form.

The cultural-historical school adopted the formal analysis of material culture as the initial point of departure for its investigations. Its objective was to find and compare as many characteristics as possible and it therefore stressed morphology. This led simultaneously to an increase in fieldwork, to more precision in its methods and to a thorough elaboration of descriptive techniques. In this way archaeology was catching up with what had been customary in biology since Linnaeus. The criteria of quality and quantity formulated by the school helped to identify centres of invention, and paths of migration and diffusion. Although it was acknowledged that basic discoveries, such as the bow, could have been created independently of each other in more than one area, the secondary phenomena (e.g. decoration) were taken to indicate some form of mutual influence. During the study of expansion, the distribution of traits in a distance-dependent way came to play an important role.

Within the cultures themselves, the followers of the cultural-historical school observed individual time periods according to similar criteria. It is also possible to use these methods chronologically (compare the so-called horizontal stratigraphy in archaeology), and to find basic strata. This school is best known for its identifying of individual cultural areas (*Kulturkreise*) and their development. In the United States the father of American cultural anthropology F. Boas, and A. L. Kroeber founded a similar tradition.

Development of the history of art

The cultural-historical school in ethnography and classical archaeology, which was mainly centred in Austria and Germany, relied to a large extent on advances made in the history of art, especially by the Viennese school of art history. The history of art and particularly the Viennese school have significantly influenced the development of classical archaeology. It is therefore appropriate to consider the prevailing philosophical trends in the history of art at the time.

G. Semper (1860) explained the development of art as a by-product of the evolution of crafts, a development where technology played a decisive role. Consequently, he saw forms of artistic expression as dependent on the media (materials), technology of production and purpose. Decorative forms of art were consequently considered as having developed at an early stage. The notion of the primary importance of the decorative elements was then adopted by the historians of art (W. Worringer 1908), classical archaeologists (A. Conze 1870, J. Lange 1899), ethno-psychologists (W. Wundt 1912) and historians (K. Lamprecht 1913). In the second half of the nineteenth century, K. F. Rumohr contributed to the development of the more precise methods of art historical analysis. Historical criticism, especially palaeography and diplomatics, which reached historians thanks to their historiographical training (T. Sickel), provided an inspiration for the new comparative methodology. The analysis of individual detail, of individual forms and of the gradual changes in style of individual scribes and agencies, which was used earlier in historical criticism, was now applied to the plastic arts. G. Morelli was among the first to identify the authorship of disputed works on the basis of such indicators, for instance the elements of personal style occurring in insignificant details such as the drawing of ears, sheets of paper, etc.

Elements of style were used in 1901 by B. Berenson to postulate the existence of a fictional artist, called Amico di Sandro, to whom he attributed a number of artworks previously thought to have belonged to other artists, C. G. Meyne searched for the archetype of an artwork, tracing its fragmentation in copies and replicas. The work by Morelli also served to emphasise the importance of detail in the evolution of style. In 1893, A. Furtwängler analysed copies of Greek sculpture in order to identify the characteristics of the original, and then proceeded to identify other sculptures made by the author of the reconstructed original. In this way, for instance, many additional works were attributed to the sculptor Praxiteles. Such methods also began to penetrate prehistoric archaeology. Thanks to his art history training, the precise methods of stylistic analysis were applied by Czech archaeologist K. Buchtela to prehistoric material.

At the end of the nineteenth century, a more formal approach to the history of art emphasised the importance of shape, especially within the 'Viennese school'. Here form was deemed more important than content or cultural-historical circumstances (F. Wickhoff, A. Riegl, M. Dvořák). The evolution of art was understood as a stylistic appearance affecting all forms of expression by means of a continuous, uninterrupted development. Art followed its own path of development, other influences were only secondary and had impact only within the framework set for them by the autonomous nature of art.

Under the influence of W. Wundt, and with the benefit of his historical training, A. Riegl introduced the psychological-historical concept of evolution into the history of art. In 1893, he began developing a global history of style, in this instance without the aid of absolute normative models. In contradiction to Semper, Riegl saw the origin of art in the imitation of naturalistically perceived reality and in artistic striving (*Kunst-wollen*). The cause of stylistic changes then occurred in the context of attempts to imitate nature and in spite of the nature of the media. Consequently, ornamentation was regarded as a later development. This view was also accepted by some archaeologists (H. Gross 1894, H. Breuil 1906, S. Reinach 1913). Riegl was also among the first to investigate popular art.

Space in sociology and linguistics

Sociology and also linguistics were among the earliest disciplines to focus on the study of spatial relationships. In sociology, space was emphasised by the American ecological school (E. W. Burgess and R. E. Park 1921). In its vocabulary, we can find terms such as migration, segregation, invasion, mobility, etc. Spatial relationships, such as those between man and his environment, or the diffusion of events in space, formed a focus of research for this school. This necessitated the development of a new methodology, involving maps, scaling of spatial measurements, and statistics. Regional perspective was emphasised by the sociological school of F. le Play. In 1898,

G. Tarde systematically studied such processes as adaptation, imitation, repetition, convergence and divergence.

In linguistics, H. Schuchardt presented a theory of geographical transformations of language elements in 1870, and V. Thomsen, a year earlier, noted the expansion of language phenomena through diffusion. While Schleicher still interpreted linguistic likeness genetically, i.e. in time, J. Schmidt in 1872 applied the opposite approach by emphasising the spatial dimension. In presenting his *Wellentheorie*, he postulated spatial diffusion of traits from their centres of origin in a wave-like advance, resulting eventually in a mutual encounter of 'waves' of different provenance. For Schmidt, the linear geneaology of Schleicher became a map of spatial distribution of Indo-European languages. In the last quarter of the nineteenth century, linguistic geography developed as a separate subject, with the task of recording geographically individual linguistic phenomena, using numerically determined boundaries (isoclines).

Finally, on the question of linguistic origins and of spatial relationships, the work of G. I. Ascoli, dating to 1886, played a considerable role. Unlike the simplified relationships depicted by the dendrograms (tree stems) earlier, Ascoli posits a substratum (the language of an assimilated ethnic group), a superstratum (the language of the assimilating groups) and an adstratum (the final product).

Diffusion in mythology and folklore

In the analysis of folk tales, the 'Finnish school' represents the diffusionist approach, equipped with a well worked-out historical-geographical methodology (J. Krohn 1884, K. Krohn 1889, 1907, A. Aarne 1910). Popular folk tales were recorded and catalogued: the list of basic motifs gathered by Aarne alone numbers over a thousand entries. This information served as a basis for the reconstruction of the centres of origin and diffusion: thus Little Red Riding Hood travelled into Central Europe from France, as did Puss in Boots. Fairytales were thought to have originated in the historical period, while myths were accorded a greater age.

In 1922, H. Neumann combined the approaches of the Finnish and the anthropological schools: this, for example, led him to postulate the existence of ancient dwellings without light, windows or adequate ventilation on the basis of the expression 'I smell, I smell a human being', so often used in Central European fairytales. (There *is* an English equivalent and one only wonders how it would be interpreted: 'Fe, Fi, Fo, Fum, I smell the blood of an Englishman!') Perhaps of greater import is the work of P. Saintyves, who in 1923 noted for the first time the analogies between initiation ceremonies and certain motifs found in fairy tales. W. E. Peuckert dated the origin of folk tales to the period transitional between the Bronze Age and the Neolithic, with the centre of origin in the eastern Mediterranean (the Minoan–Cretan theory). His interpretation is derived from ethnosociological argument which postulates matriarchal society in the eastern Mediterranean from the peasant marriage customs and initiation ceremonies. To provide further examples, F. van der Leyen derived folklore from dreams; K. Meuili from shamanistic ceremonies (1935); O. Huth from megalithic rituals (1950): demonstrably no stone was left unturned.

For many decades, popular lore was considered from the point of view of its contents, origin, diffusion and relationship to other socio-cultural phenomena. The form of the presentation was analysed only later, with the work of A. N. Veselovskij (1872) and the 'epic laws' of A. Olrik (1908). The relationship between myths and epos was investigated by G. Dumézil (1968, 1973) and V. J. Propp (1946).

The 'Indo-European theory' of C. W. Sydow, from 1909, represents the 'vertical diffusionism' in the origin and development of folk tales. Sydow's theory is based on the diffusion of a single tale (number 313 in Aarne's catalogue) which is analogous with the distribution of the two traits as interconnected, and uses megalithic architecture to date the origin of the tale. The importance of his contribution, however, rests in his emphasis on the local and social environment, tradition, and the elevation of the importance of stylistic and compositional forms.

Linguistic palaeontology

Sydow's approach was made possible by the existence of linguistic palaeontology. Initially, myths were perceived as a cultural-historical source by G. B. Vico (1668–1744), then the brothers Grimm followed with their analyses of fairy tales, and finally a word on its own was accepted as a cultural-historical document. The latter was anticipated by Leibnitz when he declared that 'words are the oldest monuments of nations'. Later, J. Amades (1950) went further by asserting that words create a better connection with the past than does stone, and that they represent a prehistoric document at least as valuable as material culture.

Linguistic palaeontology encapsulates a number of other subjects, such as comparative linguistics, comparative mythology, ethnology, sociology, etc. Its field of interest covers genetic and spatial similarities between languages (A. Meillet 1908, J. Pokorny 1938, W. Porzig 1954, E. M. Makejev 1964, H. Krahe 1954, 1964, R. Fester 1962; the Italian school of spatial linguistics) and cultural reconstruction on the basis of language. For instance, the Old Russian words for flint (*nagis*) and knife (*nož*) are related and it can be shown that the latter originated from the former, thereby suggesting that the development of the word 'knife' took place in a cultural environment where flint tools and weapons were still used or remembered.

The founders of linguistic palaeontology, A. Kuhn (1852) and A. Pictet (1859–63), still used fantasy to excess. Later workers (W. Hehn 1870, O. Schrader 1883, 1901, A. d'Arbois de Jubaiville 1889–94, A. S. Budilovič 1878–82, P. Bradke 1890, R. Meringer 1897, H. Hirt 1905–7. S. Feist 1910) adopted a more scientific approach. Linguistic palaeontology forms the basis of much of the entries in the archaeological encyclopedia *Reallexikon der Vorgeschichte* compiled by M. Ebert (1924–32). Ebert used as his source of inspiration an earlier palaeolinguistic dictionary, *Reallexikon der Indogermanischen Altertumskunde*, by O. Schrader, published in 1901. More recent developments are represented by the work of W. Brandenstein (1936), A. Nehring (1936), G. Devoto (1962), and the later work of V. V. Ivanov and V. N. Toporov (1973), as well as other members of the structural-semiological school.

Archaeology discovers space

The evolutionist additions to Thomsen's original scheme did not stand up to the trial of time. The divisions worked out by G. de Mortillet and his followers were exposed as too coarse and simplified to accommodate new cultural groupings which were more accurately defined in time and space. De Mortillet's evolutionary stages were shown to be either incidentally defined mechanical entities or cultures which were too constrained in space and time to have any stadial evolutionary significance. It had become obvious that it was not possible to explain all these phenomena inside Thomsen's structure, and that it was necessary to open its windows wide to a new factor – space.

Maps showing the distribution of archaeological cultures and other remains serve best to illustrate the disparities between the old evolutionary systems of classification and the new, forthcoming material. Although maps were already being constructed by the first half of the nineteenth century, isolated points scattered in the wide white spaces did not force anybody to take into account space along with time. After the middle of the century, the number of finds, as well as maps, was growing. In England (Ordnance Survey) and Germany (after 1878 – thanks to the Anthropological Society), the mapping of archaeological remains was carried out at a well-organised, professional level. In 1869, A. H. Pitt Rivers prepared distribution maps of megaliths; and other maps, showing the distribution of certain artefact types, began to appear. Such maps were put on exhibition in Paris (at the World Exhibition in 1867), in Copenhagen (1869) and in Boulogne (1871). Towards the end of the nineteenth and at the beginning of the twentieth century, growing numbers of finds, more thorough excavations and more accurate recording techniques, as well as the increasing use of cartographic methods and also of ethnographic parallels, all contributed to a greater understanding of the functioning of cultures and towards a more comprehensive reconstruction of human behaviour in prehistory. These advances brought to the fore a question which had been posed earlier, but only now attracted full and undivided attention: to what extent is it possible to identify an archaeological culture with the people who created it?

The first person to investigate this problem consistently was G. Kossinna. At this time archaeological culture was becoming a unit, through which the prehistoric past was described. A certain parallel to the problems of history is obvious here. History cannot be dependent on individuals, but on broader units which are represented by social groups, states, nations, etc. Similarly, culture in prehistory can be taken to correspond to social units. 'Prehistoric history', to use this unusual connection, then gives us a chronological and spatial synopsis of cultures together with their characteristics and some external bonds. For such a form of prehistory, one can find an analogy in history which would offer a chronological and spatial summary of the development of states, of their general characteristics and of some mutual relationships.

As it was obvious that units such as state, tribe, ethnos or race already existed in prehistory, the next logical question was to what extent these categories could be identified with one another, and with archaeological cultures. To what extent can archaeological culture be interpreted in terms of these notions? Spatial patterns and spatial concepts appeared to provide an ideal means of explanation, and archaeology makes itself fully accessible to these.

Migrationist theory represented one such concept, stating that almost every cultural change heralded the arrival of a new people with a different culture. And so Thomsen's structure was now becoming filled with crowds of people from different areas, who streamed in through the doors left open by the departure of evolutionism, filling the gaps which evolutionism failed to explain. Polycentric migrationism (for example, H. Breuil's) brought in new cultures from different regions, usually those which were conveniently unexplored or only little known. G. Kossinna presented a monocentric migrationist model, postulating a single centre of origin, 'the original homeland of the Indo-Germans', located in northern Germany and southern Scandinavia. As if this were a well-spring, time and again, fresh streams of Germanic people, the bearers of a superior culture, issued forth in all directions across the globe.

But the increasing number of finds gradually led to the disappearance of unexplored places on the archaeological maps, leaving polymigrationism with little scope for action. Many postulated homelands and epicentres of migration disappeared, while new ones could be found only with the greatest difficulty.

This broad concern with ethnic and ethnogenetic problems had its origins in earlier linguistic and anthropological conceptions. At the end of the nineteenth century, the Indo-European philological theory born at the turn of the eighteenth and nineteenth centuries, and concerned with the common origin of Indian and European languages, returned in full strength (i.e. T. H. Huxley 1890, I. Taylor 1890). This was after the nationalistic synonyms 'Indo-German' and 'Aryan' were introduced (H. J. Klaproth 1823, K. Penka 1883). The earlier notion of the migration of Indo-Europeans from their homeland in Asia to Europe during the Bronze Age was now replaced by Kossinna's relocation of the source of Indo-European origin into ideologically more sound northern Germany and Scandinavia.

In 1895, Kossinna, influenced by Indo-Germanic linguistics and by the Nordic racial concepts and theories, came out with the idea that archaeology was capable of isolating cultural areas (*Kulturprovinzen*), which could be identified with quite specific ethnic and national units which could then be traced back deep into prehistory. These views and their indiscriminate application, which for the most part did not survive their own time, tend to disguise and overshadow Kossinna's real contribution to the theoretical and methodological development of archaeology in the last decades of the nineteenth and at the beginning of the twentieth century.

Ostensibly, the most expressive features of Kossinna's work – the solution of ethnic identity of archaeological cultures and the investigation of ethnogenesis – had many precedents. From the beginning of the eighteenth century, we can already observe in Germany frequent attempts to relate prehistoric artefacts with one or another group listed in Tacitus' index of nations. The next wave of ethnic interpretations emerged in the course of the first half of the nineteenth century, when national schools of archaeology ascribed prehistoric finds without much ado to 'our great and brave ancestors'.

In 1869, R. Virchow turned his attention to hillforts in Lusatia, making a distinction between the hillfort ceramics – *Burgwallkeramik* – and the underlying pottery and artefacts, to which he gave the name 'Lusatian culture'. He identified the Slavs as the makers of the *Burgwallkeramik*, while the Lusatian culture, with no other chronological markers except its precedence to the *Burgwallkeramik*, is attributed to Germanic or pre-Germanic people. The identification of *Burgwallkeramik* with the Slavs is based on historical reports about the destruction of Slavonic religious sanctuaries at Arkona and Garzu on the island of Rügen in the year 1168. These sites remained uninhabited after that and the topmost layers must therefore have belonged to the Slavs. Virchow's decision to endow the Lusatian culture with Germanic ethnicity is based on the writings of ancient authors, reporting that the area which contained the Lusatian–Slavonic hillforts was inhabited until the fifth century AD by the Germans. He is, however, unable to elucidate the origin of the Lusatian culture, or to provide the date for the coming of the Germans.

Montelius also investigated the problems of ethnogenesis, although this pursuit remained on the periphery of his wide-ranging interests. He was concerned especially with the beginnings of Germanic penetration into the Nordic regions.

He started with the period when the presence of Germanic people is safely documented by the synchronisation of written and archaeological sources. From there he advanced further into the past and searched in the archaeological material of each preceding period for traits belonging to the period before the one under investigation. In this way he succeeded, albeit in an area relatively unaffected by large-scale migrations, in tracing the continuity of settlement as far back as the Neolithic period.

In carrying out his analysis, Montelius used for the first time the retrospective method, which was later adopted by Kossinna as one of the basic tools of his approach, summarised in 1911 in the following axiom: 'Scharf umgrenzte archäologische Kulturprovinzen decken sich zu allen Zeiten mit ganz bestimmten Völkern oder Völkerstämmen' (in all periods, sharply delineated archaeological culture areas coincide with clearly recognisable peoples or ethnic groups). He went on to state that in those areas where Germanic people lived in the protohistorical period, their presence was marked with burial sites and other archaeological remains much more accurately than could be assessed from historical and linguistic sources. The same must hold true for a more remote past. He believed that a nation and its culture are ancient entities with their roots deep in prehistory. Germanic people, for instance, are thought to have inhabited Northern Europe since the Mesolithic.

Kossinna then proceeded to fit the data to his theories. He did this by the indiscriminate interpretation of the former and by shifting the chronology, the object of which was to demonstrate Germanic cultural superiority and to claim that extensive Germanic migrations were settling enormous areas. In the light of his efforts (later skilfully exploited by the Nazis: see chapter 4), the reaction of other nationalist archaeologists, who employed the same doubtful methods to show the achievements of their own nation, is not particularly surprising (i.e. A. Ja. Brjusov 1952, J. Filip 1946, J. Kostrzewski 1949). (It is a matter of some irony that, at the time Kossinna was sending to the post-First World War conference at Versailles a manuscript rationalising by archaeological findings German claims to lands given to Poland, his best pupil, J. Kostrzewski, was employing the same archaeological arguments to justify Polish claims to these areas (arguing that the original settlement of these lands was by the Slavs).)

Although the approach of Kossinna and his followers became the subject of criticism by individual archaeologists, linguists and historians, only E. Wahle's thorough analysis in 1941 succeeded in discrediting the erroneous assumption which lay at the root of Kossinna's analysis: that in every period, a given culture equals a certain ethnos. By analysing archaeological sources, particularly from the protohistorical period (which can be compared against historical and linguistic evidence), Wahle demonstrated that a single archaeological culture can envelop several ethnic units or their beginnings, that a change in ethnos does not have to result in a new material culture; and that in the contrary case, a new culture does not necessarily indicate a new ethnic group.

Despite errors committed by Kossinna in the course of the application of his theories, his work had some positive features. He brought into focus the spatial relationships of archaeological cultures and the associated problems of methodology. His contribution to the introduction and the development of cartographic methods in archaeology is almost universally acknowledged. He gave theoretical justification for their use and introduced the mapping of cultures, as opposed to mere artefact distributions. At his instigation, cultural dynamics, continuity and migrations were recorded on maps. Finally, he can be credited with tackling explicitly the question of ethnicity in the archaeological material and in showing that some approaches in this direction are essentially valid, that we are dealing with a valid archaeological problem.

The crisis of migrationism was due to several causes. For the polymigrationist, an unsurmountable problem was created by the disappearance of unexplored regions from the maps. As for the monocentric migrationist, it became gradually apparent that his methods were not sufficiently precise, allowing for the reconstruction of migrations in opposing directions from the same sets of data (see C. Schuchhardt, J. Kostrzewski, A. Ja. Brjusov for interpretations conflicting with those of Kossinna). But probably the greatest blow to migrationism was dealt by its racist and political misuse, which culminated during the Second World War.

Another spatial concept, akin to migrationism, is cultural diffusionism. It postulates the transmission of cultural traits through contact and imitation rather than movement of people. As with migrationism, the development of culture in time and space is taken for granted. Similarly, too, cultural diffusionism can be polycentric or monocentric. Cultural influence is seen generally as unidirectional, extending from the more developed cultures to the less developed ones. Hence, the few original centres of civilisation are thought to have diffused their beneficial rays in all directions. The result is that in practice cultural diffusionism appears to be basically monocentric. According to the location of the original source, one can distinguish diffusionism which is pan-oriental (S. O. Müller, V. G. Childe, F. Schacher-meyer, V. Milojčić, etc.), Babylonian (F. Delitzsch), Sumerian (F. R. S. Raglan) or Egyptocentric (G. E. Smith and W. J. Perry). Moreover, in the presentation by Smith and Perry, monocentric diffusionism reaches its zenith: virtually the entire human civilisation is seen as having its roots in Egypt.

At the end of the nineteenth and the beginning of the twentieth century, migrationist and diffusionist concepts were also elaborated by L. Frobenius, and later by the so-called Viennese cultural-historical school (W. Koppers, W. Schmidt) and the ethnographic school of Cologne (W. Foy, F. Graebner), both of which expanded on Frobenius' work. The followers of this trend postulated, mainly on the basis of ethnographic material, the existence of several cultural centres, which were thought to have existed already in prehistory. Innovations were thought to have originated in one such *Kulturkreis* area, and to have diffused from there. New cultures originated through the integration of the diffused elements. In consequence, the entire history of mankind ended up being reduced to the shifting and development of a few cultural centres.

Some of the assumptions associated with the *Kulturkreis* concept found their way into archaeology, especially into Kossinna's settlement archaeology, into Rostovcev's theory of combinationism, and even into the American taxonomic school. In its later, more complex form, the same concept appears for example in Menghin's reconstruction of cultural centres during the Stone Age, according to technological (*Klingekulturen*, *Faustkeilkulturen*, *Knochenkulturen*) and economic (*Schweinenzüchter-kulturen*, *Hornviehkulturen*, *Bauerkulturen*, *Stadtkulturen*) variables (O. Menghin 1931).

Diffusion originated almost simultaneously with migrationism, but it blossomed a little later and, as a paradigm of major importance, it also outlived for some time its ideological fellow traveller. The decline of diffusionism was due to several causes, among which the discovery of ancient, highly complex civilisations in China and above all in America played a major role. Furthermore, the revision of the 'short chronology' brought about by radiocarbon dating undermined the unequivocal character of the oriental influences. These developments destroyed the notion of a few global centres of human culture and the idea of the uniqueness of innovations themselves, and led towards the opposite view that independent discovery of many innovations was possible.

The ensuing development of archaeology shows, however, that migrationism and diffusionism, if they are not misused to explain all cultural changes, but remain at the level of explanatory mechanisms for particular events, still remain valid. This has become especially clear in more recent years, when diffusionist and migrationist ideas have been elaborated and tested using new, more sophisticated methods and technological means (Ammermann and Cavalli-Sforza 1973, 1979, Doluhanov 1978a, Edmonson 1961, Jope 1973, Malmer 1962, Stjernquist 1966, etc.).

3 A digression into the natural sciences

> Every great scientific truth goes through three stages. First, people
> say it conflicts with the Bible. Next, they say it had been discovered
> before. Lastly, they say they always believed it.
>
> Louis Agassiz

So far as the division between the social and natural sciences is concerned,
archaeology sits on the fence. Essentially, this reflects the dual nature of
man: as a creator of culture and as a biological organism. To investigate
man's natural environment is part of archaeology as a discipline and this
brings it in touch with palaeontology, geology, geography and many other
disciplines. And more than that: all the natural sciences are concerned with
evolution. Their understanding of evolution is influenced by the social
sciences and in turn they provide inspiration for the humanities and
archaeology.

In this chapter, we supplement the story of the development of archaeology, described in the earlier chapters, with the account of related
developments in the natural sciences.

Uniformitarian and catastrophist theories in geology

Geology is, in essence, a historical science, aiming to explain the present
state of our planet as a result of historical processes. Descartes (1644) and
Leibnitz (1680) had already assumed that earth was initially incandescent
and that its crust was formed by progressive cooling and petrification.
More explicit hypotheses about the formation of the earth were established
in the following century (de Buffon 1749, Kant 1755, Laplace 1795, and
Lomonosov 1763).

The establishment of geology as a science would have been impossible
without empirical observations, especially without the investigations of the
origins of the earth's crust. Leibnitz had already recognised the difference
between volcanic and sedimentary deposits, but it was not until Steno's
description of stratified sediments and of their disruption by folding that
the foundation of modern geology was laid. At the end of the eighteenth
century, Lehmann recognised stratigraphically primary and secondary deposits from fossil evidence. In 1795, Hutton corroborated his conclusions.

The stratigraphic method was formed as early as 1570 by Owen, but his approach was not published until two centuries later. Steno (1699) and Werner (1786) were, however, familiar with the law of superposition (whereby older layers underlie the more recent deposits), and they also knew that volcanic layers must be younger than the primary rock through which they cut.

The second fundamental law of the comparative method in geology, the law of identical fossils, issued from the pen of William Smith in 1815. It shows that layers can be dated by the fossils they contain and maintains that layers which incorporate identical fossils must be of the same age.

Stratigraphic methodology was significantly augmented by the introduction of the concept of facies by Prévost in 1840, which he defined as different types of layers of the same age. Prevost's innovation represents the first step towards the genetically oriented explorations of sediments.

Geology entered the nineteenth century endowed with several alternative and competing schools of thought: Neptunism, emphasising sedimentation; vulcanism, oriented towards the volcanic origins of the earth; catastrophism, which emphasised the sudden nature of geological changes; uniformitarianism, which saw the present-day processes as an analogy for the past ones; and finally fluvialism, which sought to reconcile the biblical story of the origin of the earth with the record of the geological strata. While the last hypothesis was soon decisively rejected, Neptunian and Vulcanist theories were shown to describe two fundamental and comparable mechanisms active in the evolution of the earth. Uniformitarian theory, described extensively by Lyell in 1830, in his *Principles of Geology*, marks a real revolution in geological thinking regardless of the modifications to which it was later subjected. The basic tenet of uniformitarianism is best illustrated by the subtitle of Lyell's work: 'An attempt to explain the former changes on the Earth's surface by reference to causes now in operation'.

Geological stratigraphy cannot operate without the law of identical fossils. In this field, geologists cooperate with palaeontologists, whose task it is to identify the fossils. Until quite recently, these were regarded as minerals, moulded by the 'plastic force' of nature (*vis plastica, vis lapidifica, vis formativa*). Bones of large mammals, on the other hand, were mistaken for human remains. Consequently, as late as the eighteenth century, the celebrated Academy of Paris established the stature of Adam at forty metres, while Eve was supposed to be a metre and a half shorter.

Gradually the view that fossils were petrified organisms came to prevail, paving the way for the law of identical fossils and for the geological stratification of earth's deposits. In 1823, Buckland defined diluvium (earlier Quaternary deposits) and alluvium (later Quaternary deposits). In keeping with his fluvialist convictions, he interpreted the diluvial deposits as geological remains of the biblical flood. The basic division of earth's most recent deposits was carried out by Charles Lyell. Buckland's concepts of diluvium and alluvium were used along with Lyell's Pleistocene, Pengelly's Cenozoic and the French concept of the Quaternary. The Pleistocene, which originally encompassed a single ice age, was divided into two and later into four great and five short ice ages (Geikie 1874). Meanwhile, Penck and Bruckner were studying the glacial history of the Alps. They were able to recognise four major glacial epochs, interrupted by interglacials. Earlier in the twentieth century the Alpine sequence gained general acceptance. More recently, this framework has been further elaborated on a regional basis: this has been in no small part due to archaeological finds. With the continuing elaboration and the fragmentation of the earlier stratigraphic blocks, the number of stratigraphic units today is estimated at more than 100,000.

As we can see, progress in geology was to a great extent dependent on vertebrate palaeontology and on palaeobotany. In this field Cuvier can be credited with the development of comparative anatomy and the discovery of the correlation method ('show me a bone, and I will reconstruct the whole skeleton', declared Cuvier, with the characteristically Gallic lack of understatement). But how does palaeontology determine the age of its fossils? On the basis of biological notions about the organisation and evolution of nature.

The first empirical dating of fossils and deposits was not due to palaeontologists, however, but to the genius of Charles Lyell. Having discovered which fossils were recent, he ranked five geologically distinct deposits according to the number of recent species they contained. The Eocene contained 4 per cent of species still in existence, the Miocene 18 per cent, Pliocene 40 per cent and Pleistocene 96 per cent. The method apparently seemed to him too revolutionary as it was left out from the later editions of his great work, *Principles of Geology*. Consequenly, although the results of this approach are generally recognised and acknowledged still today, the method itself remained unknown.

Lamarckian and Darwinian evolution in biology

The first truly evolutionary theory was developed by J. B. Lamarck in 1794. Known as the inheritance of acquired characteristics, it could be summarised in four propositions: (1) organisms tend to increase in size and complexity to their limits, (2) the development and capabilities of new organs depend on their sustained use, (3) thus, new exertions by an animal or a greater employment of an organ would cause the organ to grow, and (4) these acquired characteristics are then passed on to the offspring, so that in time the species as a whole changes.

Lamarck used these principles to reconstruct a uniform evolutionary succession from infusorian to man. The significance of his approach was not recognised by either natural scientists or other men of learning. Unaided by the empirical evidence of fossils and geological strata, and dangerous to the established teaching of the Church, his idea seemed too bizarre and challenging in the intellectual climate of eighteenth-century Europe to gain general acceptance. Comte, for instance, objected that Lamarckian evolution could not be accepted as a basis for a comprehensive classificatory scheme and it remained without close followers until the post-Darwinian period.

The early views on ontogenesis considered evolution as a further development of original, immutable life forms and regarded evolution as identical with growth: an approach later developed by Haller and Bonnet (1754). In 1759, Wolff, observing the embryonic development of chickens, formed the opposite concept of epigenesis, whereby initially simple and uniform elements differentiate into more complex organs with separate functions. The great philosophers Kant and Diderot, among others, came to accept this view.

Even so, the idea of the immutability of the species reflected more objectively the intellectual climate of the time. Leibnitz represents this way of thinking, which extends back to Plato: nature does not indulge in leaps, and therefore species do not mutate. If evolution can be said to exist at all, it simply takes the form of growth of something which is already fully formed in miniature at the beginning. Consequently, the entire population of mankind, past, present and future, was calculated from the estimated sperm count of Adam at 200,000 million. Linnaeus, by classifying plants and grouping their external attributes, added in 1735 a magnificent scheme – carefully worked out and widely applicable – to the school of thought favouring the immutability of species.

For the evolutionary thinkers of the day, space, rather than time, was the major dimension. As Hegel said, 'Nature does not evolve, it unfolds its organisation in space.' Although that might seem absurd to us today, this is no more so than the idea of evolution through time appeared absurd then.

A popular notion at the time was the idea that man and beast were made according to the same original plan, with animals representing arrested evolutionary forms of man. This view underlies Spencer's characterisation of evolution as a process from sameness to diversity, and Herbart's conviction that the spiritual growth of each individual replicated the cultural evolution of the whole of mankind. Oken searched for the common origin of plant, animal and man. But not so long before, de Buffon contemplated the possibility that horse and ass had a common ancestor, and rejected it on the grounds that this would be contrary to the teachings of the Bible.

Despite advances in comparative anatomy and morphology, similarity between species remained a question of morphological relationships, with the genetic implications left unexplored. Such was the state of the natural sciences at the time of publication of Darwin's *Origin of Species* (1859), in which he introduced and emphasised the idea of continuous evolution of entire organic nature. In reality, biology was one of the last areas where evolutionary ideas were applied (except for Lamarck). They were already accepted in astronomy (Kant, Laplace), geology (Lyell), philosophy (Hegel), historical disciplines (Vico, Iselin, Winckelmann), sociology (Compte, Spencer) and ethnology (Bachofen, Tylor). In biology, the ground was prepared for the introduction of Darwinism by the idea of epigenesis, by the discovery of the cell and mainly by the fact that the existing approaches exhausted their possibilities.

Lamarck and those who strove to discover nature's all-embracing principles represent in biology the Continental school of rational thought, which traditionally placed emphasis on the entirety as opposed to the individual, on the state as opposed to the citizen. Nature was comprehended abstractly in terms of principles, forces and mechanisms.

Anglo-Saxon empiricism, on the other hand, anchored in experience, elevates the individual above the state, which is not empowered to interfere in his rights. As Rádl has shown, Darwin developed his theory as a sociology of nature, and moreover he illustrated it by using examples from English society. For him, nature is composed of individuals, who, rather than being subjected to laws, create laws by their actions. Historically, this view forms the basis for the shift from mere speculation to the rational formation of hypotheses. Darwin's importance takes on added significance in this light.

Darwin's theory not only postulated and illustrated the evolution of nature, it aimed at the same time to explain the actual mechanics of evolution in terms of the struggle for existence and natural selection. The idea of evolution became not just a descriptive, but also an explanatory, hypothesis. And the hypothesis was supported by the method.

As so much work on evolution had been done in biology, the whole subject of evolution became dominated by the biological sciences. One distinguished victim of this influence was Herbert Spencer. In his framework, evolution plays the role of the metaphysical integrator, fuelling progress from the amorphous to the polymorphous, from homogeneity to diversity, and from general to specific. As a result, evolution defined in such general terms merely confuses teleology with the notion of progress.

With Darwin, and the controversy generated by his work, the search for origins, the *arche*, was placed in the right perspective and research began to move. The school of thought inspired by Plato, promoting evolution as a spatial concept and interpreting reality as a hierarchical construct extending from low to high forms of life, yielded to the evolution of populations, represented individuals existing within a specific temporal and spatial framework. The similarities and differences between individuals were seen to occur not according to some predetermined concept of harmony in nature, but through genetic relationships, homology, modified through the influence of external factors. Classification was now comprehended as genealogy. Plan and purpose were now replaced by natural selection and the struggle for existence replaced harmony. Orthogenetic views (Nägeli 1865) stating that evolution follows the tendency towards perfection were rejected.

In the course of its development, the Darwinian approach profited from the economic theories of Adam Smith (1776), the utilitarianism of Bentham (1789) and Mill (1829) and the teachings of Thomas Malthus (1798). Biological theory also found inspiration in comparative linguistics, which had already proved useful in the reconstruction of the *Ursprache* and in establishing genetic links between languages. Thus, using linguistic analogy, Lyell and Darwin drew comparisons between biological species and languages. It is worth noting that while biology benefited from linguistic analogies, the application of biological concepts to linguistic did not meet with success (Schleicher 1863).

In the struggle of uniformitarianism and Darwinian evolutionary theory for recognition, the establishment of the great antiquity of the earth was one of the main objectives. With its slow rate of change, biological evolution simply could not fit within the six thousand years officially established as the age of the earth from the study of the Bible in the early 1600s (Lightfoot, Ussher). By the late eighteenth century, the estimates of the age of the earth increased. De Buffon, in an attempt to solve the problem experimentally, measured the rate of cooling of heated cannon balls. According to his calculations, the earth was 75,000 years old. In 1883, a century later, Lord Kelvin, applying the same principle, estimated the age of the earth at between twenty and four hundred million years, while J. Joly sixteen years later proposed a figure of 165 million years on the basis of salt content in the world's seas.

Biology since Darwin

Further developments in biology elaborated three principles which remained only outlined by Darwin: variability, heredity and natural selection. In 1869, while Darwin was still alive, Gregor Mendel defined his laws of inheritance. In 1902, Sutton's theory concerning chromosomes provided an operational basis for Mendelian genetics. During the first thirty years of the twentieth century, mutation (H. de Vries 1901, Korzinskij) and genetic drift (Wright 1931) were discovered, and Četverikov and Fisher (1929) combined the Mendelian principles of inheritance with Darwinian evolutionary theory. Later research into the mechanics of heredity – genes, molecular genetics, DNA (Watson and Crick 1953) – had a direct influence on the social sciences. For instance, Piaget and Jacobson have drawn parallels between the basic structures of the thought process and the information coded by genes. Similarly, Chomsky has resurrected the idea of a 'lingua adamica': an innate pattern of language.

Earlier, species were considered to be immutable, static entities, hierarchically arranged in predetermined harmony. Within such a framework, deviations were thought of as accidental or pathological anomalies. The modern concept considers species as a series of interchangeable local or regional populations, which may differ in appearance, but share the same genetic structure, the same gene pool, and are capable of interbreeding (Howell 1966).

The notion of natural selection, too, became more accurate. The vague assertion by Darwin about the survival of the fittest led to the interpretation of adaptive behaviour as the behaviour of survivors. The contemporary concept of adaptation recognises only one criterion: the ability to reproduce successfully (Dobzhansky 1962). It follows that it is not the fittest, but the most procreatively successful, individuals that survive. Consequently, the notion of adaptability of populations is reduced to the question of their reproductive success.

The environment acts in a selective manner on the pool of evolutionary possibilities, with each organism defining its own environmental conditions. In this way, the variability is conceived of both as the precondition of evolution and as its consequence. At the same time, the degree of adaptive fitness is not dependent on the level of evolution. Each change in an organism is not just adaptation to the existing environment, but simultaneously an expression of control over it.

Thanks to the evolutionary paradigm and to its application in geology, palaeontology also experienced a rapid development. Using the extensive comparative data, Depéret noted the relationship between the increase in body size and evolution. Kovalevski (1873–5) and Osborn discovered the principles of adaptive radiation. Non-adaptive evolution and mosaic evolution were defined (Kovalevski, Watson). Observing the consequences of specialisation and excessive specialisation, Kozłowski noted that those parts of the body which are in most frequent contact with the environment change more rapidly than more protected organs, while Cope maintained that generalist rather than specialist organisms have the best chances of further evolution. Doll's law postulates the irreversibility of organic evolution, which paved the way for empirical studies of evolutionary developments.

Evolution of man

For a long time, animals were regarded as functioning mechanically, or at best as creatures whose behaviour was dominated by reflex actions. As a result, science was not concerned with their behaviour: this was the province of foresters, breeders, and traders. Zoopsychology began to develop only by the end of the nineteenth century as an aftermath to Darwin's theories (1872), postulating the adaptive role of emotions in survival and drawing parallels between human and animal psychology. This new interest led to the analysis of social organisation of invertebrates (Lubbock 1882, Fabre and Forell 1887, Vagner 1907), to the analysis of animal instincts (Romanes 1882), and to the development of comparative psychology (Lloyd and Morgan 1894). The role of territoriality in animal behaviour was explored by Howard (1920), while the relationship between the environment and more complex organisms was treated by von Uexküll (1931).

Since the very nature of comparative psychology precludes introspection and since the very basic human notions about consciousness are open to question, zoopsychology provided the basis on which the discipline developed. Spencer's belief in objective psychology served as a methodological basis, while his theory of biological adaptation and selection (presented before Darwin) offered a theoretical model for the changes in animal behaviour.

These developments led to psychological laboratory experiments (Thorndike 1898, Yerkes and Watson 1929) and to the recognition of basic steps in the process of learning. It was not until later, however, that the comprehensive science of animal behaviour, ethology, developed (Lorenz 1963).

Imprudently, man had awarded himself the title of Homo sapiens in 1758, when his ancestry was still safely descended from Adam's rib and Divine Creation. The great debate about man's origins did not begin until 1860, the year of the celebrated Oxford encounter between Thomas Huxley, the defender of evolution, and Bishop Wilberforce, the godfather of creationism. The hominid finds of the Neandertal in 1828 and 1848 excited little attention, while the find in 1856 was alternatively regarded as the remains of an Irishman, a Russian Cossack or a deformed individual.

The study of human origins can be approached from three angles: comparatively, historically, and experimentally. Using the comparative method alone, similarities between man and other organisms were observed at an early stage through both classification (Linnaeus 1735, de Buffon 1749–88) and explanatory concepts (man and animals being regarded as a part of the same natural harmony). Darwin marks the genesis of the historical approach. The experimental method, based on genetic models, was not introduced until recently.

Palaeoanthropology is limited in it scope to the comparative morphological approach, even though the amount of fossil material has increased radically in the last hundred years. The contemporary primates, including man, on the other hand, are being analysed not only from a morphological, but from every possible behavioural aspect.

Using the comparative method, it is possible to combine the study of fossils with ontogeny. As a result, the 'foetalisation theory' was proposed by Bolk in 1926. According to Bolk, humans evolved by retaining the youthful features of ancestral populations, a process known as neoteny. So, for instance, our neotenic features include the large brain, the juvenile face, a strong, unrotated, non-opposable big toe, and a relative lack of body hair. These features occur in many infant primates and indeed mammals, but only in humans are they retained into adulthood. The adaptive significance of this process lies probably in the lengthening of childhood and the extending of the learning ability of a human being.

Evolutionary ideas about human origins mirrored evolutionary thinking in other disciplines. Before the development of evolutionary theory, the idea of evolution was seen in terms of variation and similarities over space (Hegel). Darwin and the majority of later anthropologists assumed unilinear evolution. Theories about parallel evolution from different origins (polygenesis) were resurrected in anthropology, as in other disciplines, only recently. Finally, there is the idea of radial evolution, through which individual evolutionary lineages emerge from common origins and remain related to one another.

As the study of genetics developed, evolution, always shrouded in vague mystery, suddenly made sense in terms of a concrete genetic process: genetic drift (random genetic mutations) modified by the selective pressures of the environment. The discovery of the principal mechanism of evolution in turn made it possible to study the effects of isolation, colonisation, and migration, as well as the role of cultural selection, the selective influence of which has been increasingly recognised (Joly and Plog 1976).

Early quantification and measurement in the natural sciences

Advances in biology, anthropology, psychology and other social sciences depend to a large extent on the application of mathematical and statistical methods. The first condition of the numerate approach is quantification and measurement. Blumenbach (1775) introduced measurement as an objective method in anthropology; at the end of the eighteenth century, Cramer defined 'facial angle' and in 1840, Retzius invented the cranial index. In 1876, Brocca founded craniometry, stimulating a number of other developments in anthropology. These advances culminated in the international anthropological convention in Geneva in 1912 and in the work of R. Martin, published in 1914.

In 1835, Quételet published *Physique sociale*, laying the basis for the statistical assessment of variability (mean values, standard deviation, normal distribution). Of fundamental significance is also the work of Galton, the biologist, who contributed substantially to the theory of evolution through probabilistic and statistical studies of the transmittance of inherited characteristics.

Galton's pupil, Cattell (1890), applied the statistical methods to psychology, developing new measures of correlation (Spearman's, Pearson's) and interdependence. This led to a new approach in the formulation of problems, which can be seen, for instance, in the 1904 attempt by Binet to find an objective basis for tests of intelligence. Anthropometric investigations and psychological tests were also carried out by F. Boas.

It is hard to overestimate the influence of the natural sciences on archaeology. For instance, even so basic a tool of archaeological method as comparative morphology owes its origins to the natural sciences, from whence it was introduced to archaeology by Virchow. Similarly, the Montelian typological method, as well as de Mortillet's evolutionary sequence, derive from Darwinian evolutionary thought (Darwin 1859, Huxley, Haeckel).

More recently, environmentally and ecologically oriented archaeologists such as Fox, Crawford, and J. G. D. Clark, as well as their successors (Brothwell, Butzer, Dimbleby, Higgs, and others), relied on a whole range of natural sciences for inspiration, analogy and explanation. The systemic approach, developed for, and applied specifically in, modern geography, was adapted to become one of the basic ingredients of 'New Archaeology': *Haggett's enormously stimulating book suggests a number of ways in which archaeologists can approach and analyse distributions in space of archaeological materials (whether of artefacts, settlements or cultural groups). It is not an exaggeration to say that we have all been working on problems which have already been solved.*

(Renfrew 1969b: 74)

In Renfrew's view, Haggett's *Locational Analysis in Human Geography* could well be renamed *Locational Analysis in Prehistoric Archaeology* (*ibid.*).

Numerical Taxonomy by Sneath and Sokal forms one of the principal sources for David Clarke's *Analytical Archaeology* (1968). As Renfrew implied, the vast majority of mathematical and statistical methods and of computer applications in archaeology are no more than modified numerical procedures which have already been applied in biology, psychology and geography. By successively emphasising concepts such as morphology, function, evolution, behaviour, environment, and system, and with continual redefinition of the notion of species, the natural sciences constantly pioneered new approaches for archaeology and have been its most reliable source of inspiration.

4 More recent history: the twentieth century

No epilogue, I pray you – for your play needs no excuse. Never excuse; for when the players are all dead, there need none to be blamed.

Shakespeare. A Midsummer Night's Dream

Sources of inspiration for the twentieth century

Not even the systematic collection of data will necessarily lead to substantial results, because, as A. N. Veselovskij, the philologist, pointed out as early as 1872, the same fact can play a different role in different circumstances. This observation forms the central theme for Emile Durkheim (1858–1917) and his sociological–ethnological school (especially M. Mauss 1923, 1924): a social fact cannot be assessed unless its relationship to the whole is taken into consideration. For Durkheim, sociology does not represent a general theory about society, about its evolution, or its structure: it is a science of social facts. Psychology and the condition of an individual no longer formed the starting point in the analysis of society; they were replaced by the analysis of the whole of society and of its collective psychology, the collective beliefs of a society. Culture was no longer defined as a collection of material objects (i.e. E. B. Tylor), of artefacts and their characteristics, but now became a collection of norms, of patterns which served as instruction codes according to which various activities were performed. In so far as Durkheim devoted his attention to a change in an archaic society, he believed that it was brought about by the division of labour and the increase in specialisation, both of which were, in turn, the consequences of population growth. Durkheim's school was among the first to emphasise binary opposition as typical for the mythological form of presentation (i.e. divine/secular, male/female, good/evil).

Durkheim's work is a source of many other schools of thought of the twentieth century. By his insistence on social fact as a phenomenon which is different from, and external to, individual consciousness, Durkheim freed sociology from the grip of psychology, and at the same time, opened the door wide for the reconstruction of collective notions and unconscious states. Functionalism is closely related to Durkheim's views, especially in the belief that social facts can be comprehended only as a part of a system.

At the same time, Durkheim's insistence that the structure of human thought process is composed of collective images which project on the outside world, the structure of human society, had a profound influence on the sociology of knowledge (K. Mannheim, 1929, M. Scheler 1926) and structuralism (C. Lévi-Strauss 1955, J. Piaget 1968) (see below, p. 100).

Ethnology

B. Malinowski and A. R. Radcliffe-Brown adopted Durkheim's functionalist approach and applied it to ethnology. They reacted against diffusionism in the same way diffusionists had reacted against evolutionism; once again, they held the prevailing paradigm guilty of excessive generalisation, and explanation without empirical foundations. As usual, too, the remedial action was seen to lie in a more empirical approach and in the verification of hypotheses. Functionalism relied on fieldwork: in the colonies among the British and French scholars, in exile in the case of Polish intellectuals sent to Siberia, and at home for many others. Malinowski (1939) summarised his ideas about culture in the following manner:

Culture thus appears first and foremost as a vast instrumental reality – the body of implements and commodities, charters of social organisation, ideas and customs, beliefs and values – all of which allows man to satisfy his biological requirements through cooperation and within an environment refashioned and readjusted. The human organism, however, itself becomes modified in the process and readjusted to the type of situation provided by culture. In this sense culture is also a vast conditioning apparatus, which through training, the imparting of skills, the teaching of morals and the development of tastes amalgamates the raw material of human physiology and anatomy with external elements, and this supplements the bodily equipment and conditions the physiological processes.

Here, culture is perceived as an adaptive and integrating mechanism which cannot be evaluated simply through the comparative method. Figuratively speaking, the emphasis is placed on the physiology, rather than on the morphology, of a society. It is purely a synchronic approach, which is based on the assumption of the existence of some equilibrium in a society, of some ideal state, around which the society fluctuates, and therefore does not offer means for the identification of change. This implies that all the remains of past societies must be considered as functional. Generally, Malinowski evaluates myths and folklore only in their psychological-social role, within the framework of the functioning of the society, and, therefore, only as its unifying, rather than identifying, element – in this respect, he is following the behaviourist perspective. Malinowski is also explicit on the question of the origins of culture, which is, to him, a 'principal base', 'a minimum of conditions sufficient for differentiating between activities which preceded culture and activities which are cultural', 'a difference between a personal habit and a custom'.

Functionalism turns out to be effective as an approach for the study of small, isolated societies, but not of societal aggregates on a broader scale. Attempts by T. Parson and R. K. Merton to introduce functionalism into sociology, although providing a source of inspiration, fell victim to the same limitations. Sociological functionalism perceives human society as a system with a given structure and function. Structure is to Merton a summary of relatively standardised relationships of individual actors, and each individual acts only within certain segmented fields of activity. These fields form the basic unit of social relationships: roles. Functions are evaluated from the point of view of their utility in preserving the system. Merton also introduces relationships which are afunctional and dysfunctional, but operating, nevertheless, within the framework of the system.

Further ethnological thought focused on the evaluation of change. J. R. Firth, M. G. Gluckman and E. R. Leach attempted to isolate the mechanisms responsible for change within the system. Meanwhile, Leach, commenting on the sophistication of Malinowski's views, compared him, perhaps a little unkindly, to a watchmaker: a mere technician. Leach already demanded an approach appropriate for engineers and mathematicians who are not interested in the classification of nuts and bolts but in processes; in his view, society is not a totality of things, but of variables. The classical evolutionism of the nineteenth century was revived in the forties by L. A. White and E. R. Service (unilinear evolution) and in the fifties by J. H. Steward (multilinear evolution).

Durkheim's understanding of social fact as a phenomenon which stands outside the human being, which is external to him and which forms a mutually interdependent system not only exerted influence on further development in sociology, but also served as a source of inspiration in linguistics and history. P. Lacombe (1894) adopted the view of a society as a system of mutually interdependent social facts: of those events which occur repeatedly, reproduce themselves, and in so doing create a common structure.

The development of descriptive methods and information processing can be considered as another major development in sociology. While, in the nineteenth century, generalising approaches were in favour (the historical sociology, synthetic sociology and macrosociology of Comte, Durkheim and Pareto), the twentieth century can be characterised by empirical sociology, which is analytical in nature and oriented towards small-scale studies. Empirical generalisations were not allowed to extend beyond observations established by the original research. Correlations, patterns and replications now become favourite subjects of research. For example, the 'cross-cultural' study by G. P. Murdock (1948) looks for the correlations among cultured phenomena.

The sociological teaching of American functionalism concerning social roles was brought into psychology by Mead. She assumes that the integrations of activity of individuals is possible only thanks to the fact that every individual 'plays back' roles of other individuals in his mind, creating thereby a common ground and an intelligible basis for co-operation.

The ethnopsychological school of A. Kardiner (1939) supported the view that individual character occurs as a result of variation in the basic structure of a personality, which is defined in a different way in each culture. It is defined not only by the natural environment and by social relationships, but above all by the ideological system of a given culture, expressed in myth, belief and attitudes. Margaret Mead, Ruth Benedict, and R. Linton, as well as other members of the Culture and Personality school, all investigated cultural patterns according to the behaviour of individuals. This information was used as the basis for the development of a configurational, culturological, organic paradigm in ethnology. In addition to the workers mentioned above, A. L. Kroeber, C. K. M. Kluckhohn and partly also the neo-evolutionism of L. A. White belong to this school of thought.

In 1934, Ruth Benedict presented an integrated view of culture arising from the study of individual Indian cultures of North America. In her view, each culture selects a certain goal, and with this goal in mind, other characteristics are selected from the range of possibilities offered by the anthropological constellation of man. In this way, culture emerges as a configuration of traits. Because the range of combinations is countless, the selective adoption of certain traits leads to the understanding and communication within each given culture. In reality, from the point of view of cultural origins, a conscious cultural goal does not exist; instead, small deviations from 'average' behaviour overlap and reinforce one another, creating a stronger, more integrated current, which may become established as a new norm: in this way, for instance, one can explain the genesis of Gothic art.

Psychology is thus revealed as subordinate to sociology, or, respectively, to ethnology and history, since every culture is collectively and in itself responsible for self-regulation and for establishing standards of psychic normality. This provides feedback for psychology: E. C. Tolman (1951), for example, considers psychology to be a study of the internalisation of society and of culture within the individual.

The thought processes of primitive man are intimately connected with

religious beliefs. This forms the subject of extensive literature in more
recent years, especially that of E. Patte (1960), G. Rachel-Lévy (1963) and
L. R. Rougier (1963).

Developments in psychology

One traditional way of explaining social events is by reference to psychological factors. Neither myths, nor folk tales, nor epic compositions require
psychological explanations. External motivation prevails in the epic and
historical works of antiquity, as well as in its literature. In early medieval
literature, predestination also plays a leading role. Psychology, and the
notion of the subjective as an explanation, found its way into the humanities only through more recent literature, and in a sense it does not extend
beyond it. In its early stages, psychology was not considered a science, and
especially not as a possible source of inspiration. Historiography, in this
respect, was fully subordinate to literature. Only historicism devoted
greater attention to psychology, not in the least because of the personal and
emotional perspectives adopted by Romanticism. The progress accomplished in the study of the past by the novel as a literary form had yet to be
fully appreciated.

In so far as use was made of psychology, this took place in two directions
– towards individual psychology, and towards collective psychology. The
former was more common in historiography, and in the Anglo-American
countries, the latter was more frequently applied in sociology on the
Continent.

Thus, Vico presumed the existence of a certain super-individual spiritual
force; for Herder, the individual was not a constituent element of history,
and for Hegel, the individual consciousness was only a part of the growing
consciousness of mankind (*Gattungsmensch*). The Romantics postulated
the existence of collective consciousness and of psychology in general. The
brothers Grimm did not consider folklore a creation of an individual, but a
product of super-personal language, which, in turn, expresses 'a soul of the
nation'.

Psychologically inspired explanation developed from these beginnings.
In linguistics and in the study of folklore it was used by H. Steinthal (1852),
A. A. Potebna (1862) and H. Paul (1880). In 1885, G. Tarde introduced
sociology as a part of psychology, interpreting language as a social space
of an idea. Myth, folktales and art in general were also explained in terms of
psychology. Associational psychology, developed by Herbart and applied
earlier in linguistics, formed the basis of a detailed framework designed for
prehistory by W. Wundt. Fundamental psychological experiences were

considered a basis for the evolution of all cultural, and especially religious, phenomena. Society was held to evolve from its primitive beginnings through a totemic stage, a heroic stage, and finally a humanistic stage. Myths were perceived as animistic narrations. In his monumental work *Völkerpsychologie*, published between 1900 and 1920, Wundt also introduces collective psychology. In linguistics, Wundt influenced H. Steinthal, J. van Ginneken (1907), and later F. Kainz (1940).

Though approached from a more popular perspective, the 'Soul of the mob' investigated by G. le Bon (1895) resulted in research revealing some interesting parallels between collective images, children's thinking, and archaic and defective patterns of thought, such as irrationality or crowd indoctrination.

The investigation of anthropological-psychological ontogensis began in the 1880s. Investigating the process of language adoption, H. Taine (1876) found analogies between the development of a child and historical process. Darwin came to similar conclusions in 1877. In 1904, S. Hall introduced the theory of recapitulation, which suggested that the psychological development of an individual replicated earlier phases in human evolution. Thus, some early childhood games were seen as analogies of hunting instincts. Similarly, E. Claparède found analogies between ontogenetic and phylogenetic evolution of consciousness.

Durkheim's school also laid the foundation for a truly collective psychology. L. Lévy-Bruhl (1910) developed the Durkheimian interest in patterns of thought which preceded rational thinking. Such patterns were thought to have been based on emotional and motor activity which did not acknowledge the existence of change. Abstract concepts merged with concrete images, and these were a part of generally shared collective notions, the basic quality of which is continuity.

Sigmund Freud stands at the boundary of collective and individual psychology (*Totem und Tabu*, 1912). The Oedipus complex represented for him not only a key to the psychology of an individual but, above all, a source of religion, morals, society and art. Myth and dreams are seen as transformations of real historical events (i.e. murder of a father figure) which are of importance to the individual psychology of participants. On the other hand, an individual is replicating tribal developments (ontogenetic theory of culture). Culture and history are here reduced to the expression of sexual forces, which are seen as the basis of naturalness. At an individual level, emotional upheavals are represented as forms of regression which can be used to study earlier stages of development.

More recently, analogies between the behaviour of people and animals, children and adults, members of archaic societies and individuals from developed civilisations, between the individual and the crowd, between men and women, and finally comparisons between pathological and normal events, became increasingly the subject of a systematic study, rather than acting as maverick inspiration. Consequently, the field of history grew in scope. M. Foucault (1963) investigated the history of madness, and T. Niperday (1973) demanded an enquiry into the history of fear, love, hope, friendship and crying. But already, a hundred years earlier, H. Taine had challenged history to investigate the basic factors affecting humankind: death, bliss, love, happiness, fatherland.

Jung followed in Freud's footsteps with his theory of archetypes. Archetypes are the collective experiences of humankind, and form, there-fore the basis of human existence. Jung's interpretation had a profound influence on psychology, psychiatry, the investigation of myths, ethnology, folklore, and the aesthetics of science and art. J. Campbell (1948, 1959, 1970), following Jungian principles, perceived mythology as a direct outcome of the neurological system and postulated a biological substrate for the archetypes. He sought support for his theory in zoopsychology and comparative psychology. E. W. Count (1960) went even as far as to try to locate symbolic activity in the cortex of the brain.

The cross-fertilisation of psychology, ethnology and sociology gave birth to sociological psychology and ethnopsychology. In 1908, W. McDougall searched for the roots of social behaviour, finding them in the social instincts with which humans are endowed by nature. In the 1930s, Thurston's school investigated instinctive reaction while motivation was analysed by D. McCleland, who saw the notion of success as the motivating force behind social events. Using the results of historical research into folklore and school textbooks as examples, he showed that the cult of success preceded economic development. In 1936, K. Lewin used the field theory to carry out a graphic representation of relationships among individuals. At the junction of psychology and sociology, J. L. Moreno began to investigate relationships between individuals in small communi-ties, an approach which came to be known as sociometrics. The work of J. Piaget and L. S. Vygotskij is of exceptional significance for the investi-gation of the individual psyche. During the first stage of Piaget's research in the 1920s, his attention focused on the process of adaptation, which he viewed as assimilation (the subject imposes its structure on the environ-ment) and accommodation (the subject alters its own organisation in response to the environment). The first state was characterised by ego-centrism and precluded communication (identification of subjective experience with objective reality). In the second stage of his research, during the 1940s, Piaget further developed the stadial framework to accommodate the development of children's behaviour, interpreting each stage as a system of operations. Vygotskij outlined the cultural-historical theory of the origin, structure and evolution of higher psychic functions in ontogenesis. He introduced a generally applicable genetic law of cultural evolution, according to which every higher psychic function inevitably passes in the course of its evolution through an external stage, because originally it had been a social function.

Linguistics

In 1907, A. Meillt allied linguistics to sociology and proceeded to investigate the relationship between languages and social structures.

The theories of N. J. Marr, in their vulgarised application of Marxism, represented the extreme sociological-evolutionary position. Here language was considered as a sub-structure following the changes in the base, so that the 'original classless societies' possessed isolating languages, tribal societies 'agglutinative', and class societies fusional ones. Influenced by Marr's teaching, I. G. Frank-Kamenickij (1932) analysed myths and O. M. Frejdenberg (1936) endeavoured to present stadial changes of *sujet* forms, which in turn reproduced certain global notions (the palaeontology of *sujets*).

Political economy

In modern political economy, the functional approach is typical, even though its roots lie in the systemic understanding of economic theories and in the immediate applicability of such theoretical conclusions. Systemic interpretations became more accurate with the introduction of mathematical and statistical methods (i.e. econometry: J. von Neumann 1932, A. Wald 1936, J. R. Hicks 1939, O. Lange 1944; macroeconomic models: R. F. Harrod 1939, E. D. Domar 1946; input–output analysis: W. Leontieff 1941; linear programming: L. V. Kantorovič 1931, G. G. Dantzig 1949; games theory: J. von Neumann 1932, O. Morgenstern 1944).

These methods were later used by archaeology and ethnology when investigating the economics of subsistence societies. The modern economic theories were, of course, aimed at the analysis of contemporary society, and their application to economic history could only be selective. Such work in the field of economic history was carried out by, among others, M. Weber (1904), W. Eucken (1934), and J. A. Schumpeter (1912). The analysis of the economic needs of an individual, rather than that of the economic groups within a society, engendered in the so-called 'vertical approaches' (i.e. K. E. Boulding 1941, F. H. Knight 1944), represented a partial return to the 'homo economicus' concepts of the eighteenth century.

Historiography

Let us turn now to historiography. After the analysis of individual aspects of society during the previous period, which nearly resulted in the formation of independent scientific disciplines, the need was felt for synthesis and depersonification. In France, H. Berr (1900) used Durkheim's work in his own investigations. The Annales school, best represented by Marc Bloch and Lucien Febvre (1929), emphasised economic history and the history of social awareness.

In Germany, historiography took a more critical view of the positivist approach. The new point of departure was adopted: Dilthey's notion of empathy (1883), which did not, however, mean an immediate psychologisation.

B. Croce (1917) introduced individuality, intuition and aesthetics into history, which led to the emphasis on the role of empathy and identification. J. E. Acton identified with this view. R. G. Collingwood saw history as the science of the unique, the task of which is to understand human existence, not some historical processes. His influence penetrated into archaeology (e.g. G. E. Daniel and I. Hodder; see below, pp. 110–12 and 131–2). H. I. Marrou is a methodological individualist: for him, historical explanation was determined merely by the intuitive understanding of the relationships between various facts. Croce, who acknowledged history only as a contemporary phenomenon, inspired a number of followers in Britain, such as R. G. Collingwood, F. H. Bradley, B. M. Oakeshott and other 'presentationists', in the United States (C. A. Beard, C. L. Becker, J. H. Robinson), and in Spain (J. Ortega y Gasset). In their work history was understood as a reflection of the present, which has to be written again and again, because the present continues to change; and thus, everyone is his own historian.

Ferdinand Braudel and his school in France were oriented towards long-term history (the study of stable geographical and institutional structures).

The question of logical explanation in history (Karl Popper 1935, 1944, 1945, C. G. Hempel 1942) served as a point of departure for a long-lasting discussion about the possibilities of historical explanation, which was shared not only by historians but also by archaeologists (see below, pp. 120, 126).

One of the greatest Western historians was, arguably, Arnold Toynbee, the author of the monumental twelve-volume creation *The Study of History*. Toynbee's work is a kind of dialectical autodynamism, in which history is represented as a mutual relationship between challenges and responses within individual cultural units.

Marxist historiography was developed in the theoretical works of A. Labriola, K. Kautsky, K. Korsch, G. V. Plehanov, G. Luckácz, and A. Gramsci, and of others. Historians of the socialist countries of Eastern Europe devoted most of their work to Marxist analysis and its development. Suffice it to mention such basic works as the methodological work of Topolski in Poland, or the approach of B. F. Poršnev in Russia, who used not only history, but also archaeology, anthropology and psychology to investigate the beginning of history.

In addition to political and cultural history, we study today social and economic history on the one hand and, on the other, the history of mentalities, emotions, behaviours and actions.

History of art

The history of art will be discussed here in some detail, because in some areas, especially in Anglo-American archaeology, its influence has been subtle and oblique rather than direct. On the Continent, where archaeology is on more intimate terms with history rather than ethnology, the history of art influenced above all classical archaeology and the investigation of prehistoric art. Prehistoric archaeology, especially the *Kulturkreis* Viennese school, also found inspiration in the history of art. Finally, let us also note that art historian K. Badt and the prehistorian E. Wahle (see below, pp. 107–8), influenced by Heidegger's philosophy, arrived at the same conclusions.

The perception of the history of art, promoted by H. Wölfflin (1904, 1915) as the 'history of art without names' – a phrase adopted from Comte (*histoire sans noms*) – envisaging a cyclic movement of two idealised types, can be contrasted with Riegel's interpretation, which emphasised the individuality and uniqueness of artistic expressions. Both authors were united in their formalised approach, concerned more with the problems of shape than with content and associated influences.

Wölfflin understands the history of art as a history of artistic optics; ways of seeing things represent to him impersonal patterns. As he notes, 'a human being sees only what he seeks, but also he seeks only what he can see'. Categories of seeing are understood as binary oppositions of 'fundamental concepts': linear/picturesque or flatness/depth, etc. In these examples, the first element of a binary opposition represents Renaissance characteristics, the second, those of the baroque period. The fundamental opposition, which is demonstrated through these elements, is the classical/ baroque opposition.

Wölfflin's model, which anticipates the structuralist approach, can be used like Mendeleev's table of chemical elements, or Goethe's metamorphosis. On the basis of Wölfflin's oppositions, E. Panofsky dealt in 1924 with the associated problem of plastic arts. Evolution of art is viewed here organically, but in an evolutionary perspective.

Structural analysis was introduced into the history of art during the 1930s, with specific orientation towards individual works of art and particular types of artwork (Q. Kaschmitz-Weinberg 1931, 'the younger Viennese school': H. Sedlmayr 1931, O. Pacht 1933). Its application to archaeology was summarised by B. Schweitzer (1938).

E. H. Gombrich finds inspiration in the critical rationalism of Karl Popper and the functionalist approach. Function is for him a circumstance necessary for the development of new forms, style is seen as a super-individual perception of reality, and both style and function can be explained psychologically. History is perceived as a space with an open ending.

K. Badt (1946), like E. Wahle in prehistory, on the other hand, is influenced by Heidegger's philosophy. History is reduced to a sequence of brilliant works emerging from the context of second-rate contributions.

Folklore

When we consider research into folklore, two opposing theories can be seen to have influenced all aspects of the analysis: the first theory, intro-duced by the brothers Grimm, owes its origins to Romanticism, and is based on the assumptions that the roots of folklore lie in prehistory. The second theory, that of extreme receptionism (W. Tapper 1868, R. Forrer 1906, J. Maier 1908, H. Neumann 1921, A. Weselski 1935), postulates that the origins of folk art are to be found as late as the eighteenth century. Despite this, Béla Bartók, for instance, was able to recognise some ancient Asiatic elements in Hungarian folk music, which must date to the dawn of history.

The analysis of prehistoric art

These considerations bring us to prehistoric art, claimed by both archaeo-ology and the history of art as their domain. The interpretation of prehistoric art was fundamentally influenced by the views of G. Semper and A. Riegel.

More than any other archaeological material, artistic expression forms a part of the spiritual sphere, lending itself readily to cultural-anthropological, ideological and sociological considerations. On the other hand, the character of finds makes it possible to apply methods of art historical investigation, even in those instances where the art in question is considered a mere expression of ritual and magic, rather than true art – as is the case with Palaeolithic art (F. A. van Scheltema 1923, R. Hamann 1952).

Stylistic analysis and comparative methodology in the history of art – concerned with such elements as motifs, symbols, ornamentation and form, their mutual interconnectedness and stylistic evolution – are similar to the typological and comparative analysis common in archaeology. As a result, the two approaches are often in juxtaposition. This can be seen in the work of E. Grosse (1894), M. Hoernes (1898), S. Reinach (1903), H. Breuil (1906, 1952), E. Piette (1907), H. Kühn (1921), O. Menghin (1925), F. A. van Scheltema (1936), A. Leroi-Courhan (1965) and, from a sociological point of view, A. Hauser (1953). Some of this work can be faulted for lacking objectivity with more than just customary negligence. Thus, Hoernes considers geometric style as a technique used by women, for women are a home-loving, orderly, pedantic gender, and the geometric style is thought to reflect these qualities. (Surely no reflection of the 'Kinder-Küche-Kirche' prejudices of Victorian gentlemen?) Kühn divides prehistoric art into the magical and the animistic. Kühn's scheme is adapted by Hauser, who elaborates further by identifying the magical with creative naturalism, common in the Palaeolithic period; man must have been a good observer, but social organisation and information exchange are simple, hence the distinction between the object and its visual representation is obscured. Animist and geometric styles, on the other hand, are put together as two artistic forms which share abstraction, standardisation, conceptualisation and rationalisation of expression – qualities which were made possible by the more complex organisation of Neolithic society.

Bounded by their geographical, cultural and chronological context, but also due to the preconceptions of the investigating art historians themselves, closed sets of prehistoric art objects were defined, and investigated in relative isolation from their cultural milieu. This was the case, for instance, with Palaeolithic art (H. Kühn 1921, 1930, G. H. Luquet 1926, H. Breuil 1952); the rock art of Eurasia and Africa (H. Obermaier and H. Kühn 1923, A. Laming 1962, H. Lhote 1959); Scythian art (T. T. Rice 1957, M. I. Artamonov 1968, 1971); Luristan art (M. I. Rostovcev 1931, R. Ghirsman 1964), *Flechtornamentik* (S. O. Müller 1881, A. Haupt 1923, W. A. von Jenny 1940); Germanic animal art (B. Sahlin 1904, F. A. van Scheltema 1923, N. Åberg 1943, 1947), etc. The increased attention devoted to prehistoric art encouraged H. Kühn, one of the leading figures in the field, to begin in 1925 a journal especially devoted to the subject: *IPEK: Jahrbuch für prähistorische und ethnographische Kunst.*

Ex oriente lux

The pioneer phase of scientific archaeology, the period of unquestionable successes, came to an end by the beginning of the twentieth century. The new knowledge was summarised in archaeological and prehistoric diction-aries, several of which appeared in the first three decades of the century (R. Forrer 1908, J. Schlemm 1908, J. Hoops 1911–19; J. Déchelette 1913–24). Among these, Ebert's *Reallexikon*, published between 1924 and 1932, and running into fifteen volumes, represents a most comprehensive summary of archaeology, ethnology, anthropology, linguistics and other social sciences. In addition, national or pan-European syntheses of the prehistoric period appeared, such as G. Schwantes' (1908) or C. Schuch-hardt's volumes (1928) for Germany, or Müller's book (1905) for the whole of Europe. The number of finds and of excavations, including the extensive aerial excavations in the 1930s, were also rapidly increasing. All this leads to the appearance of new cultures, and of new concepts. Although they differed one from another, they had one thing in common: they were all grafted on to the old Thomsenian structure, and in essence they represented its adaptation and elaboration. It can be said, therefore, that in the first half of the twentieth century, the archaeological picture of the past developed mainly through the accumulation of data. A fundamental revolution in archaeological thinking, theory and practice did not occur until after the Second World War.

The prevailing trend in the first half of the twentieth century is known as neo-evolutionism. Introduced by V. G. Childe, this school of thought combines certain Marxist concepts and the population dynamics of biology as it was then known. Models which emerged from this synthesis became widely known to student and scholar of archaeology alike. They include the Neolithic Revolution, the Urban Revolution, and their spread from the Near East, explained by the diffusionist theories. They also include a detailed chracterisation of the Neolithic period. In creating his version of prehistory, Childe used his enormous knowledge of archaeological mater-ial, which was cast across Eurasia and included first-hand experience in Western and Central Europe, Russia and the Near East. Neo-evolutionism was given its final theoretical form in 1943 by L. A. White; its main premise held that identical conditions of social process can be modified by the environment to such an extent that the resulting cultures can differ significantly from one another.

Neo-evolutionism is also implied in the work of Childe's younger contemporary, J. G. D. Clark. According to Clark, the first task of an archaeologist is the isolation of those shared traits which define a culture and which are mediated from one generation to the next. Only after the culture is defined, can a prehistorian proceed to describe its social history and its social and economic context. These goals are contingent on the accurate understanding of how societies function. In Clark's view, an archaeologist is in a similar situation to a palaeontologist who is trying to reconstruct the life of a complex organism using only a few preserved fossils. His only chance lies in comprehending the principles which control the lives of such organisms and determine their form. Social anthropology describes how societies function, and it can therefore offer a model which can then be used as a basis for prehistoric reconstruction. Clark's views evolved through several further stages, coming under the influence of Scandinavian-inspired environmental research in the 1930s and adopting an economically oriented perspective in the 1940s and 1950s (Clark 1946, 1948, 1954). His approach assumed a current form with the concept of 'bio-archaeology' in the early 1970s (1972).

Childe and Clark represent the view that the 'theoretical model of culture' cannot be constructed from archaeology alone; it must, initially at least, be adopted from outside, from sociology or social anthroplogy. These sciences, as we saw earlier, do not have a single theoretical model, but offer a whole range of them. This forms the point of divergence for our two archaeologists: Childe's thinking is based on the ideas of Marx, while Clark turns for inspiration to the functionalism of Malinowski.

Nature, the cradle of all things

In explaining cultural changes, Clark initially relied on the theory of environmentalism. Although the significance of natural environment in relation to the prehistoric settlement had been emphasised in the 1870s and 1880s (H. Schaaffhausen 1872, E. Guest 1883), the influence of the environment came to be explored systematically, especially in England and Scandinavia, only at the beginning of the twentieth century (G. S. Crawford 1921, C. Fox 1932, L. von Post 1911). According to the environmentalist view, cultural change was generated by changes in the natural environment, especially climate. Migrations or other forms of diffusion played only an insignificant role.

Such geographical determinism, although modified to a less extreme position, remains popular to the present day. This is because many cultural changes, though certainly not all such changes, can be plausibly explained by changes in the natural environment. According to the current, modified form, the natural environment is not directly responsible for cultural changes, but indirectly: through setting the limits and the range of conditions within which cultures can operate.

The combustion model of prehistory

In the first decades of the twentieth century, M. I. Rostovcev (1870–1952) was developing an approach which L. S. Klejn later called combinationism (Klejn 1975b: 98). Much of the theoretical make-up of this approach was adopted from the Viennese cultural-historical school. Rostovcev does not reject migrations or other forms of diffusion, but he also considers autochthonous traditions. He sees the genesis of a new cultural tradition in the integration of heterogeneous cultural elements. Periods of rapid social and economic change occur in the form of crisis within the historical process; consequently, they serve as catalysts for the transformation of cultural elements. New combinations of old elements are established, and this alone represents innovation. New relationships and new pressures then carry out the rest of the job, giving rise to new styles and new cultures. In this way, a rapid restructuring of cultural elements takes place, as if through an explosive transformation. Evolutionary trends, even though they envelop more rapid developments and crises, play a cyclic role in Rostovcev's model; innovations occur from a combination of the same range of elements.

The revolutionary view: with leaps through stages

Shortly after the Russian Revolution the global stage of theoretical archaeology was penetrated by the young Soviet school, and their stadial theory. Its representatives (Arcihovskij 1930, Ravdonikas 1934, 1939, and many others) embarked on a fearless and thorough reconstruction of the old structure of theoretical archaeology. They had, at their disposal, general premises of Marxism, which they interpreted and applied to the needs of archaeology; also the linguistic theory of N. J. Marr, and the archaeological research of M. I. Rostovcev – all of which contributed in a significant way to the stadial theory. Thus the ability to interpret a concrete cultural change as explosive transformation was made possible by Rostovcev. Stadialists also adopted from Rostovcev's work the careful consideration of economic and social factors as catalysts of cultural development; but they introduced a number of new elements, too.

In contrast with Rostovcev's notion of cyclic development, they reintroduced the principle of gradual evolution propounded already by the evolutionists. Rostovcev's explosions were replaced by dialectical leaps, and change did not occur in a circle, but in a spiral; consequently, transformations were now replaced by progressive evolution in stages – stadial transformations. The stadialists' understanding of Marxism lead them to regard any cultural change as an indication of the pervasive character and the rapid diffusion of stadial change into all aspects of culture. Each and every cultural change was a leap forward – a revolutionary change. This, in turn, inevitably led them to equate cultures with social and economic formations, and to bridge the gaps between cultures with revolutions. Such sociological simplification, however, encountered the resistance of the archaeological material. Stadialists, enchanted with the novelty and the revolutionary nature of their theory, responded by trying to fit all past events into their preconceived frameworks: as a result they almost entirely rejected migrations and diffusion and ended up ignoring real genetic sequences. They recognised only vertical successions in situ, which they explained entirely in terms of socio-economic determinism.

As a result of the official acceptance of the stadialist view, further pursuit of the discipline became subordinated to demonstrating the correctness of stadialist theories. In the 1930s and 1940s, the investigation of archaeological sources was remodelled so as to permit sociological revelations of law-like regularities within the historical framework, especially in the sphere of material culture. The path towards this goal seemed disarmingly simple: first, establish the chronological sequence; second, find gaps and changes in this sequence; third, generalise and fit the sequence, lock, stock and barrel, to suit the established sociological framework. Archaeology, in this way, became a history of material culture: a fact reflected in the names of most research institutes concerned with investigating the past. However, such dogmatic simplification led to crisis within the approach itself, and engendered the seeds of its downfall. The shortcomings of the stadialist approach were exposed at the beginning of the 1950s (Tretjakov 1950, Udalcov 1953) and its theories were rejected – but not before official approval was given in the form of the rejection of Marr's teaching by Stalin.

All things are measurable

On the other side of the world, the 1930s saw the development of the taxonomic school in the United States (I. Rouse, A. C. Spaulding). The most comprehensive statement of its early beliefs and aims was presented in 1939 by Irving Rouse. Thirty years later, the same scholar presented a systematic account of the taxonomic approach, which included not only the results of his own research and of the teaching experience at Yale, but also the reaction to new ideas, which have emerged in the United States meanwhile: Taylor's contextualism and the processual notions of New Archaeology.

Rouse perceives archaeology and prehistory as two separate disciplines, even though they are related. Archaeology is given an analytical function: an archaeologist uncovers remains, processes them and describes their properties through techniques of conservation, analysis, description and classification, and finally exhibits and publishes his material. The nature of archaeological material is examined further through categorisation, comparison and analysis of mutual relationships: such procedures are worked out in detail by A. C. Spaulding. This is the strategy of archaeology.

Prehistory fulfils the synthetic function: it has the job of reconstructing the past from an archaeological basis. Rouse assumes that archaeology can provide an answer to questions such as who?, where?, when?, what?, how? and why? He connects the first question with ethnic identification, the second with chronological and spatial identification, the third with the reconstruction of ethnic systems and the fourth with a change within these systems. He adopts this procedure as a strategy for prehistoric research.

All the phases of the archaeological and prehistoric procedure are saturated with the taxonomic approach. The problems of classification especially are elaborated in detail. Two terms are particularly important here: class, defined as a population of artefacts which share common diagnostic characteristics, and type, defined as a population of attributes which occur together. Class is an objective entity, while type is an abstraction created by the investigator. In Rouse's view, classes are investigated by archaeologists, while prehistorians concern themselves with types, since the latter reflect the ancient norms and standards: the mental templates.

In his explanation of the culture process, Rouse rejects both the evolutionary model of linear progress and its neo-evolutionary adaptation. He comprehends cultures as open systems, the evolution of which occurs on the basis of traditions. The concept of tradition is defined as an integration of patterns of thought which are passed from one culture to another, and undergo modification in the process, or remain unchanged. In each culture, an integration of different traditions can be observed. Rouse's view is not unlike the contemporary spatial models of culture in Europe.

American taxonomists present several models of cultural traditions and their survival. They also construct an evolutionary scheme which differs markedly from the European sequence: palaeo, archaic, formative, classic, post-classic (compare with Willey and Phillips 1965: 73).

Rouse sees a serious problem in the fragmentation of contemporary archaeology, which appears to be the result of poorly defined terminology, often having contradictory meanings, used by different schools and by people adhering to different approaches. To remove this problem, he tries to give a precise meaning to individual terms and to ensure the general acceptance of such precise terminology in his publications, above all in his volume published in 1972 which includes at the end a dictionary of archaeological, anthropological, prehistoric and sociological terms.

5   The present

Buried in their ideas, they live happily, their position and prospects
in a well-organised state are solid and secure, centuries or even
millennia cushion them from the spasms of existence, and they do
not worry in the least that these could reoccur, because what would
the police and press have to say to that?

(a comment attributed to Søren Kierkegaard)

System, model, structure and symbol

Let us begin by mentioning some of the recent ideas which have enriched
the investigation of the past and of prehistory.

The methodological problems can be divided into three large groups
(Weaver 1948). First of all, there are those problems capable of being
represented by a few basic relations (linear causality). Second, there are
those which can be explained in principle, but still not in full, by means of
clearly defined determinist systems. Finally, there are those systems whose
structure and behaviour are indeterminable.

New concepts in archaeology are based above all on theories about
systems and models. A system can be viewed as a collection of elements
which are interrelated and which form a specific, delimited unity. In
individual cases we can view the system as closed in relation to the
environment and concentrate on the study of the relationships between its
elements. Open systems, on the other hand, are marked by their interaction
with the environment. The environment acts on the system by means of
input and the system reacts in turn by output. The behaviour of the system
can then be taken as the interaction of its input and output. The behaviour
depends primarily on the structure of the system, by which is meant the
organisation of the links between the elements of the system.

A system can change by altering its structure. A system has a tendency to
reach a certain end product, for example a state of equilibrium. There are
systems which are equipped with self-regulation and self-control, mainly
through the operation of a feedback loop. Cybernetics investigates systems
from the point of view of information. Systems which can include not only
the exchange of information but also transformations of matter and energy
are the domain of the general theory of systems.

As a rule, fluctuating, vague polythetic clusters reflect reality better than
rigid, fixed and clearly defined groupings. More and more time has been

devoted to the study of these systems which are not deterministic, but 'poorly organised' (V. V. Nalimov 1966); and even in mathematics, 'fuzzy' sets are investigated along with classical sets. There are, for example, such systems where, even though the input is precisely defined and known to us, the output cannot be deduced in a simple fashion. It can only be determined with a certain degree of probability. Systems whose input cannot be described in simple fashion also belong to this category.

A model is a simplified representation of the structure and behaviour of the system in question. Models thus form certain analogies by means of which we can observe, model and simulate those aspects of the system under observation which would otherwise be outside the reach of more precise forms of investigation.

With the help of different types of models we can investigate various systems. The knowledge of the behaviour of a system enables us to study an unknown structure and vice versa. The computer enables us to simulate the behaviour of systems in different circumstances, which we can set ourselves. Modern technology thus makes possible the treatment of questions which have hitherto defied solution. The concept of a system becomes an integral part of contemporary archaeology, which is reflected in the use of terms such as 'systems archaeology'.

Philosophy and methodology of science

Let us now mention another area of archaeological inspiration – the philosophy and methodology of science. From the historical survey presented earlier, we can see how the philosophy of science had an indirect but still profound influence on archaeology (for example, Montelius: Darwinism; Childe: Marxism; Wahle: Existentialism; Clarke: neo-positivism). The same can be said about the present. The views of Karl Popper (theory of induction), C. G. Hempel (theory of explanation), R. Carnap (language of science), T. S. Kuhn (paradigms of science and knowledge), and others, and the conception of middle-range theories and the theory of experiment, have influenced theoretical concepts in archaeology (Kelley and Hanen 1985, Moore and Keene 1983, Renfrew, Rowlands and Segraves 1982, Salmon and Salmon 1982, Watson, LeBlanc and Redman 1971, 1984).

Linguistics

The linguistics of Ferdinand de Saussure draws on the ideas of Comte, Tarde and Durkheim. For Saussure *langue* (language) corresponds to Durkheim's social fact, that is a phenomenon which exists outside the individual, in contrast to *parole* (speech), which is considered to be an individual phenomenon. Language is also a system of signs and as such belongs among a number of similar systems. What sets language apart is precisely its systemic nature, its synchronic state and not its inner historical evolution – diachronics.

Saussure's definition of the two types of relationship turned out to be extremely influential. Syntagmatic relationships are linear, in such a way that each unit belongs to a sequence in relation to its neighbours. Associative (paradigmatic) relationships link in with phenomena which for one reason or another are similar.

The Prague school of linguistic structuralism (the 1926 Manifesto) developed Saussure's conception of language as a system of signs. The glossematics of L. Hjelmslev (1943, edn 1) builds on the ideas of logical positivism and gestaltism. It regards language purely formally, as a collection of abstract relations. Similar to N. S. Trubeckoj, who considers phonemes to be the basic elements of phonology, and to V. Skalička, who considers semes to be the minimal grammatical units, Hjelmslev constructs the units of meaning – figurae which are not signs but components of signs. Only their combination will supply the meaning (so the sign 'boy' is composed of the symbols for human + youth + male and if we supplant the last figura by one for a female we arrive at the sign 'girl').

The descriptive school of linguistics of the first part of the twentieth century (notably L. Bloomfield 1933) was characterised by its orientation towards spoken language and communication. This was occasioned by the need to study indigenous languages (F. Boas) and the need to teach American soldiers 'exotic' languages. Under the influence of behaviourism the relation of three components – the situation before speech, the speech itself, and the situation after speech – was studied. The foundations of objective analyses of language at the grammatical level were laid down and this was later enlarged upon by Chomsky's transformational-generative grammar (1957). According to Chomsky every sentence can be broken down into its elementary 'kernel' strings (which have their equivalents in the early language of children). These sentences can be transformed – that is, their structure can be altered (It is raining. Is it raining? It is raining!) and they can be combined (It is raining and windy).

At the same time a new linguistic trend was also developing. The central hypothesis of Sapir and Whorf's (1933, 1949), ethnolinguistics rests upon the notion that culture is *what* a society does and thinks and language is *how* it thinks. The construction of reality is, according to this approach, dependent on language norms and thinking is dependent on concrete language.

Let us mention at this point the concrete results of linguistic investigations into the origin of language and languages. Glottochronology, as part of comparative linguistics, established by M. Swadesh (1952, 1959), represents a probe into the past of languages and is based on quantification. It relies on the premises that basic vocabulary sets keep on changing, slowly and at a constant rate in all languages. Here Swadesh was inspired by radiocarbon dating. The basic vocabulary sets of two related languages can then be compared and the point in time when they began to diverge can be calculated. It is with thanks to glottochronology that the development of language can be traced deep into prehistory.

The origin of language was for a long time a forbidden theme. For instance, the French Academy refused to accept works concerned with *perpetuum mobile* and the origins of language. Because of such a prohibition, origins of language were mostly investigated by non-linguists. This resulted in the generation of simple hypotheses, which served to reinforce the prejudices of the specialists. Thus the 'bow-wow' hypothesis was created, explaining the names of animals according to the sounds they made, the 'pooh-pooh' hypothesis in which the origin of words was ascribed to the vocalisation of exclamations, the 'yo-he-ho' hypothesis, which stressed the importance of exclamations uttered while at work, and the 'ta-ta' hypothesis, which claimed that words are derived from the movements of the lips and tongue.

A respectable hypothesis was put forward by O. Jespersen in 1922. His 'sing-song' hypothesis proposed that language has its origins in the simplification of emotive 'songs' expressing feelings. Through repetition, individual sounds corresponding to individual feelings and situations were crystallised. A. L. Kroeber placed the origin of language in the context of the early Palaeolithic culture of the Abbevillian. A whole number of works dealing with this problem (Lieberman 1975 and 1984, Harmad, Stentis and Lancaster 1976, Tran Duc Thaeo 1984, Gessinger and Rahden 1988) have recently appeared.

A comprehensive thesis was put forward by Swadesh in 1972, whereby he divided languages, in an analogy with archaeological classification, into Eolithic, Palaeolithic and Neolithic. The origins of language lay in the modification of exclamations, and individual words were created by imitation and sound symbolism (similarly, Jakobson 1962). In the early Palaeolithic era language gradually became a conventional formal system. In the last ten millennia the five presumed language families gradually diversified.

C. F. Hockett (1960, edn 1) bases his investigation of language on the comparison of various forms of communication, including communication in animals. He assigns thirteen attributes to human language and then compares other systems with them. In comparison with human language, the language of bees has 4.5 attributes, the communication amongst land mammals has 5, instrumental music 6.5, primates 8 and hominids 10 attributes. The origin of language is ascribed to the signals used in biologically important situations (danger, food, sex, mothering; Hockett 1977).

Structuralism

The origins of structualism lie in linguistics, but, in the same way as functionalism, it developed into a general trend, common to most of the humanities, a trend which can also be discerned in mathematics and the natural sciences (psychology, J. Lacan; semiotics, R. Barthes; poetics, J. M. Lotman; philosophy and history, M. Foucault; history of art, P. Francastel; ethnology, C. Lévi-Strauss, etc.). Structuralism has been further developed in post-structuralism (M. Foucault), social anthropology (E. Ardner) and structural Marxism (L. Althusser), which found favour notably among anthropologists and archaeologists at Cambridge. At the same time the only thing that structuralists have in common is the fact that most of them do not consider themselves to be structuralists. This is also one of the reasons why our survey of structuralism can only be schematic.

A notion basic to structuralism (if we take the views of Lévi-Strauss as a model) is that individual kinds of human activity represent communication systems and that each one of them is subordinate to a structure independent of human consciousness. Structure is not understood as a description of external, visible connections (as are the constant and repetitive properties of the system understood by, for example, functionalists) but rather it is seen as a model of observable systems. A model is usually constructed through the collection of binary oppositions (constitutive elements). Since these are complementary and universal (for example light/heavy) a simple principle of classification can be established. What is decisive is the belief that this collection of oppositions is capable of describing any system, just as Mendeleev's table sums up all possible atoms: 'we could construct something in the nature of a periodic table, similar to the table of chemical elements, in which all the actual or even only possible customs would feature, formed in definite groups; the only thing left to decipher would be which ones would this or another society adopt' (C. Lévi-Strauss). The Prague school of linguistic structuralism, represented for instance by the works of J. Mukařovský, developed a far more concrete idea of structure. Here structure is not a characteristic of things, or of individual states of mind, but of societal consciousness.

Folklore

C. Lévi-Strauss offers a structural analysis of kinship (1949), of myths (*Mythologiques*, beginning in 1964), and of primitive thought in general (1962). His ideas bear the imprint of the influence of Durkheim, Jakobson, Jung, Cassirer and Kroeber. Myths, for instance, are seen as permutations of a limited number of basic themes, which, in turn, are composed of basic constituent elements, 'mythems'. Lévi-Strauss also considers folk tales. While myths are based on cosmological, metaphysical and natural oppositions, folk tales are based on a weaker set of oppositions – local, social, moral – which have greater scope for permutations. The Prague school of linguistic structuralism, too, took an interest in folklore.

[The] genesis of folkloric creation begins with the grouping of traditional motifs and formulas ... and the creation of a folkloric work of art stands at the beginning of an artistic process of continuous changes, which take place through the regrouping, adding or deletion of detail. Such detail provides the basic units of meaning in the development of folkloric art,

writes Mukařovský. Long before Lévi-Strauss, P. Bogatyrjov postulated that the variety of phonological and morphological structures is limited and can be reduced to a relatively small number of basic types.

The Soviet school of semiotics achieved a resounding success in their study of folklore texts. A pioneering analysis of folk tales was started in 1928 by V. J. Propp. Inspired by Goethe's morphology, he constructed a model of an ideal fairy tale, the variations of which are the various concrete fairy tales. Propp regarded folklore as a form of prehistoric literature (1976). In his view, folklore formations functioned as paradigms which people followed when reproducing and composing further texts.

Later Propp concentrated on the content and historical analysis of folklore (1946). He was convinced that evolution occurred in stages and stated that the ideas of Morgan and Engels had not, until then, been elaborated fully or brought to their conclusion. An evolutionary chain was formed, he thought, by ritual ceremonies (notably totemism and initiation), myths and folk tales. Epics originated before the beginnings of the state. The time of origin was determined on the basis of manifestations of animism, zoomorpho-anthropological phenomena, and kinship.

Propp also investigated the presentation of events in folklore. Within its framework, he concluded, time does not exist independently but is defined only through the exploits of the heroes. Similarly, space is not independent, 'the blind wander from object to object', and the only defined space is the space in which the chief protagonist currently finds himself. Thus it is not possible for a number of actions to occur simultaneously in different places.

Each persona exists only from the standpoint of action – a physical and not a psychological action. This is why heroes are only representations of characteristic attributes. The action is primary, causes are only secondary. Logic is possible but not necessary. Motivation for actions is elaborated later and for this reason it can serve as an indicator of the age of the folk tale. On the basis of this we can state that in the system of primitive thought there are neither causative relationships nor abstract concepts, that there is an entirely different conception of time, space, object, subject, reality; in summary, a different view of the world.

In stressing the importance of ritual, Propp shared the same position as schools which had otherwise differed in their orientation, notably, the Ritualistic school (A. van Gennep 1909), and the Cambridge school (J. E. Harrison 1903, R. F. S. Raglan 1936, and many others). In 1925, E. Cassirer also postulated the priority of ritual. He saw mythology as an autonomous symbolic form of culture, just like language and art. His views were further developed in the works of A. F. Losev (1930), W. M. Urban (1939) and S. Langer (1942, 1951). Losev identified stone, hunting, and magic with matriarchy, and metal, agriculture and animism with patriarchy. In line with this identification he then classified the evolution of myth. M. Eliade (1952 and later) saw myths as linked with rituals, as a conscious repetition of paradigmatic gestures which have, as their aim, unification with the transcendental. The perpetual combat of the sacred and the profane, of the fear of history and cyclical regeneration are the basic themes of his work.

On the basis of Propp's first work, dating from 1928, a systematic study of the structure not only of folklore but also of texts, especially narrative texts, was started, albeit after a long delay (C. Brémond, A. Dundes, A. J. Greimas, C. Chabrol, E. R. Leach, J. Lotman, P. Maranda, T. Todorov, and others).

In 1973, T. V. Civjan examined folk tales from a lexicographic standpoint, according to individual semantic fields – cosmological, spatial, temporal, individual and subject matter. Similarly, V. V. Ivanov and V. N. Toporov (1974) constructed a set of concrete nouns leading to the reconstruction of the archaic 'natural world' on the basis of actions, situations, personae, attitudes and empirical phenomena. Even historical events were explained in terms of empirical phenomena: for example, a winged horse signified the fact that the cult role was transferred from a bird to a horse and, consequently, that the horse began to be domesticated. The same authors also constructed a residual form of the basic Indo-European myth. But it was E. M. Meletinskij (1976) who was the proponent *par excellence* of the structural analysis of myth.

On the basis of common motifs migrations can be identified – for example, the motif of a fatherless child is common to Europe, Asia, America, Australia and Oceania.

So-called 'folk taxonomy' represented a new discipline which investigated taxonomic systems, both archaic and folkloric. These are usually based on a dual division. The study of archaic taxonomy enables us to learn about the original conceptions regarding nature, society and the way in which they were constructed.

The study of basic semantic units was started by M. Parry (1930) and A. B. Lord (1960). Central to this study is the notion of the 'formula' as the basic unit of epic language (formula = cliché). For example, the entire gigantic epic of Mahābhārata consists of about 85% formulae; the number of formulae can serve as an auxiliary dating method. A systematic study of cliché was carried out by G. L. Permjakov (1970). For Permjakov, clichés are fixed word combinations – from proverbs to riddles – from which the more complex formations such as fables and folk tales were later developed. For Permjakov, a cliché, as far as the contents are concerned, is a sign of a typical life situation.

These linguistic investigations extend into prehistory and resemble in many respects the structural analyses which were developed in archaeology (see below, pp. 130–2).

Archaeology for archaeologists

When considering the history of archaeology, the archaeologist falls into the trap of his own professional making. That is to say, he or she can deliberate on evolutionism, migrationism or taxonomy, but sooner or later he must decide which way he is going to interpret the evolution of archaeological thinking – will it be from the point of view of evolutionism, migrationism, structuralism or otherwise? (Consider the preceding chapters, for instance. Could they not be faulted for betraying the influence of environmentalism?).

The basic characteristic of the prehistoric past was its unity. The past exerted a massive influence, yet only in a condensed form, as a tradition. Nowadays, we find ourselves, to quote Nietzsche, 'amidst all the pasts'; there is enough to select from, enough to return to. For us, history is incomplete, latent and fluctuating. Like the fabled phoenix, the old archaeological conceptions rise again and with a new inspirational force, though the feathers might be somewhat different. It is, above all, the recent past which cannot be excluded from the present and cannot be dealt with in the classic historiographical way.

But then we must ask ourselves a question – in what way can we deal with it? It seems that an approach which would best take into account our own relationship with the past, especially the recent past, would be most suitable. Such an approach is now considered to be the information systems approach, which guarantees information that is both quick and synoptic and, as far as possible, representational. However, such a method can substantially differ from the historiographic approach. This, incidentally, is the approach this book strives to emulate and which is its final aim. What is presented, therefore, is a certain synchronisation of diachronic studies, a utilitarian classification and typology. The Chinese systematic division of animals into, amongst others, birds, mammals and animals belonging to the Emperor may be a source of amusement to zoologists but it was perfectly satisfactory as far as the norms of behaviour of a citizen of the Empire was concerned.

Let us then measure archaeologists with the yardstick they use for measuring others – that is, let us establish a typology, typological chains, vertical stratigraphy, geographical environment, the influence of the environment, diffusion and migration, not of artefacts, but of the view of archaeologists.

Towards the end of the 1930s the first voices can be heard claiming that the 'building of prehistory' which had taken so much time and effort to construct and which had been constantly refined and renovated was built, in part or in full, on faulty architectural plans and that it did not rest on firm foundations but on sand. In addition, the material used in its construction did not possess the necessary properties.

After the Second World War these opinions multiplied and finally they merged into a powerful and raging torrent which would, eventually, pull the whole edifice down, destroying it and scattering its remains. For almost twenty years afterwards, a significant number of people could not be found who would attempt to stem this tide or to erect a more solid structure. How did this tendency, hitherto so exceptional in archaeology, originate and gather its strength? The causes are numerous and it is difficult to say which one was primary or more significant than others. One cause, certainly, was the bad architectural planning. It has to be acknowledged that none of the theoretical concepts which had traditionally been advanced as an explanation for all the historico-cultural processes, their variability, cultural changes and successions stood its ground. When put to a critical test these concepts crumbled. This was the fate of evolutionism and of concepts regarding space (migration and diffusion), the Soviet theory of stages, of taxonomism. However, they did not turn wholly into ashes and dust: a new and raging current merely diverted them, from a river bed reserved for the 'great theories', 'scientific schools', and 'paradigms', to a tributary. Two of the old concepts – neo-evolutionism and environmentalism – preserved their vigour and even flourished in the influential works of R. McAdams, R. Braidwood, J. G. D. Clark, and other archaeologists.

But let us remind ourselves that a current is not a river and one archaeological theory does not represent the whole of archaeology. In the backwaters, concepts much older, if not the oldest, lived on. The renaissance of the theories of migration and diffusion or environmentalism we mentioned was not an isolated case.

At first, however, the new current, branching on one hand into German indeterminism with its theory of the latent formation of culture, and on the other, into scepticism, one could say hyper-scepticism, explicitly formulated by Anglo-Saxon scholars, could not be satisfied with a mere relegation of preceding theories into the background. Their failure was considered to be total and inevitable because the historico-cultural process was indeterminable, it defied laws and, consequently, any reconstruction was impossible. And if some laws happened to exist after all, then the archaeological sources (regardless of their incompleteness and fragmentation) would not be capable of reflecting the vital elements of culture or, if they did, then any reflection would be distorted. The application of ethnographical parallels was dismissed and the models from cultural anthropology were thought to be unreliable.

In the Soviet Union and other socialist countries a parallel current emerged in the 1930s in which optimism prevailed about the potential of archaeological sources as faithful reflections of past social order. However, archaeological theory was not elaborated on the basis of historic and dialectic materialism – it was simply identified with it. But what eventually transpired was that both the archaeological sources and even the very best general theory can betray our trust if we do not devote to it constant critical attention. How ungrateful!

A question, then, springs to one's mind. This infinite scepticism on one hand and the infinite optimism on the other – are they not merely two sides of the same coin? What can arise out of their coexistence?

Archaeological sources can lie

From the end of the 1930s, opposition arose in Germany to Kossinna's one-sided determinist reconstruction of the past. The new methodological and theoretical approach rebelled against the naive ideas of Nazi archaeology with its notions about the faithful reflection of ethnogenetic evolution in archaeological sources, and also against the simplistic and uncritical combination of archaeological, anthropological, linguistic, written and ethnographical sources. Until then, all these sources had fitted together snugly, just like cogs, and the wheels of ethnic interpretation had been turning smoothly and in the direction in which the regime of the time needed them to go in order to justify its geo-political claims.

The new approach developed in two directions. One line of enquiry was concerned, above all, with the methodology of analysis of all forms of evidence which constituted the past and, secondly, with recognising the limits of archaeological reconstruction. This was the way followed from 1939 by H. J. Eggers. Two years later, E. Wahle founded a new general theory of historico-cultural process – the theory of the latent formation of culture.

'Is the optimistic belief of archaeologists in the objectivity of their sources and in the faithful reflection of past reality really justified?', Eggers asked in 1950. He continued:

Is it really unnecessary for archaeologists to clean up their sources as historians do? No historian would ever believe Herodotus, even if he held in his own hands notes signed by Herodotus himself, without first carrying out an internal analysis. Are then material remains, just because, according to archaeologists, they do not represent history, free from any distortion or tendentiousness? No, this is decidedly not the case under any circumstances. Even archaeological remains can lie!

(Translated from the original German, Eggers 1950)

Until Eggers raised the question, all archaeologists, not only the Germans, were in no doubt that archaeological sources were sufficient for the faithful reconstruction of the past. They were merely aware of the fact that with increasing age one could expect fewer remains, and an increasingly poor state of preservation. For this reason they concentrated on quantitative differences and carried out only external analysis. Nobody demanded that analysis of the internal contents of the artefacts be carried out because of the prevalent view that there was no reason for material remains, assembled without purpose, to be biased (unlike, for example, the historical sources, which were written for someone's benefit or with some goal in mind).

Eggers convincingly demonstrated, however, that even amongst material remains, assemblages and monuments existed (graves, votive treasures, stelae, etc.) which were addressed to gods, contemporaries, neighbours or descendants. In such cases, people chose and arranged artefacts in such a way as to create a message in accordance with their own ideas and intentions. The dead were not buried in their ordinary clothing and quite often not with everyday objects but with things specified by ritual. Sometimes people were even satisfied with substitutes made from a cheaper or less labour-demanding material. The gods, too, were often deceived with less valuable imitations. Some of the artefacts went out of circulation fairly rapidly (for example, ceramics), while others, such as metal products, would not find themselves on a rubbish heap so quickly. Moreover, archaeological sources were found to suffer through the activities of the succeeding generations and the effects of natural processes. The concept of site formation was born.

Eggers thus drew our attention not only to the quantitative differences of archaeological sources but also to their qualitative dissimilarity. He introduced the fundamental concepts of 'living culture' (*lebendes Gut*), 'dying culture' (*sterbendes Gut*) and 'dead culture' (*totes Gut*) (*ibid.*: 49). Using ethnographic material from Pomerania, he demonstrated that within a living culture, the place of all artefacts and their functional connections are fully understood. A dying culture consists of artefacts which are not in circulation any more but where there still exists an awareness of their cultural and functional links. The time boundary between a living and a dying culture tends to vary. In the Pomeranian case, clothing is exchanged every five years, family jewelery tends to be preserved for about a century. Coats of arms of the aristocracy go back to approximately the fifteenth century and religious insignia are two or three centuries older. Within the dead cultures, there is hardly anything preserved in the tradition to give us a clue as to the status and function of the disused artefacts in the cultural system of the time. Everything has to be discovered anew.

On the basis of this analysis Eggers formulated his methodological rule: archaeological sources reflect reality with distortion, incompletely and quite idiosyncratically, compared with other types of evidence. It is therefore necessary to work out a specific methodology of inner analysis and make this a part of the archaeological research procedure (Eggers 1939, 1950, 1959).

Wahle's theory of the latent formation of culture made its first appearance in 1941, at the time when Kossinna's settlement archaeology was canonised as a constituent part of state ideology without any serious objections on the part of German archaeologists. That Wahle chose this time to put forward his theory was a mark of his personal courage, considering the political atmosphere of those days.

According to Wahle's theory, changes in culture are seen as a process of imminent internal transformation. In this process he distinguishes two periods: 'Nährperiode' – the era of creative expansion when culture is, so to speak, 'stockpiled' – and 'Zehrperiode' – the period of quiet and tranquil existence when the amassed reserves are used up. The suddenness of cultural changes and transformations is explained on the basis of a hypothesis that cultural innovations are not the preserve of large human communities but are introduced by small groups of people and creative personalities living amidst them. The new cultural traits first emerge within such small groups or from the creative activity of a genius and only then do they spread and conquer the masses and wide areas. This process of diffusion happens very quickly and this is one of the main reasons why it seems to us that culture appears all of a sudden and ready-made. However, to put it figuratively, even though its formation took place right in front of the archaeologists' eyes, it would pass unnoticed. This is because archaeology, according to Wahle, does not possess a mechanism so finely tuned that it would be capable of detecting actions of individuals or small groups from the fragmented and poorly preserved sources.

Wahle's hypothesis is based on the conviction that both ordinary people and their communities (including nations) are divided into those who create history (*die Geschichte machen*) and those who accept history (*die Geschichte erleiden*). Behind all the discoveries, inventions and innovations there is the creative personality of an individual whose activity stems only from his free will, unfettered by any social laws. That explains why the form of a new culture cannot be deduced in any way from the preceding state. And, consequently, any such endeavour is basically a quixotic adventure. The historico-cultural process disintegrates into separate periods between which all interconnections have been lost or, better still, there never were any connecting links between them in the first place.

What are the consequences of this hypothesis for practical research and explanation? Genetic sequences disintegrate and only successions of events remain, and these have to be studied within the limits of natural geographical regions (Wahle 1941, 1964).

Eggers' and Wahle's approach is further elaborated in the works of other German scholars, among them R. Hachmann, Ulrich Fischer, H. Kirchner, G. Kossack and H. Preidel.

The ideas of this school were brought to fruition in 1962 by the historian and archaeologist R. Hachmann, the archaeologist G. Kossack and the linguist H. Kuhn (Hachmann, Kossack and Kuhn 1962). Each submitted to separate analysis sources of one region in north-western Germany dating from the turn of the first millennium AD and described the characteristics of the Celtic and Germanic communities living there. A synthesis was arrived at by placing their conclusions side by side. The findings of all three disciplines coincided and confirmed one another. Hachmann carried on along this road and eight years later he published a book in which he located the homeland of the Goths not in Scandinavia, as was usual until then, but in the basin of the Vistula (Hachmann 1970). He did so on the basis of written sources, whilst the archaeological sources do not corroborate the historical sources as was the case in the previous collective work, but at the same time neither do they disprove them. They are simply neutral and we cannot but conclude that some events recorded in the written sources cannot be detected archaeologically. In his following book, devoted to the Germanic peoples, Hachmann therefore narrowed the scope of problems to those where one can anticipate their mutual comparison and verification by sources other than archaeological. This approach proved to be fruitful when Hachmann carried out his reconstruction of Germanic ritual and religious practices (Hachmann 1971a, b). Ongoing interaction between archaeological, ethnological and occasionally historical approaches is typical of West German archaeology (Bergmann 1970, Eggert 1974, 1976, 1978, Narr 1978b, Ziegert 1964).

The search for connections

In 1948, W. W. Taylor published 'A study of archaeology' (which appeared in book form in 1967) based on his doctoral dissertation, which he had written five years earlier at Harvard under the supervision of C. K. M. Kluckhohn. In his work, Taylor analyses the American approach to the study of ancient culture. According to Taylor three sciences are involved in this task: archaeology, which collects data, anthropology, which seeks a generalised understanding of culture, and history, which combines particular data with cultural generalisations and so provides an explanation for regional cultural differences and changes. Taylor points out that the majority of archaeologists – despite their claims that they do study anthropology and history – are in fact concerned with nothing more than a collection of data (an observation which did not endear him to his American colleagues). In addition, just as in the case of the 'palaeontological model', they treat artefacts like fossils and concentrate on those they consider to be good stratigraphic indicators. On the basis of formal and often remote analogies they construct higher entities – types and cultures – which are basically none other than mere projections of their own schemes and ideas. Taylor rejects the restriction of culture to a mere additive list of traits and demands a contextual study of functions and functional links of artefacts within their contexts.

There is no automatic, axiomatic assurance that the forms, types and classes established today by the archaeologist are coextensive with any separable entities that existed in the minds or life ways of a bygone people. At best, the declaration of

*any such correspondence is a matter for explicit hypothesis and testing, not implicit
assumption.*
(Taylor 1967: 121)

It is for similar reasons that already in 1946 J. O. Brew doubted the
reality of type. His ideas were further developed in the work of J. A. Ford
(Ford 1954).

Taylor called his concept 'conjunctive'. The school of thought of which
he was the founder was later called contextualism. This is because, in
contrast to the previous approach, which grouped together objects of one
type and function and, on the basis of remote associations and abstractions,
transformed them into higher entities, Taylor grouped various objects from
one more narrowly delimited locality into a complex and in this way their
functional interconnection was revealed. He therefore contrasted the
concrete context of the finds with the analogies and abstractions symptomatic of the previous approach (Taylor presumably had in mind the earlier
American taxonomists). Further, Taylor demanded that the hypothetico-
deductive method be a part of the investigative mechanism:

*It rather is incumbent upon him [the archaeologist] to derive his observational
data as objectively as possible, to differentiate between the observed fact and
derived inference, to make explicitly labelled interpretations of as detailed and full
a nature as possible and then look, either in the ground or among the data at
hand, for evidence by which his hypothesis may be tested.*
(Taylor 1967: 113)

Finally, Taylor demands that the procedures used by archaeologists
should not be vague and unexplained but, on the contrary, subject to
verification by other research workers.

Taylor's ideas (casting doubt on the reality of some more abstract entities
– culture and type) were further developed into a methodological and
conceptual system by his American followers – amongst them R.
McAdams, J. A. Ford, G. R. Willey and others. Some British scholars –
G. E. Daniel, C. F. C. Hawkes and S. Piggott – also contributed to these
developments. S. J. L. de Laet, A. Leroi-Gourhan and M. P. Malmer were
also partially influenced by Taylor's ideas. Other aspects of Taylor's work
(such as the precise definition of concepts and investigative procedures,
functionalism, the hypothetico-deductive method) inspired the 'New
Archaeology' of the 1960s.

Anglo-Saxon common sense

With the benefit of his experience as an officer in the Royal Air Force
during the Second World War, G. E. Daniel has investigated from 1943 all

the methods and approaches which archaeology has hitherto made use of in its reconstruction of prehistory. Without any sympathy and sentiment towards his elders, step by step, just like the detectives in his novels *The Cambridge Murders* and *Welcome Death*, Daniel probes, investigates and exposes the theoretical concepts of prehistory – ethnological and techno-logical schemes, evolutionism, spatial concepts, environmentalism – and, then, he delivers his judgement: all amount to nothing but a fortuitous array of platitudes and errors, without any logic or meaning, being no more than mere projections of ideas. Epochs, cultures and types are arbitrarily created conceptual research instruments. Why this singular and unqualified condemnation? Simply because, as Daniel explains, there is not, and cannot be, any correspondence between material culture and its non-material aspects. It is therefore useless to expect that the moral or intellectual culture of contemporary primitive societies living in comparable conditions with those of prehistoric societies can serve as a key to our understanding of the spiritual culture of prehistoric society. If ethnology cannot help us, where can we turn, Daniel asks.

Such reasoning leads Daniel to renounce (with exceptional elegance and charm) all the leading ideas and theories (Daniel 1943, 1950, 1962, 1966, 1967, 1975) as mere schemes, ideas and projections, incapable of aiding objective reconstruction.

The hitherto acknowledged prudence of archaeological sources does not hold its ground under Daniel's fire. Similarly, the reality of archaeological cultures and other entities and also that of boundaries of any kind (chronological and territorial) crumbles. For Daniel, all entities and any differences between them are basically conventional and relative. They do not manifest themselves in archaeological sources but are created artificially and subjectively by scholars and then made to fit the material. The investigation of cultures and their variability of changes and rifts loses its purpose since these categories are formulated purely arbitrarily and imposed on the archaeological material. For Daniel, the impossibility of the reconstruction of the cultural-historical process stems not only from the very nature of archaeological sources – they are incomplete and do not reflect the essential aspects of the past – but also from the fact that determinism is alien to this process. In this respect Daniel's position is close to the concept worked out so brilliantly in historiography by R. G. Collingwood. The similarity of the title of one of Daniel's books – *The Idea of Prehistory* (1962) – with Collingwood's *The Idea of History* (1945) certainly seems more than a coincidence.

Daniel's destruction of all previous models of explanation and reconstruction is, in a way, a new paradigm, a new model that urges us to abandon all attempts at reconstructing the past cultural-historical process. Such attempts are doomed to failure from the start. What does Daniel's 'zero model' offer archaeologists? It is the material and intellectual enrichment of the present culture by lost values. Indeterminism therefore means the disintegration of the belief in the possibility of objective reconstruction from archaeological sources.

C. F. C. Hawkes divides all information about culture into four categories – from easily obtainable information to that which is totally outside the reach of an archaeologist. B. D. Smith also stresses the general conceptual theme of the extremely limited means archaeology has at its disposal for assisting us in the reconstruction of past lifeways (Hawkes 1954, Smith 1977).

Piggott considers all explanatory models to be fortuitous and subjective. They are complementary to each other and therefore they can all, in their own way, be truthful. The criterion of their correctness is subordinate to the view of the universe held by prehistoric man. For example, if we find a bronze axe, Piggott says, we are entitled to enquire about its age, the technology of its manufacture, and the distribution of this type, etc. The application of a technological model is therefore possible; however, this model is not superior to any other model, since we do not know whether the people to whom we ascribe it valued technological progress in the same way as we do. In a certain respect, there never existed a Bronze Age. It is merely a kind of archaeological shorthand jargon. We have to admit openly, Piggott continues, that information gleaned from archaeological sources is strictly limited. If historical events, the social structure of a community, its beliefs and convictions are not reflected in archaeological sources or are not contained within them, we must acknowledge it as such and limit ourselves to demonstrating that information which is really obtainable. To ask nonsensical questions would not only be a waste of time but it would also be illogical (Piggott 1960: 5–7, 12).

It is probably true to say that the criticism of the general value of theoretical concepts by Anglo-Saxon and German archaeologists stemmed mainly from the failures encountered when reconstructing prehistory on the basis of archaeological sources rather than from their analysis (artefacts from new investigations continued to be assembled stubbornly into previously established entities). What we have to do, according to their view, is to continue to gather artefacts but at the same time to pay attention to the wide range of contexts and relationships, since an artefact taken in isolation is of little value. In practice, this act of liberation from all models can subconsciously lead to the adoption of old paradigms, and to their application without sufficient strictness. It can equally lead to methodological and theoretical open-mindedness and a deliberate commitment to empiricism alone.

At the same time this critical reckoning with the past cleared the way for new concepts. The demand that the ability of archaeological sources to contribute to our knowledge of the past be subject to examination was extremely important (especially when contrasted with the naive faith in and optimism regarding their objectivity and with their senseless application in illustrating general sociological concepts). Equally important was the introduction of a new and, one has to say, fundamental problem – the internal analysis of archaeological sources. And it was the German scholars who were chiefly concerned with this problem. Rejection of the hitherto accepted explanatory models and of the inadequate investigative mechanisms gave rise not only to a new following but also to polemics, discussion, and the search for new approaches. Archaeology badly needed such a breath of fresh air.

Theoretical hiatus: the Soviet case

The collapse of the stages theory in the 1950s occurred without being replaced by a new theory. 'For two decades we had a non-theoretical era in Soviet archaeology' (Klejn 1975b: 99). Instead, archaeologists in the Soviet Union devoted themselves with renewed vigour to empirical investigations, in the conviction that everything else would be safely explained within the framework of historical and dialectical materialism. What they failed to notice, however, was that philosophical theory then assumes the role of the theory in a specific scientific field instead of stimulating its development. As a result, a situation developed where even the most fruitful thesis built on the foundations of the archaeological material assumed a scholastic appearance and illustrative character. Direct quotations from the classics of dialectical materialism about prehistory, antiquity and material culture, often formulated only incidentally and on the basis of the knowledge of archaeology, history and ethnology prevailing at the time, were taken as the most reliable sources of reference for formulating a general theory of archaeology (Klejn 1977: 12).

Consequently, in the second half of the 1950s, some Soviet archaeologists (Boriskovskij 1960, Okladnikov 1959) returned to the research objectives of the 1930s and developed further the systemisation and interpretation of those statements of the founding fathers of Marxism which touched upon the problems of archaeology.

The position vacated by the theory of stages and not claimed by any other more significant theory was now beginning to be filled by older concepts (ethnological interpretation, migrationism, diffusion) which, until then, had maintained a low profile, that is, if they were not obliterated altogether. All these concepts, however, were conditioned and shaped by the political climate of the day. The attempts to project an ethnic division into the past and to investigate indigenous traditions of some ethnic groups, especially Slavonic ones (Artamonov 1947, Tretjakov 1948), were a reaction to the pressures of German settlement archaeology. The problem of ethnogenesis grew into the problem of the origins of the Slavs and other ethnic groups and was deemed to be one of the primary aims of archaeology.

While during the reign of the theory of stages the reconstruction of migration was tackled only very cautiously in the 1920s and 1930s, during the years following its disintegration scholars were beginning to feel less restricted in this direction. The course and directions of migrations clearly reflected the evolution of the contemporary political situation. Initially, all migrations took place only on the territory of the USSR or outwards from it (Brjusov 1952, 1957a, 1965). If they did happen to be directed towards the USSR then it was only from the neighbouring Slavonic territories (Artamonov 1950).

The attitudes towards diffusion were also undergoing a process of change. There was a transition from the outright denial of any external influences on Slavonic culture (for example, Avdusin 1953) to the admission of their existence and to the analysis of their significance in certain specific cases (Brjusov 1957b).

The rise of New Archaeology: the opening of hostilities

From the beginning of the 1960s it was obvious that archaeological war was inevitable and its outbreak was only a question of time. The adherents of 'traditional', 'subjective' or, if you prefer, 'intuitive' or 'impressionistic' archaeology together with the advocates of 'common sense' or 'indeterminism' were firmly entrenched in their positions while their adversaries were beginning to gather their arms and ammunition. And there was enough to collect from. The echoes of the first scientific and technological revolution were still faintly audible when there arrived a second one, characterised by the rapid growth of information technology, the integration of individual scientific fields, the birth of new marginal disciplines and of quite non-traditional ones. All this was accompanied by the systems approach with its attendant computerisation.

The first shots came from Sweden and France. Already in 1955, J.-C.

Gardin was the first man to voice a demand for a new methodology of description and interpretation of archaeological sources. What he saw as the chief shortcoming of the methods used until then was distilled in the observation that when one and the same artefact was analysed several times over in different periods or by a number of scholars in the same period, both the description itself and the interpretation were usually strikingly disparate. He therefore recommended that more rational methods of obtaining, preserving and utilising information be adopted. Such an aim, on the whole, demanded extensive theoretical and practical activity in various fields – the collection of materials according to a detailed scheme, the establishment of analytical codes and descriptive language, the utilisation of computers, etc. Slowly, Gardin began to accomplish his aim. He founded a Centre of Documentation Analysis in France and later he shared his experience via UNESCO. Towards the end of the 1970s, he summarised the best results of his 25-year-long effort in his excellent book *Une archéologie théoretique* (Gardin 1979).

His fellow countryman G. Laplace attacked Bordes' classification of Palaeolithic artefacts in 1957. F. Bordes and all followers of the traditional typological classification (for example, A. García Cook and J. A. Ford) regarded archaeological material as essentially capable of division and they divided it according to a priori schemes and a strictly established hierarchy of characteristics. The highest level was determined by the material from which the artefact was fashioned (stone, bone, ceramic, metal, etc.), the subsequent stage by the nature of its function, etc. The basis, therefore, was not a correlation of elements of equal value but their hierarchy, established in advance and deduced by general reasoning. In accordance with this scheme, artefacts were classified once and for all and their frequencies in complexes and strata were established. From this, genetic relationships of complexes, cultures, etc. could be inferred.

Laplace contrasted this classic descriptive typology with analytical typology, drawing on statistics and the correlation of characteristics. He rejected as one-sided the purely typometric isolation of characteristics and their combinations and instead he demanded equal weighting for all characteristics and types. He considered the hitherto accepted nomenclature of types to be semantically incorrect and replaced it with letters and figures. He demonstrated his approach in the analysis of artefacts of the early Palaeolithic and Mesolithic periods and attempted to identify their evolutionary causes. In order to explain the cultural process Laplace made use of one of the contemporary models of biological evolution. On the basis of this model, he arrived at the theory of basic polymorphism, which claims that early Palaeolithic industries were not originally specialised and only later divided into specialised complexes. According to Laplace, identical cultural elements in different localities are the result of autochthonous evolution and convergence. Migration and diffusion had no place in his interpretation (Laplace 1957).

In 1962, the Swedish archaeologist M. P. Malmer attacked 'impressionism' from his own rationalist perspective (Malmer 1962). What he calls 'impressionism' are the main principles of traditional archaeology: intuitivism, the lack of rigour and precision in the definition of terms, nebulous deductions and methods. In his studies devoted mainly to the problems of the Neolithic period, he demands, and personally adheres to, clearly defined concepts, quantified terminology, hypotheses and inferences based on strict logic, and articulated with the help of mathematics and statistics.

At the same time he developed in greater depth the typological method of Müller and Montelius which he sees as the key method which archaeology possesses. He is concerned that typological method be applied not only to the study of individual artefacts and their clusters but also to the study of localities with changing cultures. He regards material culture as an interrelated system of elements.

Malmer divided an archaeologist's work into five consecutive steps: (1) excavation and other methods of collecting material; (2) a move from a concrete artefact to an abstract concept – objective registration and verbal definition of the type; (3) spatial and chronological discussion and conclusion based on facts, typology, quantity and a combination of the finds, and stratigraphy; (4) a move from an abstract concept to a conception of the concrete historical situation; (5) synthesis – the establishment and comparison of concrete prehistoric situations, interpolation and analogical conclusions.

The isolated shots of these three scholars were not particularly heeded at the time. Nevertheless, the fact remains that most of their ammunition was stored up in the arsenal – whether intentionally or otherwise – by 'new' and analytical archaeology: the analytical approach, formalisation of description and other investigative operations linked with the application of mathematical, statistical and logistic methods, methodological autonomy on the one hand, and adoption of theoretical concepts from other sciences on the other; the recognition of archaeological material as a continuum instead of an array of elements, the recognition of causality in cultural process, the negation of migrationism and its replacement by internal transformation as a means of explaining change.

Clarke's bomb

'If my facts fall short of my theory, the worse for the facts', said G. W. F. Hegel and his theory then had to search for a reality corresponding to it. That even methods can search for their object was convincingly proved by D. L. Clarke in his book *Analytical Archaeology* (1968). If we cannot apply exact methods, the fault lies neither with them nor with reality itself and we have therefore to change our conception of reality; and we shall keep on changing it until it suits our methods. This observation might be somewhat cruel but is not untrue. Despite everything, Hegel's and Clarke's concepts are of great value and the fact that they don't correspond to reality ... well, they share that with all other theories.

Clarke's points of departure are notably 'new' geography with its systems approach and 'analytical' biology with its methods of numerical taxonomy. On the basis of these methods and enlightened by logical positivism, Clarke embarked on the methodological reconstruction of archaeology – and of the past as well.

Exact methods demand precise preliminary data and Clarke strove to obtain them by means of precisely defined elementary units. The essence of his theory is the concept of the attribute – a logically non-reducible property – which functions as an independent variable within a given system of artefacts. An artefact is defined as any object modified by human activity and this activity moulds the attributes of such an object. A type is a group of artefacts defined by a concurrent and recurrent set of attributes which are always the elements of a certain polythetic set. An assemblage is a continuous set of contemporaneous types. Archaeological culture is then understood as a polythetic set of specific types of artefacts which co-occur within a certain geographical area. A whole range of regional cultural clusters, such as sub-culture, culture, groups of cultures and technological complexes, can then be introduced. These archaeological entities undergo constant changes, and the consecutive chain of these changes is termed a process. The basic processes are ontogenesis, migration and integration. A general dynamic systems model serves as a model for entities and their systems and processes at all levels. The total system is composed of a number of sub-systems (social, economic, religious, etc.). Each of them can be investigated individually and their interaction gives rise to the total system.

Physical properties of artefacts are for Clarke the simplest facts possessing equal weight. This eliminates the intrusion of subjective opinions.

Further, Clarke studies the distribution of these properties without an a priori classification of the correlations and relationships. He therefore transforms information by means of the formal rules of analytical techniques in such a way that the unity and causality of cultural significance follow automatically. Clarke proceeds from artefacts to their properties – and then, through the subsequent correlations, from the properties to types and from the types to cultures and technological processes, to synthesis. He breaks archaeological sources into the simplest elements and on the basis of specific hypothesis he selects them for processing and then they are carried away by a strictly regulated current through the sluice gates of computers. This is expected to provide objective results which are then to be explained by means of specific hypotheses. The initial and final stages of archaeological work still remain, even after Clarke's intervention, the domain of hypotheses, because, so far, we have not been able to construct a machine capable of generating fruitful hypotheses and ideas.

Clarke's book had an explosive effect. After such a massive attack, archaeology woke up from her virginal slumbers and all the previous tentative honeymoons were forgotten (Clarke 1973). Instead of a few recipes, she was given a whole cookbook which has been, and still is, extensively used for meal preparation, even though what is cooked very rarely corresponds to Clarke's original vision. This is not surprising because, as Einstein said, 'the perfection of means and the confusion of ends characterise our age'. Let us elucidate this statement by looking at the possibilities of the misuse of statistics and modelling.

A significant symptom of both quantomania and ontology is expressed by the inscription on the facade of the Social Science Research Building of the University of Chicago: 'If you cannot measure, your knowledge is meagre and unsatisfactory.' The sense of logic is not in the formulation of new propositions – with statistics the situation is different. We reduce supplied information by means of statistical operations, and make 'shorthand descriptions' which have no meaning in themselves, but are to be interpreted in non-statistical terms. For this reason hypotheses are rejected or not rejected, but never definitely confirmed. In reality we test not only our hypotheses, but also our choice of statistical means and, often, their intuitive assumptions.

The real problem of statistical testing lies, not in measuring and evaluating alone, but in the way a hypothesis is stated and evaluated. No independent or objective way to formulate a hypothesis exists. This is the case, for example, with the classification of artefacts. The greater the number of characteristics taken into account, the more exact will be our results, altering at the same time the level of consideration. The first problem is the determination of indicators, the second, their evaluation, and the third, the choice of statistical means. By manipulating them we can perhaps prove anything.

New Archaeology as a reflection of our times

'Do you know Binford personally?'

'Yes', I finally answered. 'I was with him the day he fed five thousand undergraduates with a few loaves of bread and a newspaperful of fish' (Flannery 1976). What were these loaves and this fish?

L. R. Binford published his manifesto in 1962. Since then, processual, behavioural or systems archaeology, New Archaeology, so-called, has come of age and may justly be held responsible for its aims. Like every teenager, it claimed that its parents' beliefs were nothing but a set of dogmas when seen from the viewpoint of new and unshakeable truths. These 'eternal' truths of New Archaeology emerged thanks to hypostasis and this is a strength, but unfortunately they were also given non-specific interpretations. This was especially the case with the 'hypo-deductive method', the 'covering law', the systems approach, the idea of general measurability and quantification and, lastly, the delusion that social problems could be solved through 'engineering'.

Let us turn to the common denominator underlying all these approaches. They have limitless application, and the optimism about the possibilities of social engineering is boundless, too. Their generality is their limitation while Spinoza's 'omnis negatio est determinatio' makes truisms out of them. Take for example the 'covering law'. Its most serious problem, particularly with its application to the social sciences, is the question of how to determine the concept of law and of scientific language. Hempel reacted to this difficulty by accepting 'law-like statements'. But in this case we find ourselves with a limitless number of statements including Scriven's truisms, and can arrive at almost nothing. Consider, for instance, the value of the information contained in the statement that 'response to environmental challenges may be technological, social or ideational' (see Sanders and Price 1968: 74) – one of the most theoretical statements extant in anthropology and archaeology.

In order to explain the unique event, Hempel had to divide the rest of the world into laws and particular circumstances, a division full of Manichean dangers, just like the division into system and environment. After that, everything was simple: 'When certain cultural elements and conditions are present and in proper conditions, an invention will take place; when they are not, the invention will not occur' (White 1959: 16). If 'the law of minimal risk' (Santley and Turner 1977: 747) affirms that 'In a choice situation, the response selected will be the one which produces the minimal risk', then with the cases of Giordano Bruno and Galileo in mind, we must also ask how people conceive of risk in given situations. In the case of Bruno and Galileo we have their particular history to hand; nothing similar, however, is available for prehistory.

The problem here is that ordinary language is intermingled inconsistently with an unlimited range of 'terms' of all possible levels. Since the difference between description and explanation is minimised, almost everything can be explained, and for this reason both New Archaeology and its opponents accuse one another of proposing an explanation which is in reality only a description.

If everything is part of a system, then we can obtain a host of non-specific truisms and a system of systems – 'the culture of mankind is one single system' (White 1959: 17) – as well as an all-covering law. Let us cite two examples. P. J. Watson, S. A. LeBlanc and C. L. Redman (1971) manage to derive a substantive from the adjective 'nomological', which thus becomes one 'science of general laws'. L. A. White (1959: 29) has even located this paradise of general laws in a so-called 'analytical reality' of anthropology removed from time, space and particularities. Darwin's solution was the opposite: only individuals exist, and create laws through their activity. Clearly, English political life inspired him but, in the present case, of what is the 'analytical reality' accepted by New Archaeology a symptom? The above-mentioned 'law of minimal risk' would seem to mirror basic American belief as formulated by R. S. Lynd (1945: 28): 'people are rational, can and do know what is best for them, are free to choose, and will accordingly choose wisely'. Or, as C. K. M. Kluckhohn noted (1957: 179), 'they like to think of the world as man-constructed'. To postulate a rational agent is, however, nonsense. If all people are rational agents, the assertion is either useless or worthless, the fate of all simplifications. Alternatively, we may suppose that all people are rational, and only society and history irrational.

While 'analytical reality' is very frequent in 'New' Archaeology, reality plain and simple is in fact extremely rare. The concept of adaptation undergoes hypostasis and the problems are solved using 'pre-adaptational stages', as for example in K. V. Flannery (1967).

The cultural concept of the system derives from Malinowski as sociologically interpreted by Parson. Perfect functionalism presupposes perfect systems and must eliminate all disturbing factors as dysfunctional or afunctional. Dogmatic acceptance of the covering law leads to the acceptance of such a perception of systems: it is a case of methods developing a methodology which then confirms them. L. R. Binford had L. A. White's assumptions as this starting point. For White (1959: 27), 'technology is the basis of all other sectors of culture' (compare with Binford and Binford 1968: 22: '. . . data relevant to most if not all, [sic] the components of past sociocultural systems are preserved in the archaeological record'), and from this basis, 'to explain the minutiae of social structure in terms of technological influence, therefore, we would have to know the history of every detail of a cultural system' (*ibid.*: 21) and therefore 'the difficulties that we encounter in its application to minutiae are technical in nature rather than personal. They are the practical difficulties of actual measurement and correlation among numerous and specific variables; they are not due to inadequacies of our premises or to shortcomings of our theory' (*ibid.*: 22). Compare with Binford (Binford and Binford 1968: 23): 'the practical limitations on our knowledge of the past are not inherent in the nature of the archaeological record; the limitations lie in our methodological naiveté, in our lack of development of principles determining the relevance of archaeological remains to propositions regarding processes and events of the past'. So, from the assumption of adaptability and system properties (and of the utilitarian and functional nature of human behaviour, significant in this connection), we can arrive by deduction at the existence of common rules with measurable variability. From measure to laws, the road is clear. Friedrich Nietzsche was right when he predicted that scientific method would be victorious over science itself.

K. V. Flannery summarised this approach when he wrote that we must search for 'that system behind both Indian and artifacts' and not for 'the Indian behind the artifacts' (Flannery 1967: 120).

This kind of archaeological reconstruction of a situation is something different from our original knowledge of the situation. It is a view from a different time perspective, an impersonal view. Flow charts of social, economic, ideological and material-cultural sub-systems replicate far too many schemes from managerial textbooks. These schemes can give us only responses, not challenges, only adaptation, not selection. The method of trial and error is eliminated. All that matters is to limit a prehistoric actor to an element within a system, an element which conforms to the behaviour of a system. This is an act of cultural engineering and this is why someone such as Khomeini can surprise us. But it was E. Sapir who pointed out this danger: 'Cultures, as ordinarily dealt with, are merely abstracted configurations of idea and action patterns, which have endlessly different meanings for the various individuals in the group' (Sapir 1949: 593).

The original actors (like Khomeini) did not divide their behaviour according to a systemic framework and this meant that their responses were likely to be different from the 'rational' behaviour implied by the framework. The structure of myths is different from that of functionalist systems. Artefacts have meaning only inside the structure of a natural world. An artefact can have a role not only in economic, but also in magical, territorial, social, religious, statutory, aesthetic, ethnic and ritual senses, and is, of course, capable of conveying meanings which go far beyond its utilitarian application.

If we reduce culture to the content of a subconscious framework and then use it as a basic point of reference for our manipulations, we end up repeating the errors of 'old archaeology' – and in fact New Archaeology does this.

Another fundamental, but obscure assumption is the link between evolution and progress. The notion of evolution as progress towards improvement and optimalisation not only defines itself: it is also the basis common to all attempts at social engineering. Thus our natural world must be replaced by another world, more effective, fabricated, planned. 'Priority must be given to evolving a general theory of sociocultural change because it is of paramount importance if anthropologists are to assume a fruitful role in planning and carrying out international importance programmes', because otherwise 'we may find that the world can get along quite nicely without us' (Martin 1971: 6).

Deeply hidden in this outlook is perhaps the functional illusion of the world where everything is soluble via a group of technical and organisational strategies. A world where everything is brought down to the problem of its making, a world consequently without qualities, without a history. Seen from this perspective, can we not detect a convergence between the United States and the USSR?

These hypostasised affirmations have one other element in common: what is left over is swept under the carpet. What does not fit is a functional, old-fashioned, merely casual circumstance, only inductive knowledge, no more than tiresome historical baggage.

New Archaeology saw historiography as negatively limited, a branch of knowledge where 'scientific' methods could be applied: what then of history itself, its object? Puritans and revolutionaries distrust life and history and they know well the reason. It is not just fear. Contemporary

American anthropology and sociology, especially when descriptive and empirical, remind one of Greek historiography at its origins: a form to be filled with knowledge arising from contemporary and often commercial perceptions of the world, from 'international development programmes', practical and synchronic. Historical diachrony itself has no importance, non-analysed myths were sufficient.

'An outline of prehistory is barely at hand. And another of the goals of archaeology, the reconstruction of past lifeways, simply cannot be achieved by applying scientific techniques' (Leone 1972b: 21). New Archaeology distrusts prehistoric synthesis too. Yet we may place the same question mark after the 'scientific' used above as after 'exactness' in classification – it is the problem of the observer or the user again. When we describe only just a slightly more extensive section of time or space in the past we surpass the limits of individual observation and create an artificial perspective, the point of view of some super-observer. We create a picture no one has yet seen, yet this does not invalidate it. In the same way analytical-synchronical studies create an artificial perspective and, for New Archaeology, this is the only scientific approach (Binford and Sabloff 1982).

By the same token we get two types of observers. One will regulate his immediate behaviour; for the other dignity lies not only in consumption and manipulation but above all in knowledge, in the searching for our place in nature, and in respect for the world. But M. P. Leone (1972b: 21) today assures us that 'no one in the social sciences has ever convincingly argued that the past is valuable in itself'. Surely not only a historical picture, but also an abstract picture of the world has independent value. But when we only stress the utilitarian, we must necessarily misrepresent the past.

Methods, systems, laws – all these New Archaeology finds in anthropology, and thus it can only illustrate the latter. This 'deus ex machina' is just a huge conglomerate speaking of everything, and in various ways. It fails to investigate its own suppositions, and this is the source of its tasteless ontological assumptions and consequences. This is a disadvantage of the 'pre-paradigmatical' stage – but can we be sure that another stage is possible? Sociology lacks philosophy. The diagnosis is not a recent one – P. A. Sorokin had already written in 1956: 'These defects ... are largely due to their faulty philosophy and theory of cognition' (1958: 279). In the United States in particular, empirical sociology and its methods dominate this conglomerate. In 1931 K. Mannheim wrote in this connection: 'We must admit a very marked and painful disproportion between the vastness of the scientific machinery employed and the value of the ultimate results' (Mannheim 1953: 187) and the recent situation is very similar. We shall try to show that New Archaeology, oriented towards this sociology, shares in its properties. True, this is not the only orientation in sociology: phenomenological, structural and critical sociology also exists, for example.

From these points of view, New Archaeology is the product of a search for a common basis for modern society, especially the North American society, which would connect people to a shared history and tradition, even though it is short in time and limited in scale. This new basis is possible through the postulation of impersonal abstraction, measurement, laws (the analytical reality): what is, in fact, only a culturally determined form of rationality. History can furnish analogous situations, as in the eighteenth century, when the Austrian Emperor Joseph II attempted to unify his multi-national monarchy by artificial enlightenment, rationality and bureaucracy. We may conclude, therefore, that C. K. M. Kluckhohn's diagnosis also includes those of Sorokin mentioned above: 'the diagnostic symptom of the sickness of our society is the lack of a unifying system in canons of choice' (Kluckhohn 1941: 179).

The kind of perspective created by New Archaeology is not in itself inadequate, it is only partial. It is not an integral archaeology, but partial and specialised, its results valid only when seen in a broader context and viewed ideologically. There are no surprising statements, or perhaps it is only New Archaeology itself that is surprised.

Our remarks have been concerned with programmatic pronouncements and with ideological rather than theoretical concepts. But even the theory lacks unity in New Archaeology and the originally monolithic front of Binford's gang is beginning to splinter. Let us mention, for example, the logico-positivistically oriented wing (S. A. LeBlanc, C. L. Reman, P. J. Watson), the systems orientation (K. V. Flannery), the environmental and ecological focus (E. B. W. Zubrow) and the adherents of culture laws.

Whatever the case, New Archaeology made archaeologists conscious of new problems and this was no small achievement. Only the very fact that it turned attention to the internal processes of individual cultures and their relationships with the environment and not solely to the traditionally investigated relationships between cultures was of enormous importance. However, we must point out that while in the past this call went unheeded, the advent of modern techniques of information processing, statistical and simulation techniques, systems theories, etc., opened up possibilities of applying these requirements in practice. Similarly oriented techniques had been in existence earlier but, basically, they could not strive beyond the limits of ethnographic parallels.

No one corrected New Archaeology better and with more insistence that it did itself, and we should never forget this.

Revolution by instalments

Binford's 'fellow travellers' soon formed a whole 'Mafia' whose work we can follow in collections and books such as *New Perspectives in Archaeology* (Binford and Binford 1968), *Anthropological Archaeology in the Americas* (Meggers 1968), *Explanation in Archaeology: An Explicitly Scientific Approach* (Watson, LeBlanc and Redman 1971) and *Research and Theory in Current Archaeology* (Redman 1973).

It was 1972 when New Archaeology and analytical archaeology first met officially. This meeting took place on European soil in *Models in Archaeology* – a volume of essays edited by Clarke (1972).

At the same time, two new anthologies containing, according to the editors, key studies, and representing a powerful new perspective in archaeology, appeared in the United States. Deetz's anthology (1971) contains a fruitful discussion of the problems of classification which has been growing since the second half of the 1950s, and also discusses the application of ethnographic parallels in archaeology. Including, as it does, substantive contributions by the adherents of New Archaeology, it reflects the polemics raging at that time in North America with regard to New Archaeology. A year later, Leone's anthology presented a compendium of Anglo-American material from which New Archaeology was built.

It would at first appear that enthusiasm for New Archaeology and analytical archaeology was expressed only by young archaeologists in the United States and Western Europe. However, this is clearly not the case. For example, external similarities with New Archaeology can be discerned in Turkish archaeology and a number of Turkish scholars declared themselves openly in support of New Archaeology. A year after the publication of Clarke' *Analytical Archaeology*, a volume appeared in Turkey bearing practically the same title – *Analitik Arkeoloji – Denemeler* (Essays in Analytical Archaeology) – edited by A. M. Dinçol and S. Kantman (1969). It provides information about recent developments in archaeology in the light of the approach pioneered by Binford and Clarke, and thoughts on its application to Turkish archaeology. Also in India (Malik 1971, Mohapatra 1974) and South America (Lahitte 1977, Rivera 1979) a number of studies appeared which reflect the influence of New Archaeology and analytical archaeology and whose authors acknowledge this fact openly. Even though this does not mean that everyone accepted all the theories and methodology of New Archaeology and analytical archaeology without reservations, it is clear that the legacy of the new influence in archaeology – whether adopted totally or partially – had a wide impact and still continues to affect world archaeology today.

The first reaction of traditional archaeologists to the rejection of traditional archaeology by their colleagues was to regard New Archaeology as no more than an array of techniques, methods and impossible language, introduced from the natural and technical sciences. If they did deem it necessary to comment on the revolution in archaeology then they did so only in connection with the distinctive and sometimes rather convoluted language of Clarke's *Analytical Archaeology*, which they saw as a revolt against the Queen's English. Such opinions which flatly refuse 'dehumanisation', 'scientification' and any kind of formalisation of archaeology can be found in the works of D. T. Bayard, G. E. Daniel, J. B. Hawkes and A. C. Hogarth. It is notably D. T. Bayard (1969, 1978), J.-C. Gardin (1974, 1979) and I. Rouse (1970) who provide the most comprehensive critical analysis.

It is Daniel himself who, in *Antiquity*, provides a forum for adherents of various concepts (Agrawal 1970, R. A. Watson 1972, Clarke 1973, Isaac 1971, 1981, Neustupný 1971, Trigger 1970, 1978a, and others). Their discussions and polemics define the position of modern and traditional archaeology and contribute to the clarification of standpoints and the polarisation of opinions. Apart from the unqualified supporters and adversaries of Binford and Clarke's approach, we are beginning to witness the birth of yet another group which strives to find a point of contact between the two archaeologies.

Criticism was also aimed at the anthropological (Kushner 1970) and mathematical (Steiger 1971) foundations of New Archaeology ('Old wine and new skins', says W. W. Taylor 1972). H. D. Tuggle, A. H. Townsend, T. J. Riley and C. G. Morgan (1972) also criticised the logical explanatory model of P. J. Watson, S. A. LeBlanc and C. L. Redman (1971). Watson, LeBlanc and Redman answered their critics in 1974. In Germany, New Archaeology was critically evaluated by M. K. H. Eggert (1976, 1978) and U. Fischer (1987); in France by P. Courbin (1982); in Italy by B. E. Barich (1982).

Criticism of Clarke can be found even in his own camp. His critics charge that, despite Clarke's insistence that he presented a central archaeological theory, there is no evidence of any basic theorem which would unite all three of Clarke's models. While his analyses, classifications and integration of artefacts are well developed, the explanatory potential leaves much to be desired. One of the chief shortcomings is the preoccupation with artefacts (Moberg 1970a, b, Renfrew 1969a). Binford claims that Clarke did not, in fact, abandon the traditional, normative and additive concepts of culture (Binford 1972: 230). The latest evaluation of analytical archaeology was carried out by G. L. Isaac (1981) and I. Hodder (1982a).

In Eastern Europe the initial reaction to New Archaeology and analytical archaeology was late in coming and relatively muted. Clarke's book as a whole was described as progressive by G. A. Fedorov-Davydov in 1970. Three years later, a similar opinion was voiced by L. S. Klejn in 'New perspectives in archaeology' (Klejn 1973). In 1974, Polish scholars S. Taba-czyński and E. Pleszczyńska devoted a hundred-page analysis to Clarke's concepts.

However, in the second half of the 1970s far more attention was devoted to the criticism and application of the ideas contained in New Archaeology. This was the case, above all, in Soviet archaeology, while for other East European archaeologists (for example, Czechoslovak, Hungarian and Bulgarian) the problem somehow did not exist.

Many Soviet archaeologists (G. P. Grigorev, L. S. Klejn, B. A. Kolčin, etc.) compare New Archaeology with the Soviet theory of stages and point to a number of parallels:

At the same time the theory of stages had anticipated in many respects the 'new' archaeology – of course, on a less sophisticated and less developed level. There is the same pious approach to theory, the same passion for generalising and abstracting causes in the cultural process to the detriment of an interest in concrete historical events (what we later called 'sociological schematism'), the same disregard for delimited comparative typological studies ('simple or formal artefactology', to use the language of that time), the same striving for functional definition and the interpretation of phenomena as a complicated complex, the same fiery negation of migration and diffusion, the same indifference to ethnic boundaries and the same insistence on contrasting itself with traditional archaeology.

(Klejn, 1977: 13)

V. S. Bočkarev concentrates on an analysis of Clarke's hierarchic model of basic archaeological concepts (empirical and theoretical) which had been arranged by Clarke into one uninterrupted chain in accordance with their ascending level of complexity – from attribute to technocomplex. Accord-ing to Bočkarev, the chief shortcoming rests in Clarke's incorporation of concepts which are essentially on two different levels – that is empirical and theoretical – into a single chain. This is in direct opposition to the demand that procedure must have a rigid structure and must not allow any omission of strata or their mixing. Bočkarev himself assigns these concepts to two parallel spheres – the first consists of empirical concepts (attribute – artefact – complex) while the second derives from the first one, as a result of similarities and dissimilarities amongst characteristics, artefacts and complexes (Bočkarev 1975).

S. A. Semenov praised the positive significance of the systems approach in archaeology which had also been partially applied by Clarke. However, according to Semenov, Clarke did not manage to avoid several faulty moves. Among them is the fact that Clarke drew on neo-positivism. His research was not linked with the problems of social evolution, and artefacts were seen in isolation from their originators – human beings. He conceived of the systemic approach as absolute and in this way he impoverished it, having identified it solely with method and procedure (Semenov 1978). L. S. Klejn considers Clarke's work as monumental, especially as far as Clarke's analysis and classification of artefacts are concerned. The principal fault, according to Klejn, rests

specifically with the idea of an automatic isolation of cultural interrelations from the complexes of elementary physical properties of archaeological material by means of unselective reasoning and by mathematical interpretation lacking in focus. The practice has shown us that the results of such correlations do not have to be of any cultural significance and we cannot consider their role in interpretation. In order to construct a system of some relevance we need a preliminary selection and a hierarchy of characteristics and this is exactly what analytical archaeology rejected from the very beginning.

(Klejn, 1977: 12)

Space, behaviour, economic and social relationships

When the insurgents stormed the Bastille they found out that it was defended only by a handful of old invalids. The victory over the veterans who laid down their limbs for their country has since been celebrated as a National Day – with some justification if it is interpreted as a celebration of the courage to start anew. The battle for the Bastille united the insurgents but then they set out to look for new allies and new enemies. Up to the present, the analogy of the French Revolution with the archaeological revolution of the 1960s applies – apart from the fact that archaeologists are not so bloodthirsty.

After Clarke and Binford had their say, we can observe a slow emergence of new currents which have not allied themselves with either 'old' or 'new' archaeology. Binford and Clarke were the first as well as the last to unfold the flags of general theories. The rest make their appearance in the archaeological parliament merely in the role of representatives of various interest groups, or sometimes as their bosses. It is obvious that social, economic or symbolic archaeology always covers only a part of prehistoric reality and never the whole of archaeology and prehistory. Consequently, there is substantially less space for all-embracing theories, and for this reason, when they do occur, they often find themselves in close proximity to such specialised disciplines as, for example, urban archaeology.

As an example, let us consider spatial archaeology. New geography and plant ecology were among the chief sources of inspiration for D. L. Clarke, and it is therefore not surprising that the problem of space attracted an especially large group of archaeologists, centred at Cambridge University (for further details, see below, p. 187).

Spatial archaeology is closely connected with social archaeology; this is reflected, for instance, in the collections of studies entitled *Problems in Economics and Social Archaeology* (de Sieveking, Longworth and Wilson 1976) and *Social Organisation and Settlement* (Green, Haselgrove and Spriggs 1978). Social archaeology (Gjessing 1975, Redman *et al.* 1978, Renfrew 1973a, 1984) mainly follows the early lead of G. Childe (McNairn 1980, Trigger 1980) while the extensive progress made by Soviet archaeology in this field has been more or less ignored in the West (see below, pp. 138–46). Usage of terms such as 'centre', 'interaction' 'boundary' in social archaeology points to the influence of spatial archaeology, whilst the term 'environment' points to ecology, and terms like 'exchange' and 'transport' point to economy. Although social archaeology appears to make use of its own terminology – 'social interactions', 'community change', etc. – these terms are in fact borrowed from anthropology, as is its theory (Flannery 1976, Hill 1977, Plog 1974, 1978, Green, Haselgrove and Spriggs 1978, Redman *et al.* 1978).

The structure of behavioural archaeology was outlined by M. Schiffer in 1976 in his book bearing the same title. Schiffer investigates the variability of past human behaviour and the relationship between behaviour and the environmental context. He places a special emphasis on the investigation of all distortion which affects interpretation (Schiffer 1976).

Research into economic aspects of past societies has had a long tradition in archaeology thanks, above all, to J. G. D. Clark. The quite remarkable achievements of economic archaeology, notably in the 1970s (Earle and Ericson 1977, Earle and Christenson 1980, Higgs 1972, Higgs and Jarman 1975, Dennell 1983, Sheridan and Bailey 1981) may be ascribed to the fact that it could draw sustenance from new methods – especially modelling, simulation and experiment – and make use of the newly acquired knowledge in ecology (Butzer 1982, Jochim 1976, 1979).

Structural and semiological inspirations

Every artefact represents, constitutes and means something. Apart from its function, an artefact also has a meaning and this meaning can be realised only within the framework of a specific symbolic system. Take, for example, the symbolism embedded in the shape and design of hats or ties. The college tie alone could be the subject of a fascinating semiological study. The meaning of an artefact has a communication value and communication forms the very basis of human society and culture. Semiology, as a science engaged in the study of sign systems, represents, therefore, an ancillary but, at the same time, also an integral aspect of archaeology.

Already in 1956 the cultural anthropologist C. K. M. Kluckhohn had expressed his regret that the conceptual apparatus of cultural anthropology could not supply archaeology with such basic units as phonemes and morphemes in linguistics. He prophesied that it would be possible to obtain suitable comparative units by methods similar to those in linguistics using the concept of opposite categories. The ideas of Kluckhohn and of Chomsky and Jakobson, the linguists, inspired J. F. Deetz (1967, 1977), H. Glassie (1975), F. A. Hassan (1988), I. Hodder (1982a, b), D. Hymes (1970) and J. Muller (1968). They attempted to construct a form of grammar for artefacts and their possible transformations.

Apart from the scholars mentioned above, adherents of other theoretical concepts dealt with similar problems, for example, L. S. Klejn (1972a), V. B. Kovalevskaja (1970a, b), C.-A. Moberg (1969) and S. Tabaczyński (1971). They attempted structural analysis either of artefacts themselves or of the spatial patterns they created within the context of a site. V. B. Kovalevskaja made use of information theory methods and structural linguistics to study the ornamentation of belt buckles, perceived as a symbolic system.

J. F. Deetz built above all on the analogy with structural units in language, such as phonemes and morphemes. Deetz introduced formemes as archaeological analogues of morphemes, which he defined as the smallest part of artefacts having an independent meaning, and factemes, which are the smallest class of attributes expressing a functional value of artefacts. He wrote:

Artefacts, just like words, are the result of human motor activity produced by muscular movement, directed by intellect and carried out on a raw material. The final form of every artefact is the result of combinations of structural units – attributes. Combinations of attributes create objects with specific function in the culture which produced them. Change of any one of the attributes causes a change in functional meaning if this change is sufficiently substantial to cause a change in meaning. In other words, artefacts would be structural units corresponding to morphemes and phonemes in language. This correspondence should go beyond the framework of simple analogy and should also reflect the essential identity of language and objects in a structural sense. If this statement is correct, could it then follow that on the basis of this close similarity between the method of word formation and the method of artefact formation, words are only one of the aspects of a broad class of cultural products which would, at the same time, include all the artefacts?

(Deetz, 1967: 87)

Much time has elapsed since van Gennep and Durkheim first described primitive behaviour and thought processes with the help of binary opposites. Today, thanks to C. Lévi-Strauss, binary oppositions form the foundation of all communication codes, hidden, of course, in deep structures. A whole number of applications in archaeology derived from this interpretation. It was in the field of the analyses of prehistoric art (Conkey 1978, Leroi-Gourhan 1965, Marshack 1977), psychology (Fritz 1978) and architecture (Hillier *et al.* 1978) that this approach was first adopted, aided probably by the fact that here the scholars could find support in other structuralist studies in the history of art (Washburn 1977, 1983). It is above all structural or symbolic archaeology (Hodder 1982a, b) which is linked with structural anthropology (notably E. R. Leach). In the mother country of structuralism, France, this approach did not gain much acceptance. On the contrary, French authors display almost an Anglo-Saxon dislike for grand schemes (Gardin 1979, Courbin 1982). In contrast, structuralism is popular in British archaeology.

The greatest enemy of structuralism is probably structuralism itself – that is its infinite demands and its hypostasis of structures. The consequence of shifting the structures into the unconscious is an underestimation of conscious and individual behaviour. This explains the basis for the ahistoricism of structuralism. In one of the first structuralist manifestos in the 1920s this problem was dealt with summarily – that is by proclaiming that change and evolution are also subject to some kind of structure of evolution. This structure has never been found and one has to say that nobody has ever looked for it either. That was probably the best course of action to take.

The attempts at structural analysis in archaeology rely, on the one hand, on structural anthropology, ethnolinguistics, ethnoscience, ethnosemantics and new ethnography, where the structural methods are widely applied, and, on the other hand, on structural Marxism and neo-Marxism (Kohl 1981, Miller and Tilley 1984, Price 1982, Rowlands 1982, Shanks and

Tilley 1987a, b, Spriggs 1984), which supplemented structuralism with base, superstructure and ideology. Furthermore, these Marxists have carried the class struggle over to archaeologists. According to Western Marxist scholars, Donald Duck is racist, sexist and capitalist and 'bourgeois' archaeology is no better. Since the study of communication focuses above all on symbols, art, ritual and myth, it follows that symbolic archaeology borders on palaeopsychology (Fritz 1978, Poršnev 1974) and cognitive archaeology (Kehoe and Kehoe 1973, Leeuw 1981, Leone 1982, Renfrew 1982, Tyler 1969). Cognitive archaeology – the archaeology of mind considered by Renfrew as an independent discipline – sees as its aim the study of archaeological materials and, on this basis, the study of intelligent behaviour of their makers, the development and functioning of human conceptual abilities and practices (Renfrew 1982).

Contextual archaeology is convinced that it must study the environmental and behavioural contexts of human actions and the archaeological objects in their interrelations (Hodder 1987a). Post-processual archaeology is a summary term invented by I. Hodder (1985, 1986) for cognitive, contextual, critical, Marxist, structural and symbolic archaeology (see also Leone 1986). Besides the relationship between the individual and the social norm, post-processual archaeology is concerned with structure, mind and meaning, and the historical approach. The best critiques of the post-processual orientation have been given by A. Gallay (1986) and S. Wolfram (1986).

Marxism, like all empty formulisms, incites many diverse interpretations. While in the Eastern Block, official Marxism prefers 'iron-law history', neo-Marxists emphasise the approach of the individual to history. Such an approach is compatible with post-processualism and a revival of Collingwood, the *bête noire* of traditional Marxists (Hodder 1986, 1987a).

The return back home to settlement archaeology

K. C. Chang stated that archaeology, as a whole, is an analogy (Chang 1967: 109). According to Chang, archaeology itself has only serial and classificatory functions while interpretation is the concern of analogies. He borrows his analogies from ethnography. In keeping with the spirit of contextualism, the point of departure in his view is a small settlement. In order to study it, he applies methods of structural linguistics. He argues that the interpretation of the role of an artefact depends on its place in the structure of the site. Then, bearing in mind Gardin's and Conklin's hypotheses, he considers the possibility of competent analysis of systems of types from the perspective of the comparability of semantic and morphological structures. In this way Chang gives a concrete content to ideas expounded earlier by

Taylor. Both Willey (Prehistoric settlement patterns in Virú Valley, Peru. *Bureau of American Ethnology Bulletin* No. 155, 1953) and later Chang (1967) analysed artefacts and their configurations within the framework of defined settlement units (site, locality, settlement, etc.), their distribution, and finally the links between different types of sites.

B. G. Trigger demands the study of social relationships within the framework of settlement archaeology (this perspective is called by some archaeologists – V. M. Masson, C. A. Moberg, A. C. Renfrew – social archaeology or sociological archaeology). Trigger rejects the possibility of using archaeological sources for the formulation of laws and he equally rejects every form of determinism, especially technological and economic. On the contrary, he insists on the historical aims of archaeology. He maintains that in order to reconstruct the prehistoric past a synthesis of data from various disciplines is needed, but only after this has been independently examined by experts specialising in cultural anthropology, ethnography, linguistics, etc.

The edifice of settlement archaeology is so vast that it can accommodate quite comfortably not only contextualists and structuralists but also taxonomists, processualists, neo-evolutionists and even Marxists. This is evidenced in Chang's collection of articles *Settlement Archaeology* (1968) and in the volume *Man, Settlement and Urbanism* (Ucko, Tringham and Dimbleby 1972). In 1973 the builders of settlement archaeology were subject to appraisal by the founder and chief architect of settlement archaeology himself, G. R. Willey. Within a range of views under the banner of settlement archaeology, the adherents of optimism (for example V. M. Masson, B. Soudský) and pessimism (for example, S. Piggott, J. Mellaart) are both in the minority. The majority of scholars fall somewhere between these two extremes. The optimists continue in the footsteps of Childe's neo-evolutionism, with its concepts of Neolithic and urban revolution, and they construct a general scheme of historico-cultural evolution influenced, above all, by socio-economic factors. (We have to note, however, that although these authors consider the above-mentioned factors to be determinist, they do concede the influence of the natural environment and cultural traditions.) Pessimists, on the other hand, reject any notion of conceptual objectivity together with the search for evolutionary causes and general schemes. Most of them strive to examine evolutionary tendencies and specific rules, but they dismiss the notion that a single or several factors (economic, social, technological, ecological, psychological, etc.) could play a deterministic role. They insist that all these factors are in interaction or, at best, they may acknowledge the prevalence of one factor over others – of course, not in general but only with regard to the results of the concrete investigation of a specific locality (Willey 1973).

French connection

If we wanted to be malicious we could say that the approaches promoted by New Archaeology were novel only for New Archaeology itself, and in no way could they be considered original. Gardin's book *Une archéologie théorique*, however, represents an original approach which, all the same, leads to remarkably few innovations. Nevertheless, let us admit without further ado that in this also lies the virtue of both approaches and the source of their mutual critical comparison. It seems that Anglo-Saxon 'common sense' appears ridiculous only when it extols its own virtues; that is, at the moment when it oversteps its own self-imposed limits. Similarly, Gardin's criticisms of New Archaeology on the grounds of common sense do not extend to his own work.

Let us afford ourself the luxury of comparing both sides. New Archae-ology is strongly reminiscent of Adam Smith with his castaway tales – that is to say, it considers prehistoric reality (which will always remain a hypothetical construct) as the point of departure, and from this it tries to conclude what a science of this subject should look like. Gardin tends to move towards the opposite extreme. He takes archaeological literature as a given fact and then investigates what can be expressed through its use – in this approach he resembles his fellow countryman M. Foucault.

Within the framework of his approach Gardin defines archaeology as 'the sum of studies bearing on material objects which may help to reconstitute, in conjunction with other data, the history and ways of life of ancient peoples (specific events, daily activities, institutions, beliefs...)' (Gardin 1980: 182). The compilation of materials (artefacts and ecofacts) is primary and the commentary which represents statements on the collection of materials is secondary (for more details see figure 1).

The subject of Gardin's analysis is mainly the mental sequences which enable the transition from the material to the commentary. Since archaeo-logical literature (and not only archaeological!) basically consists of both the description of material and the commentary on the described material, together with the justification of these statements (the method of transition from the material to the commentary), it is possible to make the study of the archaeological interpretation itself the starting point:

any written text presented as a distinct unit in the archaeological literature – article, book, printed lecture, with the appended illustrations – for the purpose of exposing the results of a survey or excavation, the content of a collection, the

interpretation of an object or group of objects, or the lessons that may be drawn from any such data with respect to the history and ways of life of ancient peoples.
(Gardin 1980: 182)

The aim of theoretical archaeology is, according to Gardin, to define the formal and logical structure of constructs and their development.

Gardin discerns two extremities in constructs – that is compilation (material study) and explanation (problem study) – and he categorises his analysis accordingly. In the logistic analysis of compilations we can clearly see the many years of experience in the study of new methods of archaeographical description carried out not only by the author himself but by the whole research team of the CNRS as well, including the latest experiences in creating the artificial language SYNTOL. In his outline of explications Gardin follows mainly the logical and semantic analysis of the possibilities of typology and historico-cultural interpretation. In interpretative constructions he distinguishes initial (influences, etc.), normative (values, etc.) and dynamic interpretations (systems of behaviour). The synthesis of these results represents a universal schematisation of archaeo-

Figure 1. The processing of archaeological information; from the retrieval of finds (artefacts, monuments, organic remains, etc.) to the inferences about their meaning and function (description, identification, explanation, etc.). Source: Gardin 1980:9.

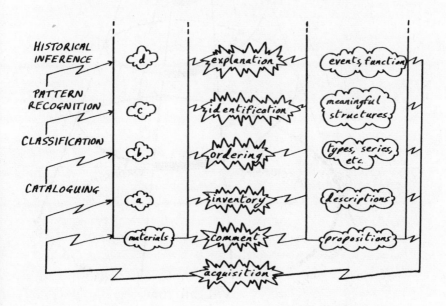

Figure 2. The succession of constructions 1, 2, 3 … (or stages 1, 2, 3 … of a given construction in the course of its composition), each characterised by positions adopted with respect to Objectives, Selection, Description, etc. The transition from state n + 1 is determined by more or less systematic validation tests. The process stops when the author decides that the gap between 'facts' and 'theories' – graphically represented by segments V_1, V_2 … – can no longer be reduced on the basis of what he already knows about either. Its metaphysical limit is the imaginary point w. Source: Gardin 1980:144, figure. 26

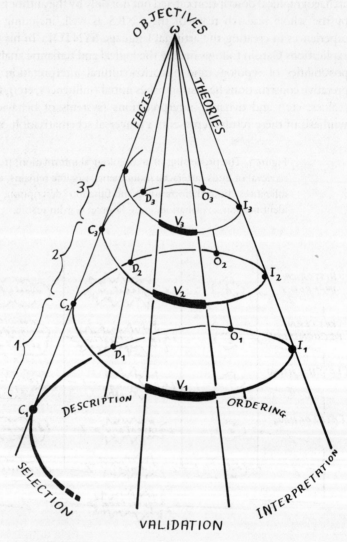

logical activity which has a cyclical character, as can be seen synoptically in figure 2.

Molière's Monsieur Jourdain improved his opinion of himself as soon as he found out that all his life he had been speaking in prose. Many an archaeologist gains self-confidence having read Gardin's book. Let us be grateful for this and also for the fact that Gardin has shown us in a non-prescriptive way what a good archaeological publication should look like.

Since the 1950s, the school of Gardin has been oriented towards documentation, codes of description of artefacts and the norms for publication (Borillo 1972, Borillo et al. 1976, 1977). Since the 1970s, the orientation has turned to problems of semiology of description and the treatment of these results with the aid of artificial intelligence, particularly that of expert systems (Gardin 1987, Gardin *et al.* 1987, Lagrange and Renaud 1984; for comparison, see Huggett and Baker 1985). If we wished to extend the comparison, we could compare this orientation with a desire to establish an archaeological 'Code Napoléon'.

A different orientation is presented by A. Gallay, but let us not forget that the extremes often meet, namely in France. It is no accident that Gallay is a professor in Geneva, a place where craftsmen make the world's best watches without having any theoretical knowledge of watches. His book (1986) is at once brilliant, serious and readable: a rare combination. He shows that a historical development and a theoretical explanation do not mutually exclude each other in archaeology (as also in biology). Gallay has attempted to practise the conception of an integral archaeology without falling prey to eclecticism. The base of the new coherence is to be found, he says, in a 'craftsmanlike thinking' (*pensée artisanale*) and not in a philosophical one: 'Craftsmanship is indeed certainly closer to science than is philosophy. The knowledge and handiwork of the artisans are veritable skills to the extent that their confrontation with the real world is daily and implacable' (*ibid*. 287). But let us not forget that Lévi-Strauss (who was no friend of philosophy) had constructed a theory of 'bricolage' (do-it-yourself construction).

P. Courbin's hypercritique (1982) of the new orientations of Anglo-Saxon archaeologists is in certain ways typical of the Continental European. The convictions of Courbin and others can be characterised, according to Gallay (1986: 57), by the following four points. (1) It is useful to admit that there are facts independent of all precise problems. The discoveries in archaeology speak for themselves. (2) The specific role of archaeology is to establish the facts, whether or not they are pertinent.

(3) Archaeology does not need to explain its demonstrations. (4) The archaeologist must, specifically, establish the facts, but he does not need to interpret them.

New trends in the East

The edited volume *Tipy v Kulture* (Klejn 1979), which includes contributions from the conference on Methodological Problems of Classification and Typification in Social and Historical Sciences, represents new currents in Soviet archaeology. The conference took place in 1974 and again in 1978 in Leningrad and it testified to the extent to which the tide of opinion has been turning in the last twenty years against views which simplified the task of archaeological theory (i.e. the identification of dialectical and historical materialism with archaeological theory). Previously, if any significance at all was attached to theory, then it was claimed that theory was the end product of many years of experience and an aggregate of a number of empirical and field studies. The theoretical work of the younger generation of scholars was considered to be an escape from the difficult and honest craft of fieldwork, viewed as a useless activity divorced from practice or at best as a kind of premature ejaculation. Consequently, archaeological theory languished in obscurity and on the periphery of individual skills.

During the 1970s it was beginning to emerge from obscurity and was becoming the centre of interest as a defining element for the further development of archaeology. The opinion that theoretical work must be co-ordinated and organised began gaining ground. The Problems Seminar of the Department of Archaeology at Leningrad University has been active since 1964 under the guidance of L. S. Klejn. Since the mid-1970s, thanks to the initiative of J. N. Zaharuk, discussions on methods of research and theory have been included in the annual spring conference organised by the Institute of Archaeology of the USSR Academy of Sciences. The Methodological Seminar of the Institute of Archaeology in Moscow and the Theoretical Seminar at the Leningrad branch of the Institute of Archaeology have been established (Bašilov 1978, Doluhanov 1978b, Grišin and Maslennikov 1978, Masson and Borjaz 1975).

In 1970 and 1972 discussions were held in Leningrad on the role of forces of production, exchange and trade in the history of society. The Leningrad symposium 'The Objects and Objectives of Archaeology' (1975) and the Moscow conference 'The Historicism of Archaeology: Problems of Methodology' (1976) were of key significance in the development of soviet archaeology.

The volume 'Voprosy teorii i metodologii arheologičeskoj nauki' (1978) was devoted to the problems of historicism in archaeology, objectives, sources and methods of archaeology, criticism of some foreign theoretical concepts and the theory and results of experimental archaeology. A survey of problems in Soviet archaeology has been provided by Bulkin, Klejn and Lebedev (1982).

In East Germany, the discussion concentrated mainly on the problems of the periodisation of prehistory, the relationship between evolution and revolution, and the possibility of extrapolating socio-economic evolution from the archaeological material (for example, Horst 1975). Since 1968 they have acquired a special place in the review *Ethnographisch-archäologische Zeitschrift* and were also represented at the international conference in Dresden (1973). In 1975 a collection of contributions to the Dresden Conference was published (Otto and Brachmann 1975) and this was followed two years later by the collection *Archäologie als Geschichtswissenschaft*, edited by J. Herrmann. A number of studies by East European archaeologists is devoted to the theoretical and methodological problems in archaeology, utilisation of written and ethnographic sources (Herrmann 1986), the problems of migration and its archaeological identification. The other view of the internal problems of archaeology in East Germany has been expounded by H. Behrens (1984).

At the same time, Polish archaeologists re-examined objectives of archaeology and the meaning of culture and type (for example, Balcer 1970, Urbańezyk 1983, Hensel 1971, 1977, Jażdżewski 1969, 1979, Kozłowski 1975, Tabaczyński 1971, Trudzik 1971 and Żak 1975). Tabaczyński, in accordance with the view of Polish culturologists, reduced culture to a semiotic system (the basis of knowledge, circulation of information, norms of behaviour in communication) which excludes anything connected with satisfying everyday needs (that is, most of human activity). According to him, in order to secure everyday needs, people do not follow models established and accepted within the framework of a given culture (Tabaczyński 1971). However, other Marxist students of culture continued to view culture as a multiform and polyaspective system (for example, Artanovskij 1973, Markarjan 1969). These strivings find expression in a volume entitled somewhat optimistically *Unconventional Archaeology* (Schild 1980): although it does introduce new perspectives into Polish archaeology, it also illustrates the relativity of the term 'unconventional'.

The pre-war school of logic in Poland gave us thinkers of the first order (Tarski, Chwistek). The great methodological conceptions arose from this group (Ajdukiewicz, Kotarbiński) which also provided the social sciences with its applications (Giedymin, Kmita). A comprehensive monograph by

J. Topolski uses these applications for history and, in turn, the monograph of Donato, Hensel and Tabaczyński (1986) uses Topolski's approach for archaeology. The result is a serious and sombre work, a case typical of the multiple applications. Nevertheless, one can find here some interesting observations. In 1969, G. Klaus, a logician from East Germany, proposed the creation of an ideal language which would bind Marxist–Leninist philosophy to mathematics, logic, cybernetics, and the theory of systems. The Polish–Italian (mainly Polish) monograph has almost succeeded in this respect. However, I suspect that this work will not satisfy the neo-Marxist archaeologist of the West. In the Eastern Block, there is one Marxism but there are no Marxists, whereas in the West, the situation is the reverse.

In Czechoslovakia, there have been a number of recent publications (Bouzek and Buchvaldek 1971, Neustupný 1971, 1973a, 1983, 1986, Pleiner and Rybová 1978, Podborský *et al.* 1977, Soudský 1967) concerned with methodology and theory (systems procedures of archaeological research, definition of theoretical and archaeological terms). The Archaeological Institute of the Slovak Academy of Sciences in Nitra even organised a symposium in 1974 on methodological problems and basic Marxist concepts in archaeology, the results of which were published four years later (Ambros 1978).

The basic problems discussed by archaeologists in the socialist countries concern the subject and the objectives of archaeology, and the way in which these problems define the place and the goals of archaeology within the sciences dealing with the past, as well as their relationship with other sciences. Two distinct lines crystallised from this discussion. The first view is held by those scholars who believe that archaeology carries out an in-depth investigation of its material in parallel with history and especially sociology (V. M. Masson, Z. Trudzik, J. N. Zaharuk). For Zaharuk, 'Archaeological procedure ... cannot be confined to specific tasks of researching solely archaeological artefacts just as it cannot be circumscribed by delimitation of contents and the sequence of stages of archaeological material.' On the basis of systems analysis, Masson concludes that 'the object of archaeology is the investigation of the laws of evolution of objects of material culture and of the diverse structures of human society which are reflected in these objects'. Trudzik believes that archaeology has an autonomous position as far as the pre-literate era is concerned and that it exercises the function of history. According to him, the cognitive process in archaeology takes place in three stages – heuristic, critical and synthetic. However, he does not mention what methods archaeology could avail itself of in order to arrive at the synthesis of non-archaeological data on prehistory. This concept is nearest to New Archaeology.

The second view taken, for example, by V. S. Bočkarev, G. P. Grigorev, V. F. Gening, I. S. Kameneckij, L. S. Klejn, G. S. Lebedev, W. Hensel, K. Moszyński and J. Żak, limits archaeology to investigations of archaeological sources, including their immediate interpretation. Archaeology is not seen as a discipline in a wider historical perspective; on the contrary, as soon as archaeology fulfils the tasks mentioned above it is supposed to hand over the results for further processing to history, sociology, psychology, culturology and other sciences. This approach corresponds, at least partially, to the concepts of Hachmann and Rouse. G. P. Grigorev maintains that the aim of archaeology is to define the laws of the evolution of archaeological objects and of relationships amongst them. Further, he thinks that there is an essential difference between the evolution of material culture, which can be investigated with the aid of archaeological typological methods, and the evolution of social forms, described by social terminology. V. S. Bočkarev constructed a hierarchical system of archaeological concepts. At the base of this system is an artefact, defined as a configuration of characteristics, and an archaeological complex, defined as a configuration of artefacts. These are combined in a hierarchical sequence of categories.

The justification of archaeological periodisation, whether based on three or more periods, and its relationship to the principle of the chronological stratification of artefacts and their complexes according to prevalent raw material or production technology (for example, Sellnow 1961, Semenov 1967, Guhr 1969a) are perceived as another important problem in archaeology. This problem is analysed in detail by L. S. Klejn (1972b), who acknowledges the limiting and schematic character of the current frameworks, but who does not agree with the attempts at their abolition or with their adaptation so as to include social and cultural phenomena – that is, combining archaeological periodisation with ethnographic and sociological schemes advanced by some workers. In his view, different frameworks are needed and each of them should be applied to a specific sphere of the historico-cultural process, and to different purposes. Klejn's approach is based on the conviction that different spheres of social life and culture enjoy a relative autonomy.

Klejn's standpoint, favouring a degree of autonomy, is contradicted by chronological frameworks which are based on the investigation of relations between evolution and revolution. These questions became a battlefield for scholars, especially in East Germany (Feustel 1973a, Günther 1965,

Herrmann 1974, 1975). Feustel's concepts are based on Childe's models of Neolithic and urban revolution. He uses the term 'revolution' also for other evolutionary leaps in human and cultural development during the Palaeolithic, in which he specialises. This is, above all, a revolution in the technology of the lithic industry. The descent of man is also seen by him as a revolution. His German colleagues object that he leaves aside biological and social factors which, in their view, should be emphasised.

'It seems to me', Klejn writes:

that both Feustel and his critics were led astray by the fact that they wanted to reduce all evolution to a simple scheme of periodisation – whether mixed as Feustel would have it, or purely social, as his adversaries preferred. Various frameworks can be worked out for various aspects of evolution, each of them with its own points of revolutionary change. In such a case, to avoid misunderstanding, it will simply be sufficient to distinguish between the terms 'revolution', 'social revolution', 'political revolution', 'cultural revolution', 'technological revolution', etc. Feustel would surely be of the opinion that we should be talking of 'technological revolutions'. If social revolutions were connected with them – and if this is so – then the extent of their involvement is another proposition.

(Klejn, 1977: 27)

In addition, the problems associated with the definition of archaeological culture, its isolation and its explanation in ethnic terms, also became a focus of interest. The debate about the nature of the archaeological culture, interrupted when considered superfluous during the reign of the theory of stages, was resumed by most scholars in the 1950s and became especially fierce in the 1960s (Artamonov 1971, Gening *et al.* 1973, Grigorev 1969, Grjaznov 1969, Hensel 1964a, b, Herrmann 1965, 1975, Kameneckij 1970, Klejn 1962, 1969, 1971, 1974, Klejn *et al.* 1970, Knabe 1959, Mongajt 1967, Otto 1953, Tabaczyński 1971, Tretjakov 1969, Zaharuk 1976).

This fertile discussion declined at the beginning of the 1970s without resolution. However, one conclusion stands clear – diametrically different opinions (for example, strict rejection of any connections between archaeological culture and ethnic groups on one hand, and the search for identifiable relationships on the other) demonstrated that the concept of culture needed to be redefined against the background of wider theoretical problems in connection with the construction of a new, central archaeological theory.

Thus, the problem of 'ethnicity and ethnogenesis' in prehistoric contexts was no closer to solution by the end of the 1960s. However, new concepts were introduced in the following decades by V. F. Gening (1976, 1983), L. S. Klejn (1981), the ethnographer Ju. V. Bromlej (1973), and the historian and geographer L. N. Gumilev (1975).

Gening began with the supposition that ethnographic sources – in contrast to the one-sided and incomplete archaeological sources – were capable of a wider characterisation of the ethnic unit. He therefore intended to interpret archaeological material, not by introducing isolated ethnographic analogies, but by means of a comprehensive, generalised ethnographic model which he attempted to construct. Gening considered the unity of culture as absolutely binding for an ethnic group and, consequently, he closely identified archaeological units with ethnic units. He did not concede the possibility of the polymorphous definition of an ethnic group and rejected the religious identity or identity arising from a common origin as possible characteristics of the ethnic group.

In contrast to the somewhat linear and schematic approach of Gening, Bromlej interpreted the ethnic group as a multi-level dynamic system. He, therefore, analysed some aspects which had not been sufficiently studied up till then, such as the relations between the ethnic group and other units, the typology of ethnic formations, the ethnic functions of culture and mental activity, the role of endogamy in the evolution of ethnic units, migration and the most specific signs of ethnic identity, etc. This polymorphous understanding of ethnos and ethnogenesis inevitably led to Bromley's demand for the synthesis of various sources, which, in practice, meant the co-investigation of ethnography with other sciences as well as with archaeology.

Original theories about ethnicity and ethnogenesis were formulated by Gumilev, who saw ethnic group and ethnogenetic evolution as an autonomous phenomenon with its own laws, relatively independent of socio-economic evolution. Its main propelling force was geobiochemical energy.

Soviet archaeologists study mainly those ethnic and ethnogenetic problems which are closely related to economics and are, therefore, tangible via archaeological sources; that is, the origin, the nature and the social structure of kinship, tribe and tribal alliance (E. K. Černyh, J. A. Krasnov, N. J. Merpert, B. A. Rybakov, A. P. Smirnov) and the problems of ethnic migrations (E. N. Černyh, P. M. Doluhanov, L. S. Klejn, N. J. Merpert, V. S. Titov). Doluhanov considers the models of population genetics as suitable for explaining the differences between the original and the immigrant culture (Doluhanov 1978a).

At the inter-disciplinary seminars held in Leningrad in 1974 and 1978, archaeologists, linguists, sociologists and representatives of other disciplines investigated the problems of culture and cultural types from the point of view of methodology – that is, in so far as it was possible to utilise the methods which had been used in biology for so long for the purpose of formalisation, classification and typification of cultural phenomena, and

also the methods contributed by semiotics and the systemic approach
(Klejn 1979). The main problem of their collective work turned out to be
the discrepancy between the emic – the external, empirically observable
distribution of characteristics in the cultural material – and the etic – the
cultural and ideational systemic distribution. The discussion concluding
the seminars indicated that the archaeologists were divided into two groups
– numerists (for example, J. A. Šer) and non-numerists (for example, L. S.
Klejn).

However, the older approach still keeps clamouring for attention.

*In order to interpret archaeological sources, a correct philosophical approach must
be adopted. Historical materialism, as the science providing the most universal
laws of social evolution, constitutes the correct point of departure. It enables us to
observe social phenomena in their context and can provide us with a solution
where other approaches fail'.*

(Pleiner and Rybová 1978: 19)

And what is the aim of Marxist archaeology?

*The goal of Soviet archaeology is the study and determination of socio-economic
laws and of structures of pre-capitalist formations. It is for this reason that
historicism forms one of the fundamental problems of methodology of the science of
archaeology. Historicism is noted not only for its pragmatic investigation of
historical material from different epochs but also for its ability to solve the most
fundamental historical problems.*

(Rybakov 1978: 5)

These are the reasons why archaeologists continued their study of the
fundamental works of dialectical and historical materialism. During the
1960s archaeologists concentrated on the investigation of those maxims and
statements of the classics of Marxist philosophy connected with archaeological problems or, conversely, Marxist concepts were illustrated by the
material from new archaeological research (for example, Crüger 1967;
Masson 1969, 1970, Wartołowska 1964). However, these approaches were
gradually rejected as schematic and scholastic. Critics also pointed out that
the classics of Marxism-Leninism concerned themselves with archaeology
only on the periphery of their interests and, as a rule, they were obliged to
draw on the then contemporary sources and ideas of specialists, both of
which have undergone a number of changes. Their statements cannot be
taken out of context and applied to any situation indiscriminately. It is
necessary to employ Marxist philosophy as an integral system in its
development (Brentjes 1971, 1972, Danilova 1968, Guhr 1969a, b, 1979a, b,
Nikoforov 1971). Constant attention is devoted to these problems in the
pages of the *Ethnographisch-archäologische Zeitschrift* edited by H. Grünert.

Grünert himself is concerned with the problems of the theory and methodology of prehistory and the economy of prehistoric societies (Grünert 1977, Grünert and Guhr 1969).

At the same time a need was felt to apply classical methods of Marxist classics to archaeological problems. This need has been fulfilled, for example, in the monographs of R. Feustel (1975, 1979) and S. A. Semenov (1964, 1968, 1974) and in the volume on Czech prehistory edited by Pleiner and Rybová, *Pravěké Dějiny Čech* (1978). These works are based on the fundamental categories of historical materialism – base and superstructure, the forces of production and relations of production, the mechanism of dialectical leap as a result of inner contradictions and as the main causative agent of evolutionary changes.

The most original concept was formulated by Semenov. Historical materialism is used by him to justify the proposition that tools are the most variable and at the same time the most determining element in the evolution of the forces of production and relations of production. When evaluating the evolution of tools, Semenov was not satisfied with a simple, formal typology but elaborated an investigative mechanism which can determine productive and functional technology relatively reliably and, by means of controlled experiments, assess productivity. A substantial part of his research procedure consists of the macroscopic and microscopic investigation of traces of manufacture and use of tools. He had been developing this methodology since the second half of the 1930s and the compilation of his results appeared towards the end of the 1950s. Semenov thus succeeded in fashioning a methodology which fitted perfectly those archaeological sources of which tools usually form a significant component. He then linked the patterns detectable in the evolution of tools with the laws controlling the forces of production and relations of production.

A striking hypothesis on the origin of Palaeolithic art based on the fundamental axiom of Marxism – the dialectical leap – was put forward in the 1960s by a Leningrad archaeologist, A. D. Stoljar (Stoljar 1978a, b). He sees the impetus in the contradiction between the biological incapability of Palaeolithic men to cope quickly with their excitement and the stored-up energy which, thanks to improved hunting tools and techniques, had not been entirely used up in hunting. The Neanderthal men solved this contradiction by imitating hunting activity in the presence of a dead animal or its parts. Stojar sees proof of this in the Middle Palaeolithic cult of the bear. In the Upper Palaeolithic, with the gradual growth of symbolic perception and self-control, people managed to curb their passions better and satisfied themselves at first with sculptures, later with bas-reliefs, and in the end with drawing or painting. At the same time these representations fulfilled more and more complex functions.

In this and similar works we no longer meet the usual approach where all changes and cracks in the archaeological material (and consequently in historico-cultural process) are explained on the basis of inner contradictions and identified with the inauguration of new socio-economic formations or with revolutions. Other explanatory means, such as the theory of migration and diffusion, external influences on Slavonic culture, etc., were beginning to be applied to a greater extent and on a more sophisticated theoretical level. The concepts of diffusion and migration were elaborated on the basis of the systemic approach and the search was initiated for more reliable possibilities of their identification in archaeological sources.

At the start of the 1980s, the theoretical discussions in the Eastern Block gave way to official and traditional attitudes. 'Perestroika' in archaeology does not, as yet, exist.

Current perspectives

The present situation is, as we have found out, somewhat unclear. It is in such a situation that prophets, utopists and futurologists thrive. All of them aspire to clarify at least the future since we cannot make any sense of the past or the present. In this situation we are all a little like Comte de Boulainvilliers who, as Montesquieu said, did not know either the past, the present, or the future. He was a historian, had a young wife, and busied himself with astrology.

However, these ironic remarks are uttered at the expense of a seemingly paradoxical truth – that the past is dependent on the future – as explained by Karl Jaspers: 'We do not know the past if we do not know its relation to the present, that is to what evolved from it. Furthermore, to comprehend the present we need to be aware of its relationship to the future which is always unknown' (Jaspers 1966: 138). However, we always have a certain notion of the future – even if it is antiquated.

Let us now try and establish some basic trends in current archaeology which, we can suppose, will be in force in the future. These are globalisation, expansion, pluralisation and integration. For comparison, see other perspectives (Melzer, Fowler and Sabloff, 1986, Moberg 1969, 1976, Trigger 1984a, 1986).

A knowledgeable commentator on current archaeology, C. A. Moberg, states that in the early days archaeology could be:

satisfied with its regional character, in the sense that there existed the possibility of concentrating on the national, Scandinavian, European, European–Oriental archaeology, or at least on the archaeology of the Old World as against the American archaeology of the New World. To a large extent it was possible to be content with a situation where everyone worked in his own field of interest. As it is, this approach brought hardly any effective results but, at the same time, it did not cause any great crises. It was possible to gather at large specialised conferences where everyone could listen to lectures and seminars pertaining to his archaeological picture of the world. In this way 'stamp collectors' could compare their 'stamps and their perforations'. Social development changed all this. The world grows together. All activity is seen in its global connections. Archaeology has been, for various reasons, markedly globalised during the past few years.

(Moberg 1969: 21, translated from the original Swedish)

This is all expressed very pithily, and let us only add that it is exactly against the background of such globalisation that the splendid and sometimes less splendid isolation into which some national archaeologies retreated stands out.

We now know enough about the expansion of contemporary archaeology, so let us recapitulate briefly. The conception of archaeological sources has become wider and wider, the amount of archaeological information has steadily grown, and more numerous methods have been used in their processing. Apart from prehistoric, classical and medieval archaeology we are introduced to their sisters – industrial archaeology, ethnoarchaeology and a broader concept of 'living archaeology'. Separate perspectives have a tendency to develop more and more into almost separate disciplines – we have economic, social, symbolic and cognitive archaeology. It seems that archaeological expansion has now reached its peak and we have before us a period of colonisation, a period of painstaking and patient work.

We have heard enough about pluralism, too, and it would be unnecessary to repeat all orientations once more. Archaeology has joined with all other social sciences and it will share their fortunes in the future, including pluralism of ideas. Why not? Voltaire noticed that the English have twenty religions but only one sauce – but what a sauce! France is a country with one religion but two hundred various cheeses. We also know of countries with one religion and one sauce or one cheese or even without any sauces or cheeses at all. Archaeology today boasts a multitude of religions, sauces and cheeses. Let us be grateful for that.

Pluralism and integration form in reality one current – otherwise there would be nothing to integrate. Integration, of course, does not mean a victory of one orientation and the destruction of all others. It is precisely thanks to the expansion of plurality that we have to find (or better, strive to find) a common language of inter-communication between individual disciplines, orientations and approaches. Integration is the language of dialogue. The archaeology of the future is an archaeology of meaningful dialogue.

6 Description, classification and seriation

A scientist, according to a simile of Henri Bergson, is like a tailor engaged in the mass production of garments. Because he wants to dress everybody, his clothes fit no one.

Towards a broader understanding of archaeological sources

Archaeology in different stages of its evolution is exactly the same as the sources it has at its disposal. It was the Renaissance scholars, collectors, antiquaries, men of the Enlightenment, and of the Romantic period, evolutionists, environmentalists and many other adherents of various trends and currents who decided and defined what constituted an archaeological record and what did not. They moulded it to fit in with their concepts and developed a variety of terms to describe it.

It was only when the Renaissance scholars discovered that some of the stones and clay pieces occasionally occurring in their collections of curiosities (hitherto thought to be the work of nature) were in fact products of ancient human generations that the story of archaeology could begin to unfold. That is, the future science acquired – its sources. In those days they were called relics of the past. By their nature they were close to curiosities and rare objects – there were only a few of them and they were found in isolation without any relation to the place of their origin or to other finds – which was in keeping with their mainly fortuitous discovery.

It was the flame of an aesthetic passion for beautiful objects, the reverence for the past as a whole, and for the past of one's own nation in particular, that motivated the succeeding generations of collectors to venture into the terrain to search purposefully for antiquities. This was the era of collectors – the antiquarian period. The collections began to grow and the antiquities, even though they still had to bear the seal of a beautiful exterior and display a good state of preservation, ceased to be just separate items seen in isolation. Sites were now registered, and their nature taken into account (though most of them were considered to be burial or sacrificial grounds or places of cult worship) and, occasionally, the distribution of antiquities *in situ* was noted (the beginnings of stratigraphy).

Antiquarians managed to collect so many antiquities that it prompted the scholars of the Enlightenment to proclaim them equal to written records. However, this statement was still only symbolic – there were still too many gaps left to realise this idea in practice. Some of these gaps were filled in by the Romantics, motivated in their endeavour by the need to prove the rich and ancient past of their own nation. A mountain of antiquities now grew in practically all the European countries: heaps of as yet unconnected facts. C. J. Thomsen was the first to manage to order them into a meaningful sequence, depending on the prevalent material or changing techniques. Antiquities suddenly became a source of new information – not only the fully preserved objects but also their fragments. Thomsen's chronological scale stressed their temporal relations, chronology and sequence. This, of course, had a feedback effect on the field investigation, where it now became necessary to discover and provide documentation for the mutual relationships of the objects of the past and their distribution within the area of finds.

The aesthetic collecting stage of archaeology then was coming to an end, and the scientific and explanatory tasks of archaeology were now beginning to gain more prominence. Importance was now attached not only to objects (whether 'beautiful' or not) but also to their relationships. Around the mid-nineteenth century the discovery was made that objects found together were once buried together. The notion of an assemblage emerged and chronological possibilities brought about by the seriation of its individual components were realised. Investigation of changes in raw material, techniques and stylistic transformations and of stratigraphically uniform assemblages lent a greater precision to chronology. During the second half of the nineteenth century, the different information value of different types of archaeological sources was acknowledged. A detailed classification of the main categories and sub-categories of portable and fixed archaeological material (settlements, burial grounds, etc.) followed. Their relations to past human activity was evaluated. All this lent a greater precision and penetration to the understanding of technological, economic and social evolution which, since the end of the nineteenth century, had been described with reference to the concept of 'archaeological culture'.

Another terminological change followed. The term 'artefact', which explicitly expresses a deepening interest in gaining knowledge of past human activity, was now used to designate archaeological sources. The word has its origin in the Latin *artefactum*, which denotes a thing created artificially. It became a matter of common usage in Anglo-American (artefact) and Central-European (*Artefakt*) areas and also in the newly emerging Soviet archaeology (*artefakt*; earlier, at the turn of the 1930s and

1940s, F. V. Kiparov coined the term 'historical thing') which was programmatically oriented towards the investigation of the results of human activity. As a term, the word 'artefact' has a wide range of meaning – it has a connotation of material substance, artifice and cultural norm. However, its concrete usage in archaeology is usually confined to tools, weapons, ornaments, and objects of cult (typically, that is, portable manufactures). It is applied less frequently to semi-finished articles, production waste, remnants and traces or non-portable objects (for example V. S. Bočkarev, I. Rouse), such as buildings, complete settlements, etc.

However, during the past decades the wide range of meaning of the term 'artefact' has become a Procrustean bed for the contemporary understanding of the archaeological record, and a limitation to artefact archaeology is criticised (Renfrew 1969a: 243, Rouse 1970: 6–7). In the meantime archaeology set itself further goals (the study of ecology and its relation to culture, and the detailed study of technology and economics, etc.), found new forms of evidence, and developed and applied methods and techniques for their identification and explanation. Food residues and food refuse, plough marks, etc. – all these could come under the term artefact. However, what to do with remains of animals and seeds, pollen, buried soils, etc. – in a word, with all those things that could throw light on the natural environment in which ancient peoples lived and engaged in their activities (even though these may not be purely natural objects untouched by human hand and intellect)?

At this point the term 'ecofact' was coined and used, especially in England, North America and Scandinavia, to denote natural objects, whether untouched or partially influenced by humans. Only very rarely do we come across the term 'naturefact', which is roughly a synonym for 'ecofact'.

Thus the latest interpretation of the archaeological record (or material sources, *archäologische Quellen* in German, *arheologičeskije istočniki* in Russian) includes both artefacts and 'non-artefact materials' (ecofacts or naturefacts) and human remains. The term 'archaeological record' was widely adopted around the middle of this century (figure 3).

If we therefore compare the earlier interpretations of archaeological sources with the situation today, we come to the conclusion that investigations of antiquities, and artefacts in the traditional sense – even though they still remain important – have lost the superiority they once enjoyed. This does not mean, however, that the concept of 'non-artefactual archaeology' is completely new. The investigation of the natural environment was called for and partially carried out during the last decades of the nineteenth century and later elaborated in detail by environmentalists. However, its wider practical application was facilitated only with the rise of modern methods and techniques of identification and of the systems approach.

Today we pay equal attention both to objects and to features typically associated with archaeology, human waste, refuse, and other traces of human activity. In comparison with the original, antiquarian interpretation

Figure 3. The division of archaeological sources into artefacts, naturefacts and mentefacts is only operational. We have to remember that artefacts are, in fact, the mentefacts of the makers, while naturefacts are investigated only to the extent of their influence by mentefacts.

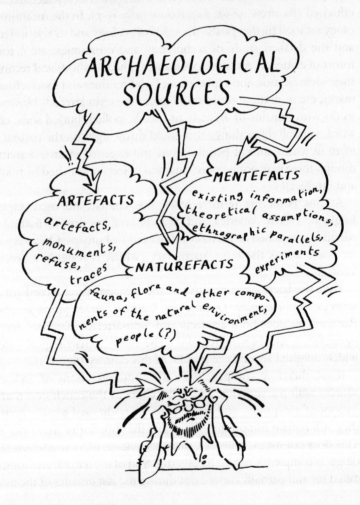

of the archaeological record, we could state, with more precision, that we take into consideration even a 'find without a find'.

Our perception of the object and methodology of archaeology, its aims and potential, depend on our perception of the archaeological record (Patrick 1985). And, in reverse, information and knowledge extrapolated from it interact with the theory and practice of archaeology in a mutually reinforcing relationship to widen and refine the perception of both.

Archaeological remains can be divided along several perspectives. Systematic classification of archaeological sources was recently carried out by D. L. Clarke (1968, 1972), R. C. Dunnell (1971) and L. S. Klejn (1978).

(1) Most commonly, we can characterise archaeological remains according to their chronological and cultural identification (i.e. the Palaeolithic, Neolithic, La Tène, *Linearbandkeramik*, etc.).

(2) Another classification can be carried out on the basis of external – that is, directly observable – characteristics of the objects (measurements, material, etc.). Such schemes are usually based on Thomsen's technological periodisation: 1 – siliceous or other chipped stone artefacts, 2 – stone used in the manufacture of polished tools, 3 – bone, antlers, 4 – ceramics, 5 – non-ferrous and precious metals, iron, 6 – wood, 7 – other organic materials (skin, woven fabric).

(3) Functional classification, such as the one presented in 1948 by W. W. Taylor, classifying data in accordance with functional clusters: food and clothing, social organisation, religion, etc. (Taylor 1948).

(4) Degree of preservation. Archaeological remains can be divided, according to the degree of preservation, into complete objects, fragments and traces.

The nature of archaeological information

A witness is a person who has observed some event. In addition to the event and the witness we have a piece of evidence – that is, a testimony about the event, formulated by the witness. A witness can tell the truth but, on the other hand, he does not have to; and, in any case, the facts provided by him have also been selected according to his own evaluation and to his choice of means of communication.

Near the ruins of fortifications of a settlement in Zemplín in Slovakia a button was found which had been missing from the grave of an old Hungarian chieftain. The dead person could thus finally be identified with the historically documented magnate called Almus. Similarly, archaeologists managed to reconstruct the last few hours of the goldsmith Makosimov when Kiev was overrun by the Tartars. However, these are exceptional cases and not of great importance – witnesses are not important in archaeology.

Prehistory differs from history precisely in that there is no evidence, verbal or written. In addition, only some artefacts were created deliberately to serve as evidence, as symbols or signs of a certain event. From its very beginnings, historiography focused on direct, explicit evidence and, consequently, on a range of events which could be rendered by direct evidence. Archaeology accompanied it along this road for a very long time and strove to understand artefacts as direct evidence of events, 'historical' events, naturally, such as war, cults, etc. In this way the selection of artefacts and their interpretation was considerably limited.

A very old tale tells us of a Greek boat shipwrecked on an unknown coast. The survivors were in mortal fear of barbarians but later they found a triangle drawn in the sand and they were immediately pacified. The triangle told them that the coast was inhabited by civilised beings. Thus, direct conscious evidence is not the only source of our information. There are no geometrical figures without intelligent beings and therefore the triangle poses as a witness-indicator. Indicators differ from explicit evidence in that they do not claim anything and, consequently, they cannot lie. They only confirm or disprove our hypotheses. What we need is a large amount of experience on the basis of which we can formulate hypotheses, and only then can we test them.

If, in prehistory (and even more so in archaeology), we have to rely almost exclusively on indicators, then it means that we cannot follow a considerable part of reality, which is the domain of historiography. Dependence on indicators further means that we have to rely mainly on preliminary hypotheses and that the experience on the basis of which our hypotheses have been formed has to be borrowed from other fields.

In a primitive society everything emerges as indicators of mythological concepts. The newly emerging world of history does not possess a sufficient temporal depth to enable an investigation of dependences other than those to which an immediate, conscious decision of the contemporaries is subordinated. Consequently, motives and psychology are studied and these are derived from indicators of behaviour investigated in an event, in action.

In the subsequent development, the number of investigated events and their attributes widens and deepens in space and time. The number and perception of indicators also widens. Theory and history not only become more complex but society itself becomes more complicated. People are forced to react more and more not only to immediate events but also to those strata of reality which can be perceived only with the help of indicators. The transformation of concrete evidence into indicators was carried out by Vico in mythology and historiography, Winckelmann in the history of art, and Thomsen in archaeology. The result is the investigation of style, processes, trends and causalities. A human being, witness and event are replaced by impersonal dependence, indicator and system or structure.

The wider conception of an artefact, the study of attributes as indicators and a continually growing number of investigated artefacts have resulted in an enormous growth of archaeological information. Further information adopted from or gained with the assistance of geology, geomorphology, palaeontology, petrology, climatology, hydrology, paedology, biology, ecology and biogeography has also accumulated. Spectrographic, fluorescent, radiocarbon, etc. analyses and tests have provided new data as well. Computers have come to our assistance just at the right time, but computers can deal successfully only with painstakingly prepared information.

Let us therefore try to establish the systematics of information observable from the archaeological material. We shall divide information into primary, secondary and tertiary information. Primary information is such information as can be observed directly from the archaeological record or its environment, and this is further divided into internal and external information. Internal information consists of data about the form (shape, surface, weight, material) whereas external information will tell us about the context (origin, spatial relations, etc.) of the observations which make up the primary information. Secondary information relates to the function, purpose and technology of production – that is, the relationship of an archaeological source to humans. This information is obtained by explication (experiments, parallels, comparison, etc.). Tertiary information is obtained by processing the primary and secondary information – that is, arranging artefacts into temporal, spatial and functional wholes (figure 4). This is only a schematic outline and it could lead to a false idea that archaeological records can give us information which does not have to be tested any further. An extensive critique of archaeological data was carried out by Menghin (1952), H. J. Eggers (see above, pp. 105–7) (Eggers 1959), J. Herrmann (1986), M. B. Schiffer (1972, 1976, 1981) and L. S. Klejn (1978).

The fact that archaeological sources can change with time was known

Figure 4. A system of archaeological research.

ARCHAEOLOGICAL ARTEFACTS

description

primary

secondary

internal description   external description

data obtained by explication (experiments, parallels, comparisons, etc.)

SHAPE 1.

SHAPE & MASS 2.

NON-FUNCTIONAL ALTERATION OF SURFACE 3. AND ITS LOCATION

TECHNOLOGY 4.

ATTRIBUTES 5. IDENTIFYING FUNCTION

RAW 6. MATERIAL

THE ENVIRONMENT 7. SURROUNDING THE OBJECT, AND THE RAW MATERIAL

QUANTITY 8.

PROCESSING

A) OF DATA IN TERMS OF ATTRIBUTES: ANALYSIS OF RELATIONSHIPS OF INDIVIDUAL GROUPS OF DESCRIPTIVE UNITS;

B) OF DATA IN TERMS OF OBJECTS: TYPOLOGY, CLASSIFICATION;

C) OF DATA IN TERMS OF CHRONOLOGICAL ORDERING;

D) OF DATA IN TERMS OF REGIONAL DIVISION;

EXPLICATION

already to Shakespeare. In answer to Horatio's objection, Hamlet answers: *No, faith, not a jot; but to follow him thither with modesty enough, and likelihood to lead it, as thus: Alexander died, Alexander was buried, Alexander returneth to dust; the dust is earth; of earth we make loam; and why of that loam whereto he was converted might they not stop a beer-barrel?*

> *Imperious Caesar, dead and turn'd to clay*
> *Might stop a hole to keep the wind away.*
> *O, that that earth which kept the world in awe*
> *Should patch a wall t'expel the winter's flaw!*

Not merely Caesar, even Lenin. 'Even Lenin someday will be buried' (Shiffer 1976: 40) or, to follow the Soviet terminology, 'archaeologised'. Unless we are dealing here with the same problem that afflicted Theseus' ark. The Athenians had preserved the famous vessel in his memory, but with the passage of time a weathered plank or a beam had to be replaced. In the end no one was sure how much of the original boat was left. However, the Greeks could have complicated the matter even further. Imagine they placed the weathered planks to one side and used these along with new ones to build other boats. In this way we may have ended up with a number of vessels and each could have belonged to Theseus.

During the process of the formation and disintegration of material culture, every piece of information must undergo a journey through a series of stages, through a number of sluicegates and filters. Every time the information is slightly altered, a part of it may be lost or distorted. In order to discover the meaning and value of an archaeological fact, an archaeologist must unveil all the stages of its formation right back to its source and, at the same time, establish how and in what way this fact is transformed by particular filters. Recent archaeological literature (Binford 1972, Clarke 1968, Daniels 1972, Fehon and Scholz 1978, Gardin 1979, Klejn 1975a, 1978, Kozłowski 1975, Raab and Klinger 1980, Schiffer 1976, 1983, 1987, Urbańczyk 1983) has usually cited a various number of the barriers, stages and filters through which archaeological records pass. Cultural rules represent the first filter, which dictates how objects are formed, passed on and adopted, used and discontinued. Schiffer's call for a set of laws, which would 'relate behaviour(al) variables to material objects or spatial relations' (Schiffer 1976: 13), cannot be met easily. People invest artefacts not only with functional, but also with symbolic and aesthetic – including the factor of fashion – value. All these values together share in controlling the number, location, use, length of circulation and manner of deposition of artefacts. Within a single culture, objects from other moribund or distant cultures can be preserved and assume other functions (see Egger's arguments, above, pp. 105–7). The above is particularly true in protohistoric period, where extensive exchange networks make it quite common for foreign imports to assume different functions in other cultural contexts.

Schiffer calls the next filter C-transforms. 'These principles permit an investigator to specify the ways in which a cultural system outputs the materials that eventually may be observed archaeologically' (Schiffer 1976: 14). Discard, disposal of the dead, loss and abandonment of artefacts can be given as examples of transforms belonging to this filter. We should also include catastrophes and wars; cynical as it may sound, it must be admitted that archaeologists like them. This is despite the fact that a good war can thoroughly confuse the pegs on which archaeological rags are hung; it must often be hard to decide, for instance, whether a damaged sword was lost, abandoned, or intentionally given as a votive offering as part of mortuary furnishing. Children should also count as favourites among archaeologists, since it is they in particular who break so many dishes, and, as we found recently, also alter the spatial disribution of sherds during their games (Hammond and Hammond 1981).

According to Schiffer, N-transforms represent the next filter, for which nature is mainly responsible. N-transforms describe the natural processes which destroy, alter and preserve archaeological materials. Archaeologists should be grateful to Mother Nature for her kind treatment of pottery in particular: thanks to the carelesness of housewives and clumsiness of children, the average life of a ceramic vessel is no more than three years, giving archaeologists plenty of material to work with in building their chronologies. Processes of ageing, weathering and disintegration of archaeological materials form the subject of taphonomy. Natural processes such as floods can also relocate archaeological remains far from their original location (Turnbaugh 1978). Last, but not least, the size and the weight of the object play an important role in such events (Baker 1978). The collusion of unpredictable events can also play its part – for example, we can archaeologically document very well an insignificant battle at Živohošť in Bohemia in 1419, but we cannot do so with a historically significant and monumental battle of Alexander Nevskij against the German crusaders on Lake Pejpus in 1241. We have to include archaeologists themselves, especially the older generation, among the destroyers of archaeological records. We can say that Schliemann not only discovered Troy but also destroyed it. Sir Mortimer Wheeler was certainly right to maintain that 'excavation is destruction'.

The meaning of description

Archaeological evidence and its interpretation includes an extensive but unclear area which until recently archaeology simply had to put up with. In brief, this is the area of description and classification. Naturally one does not always have a simple sequence: sources – classification – interpretation; hypotheses need their own indicative evidence just as methods of analysis need their own specific data and defined aims. In spite of this the area of description and classification has its own rules of play, and one must keep to them. There are methods which objectively record for us certain non-random connections between data. But there are also methods which conceal unspoken preconceptions. These too have a meaning, that is, if we are conscious of the interpretations hidden in them. This section is devoted to a survey and analysis of the rules of play, to particular methods of classification, and to those unspoken preconceptions.

Now that we have an archaeological record before us, what is the next step? One of the methods was described by Swift in *Gulliver's Travels*. In the Great Academy of Lagado he met sages who only trusted *things* and not the names for *things* and for this reason it was necessary for them to move about carrying their *things* with them in a bundle and, when the need arose, show them to each other without speaking:

I have often beheld two of these sages almost sinking under the weight of their packs, like pedlars among us; who, when they meet in the street, would lay down their loads, open their sacks, and hold conversation for an hour together, then put up their implements, help each other to resume their burdens, and take their leave.

(Swift, *Gulliver's Travels*)

We do not share the mistrust of language but, unfortunately, there are so many archaeological remains that they would not fit into any sack. There is nothing else to do but to attempt an objective description of their attributes. To decide what came first, chicken or egg, theory or description, is impossible and this question does not make sense anyway. Description and theory are only two mutually complementary components of one process and we can only distinguish between them within the framework of a textbook explanation. Already the first question of description, what to describe, is inseparably bound up with the whole of theory. Only on the basis of theory can we then lay out our investigation and separate its individual features. There are feedback loops between description and theory which always lend a greater precision to the existing investigation, or occasionally establish anew what is to be described.

The interpretation of the description of archaeological records usually begins with the description of artefacts. Artefacts are understood here in the widest sense of the word, that is, as all objects not only formed but perhaps only touched by human activity (it can be just mental activity for example). Each artefact is, at the same time, necessarily an ecofact as well, a part of nature independent of humans. This double side of each object has a direct consequence for its description. Artefacts are studied because they are manifestations of human activity and it is precisely this activity that we want to study with the help of artefacts. We can study, for example in stone-working, the direct traces left by this activity, such as production and functional traces (drilling, sawing, polishing, wear caused by use, etc.)

However, we can also study those ecofactual signs which provide evidence of human activity in the sense that the material used was chosen because of an attribute specific to it (hardness, the ease with which it lent itself to manufacture, colouring, etc.). In addition, we can also take into account those attributes of artefacts which their creators themselves did not sometimes consider (the possibility of discovering the location of a raw-material source, temporal definition). Older archaeology was concerned practically exclusively with the description of artefacts as such, concentrating on their shape and ornamental attributes and leaving aside the description of their relation to the environment and the circumstances of their find (stratigraphy, position, relation to the surrounding environment, etc.).

One of the systems of archaeological description (similar to the systematisation of archaeological information mentioned earlier) can be seen in figure 4. It is based on the determination of a sufficient number of attributes of internal description (shape, size, non-functional modifications of the surface and their position, technology, function, material), external description (ecology of the artefact, provenance of the material, distribution) and finally, attributes of secondary description (explication – experiments, parallels, systemisation, etc.). They should be arranged in such a way that the definitions of individual attributes fulfil the demands of objectivity, non-apriority, logical independence, standardisation, the replication of procedures, precision and adequate refinement.

If we want to describe an artefact and, naturally, the whole complex of the find, the locality, we must accurately distinguish these individual aspects of description, determine relevant attributes for each aspect of the complex and consider the size of the sample. Apart from recording the conscious activity of the prehistoric people – such as the selection of materials, their functional treatment, decorations chosen – we can also follow the unconscious selective processes which the original makers did not or even could not perceive or of which they were not conscious at all, such as the gradual changes in the shape of vessels.

We can view description from yet another perspective. The function of description is to help us to differentiate between the phenomena under investigation and to determine their common characteristics and relationships. Description can serve for classification purposes if it has, in the first instance, a systematic function – that is, it will at least enable us to find bearings in the deluge of individual, externally unconnected artefacts. However, if a description is to be of service to systemisation it has to be, in turn, dependent on it – the problem of determination of the number of attributes also depends on the number of investigated objects. In order to differentiate and classify a small number of objects, a smaller number of attributes is sufficient and vice versa. In summary, the size of our sample will determine the range of attributes which can be investigated.

In historiography, archives can serve as an advanced stage of analysis, during which a preliminary selection of material can be carried out. In archaeology, in contrast, no facts are ruled out in advance if they can be described, processed and evaluated. In practice, description is always incomplete but it can be augmented by a compilation of reports on the finds of all archaeological material which has been discovered and, in addition, we can make a conscious decision to leave the prehistoric remains or their fragments undisturbed. In comparison with history, the relatively monotonous nature of artefacts enables us to use different and more effective methods of description and, above all, better methods of description processing.

The basic precondition of modern taxonomy, which will be discussed later in more detail, is the determination of equal importance – weighting of attributes. Consequently, we have to deal with a whole series of attendant problems concerned with the composition and enumeration of attributes of artefacts. For instance, in order to define a shape we can use a large number of methods which will differ in the number of attributes used in its description. Depending on the quantity of other attributes, the description of the shape will then play a greater or lesser role within the overall description. How should we then deal with reclassification of objects when new attributes are introduced? If we do not accept the proposition of equal weight we have to deal with still further problems. On what basis can we determine a hierarchical order in population of attributes?

There are further problems of an external nature. How can we define and systematise our description of attributes? This is a question of the recurrence and objectivity of description. But the complications do not end here. Each attribute – for example the attribute of colour – has a number of modes or states (in the case of colour there are individual modes, such as black or blue). A different terminology designates colour an attribute class or a variable, and its mode as an attribute (see Cowgill 1982). The modes of attributes and attributes themselves are usually divided into quantitative, comparative and qualitative categories. Quantitative categories are those which can be measured or counted (for example the length of an object); comparative categories can be ordered (different grades of hardness); and qualitative ones can be neither measured nor ordered (for example, bell-shaped or funnel-shaped) (see Cowgill 1982). Consequently, the values assigned to the modes of individual attributes differ considerably and their mutual comparison does not necessarily make any sense. We shall try to explain as simply as possible in principle that the values are mutually comparable.

In order to continue our train of thought we have to start from the premise (even though this may not be justified) that all these problems of description have already been solved. However, this is more a question of practice and convention than theory – many athletes lack technique but

Figure 5. A matrix with m rows and n columns, where the first number corresponds to the membership in the row and the second to the membership in the column.

they still produce good results. To take this analogy further, archaeologists resemble athletes in that their individual techniques and conventions are highly idiosyncratic and differ from one another, and so it is usually left up to the reader to find out which rules, practices and conventions apply in any particular case. When the description of objects has been finalised, our starting point will always be some kind of a matrix with *m* rows and *n* columns (figure 5).

In the case of artefacts such a matrix can be illustrated more graphically in the form of a specific table (figure 6), in which letters represent objects and Roman numerals attributes: 1 signifies the presence of an attribute, o its absence. If we take the object A as an example, we can see that it possesses the attributes 1 and 2 but that the attribute 3 is lacking.

In order to illustrate the subsequent hypotheses it would be best to construct a geometrical model of such a table. If we take attributes as the axis of co-ordinates with unit distance in three-dimensional space, then the objects A, B and C will be represented by points in the resulting space (figure 7). In this way, we have managed to place objects in the dimension provided by attributes. However, we can equally place attributes in the dimension provided by objects.

If we consider more than three dimensions we cannot then rely any more on pictorial representation, but we can study the n-dimensional space by means of a relatively simple mathematical operation. The geometrical model or relationships between objects or attributes can also be created on the basis of other types of spaces (metric, non-Euclidean, non-metric). Let us now return to our initial table (figure 6). The collection of data represented by the table forms a complete registry of all our observations. In the case of a more extensive table dealing with dozens of objects and

Figure 6. An example of a concrete hypothetical table. Rows marked by letters correspond to objects and columns marked by roman numerals correspond to their attributes. Number 1 denotes that an object possesses a given attribute, o means it does not have one.

	I	II	III
A	1	1	0
B	0	1	1
C	0	0	1

hundreds of attributes we necessarily lose our orientation. We have, therefore, to simplify data to such an extent that the scheme is manageable. Obviously, not every simplification makes sense – it has to be such that with its help we can reach conclusions which will reveal certain features that are common and similar and this, in turn, will enable us to generalise about the objects or their attributes on a higher level.

The basic operation in this sense is the determination of relationships between two rows or two columns of the matrix (figure 5) or a table (figure 6) – that is, relationships between objects or relationships between attributes. We can therefore trace the degree of similarity between any two of the attributes on the basis of a measure of difference which we can establish as the ratio of the number of objects where both of these attributes are present to the number of objects where only one or the other attribute is present. In a similar fashion, we can trace a similarity between two objects. They will be (taxonomically, within the framework of the matrix) identical if all their attributes correspond. The ratio of the quantity of corresponding attributes of two objects to the quantity of discrepant attributes forms the basis for establishing the degree of similarity of two objects.

However, here we come across further problems. In the first instance we have assigned equal weighting to the attributes under investigation (and, naturally, to the object, too, which, however, is perfectly legitimate), and we have done so even in the simplest case when we are dealing only with two-value attributes (that is, attributes either present or absent in a specific

Figure 7. Abscissas I, II, III represent the axes of co-ordinates of a three-dimensional space which is bounded by the unit distance of the ends of abscissas from their point of intersection. If they are taken to represent attributes, then according to the table in figure 6, point A, for instance, will be located in the top left corner (I + 1, II + 1, III + 0).

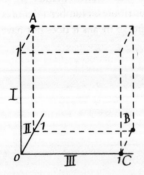

object). However, how are we to evaluate a negative match of one attribute between two objects? Can we assign it the same weighting as a positive match (that is, when both objects possess the same attribute)? And what if we take into account all other objects? If we have, for example, ten objects and nine of them possess both the investigated attributes while in one case these attributes are absent, then such a correlation – even though it is a negative one – can be taxonomically of greater importance than an individual positive match. Or, to give a different example, the probability of a correlation of two bi-modal attributes is given by the distribution of their values. If one attribute occurs in nine objects out of ten and the same goes for the other attribute, then a simultaneous discrepancy of two attributes in one object is highly improbable. In this case, of course, if such a negative match really occurs, we have reason to consider it more significant. In this instance we evaluate the similarity of two objects on the basis of relations to all other investigated objects (Smirnov 1969). On the basis of various approaches we can formulate a definite coefficient of similarity by means of which we can state the measure of similarity between two objects, or between attributes respectively. However, we have to decide further which coefficient to apply, and this problem will be discussed subsequently.

Let us start with one of the simple and, at the same time, most efficient coefficients of similarity – the coefficient of Sokal and Michener – called the simple-matching coefficient. This coefficient states the measure of similarity (S) of two objects (A, B) as the ratio of the number of the number of coinciding attributes (p) out of the number of all attributes (n): $S(a, B) = p/n$ in the case of our first example $S(A, B) = 1/3$; $S(A, C) = C$; $S(B, C) = 2/3$.

Let us now return to the possibilities provided by the geometrical model with unitary distance (figure 7). Here we can interpret the identity of two objects as an identical location of the points created in this way in space. The distance equalling the edge of a cube represents a similarity of $2/3$, the distance equalling the diagonal through the side of the cube represents a similarity of $1/3$, and the distance equalling the diagonal through the cube represents a zero similarity.

Having established the similarity of all the pairs of objects (and, similarly, of attributes) we can construct a new table, a table of similarity (resemblance) (figure 8), where the values which can be read off in the intersection of columns and lines state the values of similarity of those elements which are represented by a line or a column.

The relationship between the pairs of columns (or rows – for the sake of brevity we shall talk about columns only from now on) is the domain of such statistical techniques as a simple regression and correlation analysis by means of which we can compare even multiple-value attributes. Let us take two columns. First of all we have to establish the characteristic quantities for each column separately, such as the central value, measure of deviation, variance and standard deviation. By means of these characteristics, regression analysis investigates in what way one column is dependent on the other – that is, how to estimate, provided we know the values of one column (the independent variable), the values of the second column (the dependent variable). The sequence of the investigated dependency of columns can then be reversed. Correlation analysis investigates the measure of the mutual relationship of the columns. There is a whole number of correlative coefficients and they depend on the nature of the input data (sequential, alternative, etc.).

When comparing two columns we can, on the basis of similarity, also investigate the phenomenon of tendency, which expresses the trend of differentiation between objects or attributes. Let us then interpret this phenomenon in three-dimensional space, and in order to gain a better idea we shall consider only multiple-value attributes. If we take the attributes as the axes of co-ordinates then, in the case of the given matrix (figure 5), we shall obtain the spatial representation seen in figure 9. The distance between the objects is interpreted as resemblance. The higher values of attribute 2 shift the object to the right, while the higher values of attribute 1 shift it upward, and attribute 3 shifts it backward. The position of the

Figure 8. A table of similarity of objects A, B, C in figure 6, where the individual measures of similarity are calculated on the basis of the coefficient of simple correlation. 1 denotes the maximum similarity (A is identical with A), 0 denotes no similarity (A and C do not share a single attribute), 1/3 and 2/3 expresses a degree of similarity (in our case, one or two characteristics out of three). If we divide the picture diagonally from the top left corner we find that the two halves are identical. The information in picture (b) is therefore sufficient.

(a)	A	B	C
A	1	1/3	0
B	1/3	1	2/3
C	0	2/3	1

(b)	A	B	C
A	1		
B	1/3	1	
C	0	2/3	1

abscissa connecting the two points determines the tendency of both points, and the position and direction of the abscissa determines the tendency of one point in relation to the other. If we consider the length of the abscissa we can establish the extent of the tendency (its value is in inverse proportion to the measure of resemblance). If we therefore choose a certain tendency we can, on the basis of it, arrange all objects into a sequence which is useful, above all, when the given tendency can be interpreted from the point of view of content (for example, from the point of view of function, space and time).If we, on the other hand, investigate attributes on the basis of objects we arrive at the tendency of changes in attributes.

We have, for the time being, investigated the resemblance between two objects. If we compare an object with itself we arrive, according to the simple-matching coefficient, at an intuitively clear and self-evident result, – the value of 1, which signifies total identity. However, if we apply Smirnov's coefficient we arrive at a seemingly paradoxical result – the resemblance of an object with itself does not necessarily have to equal 1. This is because with the help of this coefficient we evaluate the status of the object in relation to all other objects in the table – we establish its degree of resemblance to an average object of the given table – that is, its typicality. The notion typicality can then be used with all other coefficients of resemblance. On this basis we can compare objects according to the extent of typicality and find the most typical elements. Similar investigation can of course be carried out also where attributes are concerned.

Figure 9. A representation of three-dimensional space, which is not defined by unit distances, as was the case in figure 7. Such space is not limited by a simple binomial opposition (presence/absence of attributes), but can incorporate different states of the attributes (such as different heights of vessels). A higher value of each attribute is then represented by a greater distance of the object which possesses such attributes from the point of intersection of the abscissas.

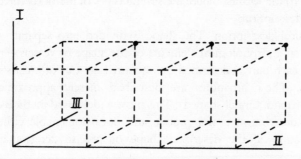

The description of shape

One of the first scholars to investigate the description of shapes and their classification was an unknown natural scientist who, according to G. C. Lichtenberg, classified animals by the shape of their excrement. He established three categories: cylindrical, round, and pancake-shaped. Let us bow to his memory and carry on with our task.

Let us begin with animals, and let us take dogs as an example. There are many different sorts of dogs, some rather dissimilar to others. Despite this, no small child, on the basis of the recognition of a single dog, will confuse any other dog with a cat, for instance, even though some dogs may look more like cats than dogs. A child acts on the basis of its intuitive 'pattern' of dog. A discipline, known as 'pattern recognition', therefore, does no more than systematically study the recognition of such patterns, of that which integrates form, unit, shape, interconnectedness, Gestalt (Lesman 1979).

Here we shall concentrate primarily on the problem of study and description of the shapes themselves from the point of view of the investigation of their exact mutual resemblance. The methods of pattern recognition, on the other hand, deal primarily with the formation of classes of objects and assigning the object into them. However, these are not fundamental differences, rather a different emphasis.

Further to the problems of description of the shape itself, in many cases the concept of description does not only stem directly from other analytical methods but is even interchangeable with them. For example, if we express shape by the enumeration of its selected co-ordinates in two-dimensional shapes, it is perfectly possible to make this description by means of analytical geometry. Furthermore, many of the given forms of description can be mutually combined and their specific advantages can be made use of. In fact, many methods stem from each other and for this reason we cannot reject any of them a priori.

Shapes are basically two- and three-dimensional. We shall, initially, limit ourselves to the former. There are several types of methods currently used in shape description:

  1. Classical description. The shape is divided into separate parts (for example, six morphological elements of the shape of vessels – rim, neck, etc.) and each part is described by one attribute out of a class of chosen attributes. These attributes are described merely approximately (for example, round, funnel-shaped). This most widely used method of archaeographic description is not precise and does not enable either reverse reconstruction of the described shape or precise determination of a

Figure 10 (a): Basic dimensions of description. To describe a given section of a shape we can use a three-digit number, where the first digit denotes length, the second denotes slope and the third denotes curvature. (b): Using information illustrated in (a) we can describe 7 × 6 × 5 = 210 basic shapes. Six examples are illustrated here. Some of the compound forms, which can be described by the means of such an 'alphabet', are illustrated in section (c). Source: Uhr 1973: 166.

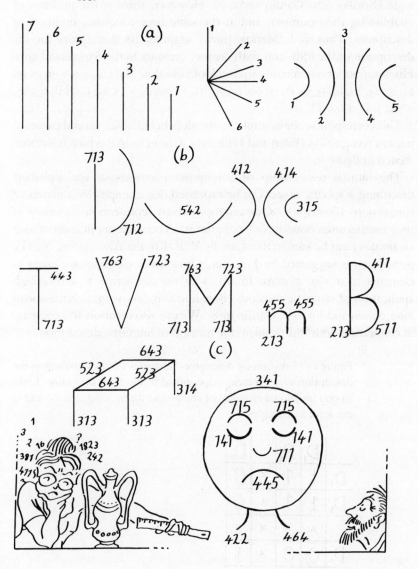

resemblance of the shape. It leads to the establishment of monothetic groups.

2. Description by means of descriptors. This method stems from the classical description but it differs from it in that it is based on a systematic dictionary of descriptors which are specific to each area under investigation. This enables coding and lends itself to computerisation. This method is widely used by the French Centre d'Analyse Documentaire pour l'Archéologie (Borillo 1975, Gardin 1958a, b). However, there is the problem of establishing the optimum, and at the same time adequate, numbers of descriptors. Thus B. I. Maršak (1970) suggests 258 descriptors for the description of the fifth- and sixth-century ceramics in the Samarkand area. His notation for one ceramic artefact looks like this: $1, 2, 3, 4, 5, 6, 7, 9, 17, 19, 22, 23, 23, 29, 50, 53, 55, 57, 58, 60, 61, 70, 73, 77, 79, d_5, a°, 3, a_1, 3, 5, H^1, 7, 5, a_2, h^2, 4, 5, D, 10, 5, H, 15$.

This corresponds, for example, to the alphabet of abscissas and curves in pattern recognition (Eden and Halle 1961, Uhr 1973: 166) which is demonstrated in figure 10.

The mutual relationship of descriptors (elements of the alphabet) describing a specific object can be expressed, for example, by a matrix of connections (descriptor × descriptors) which represents a summary of their mutual interconnections (see figure 11). A concrete application of such an alphabet can be seen in the study by V. B. Kovalevskaja (1970a, b). The principle was suggested by J. A. Šer. Ornamental elements are taken as elements of a sign system. In this way we can arrive at a thorough application of syntactic methods (Breeding and Amoss 1972, Narasimhan 1966, Swain and Fu 1972, Gardin 1978). We can also mention and compare in connection with this problem the method of linguistic description.

Figure 11. Links among descriptors (elements of the alphabet) in the description of a concrete shape, noted in the form of a table. Links among individual elements of compound forms in figures 10c and 13 can serve as examples.

	D_1	D_2		D_n
D_1	1	1	×	0
D_2	1	1	×	0
	×	×	×	×
D_n	0	0	×	1

How the method of description by means of the dictionary of descriptors works can be illustrated by a simple example, for instance the description of one type of animal (Kameneckij, Maršak and Šer 1975: 62–3). In figure 12 the descriptors a and b record the method of the depiction of legs; c and d depiction of horns; e and f of eyes; g and h of whiskers; i and j the number of ribs; k and l the depiction of the tail; m and n of ears, o of muscles of the right leg. The matrix in figure 13 corresponds to such a description.

3. Description by means of points of intersection. The shape is entered on to a plane dissected by horizontal and vertical lines, which are parallel and equally distanced. The points of intersection of the entered shape and these straight lines (either only horizontal or only vertical or both) can serve as the selected points for the description of the shape. The value of these

Figure 12. Description of figures by means of a dictionary of descriptors. Source: Kameneckij, Maršak and Šer 1975:63.

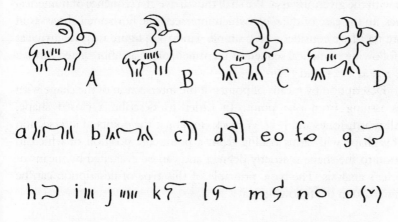

Figure 13. A concrete example of links among descriptors used in figure 12, expressed in the form of a table. Source: Kameneckij, Maršak and Šer 1975:63.

	a	b	c	d	e	f	g	h	i	j	k	l	m	n	o
A	1	0	1	0	1	0	0	1	0	1	0	1	0	1	0
B	1	0	0	1	0	1	0	1	0	1	0	1	1	0	1
C	1	0	1	0	1	0	1	0	1	0	1	0	1	0	0
D	0	1	1	0	1	0	1	0	1	0	1	0	1	0	0

points can be given by means of co-ordinates. The sequence of numerical values of the co-ordinates (arranged according to a specific convention) then corresponds to the description of the shape (Vašíček and Jičín 1971).

The points of intersection can be given not only by means of the network of straight lines but also by probes. The probes are those chosen abscissas which are necessary to distinguish a certain kind of pattern. For example, in order to distinguish arabic numerals, one set of many possible sets of probes was worked out (figure 14; Arkadev and Braverman 1971). Each of the numerals always intersects only one sub-set of probes.

Another method, by means of which we can ascribe numerical values to selected points, is the *wind-rose method* (Schröder 1969, Wilcock 1971). Here we start with the points defined either by horizontal or by vertical straight lines. The adjoining points, where the *shape* intersects the straight lines, are then connected one by one by abscissas. We then assign to each abscissa a numerical designation of the direction of the *wind-rose* which corresponds best with the given abscissa. We shall thus arrive at a sequence of numerical values. In the case of the *shape* which intersects the horizontal abscissas in figure 15a (if we consider a very simple wind-rose, figure 15d), we arrive at the following numerical sequence: 1122111666, or, in an abbreviated form, 2 × 1, 2 × 4, 3 × 1, and 3 × 6.

4. Description by means of points of the intersection of the shape with arms issuing from one point. In order to describe a closed shape, P. Allsworth-Jones and J. D. Wilcock (1974) use the points of intersection of this shape with arms issuing from a point, the position of which in relation to the shape is strictly defined and can be evaluated by means of Fourier's analysis. The basic principle of this type of description can be summarised in the following way:

Figure 14. A characterisation of numbers with the help of 'probes'. These consist of a given number of abscissas in a defined configuration. A configuration is selected in such a way that numbers do not intersect with the probes.

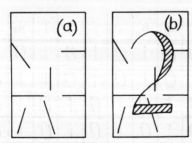

(a) we find out the strictly determined point (usually the centre of gravity);

(b) this point then becomes the centre of the system of polar co-ordinates (see figure 16a) and the polar axis is defined (for example, this could be the axis tracing the maximum length of the shape);

(c) we then measure the distance between the centre of the co-ordinates and the points of intersection of the arms issuing from this centre with the shape;

(d) these distances form a set of numerical values which can then be compared graphically (figure 16b);

(e) with the help of Fourier's analysis we can assign specific values of coefficients of Fourier's development to this set of numerical values;

(f) we compare the values of the coefficients in order to define the similarity of the shapes.

When using this method it is necessary to establish the starting point precisely. Each side can have only one point of intersection with the shape.

Figure 15. Different methods of shape description: (a) where a shape intersects with a simple grid; (b) where individual smallest areas created by the grid are considered as receptors; if such receptors are then aligned from the top left corner to the bottom right, we obtain a notation 01110100100100110011; (c) where points of intersection of a grid and the shape are connected with abscissas, each abscissa receiving the direction of a 'wind-rose' (figure d) which best corresponds to the given abscissa; in this way we obtain a numerical notation 666655554444.

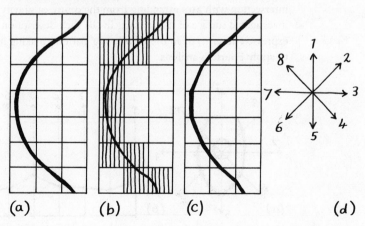

(a)   (b)   (c)   (d)

When different sizes are involved, different values of coefficients are obtained and therefore it is necessary to convert the shape to the same size.

The numerical values of the distances of the points of intersection of the shapes from the sides can be compared not only by means of Fourier's method but also with the help of polynomes and other methods cited here.

5. Description by means of characteristic points. Shapes can be described and evaluated on the basis of exclusively formal criteria without going into the meaning or description. Method No. 3 is an example of such a formal system of description. Another approach is, for example, determining the length of the outline of the shape, establishing a starting point and dividing the length of the outline by a stipulated number. The starting point and the points determined by the multiples of the segments then form a system of selected points. Method No. 7 uses a similar approach.

Thus, for example, according to H. Freeman (1961), we can establish a unit of length T by means of which we divide the curve under scrutiny into equal lengths, and in this way we in fact convert it into a strict sequence of abscissas (see Method No. 3 for comparison). The curve is then described by the sequence of angles which the individual abscissas form with one of the axes of the co-ordinates (figure 17).

In this case the sequence is as follows: 11°, 28°, 87°, 100°, 46°, −6°. If we establish a unit angle of 18° (we shall thus arrive at a scale of twenty standard angles) we can obtain a simplified notation: 1, 1, 3, 5, 6, 3, 0, 19. Other methods of curve-following are given, for example, by C. R. Brice and C. L. Fennema (1970).

However, the majority of scientific fields have elaborated a specific

Figure 16. A description of a shape of a battle axe using points of intersection with axes extending from the centre of gravity of the investigated surface of the artefact. In (b) such description is expressed in terms of an irregular 'wavy' pattern, making it possible to apply Fourier's analysis.

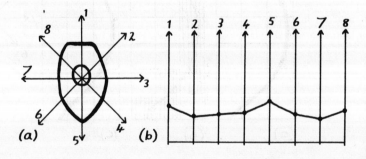

system of selection of characteristic points which are based on the supposition that the comparison of shapes is meaningful only in the case of a functional, morphological, genetic or other dependency. These dependencies should be expressed by a greater number of selected points in the individual parts of the shape we are describing.

The shapes under investigation are thus reduced to a system of corresponding points (for example, anthropometrical, craniometrical, morphological, etc.) which P. H. A. Sneath (1967) calls 'h-points'. Their selection, location and number are determined by the practices of a given branch of science.

The location is then defined, above all, by the mutual relative position. The position of the points on a plane is not usually expressed, but their mutual relationships sufficient to distinguish individual shapes are given, even though in many cases their shape cannot be reconstructed. The sequence of values of mutual relationships of characteristic points expressed numerically in a corresponding number can be considered to be the description of the shape. Another method is that of stating the values of the co-ordinates of each characteristic point on a plane (Sneath 1967).

6. Description by means of parameters. We look for such parameters which do not describe the shape directly but describe some of its attributes. For example, its circumference, area, length of the largest axis, radius of the circle inscribed into the shape, that of the concentric circle, etc. We can also

Figure 17. A description of a curve using the values of angles. A curve is divided by a selected unit of length. Points on the curve obtained in this way are then connected by abscissas. The angle formed by the abscissas with one of the lines running parallel with one of the co-ordinates forms the angle of description. In (b), for example, we elect a unit angle of 18 degrees for description. Source: Freeman 1961.

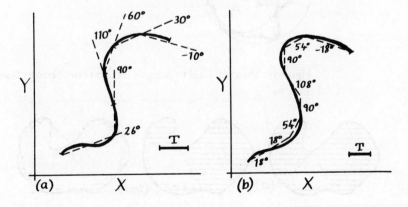

study other characteristics (such as the distance between the centre of the inscribed and circumscribed circles) and the mutual relationships of these characteristics (for example, the ratio of the radii under investigation). Such methods are used, for example, in sedimentary geology (Krumbein 1959) and geography (in studies of town territories, Gibbs 1961; figure 18). These methods could be utilised in archaeography, above all in the study of the shape of settlements or of different tools.

W. Bunge's method of description is based on two premises (Bunge 1962):

(a) all shapes can be identified with sufficient precision with equilateral n-polygons whose length can vary; the more sides there are, the greater the precision of identification (figure 19);

(b) the mutual relationships of the vertices of the n-polygon give a sufficiently precise characterisation of the n-polygon and, therefore, the shape corresponding to it (figure 20).

The principle of Bunge's usage rests with the determination of mutual distanced vertices. According to convention, we further divide the distances and determine within individual groups their total and the total of

Figure 18. Description of urban areas with the aid of the following parameters: A – area, P – circumference, L – longest axes, R_o – radius of circle drawn outside the circumference, R_i – radius of a circle drawn inside the circumference of the urban area. Source: Gibbs 1961: 101

Figure 19. Illustrative aid to Bunge's theorem one. Source: Bunge 1962: 94.

these distances raised to the power of two. For example, in the case of an octagon (figure 20), one group will consist of distances between every other vertex (1–3, 2–4, 3–5, 5–7, 6–8, 7–1), the second group will consist of distances between every vertex but two (1–4, 2–5, 3–6, 4–7, 5–8, 6–1, 7–2, 8–3), and the third group will consist of distances between every vertex but three (1–5, 2–6, 3–7, 4–8). In this way we obtain a sequence of numerical values S_1, S_2, S_3, S_1^2, S_2^2, S_3^2, where S_i indicates the total of lengths of the i-group and S_i^2 the total of the lengths raised to a power of two in the i-group.

7. The analytical method of description, in the terminology of M. J. Brajčevskij (1970), is not, in the strict sense of the word, a method of description proper since it is based on an already established system of points (selected by various methods) and this system is then described by it. The system of the points selected can be interpreted as the vertices of a polygon whose sides are formed by the connecting lines between these points. The description of the polygon can be carried out by means of various methods using analytical geometry. For example, it can be separ-

Figure 20. Illustrative aid theorem two. Source: Bunge 1962: 95.

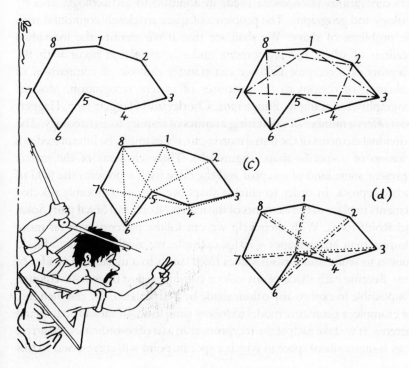

ated into triangles. Each two similar triangles are determined by two angles. If we then arrange the inscribed triangles into a sequence determined by a given sequence, we arrive at a sequence of values of angles which fulfil the demands of a uniform description. Another record can, for example, stem from the angles and from the ratios of the lengths of sides. We can also use other measurements if these are sufficient for the transfer of values. In this way we obtain a sequence of numerical values which represent the description of the shape of a chosen object.

8. Fourier's analysis was used in connection with the problems of description for the first time by E. S. Smirnov (1928) and later by other scholars (for example, Allsworth-Jones and Wilcock 1974, Lu 1965, Sneath 1967).

The position of the centre of gravity of an area and the values of Fourier's coefficients can also be determined with the help of machines such as harmonic analysers or computers.

9. Description by means of receptors. We shall devote more time to the problems of this method of description because it is closely connected not only with the problems studied by methods of pattern recognition but also with an important problem of illustration and evaluation of spatial relations between various phenomena used, in addition to archaeology, also by geology and geography. The problems of space are closely connected with the problems of shape. We shall see that if we identify the individual localities of where the phenomena under investigation occur with the receptors of a receptor field we can transfer the role of comparison of evaluation of regions to the processes of pattern recognition. Modern geography (for example, Bunge 1962, Chorley and Haggett 1967, Haggett 1965) offers a number of interesting avenues of enquiry to archaeology. The individual elements of the initial matrix can, for example, be interpreted as a notation of a specific shape (figure 15b). These elements of the matrix represent some kind of receptor and the table itself represents the field of such receptors. In order to enter a shape we can use randomly selected elements in place of the elements of the matrix (Rohlf and Sokal 1967, Sokal and Rohlf 1966). With their help we can follow patterns even far more complex than linear shapes – if, for example, we ascribe value 1 to black, value 0 to white and various values from 0 to 1 to a number of shades of grey. Because each shade of any colour is composed of three basic colours, it is possible to express any colour shade by a triple ratio. We can then use, for example, a geometric model to follow similarities of various shapes and patterns. If we take each of the receptors as an axis of co-ordinates, we arrive at an n-dimensional space in which a specific point will correspond to this

pattern. In this case description is given by a matrix. We assign the sequence of columns or lines to a matrix consisting of one line (column) to which the sequence of numbers corresponds (in the case of the shape in figure 15b this is as follows: 000100110110110010001100010001000110011, if we take the lines from left to right and from top to bottom). A shortened notation can be constructed in a similar way as with Method No. 3. As we have already stated, we can, in the same way, also render decoration formed by various colours or a different intensity of colour. By comparing the distances of a different point corresponding to a different pattern, their mutual similarity can be studied. We can thus distinguish, compare and evaluate the shapes and patterns of artefacts and also the spatial distribution of the phenomena investigated by archaeology.

A number of specific methods (Bunge 1962, Wilcock 1971), trend analysis (Sneath 1967) and, above all, the methods of pattern recognition are based on such types of shape description. The shape is studied by means of sequential chains (1 in contrast to 0 signifies a coincidence of the shape and receptor) which can then be fed into a computer and analysed. These sequences can be not only vertical or horizontal (columns or lines) but can also be applied in more complex instances such as curves. In order to follow curves, a method, the principle of which was explained under the name of wind-rose (figure 15) and which is also illustrated in figure 21, is used (see McCormick 1963).

10. Description by means of a matrix of differences. This method is highly developed in pattern recognition and is based on the possibilities provided by a field of receptors. The pattern (figure 22a) is converted into a sequence of 1s and 0s (figure 22b) – description by means of receptors – and on the basis of this a matrix of differences is constructed (figure 22c). In this matrix the value of each receptor is given as the difference between

Figure 21. Picture (b) illustrates the values of the individual axes of co-ordinates corresponding to the individual directions of the wind-rose in figure (a) (1–8), which we can employ to describe a curve of a shape. Source: McCormick 1963.

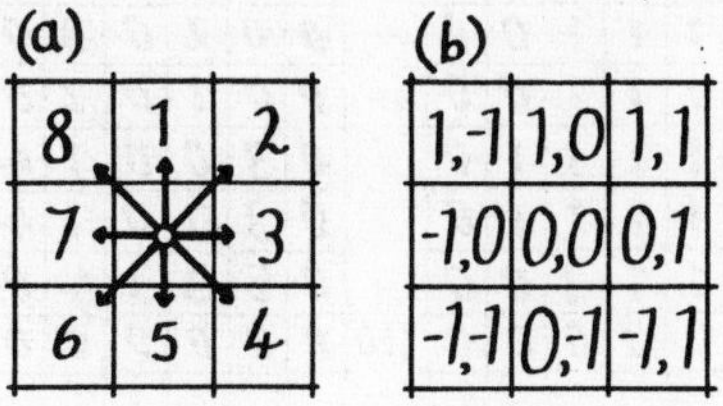

(a)

8	1	2
7	✳	3
6	5	4

(b)

1,-1	1,0	1,1
-1,0	0,0	0,1
-1,-1	0,-1	-1,1

the sum total of all adjoining receptors. The values for o receptors are not given.

Consequently, a specific form of curvature corresponds to a specific value – for example, 5 corresponds to a 90° angle, the sequence 3 corresponds to a straight line, etc. And because receptors inside the pattern bear a o value we obtain an outline – a shape.

There are many more highly complex and differentiated preconditions for establishing a local function. For example, we can take into consideration even the more distant receptors and the ratio ascribed to them is inverse to their distance.

II. Linguistic description. This is based on a classical description but individual stages of it are formalised. The description is based on a vocabulary of fragments (part of a shape; for details see below) and a vocabulary of places (placing fragments into an area). The description of each shape can then be rendered by a matrix of the type 'fragment × place'. Both sets of vocabulary are constructed purely mechanically without any subjective evaluation or a priori selection of ideal geometrical shapes, which can be the case when a classical description is applied. Consequently, description of individual shapes and their comparison and classification can also be carried out mechanically.

Since we do not know of a case in archaeology where this method would be used – despite its undeniable advantages – we shall attempt to show here

Figure 22. A given shape (a) can be described using receptors, expressed in terms of their presence (1) or absence (0) (figure b). Then, according to a formula, we can mark the local function of each of the receptors (figure c). In the present example, we can calculate the function of each square (receptor) by subtracting the number of neighbouring squares with the value of 1 (indicating presence) from the maximum possible value of 8.

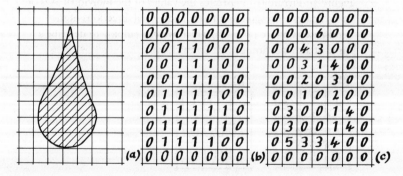

in a more detailed but still a simplified, way how such vocabulary sets are constructed (Arkadev and Braverman 1971):

(a) we start with inscription of the shape in a field of receptors (figure 23);

(b) we construct a 'window' in such a way that (1) the number of receptors is smaller than the total number of receptors in the field in which we investigate the shape and that (2) the number of receptors in columns would equal their number in lines; then to each of the receptors from the 'window' we assign a numerical value which must be highest in the middle and which gradually diminishes towards the edges (figure 24);

(c) we place the 'window' on the receptor field in such a way that its middle field overlaps with a receptor in the receptor field;

(d) to each position of the 'window' where its field overlaps with at least one of the receptors of the original receptor field (this is the

Figure 23. An illustration of a shape in a field of receptors.

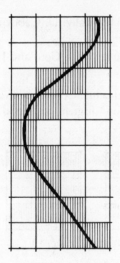

Figure 24. A field of receptors expressed as a 'window'.

1	1	1
1	2	1
1	1	1

field which records the shape) we ascribe a numerical value
which equals the total sum of the values of the window-
receptors which overlap with receptors of the shape;

(e) we select those fragments of the shapes covered by the window
which have the highest numerical value (in our case the
fragments shown in figure 25);

(f) the vocabulary set of places is constructed in such a way that we
provide a list of sectors in which the individual fragments can
join each other; in our case a two-term vocabulary set – up,
down – is sufficient;

(g) we construct the description by means of a matrix of the type
'fragment × place' (figure 26);

(h) in the case of a description of a whole class of shapes we proceed
as in steps c–e; the corresponding parts of the class and from the
fragments obtained in this way – which range from a specific
minimal value – we construct on the basis of their similarity
classes which then form a matrix of the type 'classes of fragments × places'.

Shapes can also be recorded purely mechanically. D. Gabor (1965) uses
holography for descriptive purposes.

Recently, H. L. Dibble and P. G. Chase (1981), J. Gero and J. Mazzullo

Figure 25. Fragments of shape with a highest numerical value,
obtained with the help of a 'window' diagram, applied to a shape
placed in a field of receptors.

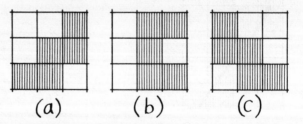

(a)   *(b)*   *(c)*

Figure 26. Matrix of a type 'fragment × location'.

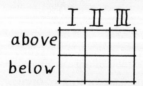

(1984), S. J. Shennan and J. D. Wilcock (1975) and J. A. Tyldesley, J. S. Johnson and S. R. Snape (1985) studied the problems of shapes.

The ideal method of a detailed description of a shape of an artefact – and we can formulate it now that we have outlined a number of methods – would be such a system of the basic elements of description (that is, those to which the shape is reduced) as would have the following qualities:

(a) it would be independent of the size of the shape;
(b) it would be independent of the position of the shape;
(c) the position of each basic element of the description in a shape would be strictly determined;
(d) in the cases of definition of size, position and orientation, the position of each element in a plane (or space) would be given;
(e) the position of individual elements in the plane could be reconstructed from the notation (entry);
(f) the difference between the shape described and the shape given by the description would be minimal;
(g) each two differing elements of description would have a different entry.

Conditions (d) and (g) indicate that changes in entry are proportionate to changes in position and, consequently, to changes in shape. The conditions (a) to (c) can be eliminated by selecting identical conditions or their descriptions can be adjusted in such a way that these categories would be identical for all the compared descriptions (Sneath 1967, Sokal and Rohlf 1966).

The methods of description quoted (apart from the classical description) provide a number of numerical values arranged either in a sequence or in a matrix. We can then follow the similarity of shapes on the basis of various coefficients of similarity providing that we always compare the same number of values. If we use a matrix of the type 'fragment × place' we can also ascertain the extent of overlapping with the help of Jaccard's coefficient. On the basis of the matrix of similarity or of the position in a space, the given shapes can then be classified.

Three-dimensional shapes can best be described on the basis of characteristic points either by locating their co-ordinates in space, or by establishing mutual relationships between them (for example, in anthropometry). Here we often come across practical problems stemming from the fact that it is difficult to establish sufficiently precise input data. It is a matter of practice, established usage and the purpose of a given description and classification to reduce the number of input data (and also the degree of their precision) in such a way that they yield sufficiently precise results. This problem is equally topical also in the case of two-dimensional shapes where we have to bear in mind the problem of the number, distribution and extent of the precise determination of the basic elements.

In certain specific cases (such as coloured maps and plans, ornament, etc.) we can use description by means of a receptor field if we identify the height with the colour shade.

An interesting problem in the study of shapes is posed by the surface-trend analysis which is well established in the construction of geological maps (Haggett 1965, Krumbein 1959, Merriam and Sneath 1966) and also used in numerical taxonomy (Sneath 1967). In the case of shapes the trend is understood to be an expansion of some of the parts, or, if need be, of the whole shape in relation to another shape. D'Arcy Thompson established transformation networks for investigation of different patterns (Thompson 1917). The shape on the basis of which the comparison is carried out is covered by a right-angled network (description by means of points of intersection). The network of the second shape comparable with the first shape is constructed in such a way that the lines of the networks are altered to correspond with the characteristic points of the second shape. In this way we obtain a transformed network which can then be compared with the right-angled network and which demonstrates graphically the trends in the changes of the shape. The distortions of diagrams can be measured numerically with the help of the coefficients of trend equations (figure 27). Further, we can determine the extent of similarity based on the comparison of trends. The analysis of trends of a surface is of special importance in the study of evolutionary sequences and can be used to determine the temporal seriation of phenomena (Bove 1981, Roper 1976).

The description of space

Space forms another major variable used in the description of archaeological material.

Apart from such data as orientation, stratification, etc., the classification according to location plays a most important role. No phenomenon can exist without its place of occurrence and every such place of occurrence is designated as a location. The spatial dimensions of location can vary with the attributes of a given object or feature. In archaeology, location can be identified with a findspot, a site, or, as the case may be, with a complex of sites. A region is then an aggregate of those locations in which the investigated object is represented; it is a class of locations.

When studying the mutual similarity of objects, the classification according to locations does not have any significance because the fact that two objects originate in the same location does not provide us with any information about their mutual similarity. It is therefore advisable to construct a special matrix of data when considering the relation of objects and space.

A matrix, in which the lines and columns can be interpreted as objects and location and the elements of the matrix can be interpreted as the presence or absence of a relationship (... it is present at a location...), forms the basic description of the spatial classification of objects.

If such a matrix is subjected to the procedures already quoted – those which study the link between objects – we obtain information about the mutual relationships between those objects which are found, to a lesser or greater extent, together (such dependencies can be interpreted as, for example, due to tradition, functional dependency, etc.)

When we study the mutual links between locations we do, in a sense, gather information concerned with the spatial classification of the objects

Figure 27. Relations between two-dimensional functions and their appropriate three-dimensional surfaces. Source: Haggett 1965: 273.

two-dimensional

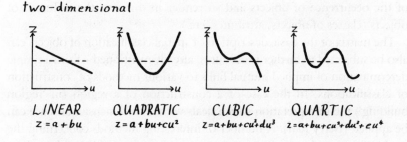

LINEAR
$z = a + bu$

QUADRATIC
$z = a + bu + cu^2$

CUBIC
$z = a + bu + cu^2 + du^3$

QUARTIC
$z = a + bu + cu^2 + du^2 + eu^4$

three-dimensional

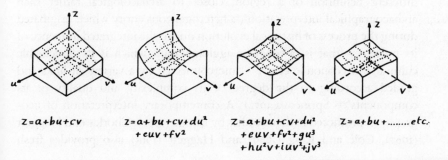

$z = a + bu + cv$

$z = a + bu + cv + du^2$
$+ euv + fv^2$

$z = a + bu + cv + du^2$
$+ euv + fv^2 + gu^3$
$+ hu^2v + iuv^2 + jv^3$

$z = a + bu + ... etc.$

under investigation. In this case we arrive at a formation of classes with spatial implications. In connection with the basic description of the objects we can determine the regions, not of objects, but of occurrence of these attributes. We can thus investigate, for example, the spread of a certain decorative element or of the raw material used.

In the case where the classification of objects on the grounds of a basic description has already been carried out we can construct a matrix of data of the type 'classes of objects × locations'. The conditions which we take into account while assigning locations to objects of a given class can be specified. For example, we can insist that all of the objects of a given class are present in each locality or that at least a certain number of objects of the given class is present. In a case where higher taxonomic units are concerned we can, in addition, assign a different measure of probability, depending on how many objects are included.

If we consider the number of individual objects (and, equally so, the classes of objects) in locations, we come to a self-evident conclusion that the sizes of locations can be compared according to the number of objects found in them. And if we continue to study this relative number we can eliminate the differences which are due to a different size of location. More importantly, we can also follow the borders, foci and dispersion of intensity of the occurrence of objects and so render in this way the diffusion of objects (classes of objects, attributes, etc.).

The matrix of the basic description of spatial classification of objects can also be subjected to further procedures, already mentioned – from a simple determination of implied mutual links to various methods of construction of classifications. In the case of a construction of a region (in 'region building') the interpretation which deals with an n-dimensional space can be applied (Berry 1961). A number of interesting methods concerning the study of regions has sprung up recently in a newly established branch of geography – so-called economic regionalisation. However, in this instance, the study of a region has a different aim and, consequently, there is a different definition of a region, closer to archaeological rather than archaeographical interpretation ('a heterogeneous entity which originated during the process of historical evolution due to the integrated influence of its nucleus – that is, a town or agglomeration which is its undeniable cultural and economic centre – interconnected by a variety of links and graded according to the degree of its complexity and quality of its components' – Šprincová 1972). A contemporary interpretation of geography as promoted in their studies by Bunge (1962), Chorley and Haggett (1967), Cole and King (1969) and Haggett (1965) also provides fresh inspiration for the study of archaeological phenomena in space. For example, locational analysis can investigate the spatial distribution of a phenomenon (Hägerstrand 1967) such as dispersal of farming in Europe (Ammerman and Cavalli-Sforza 1973, 1979).

If we identify individual locations with receptors, they can then be pictured in n-dimensional space, and if we adopt some other concepts (such as border and inner locality) we can convert the task of constructing, comparing and evaluating regions to the procedures of pattern recognition.

Finally, in regional studies we have, in many cases, to establish yet another parameter – time.

As far as spatial classification is concerned, we can investigate archaeological relationships (functional and structural) which go beyond the archaeographical field. The theoretical study of space with its concrete application has recently made great strides and practically developed into a new discipline – spatial archaeology. The collection of articles *Spatial Archaeology* edited by D. L. Clarke (1977) and Hodder and Orton's book *Spatial Analysis in Archaeology* (1976) have set the standards for this approach. Both books put forward new ideas at both the methodological and the theoretical level about the applications of spatial relationships in archaeology. Studies by Carr (1984), Hietala (1984), Hietala and Stevens (1977), Hillier *et al.* (1978), Hodder (1977, 1978a, b), Hodder and Orton (1976), Kent (1984), Kintigh and Ammerman (1982) and Simek (1987) also merit attention.

Seriation and time

Until now in our study we have not gone beyond the framework of the input table. We have considered nothing else but its data. However, the selection of suitable coefficients of similarity and methods of grouping is influenced by considerations other than the data contained in the table, since their power of inference can only be determined empirically. If further empirical observations are added to the table we arrive at the possibility of studying further relationships.

The basic problem facing archaeography is that of determining the chronology of material, its seriation. The basic empirical assumptions which would enable us to interpret the information contained in the table from the point of view of chronology are roughly as follows:

(a) the existence of functional evolution – functionally optimal objects are more recent than less optimal models;

(b) the existence of stylistic evolution – the evolution of style is characterised by certain common relationships (for example, a large number of attributes in the culminating phase of development);

(c) a chronological proximity of locations with identical or similar composition of artefacts (statistical typology – Bohmers 1963);

(d) the existence of parallelism – that is, typological evolution of various types of artefacts must be, in principle, similar;

(e) the existence of a causal relationship between the material, functional and formal similarity of artefacts and their temporal proximity;

(f) and, finally, the assumption that the attributes of an artefact are subject to gradual change.

These assumptions and their general application have enjoyed widespread attention (Almgren 1965–6, Angeli 1958, Bartra 1964, Dethlefsen and Deetz 1966, Eggers 1959, 1974, Ford 1954, Kameneckij, Maršak and Šer 1975, Kunst 1982, Meggers and Evans 1975, Read 1982, Sangmeister 1967, Schweizer 1969, West 1983–4, Whallon 1977). At the end of the 1960s and in the 1970s, studies concerned with these problems all strove to point out the possibilities brought about by developments in statistics, information technology and computerisation (Dunnell 1986, Gräslund 1974, Hodson 1980, Klejn 1978, 1982, Narr 1978a, Whallon and Brown 1982). Gräslund's critical analysis of typological methods originating in the North formed the basis for a more extensive discussion published in the *Norwegian Archaeological Review*. Klejn's and Narr's approach is even wider – they evaluate the development and the contemporary state of classification, typology and seriation in archaeology and discuss the meaning of the terms 'type' and 'class' and also the use of type archaeology as a tool of scientific systemisation on the one hand, and as a concept for expressing cultural norms on the other.

A whole series of specific techniques – from the simplest to the most complex – was developed in order to carry out seriation and we shall deal with some of them in this study. For example, it is presumed that, using proximity analysis, it is possible to express precisely the relationships of similarity between objects in one-dimensional space (figure 28). The sequence obtained in this can be seen as a basis for temporal analysis. Or the matrix. analysis is based on the last assumption mentioned above (f) (figure 29) (for example, Clarke 1965, 1968, Flanders 1960, Gelfand 1971, Matthews 1963, Tugby 1958, True and Matson 1970). The basis of most seriation techniques rests on the expectation of a lenticular trend in the number of artefacts of a certain group. The principle of this hypo thesis is simple (figure 30). Suppose that we have six groups of finds (1–6) and we know nothing about their temporal seriation. We establish that these finds contain artefacts of one functional group (for example, tombstones) which can be divided into five types (A, B, C, D, E). We then compile a percentage summary of the occurrence of these individual types within each of the layers (individual lines; figure 31). We then assume that the number of artefacts in the middle phase of their development is the greatest, while at the beginning and towards the end, it is smallest – that is, we obtain a

Figure 28. Measure of similarity expressed in different forms of space: (a) a measure of similarity of objects 1–6 expressed by distances between points in a three-dimensional space, (b) a measure of similarity of objects 1–6 expressed by distances in a two-dimensional space, (c) the same, expressed in a one-dimensional space, (d) the same, expressed sequentially (by unit distance) in a one-dimensional space.

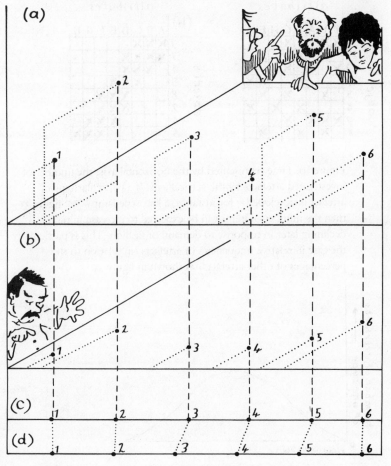

lenticular or 'battleship' shape. We then move the sequence of individual
layers in such a way as to arrive at a final sequence which would produce the
'battleship' sequences (figures 32 and 33).

It is obvious that in a case of numerous sets such manual manipulation
would be impossible and for this reason a number of mathematical
methods have been developed (Cowgill 1972, Djindjian 1985a, b, Dunnell

Figure 29. Assuming that attributes of objects change sequentially
with time, we can attempt to order objects into a sequence according
to the degree of change they undergo. This will enable us to proceed
from figure (a) to a sequence illustrated in figure (b) where the
sequence is 3, 7, 1, 5, 8, 2, 4, 6; or the reverse, because such ordering
will not reveal the direction of change. Source: Tugby 1965: 5.

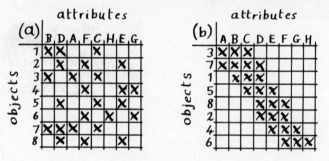

Figure 30. Time represented by the horizontal axis, the number of
investigated artefacts by the vertical axis. If a particular type of
artefact is developed – for instance, a kerosene lamp – see figure 33 –
then the number of items can be expected to increase initially,
declining later in response to demand or fashion. This is particularly
the case in relative frequencies of artefacts (in relation to the
percentages of other artefacts) as shown in figure 33.

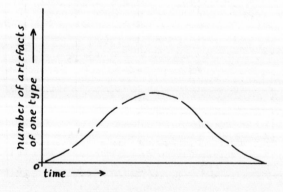

1970, Goldmann 1974a, b, 1979, Hole and Shaw 1967, Ihm 1977a, 1983, Johnson 1972, Kendall 1971, Laporte and Taillefer 1987, Marquardt 1978, Regnier 1977). In addition, heuristic techniques which evaluate the known temporal relations are also used for the purpose of seriation (Doran 1972).

However, let us return to our case in question (figure 31). In the case of the artefact 'type C' we have, at the same time, formed a typological series of

Figure 31. Initial phase of a chronological seriation. Numbers 1–6 represent undated assemblages, the mutual chronological links of which are unknown. Assemblages may consist of five types, each assemblage composed of different proportions of types.

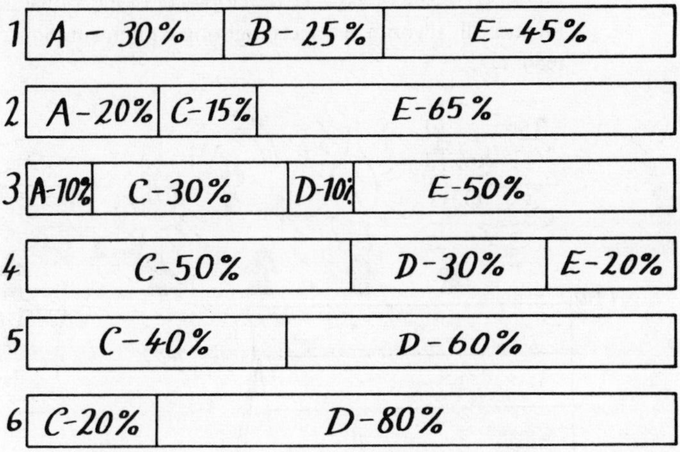

1	A – 30%	B – 25%	E – 45%
2	A – 20%	C – 15%	E – 65%
3	A – 10%	C – 30%	D – 10%	E – 50%
4	C – 50%	D – 30%	E – 20%
5	C – 40%	D – 60%
6	C – 20%	D – 80%

Figure 32. A final phase of seriation. This is based on the observation that the sum of all types in each chronological zone amounts to 100%, on the assumption that the percent zones will be similar, and, further, on the assumption that in the case of two chronological zones, frequencies of each type will follow an increasing or decreasing trend. The individual assemblages are then ordered according to these assumptions. In our particularly simple case, the chronological ordering does not differ from that shown in figure 31.

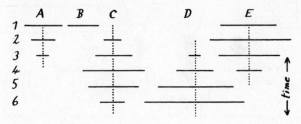

this type (similarly, see figure 34) – that is, we established a precise chronology which has temporal and genealogical meaning. Both forms of chronology (they are very often closely linked) have to be distinguished from one another. A genealogical chronology (for example, the affinity determined by common origin in biology) is an autochthonous chronology where individual typological sequences cannot merge or influence one another (figure 35a). In contrast, a temporal chronology of artefacts expressed by their typological sequences allows for both merging and influencing of two or more typological sequences (figure 35b). This is one of

Figure 33. A case of lens-like development of individual groups of functionally identical artefacts: lighting equipment. Source: Moberg 1969: 147.

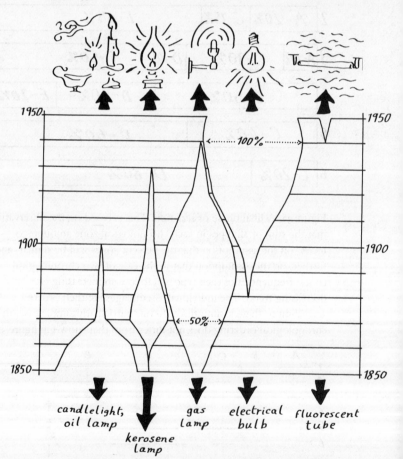

the reasons why, in archaeology, we have to exercise great care when studying hierarchical classifications, and why, if we adopt cluster or association techniques which combine temporal and spatial meanings, we cannot expect to arrive at unequivocal results.

Classification

Classification and the way it is applied has a deep influence on archaeology. The exponential growth of newly discovered artefacts and more exact methods of their description will exert greater and greater demands on classification. For this reason the problem of classification has to be evaluated in some detail.

Classification is one of the first prerequisites of learning itself and of science in general. This of course applies to archaeology as well. Classification permeates our lives and we take it totally for granted. And those people who make classification their *raison d'être* tend to go even further!

Figure 34. Seriation of stylistic changes of a particular type of gravestone from New England. Source: Deetz 1967: 34–5.

Linnaeus was so deeply immersed in classification that in his speech given in honour of the King's coronation he presented a systematic classification of kings. He also used classification to settle accounts with his friends or enemies. He gave names of his friends (Celsius, Cliffort, Rudbeck) to beautiful flowers and on unattractive flowers or animals he bestowed the names of his adversaries (Adanson, Heister, Siegesbeck). The French aesthete and natural scientist Georges Buffon got the worst of the deal – it is the toad (*Bufo bufo*) which bears his name. Classification also dominated D. I. Mendeleev's life – he classified books, offprints, furniture and, of course, chemical elements.

Our 'natural' everyday world is formed by classification. This stems from arranging objects, things, into a nomenclature. The crucial role of classification in our lives becomes obvious only when the capacity to classify is impaired due to mental disease. The problem of classification was illustrated, for example, by A. R. Lurija's expedition to Uzbekistan in the 1930s. The Uzbek shepherds classified objects according to their use in the context of different activities. The initial classifications are determined on the basis of the objects' immediate relation to activity, to which they are connected through their function. It is only later that they are described and, consequently, divided with the help of binary oppositions.

Aristotelian classification uses a similar technique. However, it systematises the selection of attributes which was more or less arbitrary in the mythological world. Philosophy culminates in the system of universal categories. To these a hierarchy of entities according to the degree of their universality is subordinated and in this way a hierarchy of attributes is constructed.

Linnaeus' classification represents a kind of hybrid – its species, genera, classes, etc. are formed on the basis of universality. However, the attributes which characterise each taxon are real in that they are based on external, observable similarity, and groups are not always created by the dual system of description.

Darwinian classification established a different principle – division

Figure 35. Genealogical (a) and typological (b) succession of artefacts.

(a)   (b)

according to genetic affinity: simple external similarity was not enough. For example, the rabbit had to be taken out of the category of rodents because it had kept its origin secret. This leads us back to one of the oldest classifications – genealogical classification. The Spanish expression for a nobleman – *hidalgo* – can serve as a useful example. It originated from *hijo de algo* – 'a son of somebody'. The whole basis of Darwinian classification, systematisation and taxonomy rests on the simple fact that there is no inter-species cross-breeding. This, however, also sets the limits of their applicability.

The botanist M. Adanson, who antedated Darwin, understood classification differently. His interpretation has been found to be relevant only now – 150 years later. Adanson saw the flora of Guinea as an enormous chaos, impossible to cram into the usual pigeon-holes. He saw the selection of characteristic attributes, specifying individual taxa, as arbitrary and therefore suggested a classification which would not be based on a limited selection of attributes but would take into account all attributes. After all, this had been a valid technique even before Adanson.

It is because Linnaeus had known his flora so intimately that he selected only certain attributes for taxa. He deemed taxa to be natural, created by God, or – more precisely – he considered that the appropriate attributes were selected by God himself. Adanson was far ahead of his time and it was impossible to develop his scheme because of the enormous amount of work this would involve. The problem surfaced again in the 1950s with the developments in microbiology. In microbiology we come across a whole number of morphological attributes, but, in addition, there are also attributes of a chemical nature which do not lend themselves to systemisation. Moreover, it is only with great difficulty that evolution can be followed in this area and, finally, more than anywhere else, we come across here the dependence on human needs and intentions. This being the situation, it was necessary to put classification on a new footing and gradually create new disciplines called numerical taxonomy and automatic classification.

It was not only Adanson who elaborated new approaches to classification; there were also others. The first breakthrough as far as the old type of classification was concerned was achieved by bureaucrats. They improved on the usual criterion for advancement in service – the number of years served – by multiplying certain years (for example, those spent in the war) by a specific coefficient. So a situation could have arisen whereby some lucky soul could have been serving in the office before he was even born! A similar method was used to create indices which would unify a number of incomplete data (anthropometric indices).

Another problem was pointed out in the 1920s by E. S. Smirnov, with his principle of congregation. According to Smirnov a group includes objects which resemble each other more than any other object not belonging to the group. At the same time it became obvious that many taxa in the natural sciences could not be characterised by one attribute only or even by a larger number of attributes which would remain constant. Such polythetic taxa can be defined only by a number of attributes and each individual belonging to the taxon must possess the majority of them. In a similar way, Wittgenstein arrived at the description of family resemblance – family resemblance reflects a chain resemblance, where each two neighbouring segments of the chain resemble each other in the majority of attributes; however, the first and the last segments of the chain do not share any common attribute. In this way a reality, not subjected to the conventional requirements of classification, is revealed. Librarians also came across similar problems. In the old classification of monastery libraries the section miscellaneous became larger and larger and even the Prussian Royal Library Regulations could not cope with it. One of the first modern classificatory systems was Dewey's system of classification and later decimal classification, which was notable for its capacity for detailed simultaneous sub-division and the creation of new units.

However, it is R. S. Ranganathan who can be credited with the first wholly untraditional system of classification. Ranganathan was inspired by Meccano, the toy construction system for children which enables one to construct a great number of configurations from a few basic parts due to their compatibility. Anything we want to consider can be described (but not divided) by a few basic categories. (Ranganathan gives five.) Every category is then separated into sub-categories. If we are then in search of information, or a book, we can specify what we are looking for by a sequential chain of individual sub-categories, and because the librarian has almost certainly specified the book in the same way, we can usually find it. In this way we arrive quickly and safely at what we want, but, basically, there is an absence of any kind of classification, because it reflects nothing more than the organisation of our requirements.

Let us return to our table, however, which we used in the earlier calculations.

We gradually progressed from the relationship of two columns of the table to the investigation of relationships between more than two columns (and, of course, rows). Let us establish a concept of similarity in a class of elements, which is equal to the similarity of all elements of this class. The value of mutual similarity of a two-object class then equals the value of similarity of these objects, and the value of mutual similarity of a class with more than two elements can be defined, for example, as an arithmetic average of values of similarity between all possible pairs of this class.

It is obvious that classes of objects which possess a great degree of mutual similarity have also a greater information value and we can, therefore, on the basis of attributes of one object, ascertain with corresponding probability the attributes of another object, about which we know only that it belongs to the same class.

On this basis we can attempt to reconstruct and reduce our input table in such a way that it is, as far as possible, simplified but at the same time contains a large amount of the original information. This makes systematic and organisational sense, which helps us to perceive patterns in seemingly disparate data. But, at the same time, there is yet another, deeper meaning to all this. As Aristotle said, 'we recognise things only as far as there is unity, uniformity and universality'. We can, therefore, suppose that if we compare objects according to their similarity this external similarity will, at the same time, be a sign of some deeper links, for example, genetic, causal or temporal or, in the case of attributes, that it will be symptomatic of factors which influence the individual attributes. For the present we shall consider only the formal possibilities provided by operations which can be carried out within the framework of the table without analysing the content of such operations.

How should such a reorganisation of the table be carried out? Let us formulate this demand at a different level. Our task will only be achieved if we can construct such sub-classes of the objects of this table which would fulfil the following demands:

(a) the elements of the sub-classes would all be the objects under consideration;

(b) the individual sub-classes would possess the maximum value of mutual similarity;

(c) each object would be an element in one sub-class only.

Every one of the sub-classes created in this way can then be subjected to the same procedure and in this way we would arrive at a descending sequence of classifications which ends with individual objects of the initial table. However, in practice, condition 'c' often affects the lower level of similarity of the sub-classes. This is why we often subordinate this condition to condition 'c_1' which demands that individual sub-classes should have the smallest possible number of objects in common.

In order to establish classifications which would form such sub-classes, called clusters of objects or associations of attributes (Cowgill 1982), many methods were developed which differ in their techniques and conditions. Let us choose one of the simplest techniques of cluster analysis and demonstrate graphically the method of cluster formation. Let us convert the input table (figure 36) by means of the simple matching coefficient into a table of similarity (figure 37). We take the highest value of similarity appearing in the table – e.g. the value 1 (each object is identical with itself = 100%). We thus obtain the list of all objects. We then select the next highest value of similarity (in this case 75%), which is met satisfactorily by similarity of objects (A, B) and, naturally, by the one-element classes such as C, D, E and F. The next level of similarity, 50%, is fulfilled by the classes, A, B, D, E,

Figure 36. An initial data input table with four rows and six columns.

	1	2	3	4
A	1	1	1	1
B	0	1	1	1
C	0	0	0	1
D	0	0	1	0
E	0	1	0	0
F	1	0	0	0

Figure 37. A table of similarity created by applying the simple correlation coefficient to data in the table in figure 36.

	A	B	C	D	E	F
A	1					
B	¾	1				
C	¼	¼	1			
D	¼	½	½	1		
E	¼	½	½	½	1	
F	¼	0	½	½	½	1

G and F and the classes A, B, C, D, E and F, reaching a 25% level. On this basis, a dendrogram (figure 38) can be constructed, giving us a graphic representation of these relationships.

For the application of cluster analysis in archaeology, see Johnson (1972), Aldenderfer (1982), Aldenderfer and Blashfield (1978) and Christenson and Read (1978).

We shall again mention the geometrical representation with the help of which objects can be depicted as points in space and where the distances between the points correspond to the degree of similarity of the objects. In a similar way the task of cluster determination can be converted into a task of defining the points nearest to each other.

Figure 28 will show us in a hypothetical case how the loss of a dimension leads to a simplification of mutual relations between objects (given by the distance in space) but, at the same time, also leads to changes in their information value. The ratio of distance 1, 2 to the distance 1, 3 is very different, especially in figure 28a and, above all, in figure 28c. This method is similar to the cluster formation method used in proximity analysis (multi-dimensional scaling, Kruskal 1971, Sibson 1977), which is based on conversion of similarities into distance and formation of optimal configuration of points in a space with the smallest possible number of dimensions.

Classification of objects can also be carried out by means of the 'q' technique of factor analysis, but the 'r' technique, which is used to group individual attributes of objects into one factor is also convenient. The concept of factor is based on the supposition that if certain attributes are closely connected then it is possible to interpret attributes as a manifestation of yet another attribute – a factor, which is relegated into the

Figure 38. A dendrogram created on the basis of tables in figures 36 and 37, expressing the succession of individual objects, which can also act as a hypothesis for the testing of genetic or chronological succession (F evolves independently, other objects have a common base, from which they diverge).

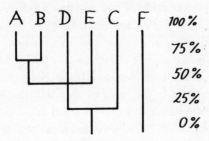

background and cannot be observed directly but which can have a causal relationship with the attributes which are observable. Factor analysis is, therefore, of crucial importance in cases where observations cannot be carried out. It is a kind of hypothesis on the structure of attributes whereby we construct a new matrix of data – 'objects x factors' – which arises as a result of the reduction of non-essential information. However, the meaning of a concrete factor depends on the interpretation of its content. Consequently, if we construct a correlative matrix of factors their inter-correlations can be explained by means of a more universal factor. This process can then be repeated again. Factor analysis thus reduces, structures, and classifies, the input data. Factor analysis has been applied in archae-ology by many scholars: Sackett (1967), Rowlett and Pollnac (1971), Vierra and Carlson (1981), Christenson and Read (1977, 1978).

The relationship between a larger number of columns and lines is studied above all by means of multivariate statistical techniques (for example, Spaulding 1953, 1978, Benfer and Benfer 1981, Redman 1978, Doluhanov and Kozłowski 1980). Multiple regression analysis estimates the value of one column on the basis of knowledge of values of a greater number of columns (in archaeology, see for example, Longacre 1964). A. C. Spaulding (1953, 1978) searches, with the help of statistics, for positive, non-random attribute associations. Multiple correlation analysis studies the means of dependence of one column on the values of several columns. Discriminant analysis assigns the columns into groups determined in advance. Numerical taxonomy, which in its wider interpretation extends beyond the framework of statistics, provides us with a whole complex of methods of classification (Sneath and Sokal 1973, Kronenfeld 1985). A survey of classification techniques is provided by Voorrips (1985).

The units which have been formed can be either monothetic or polythe-tic. Monothetic units are those where we have a set of attributes common to all the objects which form the elements of this set. However, such a set of attributes is sometimes impossible to find. If we consider that the elements C to E (figure 36) form one group we later come to the conclusion that they do not, in fact, possess a common attribute and that this polythetic group is characterised by the fact that the percentage of similarity of its elements is 50%, whilst each of the attributes occurs only once in each element.

We thus arrive again at the concept of classification itself which was the standard conceptual form in the past, but which has been preserved in archaeology up to the present. On the basis of the Aristotelian type of classification we class objects in such a way that we select a specific attribute and deem it to be a basic one. With its help we divide all objects into two groups. Within each group we always select another attribute which leads to a further division of the group. We can continue in this way until we reach a final division into individual elements. It is obvious that if the attributes are selected in a responsible fashion they thoroughly classify the objects and such classification cannot be faulted as far as its formal aspect is concerned. However, the selection of attributes is debatable. This objection pales somewhat if we consider that the classification process is usually an additive one – classes are established intuitively on the basis of similarity. We then search for attributes which would separate them from each other. An example of such classification is the classical diagnostic key which assigns objects into groups established in advance. As an example here we shall use the key (figure 39) designed for defining the objects in our example in figure 36. The method of construction and evaluation of monothetic keys is shown, for example, by R. Jičín, Z. Pilous and Z. Vašíček (1969). The keys of polythetic groups are far more complex.

People in non-literate societies, as Lévi-Strauss (1962) has shown, construct their classification on a similar basis. This served as a stimulus for R. Whallon, Jr (1972), to set up an experiment whereby he reconstructed the classification of artefacts according to principles similar to those used by their makers. It follows that in archaeological classification, two basic approaches are possible.

(a) Typologies are constructed according to the morphological, technological and functional similarity of individual artefacts. It is assumed that other social phenomena are causally connected with this typology.

(b) We try to reconstruct a typology that resembles the classifi-

Figure 39. A diagnostic monotypic key. Let us select any object from the range described in figure 36. Let us determine the presence or absence of attribute 4, grouping it accordingly into the range of typological A–C (present) or D–E (absent). Let us then determine the presence/absence of attribute 3. If it is absent, the object belongs to type C.

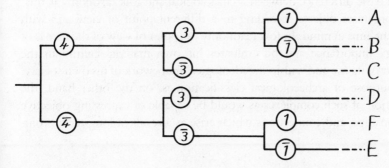

cation developed by the original makers and users of the
artefacts. There is no doubt that such classifications did exist;
we can observe them in contemporary primitive societies.
We also have to be aware of the fact that the term 'original makers and users'
is very wide. It embraces too many people differentiated in time, space and
social position. J. P. White and D. H. Thomas have drawn attention to this
problem, noting variations in the conceptual definition of artefacts ranging
with time, space and persons concerned (White and Thomas 1972).

Even though both of the above mentioned approaches are different this
does not mean that they are mutually exclusive. If, for example, a fish
expressed its opinions on the classification of fish it would, no doubt, be
very important and instructive as far as ichthyologists were concerned.
However, its influence on ichthyological classification would be minimal.
In this way we would have obtained knowledge about fish as such, but not
about the classification of fish. In many instances we understand the
description, similarities or differences of artefacts quite differently from
their makers. In extreme cases we can be unaware of major similarities just
as the people who produced the artefacts might have been. It is probable
that the makers paid greater attention to functional attributes than to
morphological attributes whilst, out of necessity, we have to stress the latter
group. Compare, for example, extremely detailed archaeographical description and classification of Palaeolithic leaf-shaped spear tips (Allsworth-
Jones and Wilcock 1974) with the much less rigid contemporary folk
taxonomy of New Guinea. The latter divides similar tools according to two
basic characteristics: edge-form and tool size, where the functional edge of
the tools is of a primary, and the size of a secondary, importance. However,
it disregards such important technological differentiation as the difference
between flakes and cores (White and Thomas 1972).

From ethnology we know of many examples of folk taxonomy and we
know that their principles, selection of attributes and establishing of their
values differ basically from the methods of modern classification (Lévi-
Strauss 1962).

The basic difference between archaeological and folk taxonomy is this:
each organises objects according to a different point of view and with
different aims in mind. In folk taxonomy the point of view of the user is of
primary importance and he evaluates his own material culture in the
context of its use and within the ideological framework of his own society.
The purpose of archaeological classification is, on the other hand, the
formation of such complexes as would be capable of expressing objective
relationships, and connections which arise as a result of long-term evolu-

tion and which are the consequences of changes beyond the comprehension of the original users, because such changes were outside the temporal and spatial scope of their experience.

Both these types of classification describe, therefore, quite different structures, which does not mean, however, that they are irreconcilable. In summary, we cannot make direct correlations between the views of a prehistoric maker and the fact that the type we have defined represents a certain norm, standard or mental pattern (Deetz's definition of a type, Deetz 1967).

We should also mention those typological classifications which are fairly frequent in archaeology, bearing in mind the range of meanings conveyed by the archaeological notion of 'type': summary equivalent of (1) a taxon, (2) a type proper, (3) a typical individual and (4) a classificatory unit as a whole. As often in archaeology, the definitions of type and of typology are not one and the same. The question what is a type is strictly unanswerable (Cowen 1969). A long time ago, when the concept of type was created, two models stood at its cradle, and because they have never been analysed, those two models are still in force. On the one hand there is the conception which has been the norm in other scientific specialisms since antiquity: for example, the typology of character (the irascible, the phlegmatic, etc.). In this case one divides a particular population according to a relatively small number of common attributes. In an extreme case it can even be based on a

Figure 40. A division of population of attributes by axes expressing the intensity of selected attributes. In this example, the horizontal axis expresses the degree of hardness, the vertical axis expresses size.

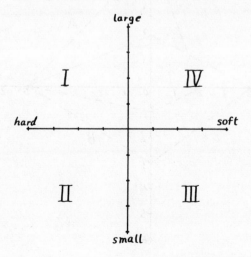

single attribute (monotypic scheme) or on polarity of two attributes (bipolar scheme). A typology of attributes based on a greater number of oppositions (polytypic scheme) is more realistic, the most common being typology stemming from two oppositions (figure 40). According to this scheme we arrive at four types (I – hard and large, II – hard and small, III – small and soft and IV – large and soft). Since it is only on rare occasions that we can assign an individual to a specific type, we can, bearing in mind the grading of individual oppositions, also study the more concrete form of an individual that had been evaluated in terms of such oppositions (figure 41). When a greater number of attributes is used, typology changes into classification.

The second basic idea in the creation of types is the Darwinian idea, used by Montelius, of the evolution of forms, which orders types into typologi-

Figure 41. In this example, every arm of the axis issuing from its point of intersection (o) denotes a single attribute, and the distance from o corresponds to the intensity of the attribute. Each object under investigation can be described in terms of a quadrangle drawn by connecting the points on the axes, which indicate the intensity of the attributes of an object. The ratio of areas of such quadrangles is then equal to the degree of similarity of the corresponding object.

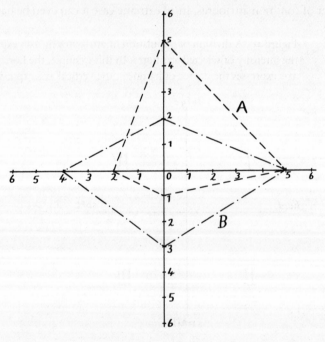

cal sets. It supposes that types are chronologically linked to themselves. American archaeology, of course, is inclined rather to the spatial interpretation of types; this may be a result of the relatively slight time depth of American prehistory and the enormous physical area. If one defines an association or cluster as a type on the basis of similarity in a greater number of attributes (e.g. Spaulding 1953), misunderstandings can easily occur because units formulated in this way do not have a previously defined interpretation in temporal, spatial or functional terms.

The choice of appropriate coefficients of similarity depends largely on the nature of the input data. The same applies to selecting a method of classification. General problems of archaeological classification have been covered by W. Y. Adams (1988), J. N Hill and R. K. Evans (1972) and by contributors to R. Whallon and J. A. Brown (1982). C. Cullberg has attempted to apply the theory of graphs as an aid to classification (Cullberg 1968), a method subsequently discussed in the pages of the *Norwegian Archaeological Review* (Voss, Malmer and Cullberg). The comparison of intuitive, impressionistic and automatic classification has been carried out by B. Solberg (1986). The problem of classification was also studied in detail by a group of Leningrad archaeologists, linguists and scientists towards the end of the 1970s (Klejn 1979, 1982) as well as by J.-C. Gardin in his monograph *Une archéologie théorique*; an exhaustive survey of approaches to the methodology of classification in the United States has been carried out by R. Vossen (1970).

Apart from attributes, the matrix of description can also contain the description of mutual relations between objects. The table can contain more than one relationship, and can also record more than one value for each relationship. Such data can be combined with the attributes. The data contained in the table can then be analysed by the methods we have already described.

Thus far we have always referred to the basic matrix (figure 5) in which rows are interpreted as objects and their characteristics or relations are studied. Not only individual artefacts but also their groupings can be considered to be objects. However, in such a case, characterisation becomes somewhat more complex because we have to consider the presence of attributes as probable, rather than certain (for example, the attribute 'black' can belong to only 90% of the objects included in the taxon). The table, therefore, has also to include the concept of probability – the probability of both rows and columns and also of individual data – elements of the table. This enables us to elaborate and evaluate further the information we thus obtained. Apart from the artefacts themselves we can, from this table, study their groups. With the help of artefacts, archaeologists can also study broader entities of a more abstract nature, such as events, or processes. They can all be investigated in a similar way: all such abstract entities can be divided in archaeology into several basic trajectories, such as time, space, situation, activities, and so on. If we take into account the possible mutual relations of these trajectories, we obtain information which can be expressed as a matrix of data and which, at the same time, is itself a method of analysis of archaeological material (Malina 1977: 25).

Types, groups, patterns and all other statements about the material under investigation are, at the same time, also hypotheses which can be tested statistically. With the help of statistics, we are in a position to investigate sets of events, consider the optimal size of the sample and decide whether the data are interdependent or not. Moreover, we can use statistical means to test hypotheses and to construct chronological sequences. (Eggert et al. 1980). Finally, we can also apply statistical methods to the reconstruction of causal relationships.

Fortunately for us, we have now left the pioneer times of statistics in archaeology behind. A whole range of books, explicitly concerned with the application of statistics and mathematics to archaeology, now exists (Carr 1985, Doran and Hodson 1975, Ihm 1978, Moscati 1987, Orton 1982, Richards and Ryan 1985, Voorrips 1985), while the range of methods and procedures appropriate to the solving of archaeological problems is becoming standardised.

The development of computer technology has simplified the task significantly, while the exponential growth of new archaeological material, clamouring for analysis, as well as the more exacting demands placed on method and analysis by the new theoretical concepts, make the statistical approach and the use of the computer all but inevitable. Renfrew has argued that the days of the innumerate are numbered. On the history and future of these methods, see Clark and Stafford (1982), Cowgill (1986) and Doran (1986).

A framework for basic information processing

Below, we shall try to summarise all the previous approaches into some kind of ideal six-phase scheme according to their sequence.

I Finds from one temporal layer are divided into categories of artefact (axes, daggers, swords, pots, etc.). The individual objects are grouped into clusters or associations and the proportion of categories and clusters (associations) within individual sites is established per layer (figure 42).

II Seriation of individual chronological layers is carried out (figure 32).

III On the basis of steps I and II typological series of individual types of artefacts are constructed (for example, figure 34).

IV Investigation of mutual relations of individual typological chains (divergence, convergence, splitting, merging, oscillation, parallels; figures 43, 44) is carried out.

V Investigation of spatial distribution, clusters, associations and

Figure 42. Structure of an assemblage: categories of artefacts (A, B, C); clusters of artefacts (a, b, c, d).

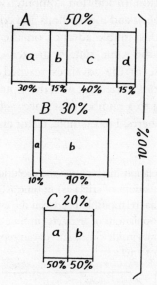

Figure 43. Different types of relationships which can occur between artefacts in a chronological perspective: (a) parallel, (b) divergent, (c) convergent, (d) nucleating, (e) merging, (f) oscillating.

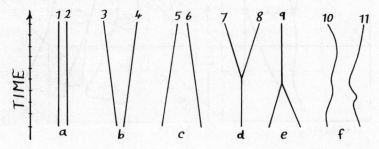

types of artefacts and their mutual ratio (figure 44a) is carried out as well as spatial analysis. The construction in time and space of entities of homogeneous localities (cultures and higher entities; figure 44b) takes place.

VI Finally, relationships between cultures and further entities (tragectories) are investigated.

This chapter was devoted solely to a summary of the techniques of description and classification. All of them have, to a lesser or greater extent, been used in the past and they continue to be used also at present. Exact formulation raises the possibility of employing computerisation without which it would be impossible to study in depth the increasing amount of archaeological material and information. In addition, computerisation also enables suppositions to be made explicit and the methods and conclusions reached to be checked. This is a favourable advance on the methods hitherto used in archaeology. At the same time a greater degree of abstraction enables us to make use of the advances reached in other sciences, since the numerous operations carried out with the input data and the methods employed are common to a number of sciences – that is, to their descriptive and classificatory spheres. For example, factor analysis has

Figure 44. (A): A mutual relationship between the evolution of individual artefacts (or populations of artefacts) in time according to their similarity. (B): A mutual relationship betyween the evolution of individual artefacts (or populations of artefacts) in time according to their spatial location. Points inside closed curves can represent individual types or clusters of artefacts.

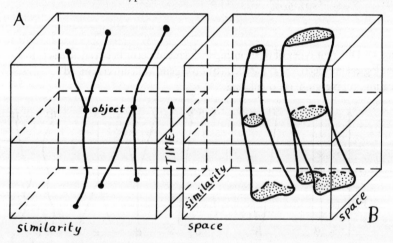

its origin in psychology and the techniques of clustering can be traced back to biology.

We started our account with thoughts on artefacts and their attributes. This formed the basis for the formulation of a number of empirical concepts, such as concrete clusters, associations, typological sequences, temporal seriation and, partly, also the concepts of culture and diffusion. The next stage will consist of a shift from empirical to theoretical concepts and hypotheses. However, even here, we can make use of the same techniques we have described so far – albeit on a different, more abstract level. Consequently, the matrix in figure 5 forms the basis for all our hypotheses, if these are, indeed, capable of being formulated within the framework of attributes and entities.

7   Archaeological hypotheses

'Good morning, Mr Kohn.'
'Sorry, have we met before?'
'We haven't, but you've come up in my calculations.'

A Jewish anecdote

The construction and verification of hypotheses

In every social science there is always a contrast between the empirical and the theoretical level of enquiry. In cultural anthropology this difference is expressed by the "emic–etic" distinction: emic operating from concepts derived directly from the group under study, etic describing the group by means of concepts created by the researcher (Pike 1967, Waterhouse 1974, Feleppa 1986). This contrast is also felt in archaeology, and is often explicitly expressed, and, what is even more important, it is associated with different theories and research methods: C. Ankel and R. Gundlach (1969), Moberg (1969: 41–3, 1976), Rouse (1973: 23, 25–6), Gardin (1979: 134–43), Klejn (1981).

On the basis of archaeological material, ordered through description, classification, and seriation, we are creating specific notions, and thus proceed from archaeography to archaeology and prehistory. This method enables us to describe entities which are basically unobservable and, therefore, we have to be cautious when choosing methods to construct, verify and characterise our observations and statements.

In the case of a hypothesis there is a tendency towards generalisation and abstraction. It would seem that the purpose of a hypothesis and similar theoretical notions is nothing more than the adoption of a level of abstraction which would allow us to summarise all the facts, which at the original level of resolution appear too fragmentary and without any patterning. This shorthand description (in T. Parson's words) can, of course, be subjected to descriptions at more abstract levels.

The shorthand description must be compatible with the 'initial' description, i.e. it must be compatible with all the available data on the subject. The derivation of working hypotheses and their subsequent testing and verification based on the analysis of data is called the hypothetico-deductive method.

In creating hypotheses, we usually adopt the following procedure.
- (a) We articulate a preliminary working definition of the problem/ subject.
- (b) We state the dimensions of the problem/subject – by which we mean groups of characteristic features which define the subject under consideration. Each of the possible features belongs to one of these dimensions. In archaeology it is possible to obtain these by a very general method, e.g. by asking questions that relate to dimensions such as the following:
  1 Who? (Subject)
  2 What? (Object)
  3 Where? (Space)
  4 When? (Time)
  5 Why? What for? (Purpose)
  6 By what means? (Means)
  7 How? (Process).
- (c) In response to these questions, we can then make a detailed list of features such as:
  1 groupings of inhabitants according to their age, sex and descent;
  2 description of categories, clusters and associations of artefacts;
  3 description of the area under consideration;
  4 description of the time under consideration;
  5 description of the type of transport, the type of production or hunt, and rituals;
  6 description of the kinds of material used;
  7 description of the technology.

It is further necessary to define the relationships within each category, by subdividing the variables and looking for the possibilities of measuring their scope and intensity.
- (d) Then we must find those empirical features by which individual dimensions are to be found in the existing archaeological record, i.e. indicators of those features. For example, matrilocality is often indicated by a certain frequency distribution of certain stylistic elements of the ceramics in the settlement; a given frequency distribution of certain artefacts is an indicator of a certain kind of technology, etc. Finally we must make a list of selected indicators which satisfactorily defines the subject under consideration.

One of the advantages of this method, i.e. breaking up the subject/ problem into indicators, is the possibility of finding to what extent our conclusions agree with those of other researchers. 'An ideal solution would be to carry out a systematic analysis of all the notions and definitions in literature in order to arrive at a "right" definition and an "appropriate" term' (Stoetzel and Lazarsfeld 1965). In any case, this approach makes it posssible to describe exactly the differences between different notions and to compare them.

As an example of relationships among different dimensions, indicators and selected indicators, let us mention the problems involved in the study of religion. We will use this example to point out close links among those sciences which study religion, i.e. history, prehistory, anthropology, and sociology. Another reason for such investigation is the fact that ritual objects are a large and important part of the existing archaeological material.

C. Y. Glock, a sociologist of religion, notes four dimensions involved (in the brackets are some of the indicators):

1 the dimension of experience (emotions, experiences, spiritual and religious life);
2 the dimension of the ritual (cults, prayers, liturgy, denominations, etc.);
3 the dimension of ideology (faith, belief, one's views on nature, deity and eternity);
4 the dimension of consequence (relationships among people resulting from other dimensions) (Glock 1965).

Formulating these dimensions will alone restructure our knowledge, for example, by the simple fact that we attribute to each dimension the same significance in the system. What we must do next is to find the right indicators, selected indicators, and define them so that they can be universally used in the study of the religion. In the case of prehistoric studies it is only the dimension of ritual which is available for research: all the others can be studied only from secondary, auxiliary sources, and often not at all.

The indicators can be further divided into quantitative and qualitative ones, that is, the extent and the type of religion, e.g. animism, totemism, etc. In the case of quantitative features it is possible to arrange them according to their intensity.

Let us return to religion. W. J. Goode examined religious systems according to five categories:

1 religious personnel with two modes of variation:
    (a) the extent of formal religious training
    (b) the extent of identification of the secular with the sacred leaders and followers;
2 societal matrix:
    (a) rationality
    (b) self-interest
    (c) universalism
    (d) functional specificity
    (e) impersonality of daily social interaction: features (a) to (e) can further be subdivided into rural and municipal communities;
3 sacred entities:
    variation from highly abstract entities to concrete ones;
4 ritual:
    the extent to which it has been elaborated and the degree of its symbolism;
5 belief:
    its expression in relationship to soul, ritual, creation myths, etc. (Goode 1951: 227–36).

On the basis of these categories it is possible to characterise all kinds of religious systems.

When it comes to classifying and characterising religious indicators in the prehistoric material, Goode's categories are more useful than Glock's categories. This is mainly due to the nature of Glock's work, which is sociological, especially when studying religion, while Goode's work is more of an ethnographical and classifying nature. He investigates religious communities rather than religion: his is not a direct study of the religious systems themselves.

On the basis of working definitions, dimensions, features and indicators we can then describe the investigated phenomena. To give a simple example, let us consider three dimensions only and within each of them only those features which are mutually comparable for their intensity. Thus we shall have a three-dimensional space in which we can define the phenomena under consideration, taking into account their similarities (as we have shown in the survey of archaeological description). If we place the events under investigation into a spatial perspective, it will enable us to assess their mutual similarity (compare figure 7).

When testing a hypothesis, having established its dimensions, features and indicators, we can look for the extent to which the indicators are present in the studied material and thus prove or disprove its validity. When some of the indicators are incompatible, we have to correct, rewrite, or even abandon it.

Let us quote one example. In his work on Broken K Pueblo, J. N. Hill writes that during his excavation work there were obvious differences found in various rooms of the pueblo. He examined these differences from the point of view of their function and the behaviour of their inhabitants. Then he gave a detailed description and statistical account of all the rooms and came to the conclusion that there were two main types of rooms at the pueblo as well as several specific ones.

He formulated several hypotheses about the function of these rooms based on the comparison with the present-day ones. These were further tested on the assumption that different functions of the rooms will correspond to different kinds and types of artefacts and similar objects found in them. There were sixteen possibilities. The results confirmed the hypothesis that there was a connection between different types of rooms and their function as living, storing or ceremonial place. Those assumptions (of the sixteen) which were not confirmed were important as well because they supplied new information. They could not be confirmëd by the ethnographical research. To explain them Hill formulated further hypotheses, defined their archaeological indicators and continued to test them.

This is the author's conclusion:

It is evident, then, that archaeology can contribute information of its own: propositions can be generated and tested, and a great many things can be learned that have not previously been known or speculated about before. In addition to making use of available ethnographic evidence, it is possible to discover new information that will be of use to ethnographers and social anthropologists. This general methodology of generating and testing propositions is, of course,' not restricted to use in the American Southwest; it is universally applicable.

(Hill 1968: 140).

Subsequently, J. J. Lischka has shown that Hill's conclusions are not statistically reliable (Lischka 1975).

Analogies can serve to formulate specific hypotheses. For instance, we have found a site with a great number of finds. By analogy with our previous experience, which can be personal, taken from literature or based on ethnographic/archaeological research, we can formulate the following hypotheses.

Finds were:

    I (a) deposited in the event of wars
        (b) deposited for ritual reasons
        (c) deposited purely for storage reasons
        (d) deposited as loot
        (e) deposited by a merchant.
        Finds are of:
   II (a) local provenance
        (b) foreign provenance
  III (a) simultaneous origin
        (b) gradual origin.

Each of the specific hypotheses is tested by special indicators (e.g. the origin of raw materials, number of inhabitants, coins and locks found on the site). The final hypotheses must integrate special ones from all the three categories (I–III). For example, if propositions Ic, IIa, IIIb hold true, this would suggest that there was apparently a production centre on this site. The final hypothesis must be further tested by other indicators. As is often the case, some of the indicators prove the hypotheses while others disprove it. The latter can be divided into those which are neutral as far as the hypothesis is concerned and those which are clearly incompatible. A hypothesis which does not have any incompatible indicators and very few neutral ones is a highly reliable one, the more so if it is compatible with other hypotheses about other artefacts found in the area under consideration.

Let us quote another example. Social structure can be studied only because it is connected with spatial relationships. This was pointed out by C. Lévi-Strauss, using the layout of a Bororo village as an example. The layout of the village reflected family relations, various activities and even mythical notions of the inhabitants (Lévi-Strauss 1955).

At the core of the study of intra-communal social relationships based on the investigation of the relationships between artefacts and spatial units within a site, ethnographic analogy plays a large role. In 1934, P. N. Tretjakov expounded the following theory: fingerprints found on ceramic objects show that they were made by women. In communities charactertised by matrilocal distribution there will probably be less variation in the ornaments than in patrilocal communities, the reason being that in this case there will be a number of women from different tribes meeting at the same place. This premise was also used in 1960 by J. Deetz in his Ph.D. thesis, in which he studied the correlation between changes in social organisation and the distribution of features used in decorating ceramics. C. Cronin applied a similar approach (Cronin 1962: 105).

Let us mention another example. W. A. Longacre investigated a pueblo site in eastern Arizona in the period from AD 1100 to 1250 (Longacre 1964, 1968). Following ethnographic parallels, he proposed that local matrilineal groups inhabited the site and that ceramics and their decoration were made by women. In the sample of six thousand fragments he found 175 design elements. Then he studied their distribution within the locality. It appeared that there was a connection between various groups of these units and certain areas. He then studied their frequency by means of multiple regression analysis. The results demonstrated the existence of three groups of localities, each of which was associated with a kiva (a ceremonial structure) known from comparative ethnography.

He then found different types of rooms. Again using multiple regression analysis he was able to define the connection between different types of ceramics, i.e. different types of activity, and different types of rooms. These findings corresponded to the results obtained from the present-day pueblos. He further discovered the connection between certain types of vessels used for rituals, associations between structural parts of the village on the one hand and certain graves and objects made by men on the other. On the strength of ethnographic analogy he formulated a hypothesis which gave positive results when tested on the material found on this sitè. A similar approach had been applied earlier (by Kalgrem, Lothrope and others). It is only today, however, that, due to statistical methods and computers, it is possible to study these very complicated relationships in greater detail. Similar research was carried out by J. Deetz, who used additional statistical methods (Deetz 1965), and R. Whallon (Whallon 1968, sequential analysis).

The conclusion is a little ironic – the original idea that it is possible to differentiate between male and female fingerprints is wrong (it may be true of the size of the outline but not of the papillary lines).

Maybe at another time we will arrive at better results than archaeologists of the year 5868, whose knowledge of General Grant was preserved thanks to Mark Twain in his book *The Innocents Abroad*:

Uriah S (or Z) Graunt – popular poet of ancient times in the Aztec provinces of the United States of British America. Some authors say flourished AD 742; but the learned Ah-Ah Foo-Foo states that he was a contemporary of Scharkspyre, the English poet, and flourished about AD 1328, some three centuries after the Trojan War instead of before it.

Formulating a hypothesis at any level requires inventive thinking which must be based on something other than just the material. Artefacts on their own do not give any evidence – they have to be described, classified and serialised. The description, classification and serialisation of the artefacts, no matter how exact and objective they may be, are made in a certain language which is a system in its own right, the individual parts of which are defined and determined by one another. After all, even the simplest classification is, in fact, a hypothesis, i.e. a hypothesis about the rules and conditions of the classification.

A hypothesis is always formulated in a language of non-indicators, in this case, non-artefacts. It is obviously a different system (in this case the language of archaeological theory and prehistoric interpretation). Therefore, when formulating hypotheses, we have to apply systems other than just artefacts.

In the first place there are analogies, experiments and theoretical concepts of other sciences. Obviously the most frequent starting point of any archaeological hypothesis is the theory of archaeology itself, i.e. its terminology and syntax, which is, at the same time, a point to which all the hypotheses return.

According to R. Carnap (1959), 'it is a matter of taking potluck' when you want to arrive at the right hypothesis, as there are no rules on how to think creatively.

The problem of archaeological terminology

When formulating hypotheses, archaeology provides us with a whole range of concepts which we can use to express our statements. It is 'traditional archaeology' which can be described as that which uses only its own specific concepts in order to formulate statements.

In the course of decades archaeology has created and specified a number of terms expressing facts as well as general ideas concerning the past and the future development. Each of them is a small hypothesis, which is being changed all the time.

The meanings of individual concepts are mutually related. They complement one another and together they represent a certain theory, a very general theory that includes many partial interpretations. Therefore, many archaeological terms appear to lack precision, i.e. they are more clearly defined only by their context. Let us illustrate this with a detailed analysis of a single concept, an archaeological culture, in the hope that it will clarify the position of other concepts as well.

The history of the terms 'culture', 'civilisation' and 'history' characterises, in brief, the development of history itself. In the course of the eighteenth century the meaning of the term history became unified, as illustrated in German by the transition from plural to singular (*die Geschichte*). And indeed it was at that time that the world became integrated through increased communication and the term 'world history' was born. Similarly, the terms 'civilisation' and 'culture' appeared at that time; originally in the singular, later they began being used in the plural. 'Civilisation' dates back to France in 1766 where it was used to express the opposite of barbarism. Having in mind the new social development, it is necessary to distinguish between the barbarians of the past and those of the present. Civilisation (as an equivalent of Enlightenment) had to be fought for and brought to others – a typical Enlightenment attitude. It was only after 1850 that the right to have 'one's own civilisation' was discussed. That is how we came to have several civilisations – the plural. The word was increasingly used to mean material aspects of civilisation – it became a symbol of manufacture and trade.

At that point the term 'culture' appeared in Germany. J. G. von Herder juxtaposed material civilisation and culture of the mind (*Geisteskultur*), which became the object of *Kulturgeschichte*.

In 1871, Sir Edward Tylor introduced the term 'culture' into anthropology and archaeology. 'Culture' is a complex term including all parts of social life and increasingly used in the plural. 'Civilisation' is a collective term describing a number of similar cultures. In 1975, G. E. Daniel observèd a shift in the opposite direction: 'from a study of cultures to a study of culture' (Daniel 1975: 318).

However, this applies only to anthropology and archaeology; in other humanities (history and philosophy) the words still retain their original meanings. According to Oswald Spengler culture is the 'spring' of society, civilisation its 'autumn'. For P. Bagby culture is the non-urbanised countryside and civilisation means towns. In 1954, A. Cuvillier found twenty different meanings for 'civilisation'.

The term 'culture' is interpreted in realistic philosophy as a metaphysical idea, or as a heritage of ideas and traditions; in nominalist philosophy as a system of external features which, in turn, determine its nature – for example, the kind of activity, ideas and achievements which are characteristic for a particular culture (A. L. Kroeber defines culture as an extrasomatic product of a society transmitted through mechanisms other than heredity). It can also be used as a means of classification (Kroeber writes: 'It helps us to arrange a number of facts into categories'); it can be interpreted in terms of organicism (Oswald Spengler: 'culture is an organism'), or in terms of functionalism (B. Malinowski: 'culture is a functional phenomenon'). Interpreted as a system of conventions, norms and standards, it can also be explained in terms of transcendentalism or in terms of social history.

There is a parallel with other terms: for example, that of style in the history of architecture and art; some terms used in history; and the term 'kind' used in biology. Even with these terms, there is no uniformity. For Linnaeus the 'kind' is a constant unit determined by external conditions, while Georges Cuvier explains it as an anatomical unit of a higher order. Nowadays it means a constantly changing and developing population. Such interpretations can also lead to ontological conclusions and vice versa.

Thirty years ago A. Kroeber and C. K. M. Kluckhohn found 164 different definitions of culture in anthropology. They can be divided into seven categories (Cafagna 1960):

(a) those emphasising cultural inheritance – every socially inherited element whether material or metaphysical belongs to culture (Sapir);

(b) those emphasising learnt behaviour – culture is a sociological term for learnt behaviour (Benedict);

(c) definitions emphasising ideas – culture as an association of a complex of ideas (Wissler);

(d) definitions emphasising accepted behaviour – culture is a set of more or less accepted ideas, attitudes and habits (Jahn);

(e) definitions emphasising the extra-organic nature of culture – it is a set of extra-somatic and extra-biological means of adaptation (White);

(f) definitions emphasising the name of the category, the thing or the event – culture is a word for a category of phenomena, things or events (White).

The term culture is one of the most frequently used in archaeology. Or rather has been (Wolf 1984). In one of the latest synopses of the state of archaeology by Moberg (1969) it is not used at all. In 1972, J. Lüning presented a detailed list of different concepts of culture as they were used in Anglo-American and German archaeology until the end of the 1960s, similarly L. S. Klejn (1982). K. C. Chang's suggestion in his book *Rethinking Archaeology* was to start anew, using quite different concepts. The term 'culture' was rejected by R. Braidwood, J. B. Hawkes, G. E. Daniel and to a certain extent by A. C. Renfrew, H. Müller-Karpe, S. Piggott and others. Even in the past there was no uniformity in what the term culture meant. In fact, it was not even necessary as all the meanings were more or less compatible with the general trends in prehistory. The old concept of prehistory has now been abandoned, however; prehistory has expanded and developed, and it is time now to rethink the term culture as well. In the past, prehistory and archaeology concentrated mainly on the general direction of thought in dealing with archaeological material, i.e. sorting those fifty to a hundred million pots which had been excavated. It was then that the term 'culture' was first used and proved to be very useful.

Culture was interpreted in many different ways either by evolutionists, or those advocating the theory of migration and diffusion, or by classical taxonomists, or those emphasising the influence of the environment.

There are many different views about archaeological culture. Below is an example of different perceptions of culture which prevailed among Soviet archaeologists at the end of the 1960s.

1 (a) we can work without the term culture (Šer)
   (b) it is an essential concept (Klejn)
2 (a) its content is sufficiently clear (Smirnov)
   (b) it is not well defined but it is a matter of 'the party discipline of archaeologists' (Grigorev)
3 (a) 'culture' is an auxiliary means for classification (Mongajt)
   (b) culture is a realistic concept based on tangible evidence (Grjaznov)
4 (a) culture corresponds to ethnic units (Brajčevskij)
   (b) there is no connection between historical evidence and culture (Lebedev).

Culture can further be defined as:

1 (a) similar forms (Blume, Jahn, Kilian)
   (b) stylistic uniformity (Schuchhardt)
   (c) internal functional relationships (Childe)
2 (a) a system of forms and features (Šer)
   (b) a complex of sites, finds and artefacts (Brjusov, Zaharuk)
   (c) a territorial unit characterised by similar artefacts (Jahn, Kilian).

It is the concept of culture used until recently in 'prehistoric history' which is most often the object of criticism. The most recent approach is either to leave it out altogether or to incorporate it into a system of ideas where it loses its previous exclusive position. This trend leads us from traditional archaeology which could be described as 'narrative' to modern archaeology which is systematic and sociological.

There is a similar range of variation concerning other archaeological terms, for example, 'type', 'stage', 'period', which could be analysed in a similar way.

Let us mention them briefly. They occur in the same context as culture and their position is largely determined by that fact. This is relative, of course, because we could have based our considerations on a term other than culture.

Below is a survey of different archaeological terms. We shall mention also terms loosely linked with archaeological sources and the methods of obtaining them. More information on this subject can be found in Dunnell (1971).

Every science has its *object*. In archaeology there are several terms used at this level – *find*, *record*, *antiquity*, *source*, *remains*, *material*. Their meanings often overlap. Differences occur when one of them emphasises a particular aspect or a specific feature of an archaeological object, both of which are often contingent on their use in the context of a certain stage of the archaeological procedure.

Archaeology finds its object of study primarily in *sites* or *localities*. The term 'site' is very vague and very broad. It usually appears at the time when we still do not have enough information about the place of our study. 'Locality' in Anglo-American literature means a geographical area in which we expect homogeneous cultures in every stage.

We can discover *things* (*artefacts*), *buildings* (*objects*), *deposits* and *layers* of different cultures, *ecofacts* or *natural material remains* (skeletons).

Artefacts (things) and buildings (objects) form a set of finds or an inventory. These, together with deposits (which usually provide a kind of cover), can be grouped into a closed or semi-closed complex. Apart from them there can also be isolated finds and unique finds.

The basic units and a starting point of any consideration are the notion of the *attribute* (a constant feature of an artefact or a system which cannot be further divided) and that of the *artefact*. Artefacts can be classified, or grouped into *categories*, *classes*, *types* and *variations*. In archaeology (even present-day archaeology) the notion 'type' often represents several meanings and is often wrongly used in the sense of 'class'. Artefacts are produced or created according to the methods and types inherent in a given culture.

The conclusions we made about 'culture' can be applied to 'type' as well. The next important term is *industry*. Every artefact is a remnant of a certain *activity* or *event*; it demonstrates something. Activity is closely linked with behaviour. The behaviour of people is based on norms which were quite rigid – especially in prehistory. A number of sites with similar types of finds which belong to one culture (usually with a centre) is called the *region* of this particular type (micro-region), or *culture*. Sometimes the same geographical area, without being studied in different periods, is called an *area* (micro-area). It is often confused with *space*, which always means a unit of a certain culture. If we study certain artefacts, types or cultures (archaeo-logical entities) found in different places we can talk about the *horizon*. A *settlement* is a local group within the horizon. If we study artefacts, their sets, types and cultures from a chronological point of view, we talk about *stages*, *phases*, and *sub-phases* (micro-phase). They denote a certain section of our study whose time and content features are consistent. In relation to a certain place the phase is seen as a *component*. This term is used in Anglo-American literature. A series of components is described as a *local sequence* and a *regional sequence*. The connection between the entities of the previous and the following stages is expressed by the term *tradition*. When studying the development of one particular entity, e.g. *culture*, *group of cultures*, or a *complex of cultures*, we usually talk about *stages*, *periods* or *epochs*. On a wide scale we can talk about different *periods of culture* or *civilisation* in general (savagery, barbarism, urban civilisation).

Every archaeological entity is in the process of constant *development*, i.e. going through different stages and bringing about changes which, in turn, are a cause of further development. In this process we distinguish the beginning, peak and declining stages. The process of change can be described by means of such phenomena as *innovation* (invention), *adapt-ation* (ecological, morphological, psychological), *assimilation*, *cultivation*, and *convergence*. They describe the origin, the introduction of and adapting of new ideas, behaviour and their material signs within one entity. A *change* can be transferred from one culture to another by means of *migration* (invasion), i.e. movement of individuals belonging to one population, and by means of *diffusion*, i.e. gradual spreading of changes by adaptation. Both migration and diffusion can eventually become peripheral. To conclude our survey let us recapitulate and summarise the different levels at which the concept of archaeological culture can operate. Their mutual relationships reveals archaeological culture in its complexity and diversity.

Archaeological cultures can be divided into lower entities, e.g. a *sub-culture*, or a group (terms 'type' and 'facie' are also used, which, however, also have other meanings in archaeology), or they can be parts of higher entities e.g. a *group of cultures*, areas of the same culture, a *complex of cultures*, *techno-complex* or *civilisation*. Such archaeological entities as the type and the culture can have corresponding anthropological (cultural and social), historical and sociological terms. They describe a certain *population* formed by ethnic, social, linguistic, professional and cultural features. Here we can mention such terms as *community*, *population*, *ethnic group*, and *ethnicity*.

We must bear in mind, however, that these concepts are just a very general explanation; in fact, they are nothing other than a description. The way we divide the material into different cultures, describe their character-istic features, define their area and time, describe their neighbours, higher entities, and describe the whole process by means of migration, diffusion or innovation, corresponds closely to any historical narrative, i.e. with little regard to explanation.

Analogies and parallels

At the core of archaeology as opposed to archaeography is the concept of analogy. By analogy we mean a certain way of thinking whereby, on the basis of similarity of some properties or relations of two phenomena, we assume similarities in all the other phenomena. Analogy is comparing one thing with another. The structure of comparison is always determined by our previous experience, including our aims and our thought patterns.

We assume that certain facts from our ethnographical material will in similar circumstances give similar results, e.g. in prehistory (Kramer 1979, Orme 1981). Classical evolutionary assumptions, however, maintaining that the way of life of present-day primitive societies is an exact replica of the way of life and behaviour of ancient societies, which can, therefore, be used as a direct model for reconstruction, have now been abandoned. The optimism of the nineteenth century has been forgotten (Orme 1974). Most present-day researchers believe that ancient 'primitive societies' had under-gone a very complicated development and, therefore, present-day ethno-graphical material can only be used after critical examination and com-parison with other observations (Ascher 1961, Wylie 1985). That is the reason why so-called ethnoarchaeology (archaeological ethnography, living archaeology, action archaeology), which studies the relation between cultural dynamics and archaeological statics in living communities, is becoming important (Binford 1978, Carmack 1972, Cazella 1985, Charlton 1981, Gould 1978, 1979, Gould and Schiffer 1981, Gould and Watson 1982, Hodder 1982b, c, Kramer 1979, Rathje 1974, Stiles 1977, Yellen 1977; from the theoretical standpoint, Salmon and Salmon 1982, chapter 4).

It is thanks to ethnoarchaeology that the number of hypotheses about matters which could not be studied until recently has rapidly increased. This is especially so in the area of symbolic meaning, which in the past was closely linked with social, economic, and spatial organisation, and through them, with material culture as well (structural, symbolic archaeology). However, there is a danger of inadequate interpretation in this field, mainly because there is a great variety of symbols and because they are subject to frequent changes. Ethnoarchaeology contributed to the abandonment of a large number of recent ethnographic parallels (see David 1971). Ethnoarchaeology has significantly increased the possibilities of prehistoric interpretations, but, at the same time, it has made us aware of the pitfalls of ethnographic analogy.

It is obvious that analogy is merely a means of explanation. Even the highest degree of similarity between two objects cannot guarantee similarity in *all* their features (Moberg 1981).

As analogy (as we have just described it) is a basic method of archaeological research, we must examine carefully every case of analogy and compare the results attained by this method with those of the whole system. Furthermore, we must examine all the existing prejudices (collectively shared analogies). For example, A. Laming-Emperaire, when studying cave art, pointed out that the ethnographical material these pictures were being compared with was obtained ten years earlier by anthropological methods which had since been abandoned.

Knowledge attained in exact sciences, e.g. physics, undergoes little change, regardless of its age. Facts of archaeology, on the other hand, their selection, classification and interpretation, must constantly be compared with the latest results. One of the tasks of archaeology is to update older data (Clarke 1972).

Analogy itself cannot deceive us because it does not claim anything. Where we can be deceived is in our interpretation of analogy, explanation or hypothesis which has been obtained by analogy. The fact that there is a certain number of similarities between pre-Columbian cultures and ancient Egypt is unambiguous: what is problematic is the explanation of this fact.

Experiment

The contemporary understanding of experiment is concerned with practically the whole field of archaeology (Malina 1980a, 1983). It might, therefore, be fitting to include a summary of possible applications of the experiment in archaeology (Coles 1979, Malina 1980a).

We will deem an experiment to be a situation where the observer either controls or deliberately manipulates an object or a set of data and then compares the initial and the final states. An experiment, is, therefore, an extension of a purposeful, planned and controlled observation carried out to test a certain hypothesis. S. Jevons, in a classic study of the methodology of science and logic, wrote in 1874 that 'there is not a strictly defined border between what is purely an observation and what is definitely an experiment'. The perimeter of experimental methods is not only very wide but also fluctuating and not sufficiently precise. A whole host of methodologies pertaining to experiment is also represented in archaeology. Unfortunately, we often find ourselves in a situation in which the methodology of experiments is a matter of oral tradition rather than a matter of explicit explanation. In addition, the experiment is usually identified with the traditional laboratory experiment appropriate to the natural sciences, and its other numerous variants are not widely known.

The so-called classic experiment, which originated in the natural sciences (Francis Bacon, Galileo) and became prevalent in the methodology of this area, and which was, for a long time, considered to be the ideal or sole form, is not really of great use to archaeology.

The strategy of the experiment independent of the demands of the experiment in its classic form is studied by a discipline called Experiment Design, or sometimes the Mathematical Theory of Experiment, first expounded by R. Fisher as early as 1935 in his book *The Design of Experiments*. Revolutionary developments are taking place in this area at the moment, with far-reaching implications for the applied sciences and industrial production.

The beginnings of Experiment Design lie in the application of experimental methods in disciplines where it was not possible to carry out tests in purely laboratory conditions, as in physics or chemistry, for example. Such experiments were first carried out in agrobiology.

Before we embark on a more detailed explanation of Experiment Design we must return once again to the question of observation – the basis of experimentation. What we have in mind here is a planned observation which is termed a passive experiment. Let us consider a simple example of finding out the productivity of a particular agricultural crop. In certain instances we do not have to sow such a crop – we can merely observe its natural occurrence. In this case our observation may be subject to the same design (for example, by means of various methods of random selection). Procedures used in the design of truly pure experiments can, therefore, also be employed in cases of scientific observation. This is of special importance to archaeology, since the range of application of the classic experiment in archaeology is relatively narrow. However, the range for testing and planned observation is wide. This is nothing new since archaeologists have used many such methods fairly regularly, albeit in their vague and intuitive form.

However, a thorough application of these methods in archaeology is only possible after precise, objective and standardised processing of the finds has been fulfilled. This has been facilitated by the developments in information technology which enable us to find with speed the data relevant to our demands. As we will see later, the Mathematical Theory of

Experiment affords so many possibilities that it can significantly supplement the methodology hitherto used in archaeology and prehistory. Experiment also brings to archaeology the use of methods from other disciplines (information theory, theory of games, graphs, decision-taking and systems analysis) and enables us to summarise their essential features.

The Mathematical Theory of Experiment is today a very extensive discipline and therefore we have to limit ourselves to only a brief summary, the aim of which is to arouse attention rather than to satisfy curiosity (cf. Malina 1980a).

The analysis of dispersion represents a first major approach. The result of an experiment is influenced, on the one hand, by the factors under investigation, and, on the other hand, by unknown factors or by those factors which are not the subject of our experiment. The methodology of classic experimentation demands that the uncontrolled factors be held constant and the activity of the investigated factors be studied against the invariable background of these other factors. This, however, leads to a number of difficulties because stabilisation and isolation are not necessarily an easy matter. On the other hand, all factors can be taken as random. This is achieved by making the conditions of an experiment random: randomised blocks, Latin squares and rectangles, Graeco-Latin squares, etc.'

For example, if we investigate the effectiveness of a manipulation on certain objects, their parameters, such as the sample, experimental squares, etc. will never be identical, despite all our efforts. Their reaction to the manipulation will vary. The aim of the experiment will be to define the extent of the effectiveness of the manipulation, which is only possible to achieve by the stabilisation of experimental errors which had occurred as a result of the non-homogeneity of the samples.

In the instance where the same sample cannot be subjected to all intended manipulations (it is distorted by the first manipulation; it is not at our disposal in the case of a passive experiment, etc.) it is a good thing to investigate all combinations (table 1).

In the case of a large number of combinations we select from the possible

Table 1. Three-member combinations for four elements, A, B, C, D: interventions 1–4 are a specific series of interventions called blocks.

1	B	C	D
2	A	C	D
3	A	B	D
4	A	B	C

combinations a smaller number by means of random selection. From the obtained results we find, by means of normal statistical methods, the extent of the effect of individual manipulations (randomised blocks).

Reduction can be systematised with the help of counterbalanced, incomplete blocks. Thus, for example, we arrange the results in a Latin square randomly in such a way that in each column and in each row every result appears only once (table 2). Randomisation is achieved by selecting a Latin square randomly for all possible Latin squares of corresponding measurements. This approach can then be extended to even more complex tasks (Graeco-Latin square, etc.).

These methods leading to the analysis of dispersion can also be used in the case of a passive experiment – that is, where we have at our disposal the result of a simple observation or results obtained by testing. In the case where we have, in archaeological practice, set blocks of observation (for example, types of artefacts) and factors (a climax of development, identical manufacturing conditions) it is not decisive whether or not these factors were created artificially or whether or not they can be controlled. As a rule, blocks of observation are not complete and therefore the selection according to the above-quoted principles can be applied. Results will not, of course, be as satisfactory as in the case of an active experiment because individual samples may be considerably heterogeneous.

These methods can also be applied profitably in an archaeological reconstruction of the very thing for which they had been originally developed – that is, agrobiology. On experimental fields we can study the yield of produce cultivated with ancient technology. The same application is possible and necessary in many instances of research into technology if this is carried out at different times, at different places, with different material, etc. This methodology can be used equally successfully both during excavation (Binford 1964, Neustupný 1973b) and with the evaluation of the finds obtained (Daniels 1972).

The multi-factor experiment offers us even further possibilities. Let us suppose that by using either a test or an experiment we are to find out the effect of two independent factors (A, B). This can be done by carrying out a

Table 2. Latin square for four elements.

A	B	C	D
B	A	D	C
D	C	A	B
C	D	B	A

series of three single-factor experiments (row 1 to 3 of table 3 indicate the control experiment – row 1, neither of the two factors is operative).

There is yet another possible approach using the same number of experiments which is, however, more precise. This is illustrated in table 3, rows 2 to 4. In this case, for example, the effect A equals half the difference between the total of 3 + 4 and 2, that is $[/(3) + (4)/ - (2)]: 2$. Thus, in contrast to a single-factor experiment, the effect of each factor is measured by the results of all three steps. So far we have dealt with the method of finding out the effect of two factors. However, it is not only single factors which operate separately, but also their combinations. We say that two or more factors operated in interaction when the result achieved differs from the total of the results of individual, independent factors.

In the case of the two factors A and B, the number of factors and their possible interactions equals four (we take into account also a case of absence in both factors), but in the case of seven factors we get 128 combinations (expressed by equation – the number of factors equals 2^n, where n is the number of factors) – that is, a number which is difficult to verify by testing. It is therefore necessary to make this method more effective or, as the case may be, even possible. In the case of two factors we mentioned earlier we used three steps to find out the effect of both factors and their interaction; the effect of each factor (excluding interaction) was verified two times. In the case of interaction between A and B we can immediately see the difference between the effect of a factor investigated separately and the effect given by the total result. The simplest case would be to investigate the effect of individual factors in isolation. In such a case we have to bear in mind that:

(a) individual factors must be isolated, which is not possible in all cases;

Table 3. Combination of two factors (1 = presence, 0 = absence of factor). In the case of a single-factor experiment, 1 is considered as a control experiment.

	A	B
1	0	0
2	0	1
3	1	0
4	1	1

(b) the result of our measurements cannot be compared with additional measurements;

(c) we have no information about all possible interactions.

An interaction of a lower order (a smaller number of factors) obviously influences an interaction of a higher order and vice versa; we can find this out on the basis of interactions of a higher order and values of individual factors. This system of a mutual interlinked network of the resultant values of interactions and factors enables us, in certain cases, to determine missing data. Still further reduction in the number of experiments used to investigate the values of individual factor combinations can take place when we work on the supposition that the interactions of a higher order are not essential and can, therefore, be disregarded.

Taking such suppositions into account we arrive at different degrees of reduction of the total number of factor combinations. For example, as we have already stated, in the case of seven factors we have a possible total of 128 combinations, which, however, can be investigated on the basis of a sample of only eight combinations (table 4).

If we have at our disposal data obtained by observation only, without experiment, the situation is, as a rule, similar to that where we have at our disposal data gained by experiment. The difference, which can, however, be substantial, lies in the fact that the homogeneity of conditions is not guaranteed in cases of mere observation. Different conditions can substantially distort the result or can make a complete nonsense of it. This danger is quite obvious if, for example, we consider artefacts as indicators of a certain social phenomenon. If we investigate formal changes in the shape and decoration of artefacts only, the homogeneity of assemblages

Table 4. Summarised matrix of the type 2^{7-4}.

	A	B	C	D	E	F	G
1	0	0	0	1	1	1	0
2	1	0	0	0	0	1	1
3	0	1	0	0	1	0	1
4	1	1	0	1	0	0	0
5	0	0	1	1	0	0	1
6	1	0	1	0	1	0	0
7	0	1	1	0	0	1	0
8	1	1	1	1	1	1	1

increases. In any case, the application of this strategy will enable us to orient ourselves with regard to our material – even though we cannot perhaps use it to test a certain hypothesis, it can help us to formulate a new hypothesis for which additional indicators can be found in our material.

These methods play an important role, especially in archaeology. They enable us to orient ourselves on the basis of even incomplete information in the material.

Factor experiments can be utilised in archaeology above all where factors are localised in space. They have also been applied in the study of influences that regulate the location of investigated phenomena in geology (Krumbein 1955, Melton 1960) and geography (Haggett 1961). Haggett, for instance, used this method to study water divisions in Brazil. Following his method the total area under investigation is divided according to localisation of the investigated factors and their combinations (figure 45), and the significance of individual factors or their combinations is then determined by statistical methods. Similar approaches have also been adopted in archaeology (Chenhall 1975, Davidson, Richer and Rogers 1976).

Factor analysis, component analysis and methods of cluster analysis can also be used in order to determine the experimental strategy. Let us consider the following example: we know the initial situation, more than one possible outcome, and a common factor. It is obvious that the common factor can be split into a number of separate factors: various types of combinations of their mutual associations that cause different outcome situations. The individual factor combinations causing different outcomes can be determined by, for example, discriminant analysis or clustering. The results can, in turn, be subjected to a component analysis or clustering and, in this way, after the contents have been interpreted, we obtain the factors standing in the background of the process. Again, it is not decisive, whether

Figure 45. A procedure in a regional sub-division of a region using three factors, A, B, and C (Ā denotes negation of A, A conjunction). Source: Haggett 1965: 300.

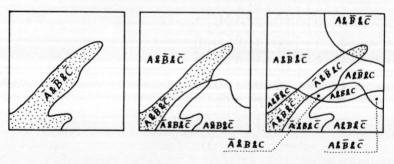

the manipulations (factors) originated as a result of our activity. What is decisive is the fact that once we have formulated our subject matter in this way a whole range of statistical methods are at our disposal.

The investigation of optimal characteristics of some event, for instance of technological processes, forms another area where factor analysis can be usefully employed. Here our task would be to find the optimal conditions of a certain phenomenon, that is, such a combination of levels of individual factors as is most effective from the point of view of our demands. A polynomial model will serve us for this purpose. This task can be interpreted in its geometrical design. Let us consider a factor space which is given as an n-dimensional Euclidean space (n = the number of factors). The individual possible combinations of different levels (orders) of all factors are represented by points in this space (figure 46). A complex consisting of these points forms the experiment field (surface design) which can be described by means of polynomes.

Let us now imagine that we know the values (the measure of their effect) of all possible combinations of factor levels (orders). If we then connect the points of equal value by lines, we obtain a kind of contour map which shows how the effects of individual combinations are rising, falling and linking. The optimal combinations are represented on this 'map' by the maximum, or extreme values (or, in other cases, the minimum, according to the design) – that is, the 'mountain summits' ('valleys') (figure 47).

However, in order to construct such a map we have to know all the

Figure 46. Three-dimensional space created by three factors (A, B, C), each factor being defined at two levels of resolution (i.e. assigned two values or attributes, such as rich/poor). This raises the number of factor combinations to eight, creating an experimental area in this space.

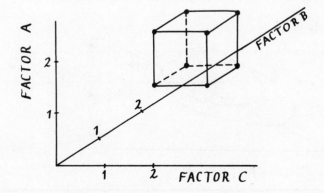

possible combinations, which is neither effective nor, in some cases, possible. For this reason we carry out a series of experiments in such a way as to reach the summit as quickly as possible (the remaining terrain is of no interest to us) – that is, by way of the steepest ascent. However, our journey will only be successful if the surface is continuous and smooth and if there is one optimum only. Consequently, we have to carry out a series of steps (experiments) in such a way that each step leads to new information on the basis of which we can then carry out the next step (the step-by-step strategy). This strategy has far-reaching implications in archaeology. It is envisaged that this method can be applied in the study of artefact evolution, or evolution of technological processes, above all in the case of artefacts which evolve towards functional optimalisation. In this case we can take as factors, for example, the morphometrical data, the combination of which is optional as regards the function of the implement. This, of course, demands precise measurements of efficiency, for example by ergonometric tests. A grouping of individual types of artefacts according to their effectiveness can then help in determining their temporal seriation. Apart from the functional optimum, certain cases of stylistic revolution can also be studied, providing we know its culmination. The applications and possibilities stemming from the concept of optimalisation, above all in biology, are discussed by R. Rosen (1967).

The investigation of palaeoeconomic systems, often directed towards the reconstruction of optimal technological and economic strategies, offers further opportunities. As an example, one can cite the analysis of the economic cycle of the Shoshone Indians (Thomas 1972), agrarian strategy

Figure 47. Three dimensional factorial space, where contours are defined as links between points of the same value.

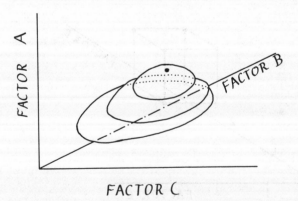

(Gould 1963) and location strategy (Barth 1959–60). A computer model of the system behaviour can be used to simulate the changes in conditions and behaviour of the system (Keene 1981). The determination of the optimal variants of a strategy of a certain system can be done by carrying out experiments within the framework of simulation. The degree of optimality and adaptability can then be compared with, for example, the age of the society being studied.

Geometric interpretation in n-dimensional space, where the connecting lines between the points with the same effectiveness represent contour lines, can also be used in solving other problems.

If we construct in this way a surface representing the efficiency of a certain artefact ('surface of efficiency') we can follow, on the contour map we thus obtain, the way in which a local tradition influenced the method of solving the problem of optimalisation (the different paths leading to the summit – e.g. the optimum) (figure 48) or, as the case may be, discern whether there existed perhaps some local extremes which would delay this process (figure 49).

Contour lines linking points of the same attributes can illustrate the numerous relationships between such categories of artefact properties as for example time, space, individuality, raw material and activity. These relationships can then be expressed numerically. Such possibilities are systematically discussed by J. Malina (Malina 1977).

Yet other possibilities, especially the surface trend analysis (Haggett 1965,

Figure 48. Points p_1–p_5 and points r_1–r_5 represent artefacts (or technologies, economical strategies) from two different regions (or different ethnical, cultural or other units), p and r. Their chronological succession within each region corresponds to the sequence from the bottom to the top. Dotted lines denote local tendenies leading to optimisation.

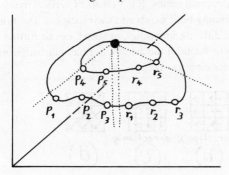

Sneath 1967), stem from the representation of surface data in n-dimensional geometrical space by means of polynomes.

Further possibilities of application of the geometrical interpretation are offered by the graphic representation of trend, tendency and movement in n-dimensional space, and also modification of this space through such influences.

The values of the input matrix are interpreted as speed potentials (figure 50a) (for example, as the height of the terrain which influences the speed and direction of the current or diffusion). We can then find out the horizontal (figure 50b) and vertical (figure 50c) vectors. When we add up the vectors obtained in this way we arrive at a final table which includes the

Figure 49. The optimal state of an investigated phenomenon is represented by formation (a), local optima are represented by formations (b) and (c).

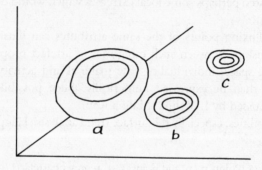

Figure 50. (a): Hypothetical matrix of initial input data. We are working under the assumption that direction of movement leads from lower values to higher values; and we are considering relations only between those cells which share a common boundary. (b): Vectors of horizontal trends. (c): Vectors of vertical trends. (d): Vectors combining both trends and their location. Their orientation is 135 degrees; different intensities, or speed, can be further illustrated by the length or width of the arrows. Source: Harbaugh and Bonham-Carter 1970: 211–13.

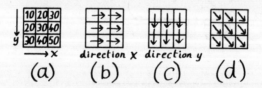

oriented vectors and, possibly, an indication of their intensity (figure 50d). We can then simulate the course of complex designs on a computer by changing the matrix design, the introduction of input and output with various locations, etc.

Models and modelling offer wide possibilities for experimenting. The initial state of an experiment can take a number of forms. We can begin by setting out the limits of our study, which are bound to be related to its aim, without removing the subject from its original environment. However, even in this case we create a certain amount of isolation by studying only those aspects of the situation that we have selected. An idealised object – a situation in a mental experiment – serves as an example of the other extreme. In many cases it may become clear that the only meaningful, or perhaps the only possible, way is to study the situation indirectly by means of a model.

In model experiments, therefore, we are not testing the situation itself, but its model. If the model corresponds to the investigated object such substitution does not change the structure of the experiment.

It is obvious that different types of models lead to different types of experiments and that not all of them find their full application in archaeology. The oldest and most widely used types of experiments are experiments with material models based on a spatial and physical similarity. They can be divided into two basic kinds – a replica and a scale model. A replica is a model where more or less all the characteristics of the model correspond with the original in such a way that the replica and the orignal can be interchanged. Replicas are mainly used in instances where the original is not at our disposal (reconstruction) or when we do not want to damage it. A material model – a scale model – is used in instances where we investigate the characteristics of the original by means of the identical or almost identical characteristics of a model, but on a different scale. These types of models are connected with the oldest form of experiments which were carried out in ancient societies.

When describing and, naturally, interpreting objects, numerous observational errors are often made and it is therefore imperative that the individual sources and the extent of the errors are identified. To this end, we can employ an experiment in which we subject a physical reconstruction of a prehistoric object (for example, a house) to destruction (fire, etc.). In this way we can discover the sources of individual variations (by repeating the experiment or carrying it out on a larger scale) of the changes in the object after destruction and systematise our observational errors.

In a similar way we can carry out the reconstruction of objects of which only depictions are known (for example, ploughing implements or vessels engraved or painted on rock) and determine by means of experiments their characteristics (including the technology used in their production). The reconstructions carried out by Heyerdahl and Severin belong to this category.

Among these types of model experiments belong, above all, experiments which serve to investigate technology and function: for example, the acquisition of food by hunting and gathering, forest clearance, soil cultivation, sowing of various cereals and other crops, harvesting and storage of the harvest, preparation of food and its consumption, building and deterioration of buildings, transport and transportation, working of stone, wood, bones, leather, production of ceramics, glass and metals, artistic techniques, art and music.

A specific event (for example, the production of chipped stone implements, cutting of trees by a stone or bronze axe, preparation of 'Neolithic' fields, production of iron on old shaft stoves, etc.) is imitated while preserving all of the known, original conditions. Where a significant correspondence exists we can assume that our methods and the original methods are similar.

However, problems emerge when carrying out experiments the purpose of which is to identify technological and functional capabilities and attributes of old material culture. This is because the result of the experiment is always concrete but it has, at the same time, an undefined temporal and spatial validity. We cannot decide, on the basis of such an experiment:

(a) that the technological process was carried out in the past in exactly the same way as in the experiment. On the other hand, a demonstration that a process was carried out at some place in the past in a different manner is not proof that this had been the case every time and everywhere;

(b) the temporal range in which the process was in operation;

(c) the area where it was used.

This problem, however, can be mitigated when carrying out reconstruction by:

1 using the same material as that used in the original objects;

2 making the reproduction as precise as possible;

3 using appropriate technology;

4 carrying out the reconstruction in the simplest possible way.

Furthermore, it is necessary to isolate during the experiment all the byproducts, waste matter, traces and other indicators characteristic of the activity performed in a certain way and then to look for its counterparts in archaeological sites.

Many of these difficulties are overcome by organising expeditions and centres of experimental archaeology, where experiments are carried out within the framework of the total technological complex of the culture and natural environment.

Other types of models are analogical and symbolic models. In analogical models certain characteristics of the original are substituted by other physical quantities and analogical relations.

The aim of simulation is to investigate the behaviour of the model under changing conditions. A material model can be subjected to a mechanical simulation and the behaviour of an ideal model can be simulated by symbolic equations and carried out directly on a computer. For the application of simulation models in archaeology, see Clarke (1972), Earle and Christenson (1980), Gardin (1974), Hodder (1978a), Sabloff (1981).

For example, by simulating natural conditions on a computer we can verify an economic strategy and investigate the corresponding spatial dispersion of artefacts (Thomas 1972, 1973). In a similar way we can simulate the course of population diffusion in a certain area – this can be done on the basis of the mathematical theory of diffusion. In archaeology, simulation is usually used when modelling the natural environment. In this way we can test hypotheses about processes where an enormous time span is involved (for example, a test of the hypothesis concerning the process of the origin of crude oil) and, equally, the hypotheses concerning the processes which took place in exceptional conditions (geological and archaeological processes) can be tested.

Simulation experiments are often employed in the study of diffusion; stochastic (random) models, based on the Monte Carlo method, have been successfully used in this area. The study of erosion, sedimentation, diffusion and flow of simulations is often carried out by means of icono-symbolic models in geology and related sciences (Bonham-Carter and Sutherland 1968). Similar methods can be used in archaeology to study the formation of layers, the erosion of mounds and buildings, destructive processes, etc. The model of sedimentation by evaporation in the Michigan basin in the late Silurian period can serve as a perfect example (Briggs and Pollack 1967). It allows us to experiment with the:

(a) shape of the basin
(b) number and location of inlets and outlets
(c) volume of flow through inlets and outlets
(d) speed of evaporation.

Methods of simulation were also used by D. Davidson, S. Richer and A. Rogers in their study of the influence of environmental factors on settlement location. They investigated whether any correlation existed between the distribution of settlement and selected environmental characteristics in the Orkneys, and tried to determine those factors which had an influence on the distribution of sites. They simulated quite a large number of possible distributions (each of them with given environmental factors) and the result was compared with a real distribution of settlement. The influence of each factor was then determined by the distance between the real and the simulated pattern (Davidson, Richer and Rogers 1976).

The progress of individual changes, which incorporates stochastic variation leading to optimisation, can be simulated by computer. Vértes adopted such a procedure, for instance, in his investigation of the rate of evolution of the Palaeolithic industry (Vértes 1968). Cavalli-Sforza used a simulation approach in modelling the links between biological and socio-cultural evolution (Cavalli-Sforza 1971, Ammerman and Cavalli-Sforza 1973).

It now remains to mention some specific types of experiment, namely social and sociological experiment, which was the last to appear in its explicit form (the first socio-psychological experiment was carried out by N. Triplett in 1897; socio-industrial by E. Mayo, 1923–4; sociometric by J. L. Moreno in the 1920s and 1930s). This was brought about by a change of orientation in sociology which turned from the universal concepts which were prevailing in the nineteenth century to the micro-sociological study of individual social groups. Sociometry is characterised by the direct study of groups and their dynamic structure, in which social, cultural and psychological factors are interwoven, and by the study of their measurement.

The social and sociological experiment cannot be implemented in its pure form in our area of interest, simply because the societies we study do not exist any more. It is possible to do so in the recent pre-literate societies, which is the domain of ethnography, and the results can be of interest to archaeologists. However, experimental archaeology and ethno-archaeological research offer some specific possibilities.

Archaeology is, in its entirety, a social science even though it makes more use of the methods of the natural sciences than do other historical sciences. The aim of the study of artefacts is precisely to gain knowledge about society. If we interpret archaeological material within the terms of archaeological theory we obtain a description of a higher order, which can in turn serve to explain the material. Inferences of this order are hypotheses, with archaeological material as their indicators.

The testing of archaeological and of general historical hypotheses is sometimes identified with the historical experiment (Rakitov 1969: 181–3). The perimeter of a simplest form of experiment can be transgressed only if we employ the methods of passive experiment, which allow for choice of observation strategy. Just as E. S. Dethlefsen and J. F. Deetz verified in 1966 the correctness of the methods of seriation on dated material, K. J. Kansky (1963) verified his model of the railway development in Sicily by a comparison with the real situation.

One of the reasons why the mathematical apparatus of the natural sciences differs substantially from that of the social sciences stems from the difference between a well- and a poorly organised system. In this situation one of the few instances in which modern methods can be applied is the so-called passive experiment. A sociological quasi-experiment carried out by H. F. Christiansen (Schulz 1970: 91) illustrates its possibilities in this area. Christiansen investigated the validity of the hypothesis of a relationship between school results and subsequently attained social status. She selected over two thousand people who had left school nine years earlier and divided them into a group of those who finished school and one of those who did not. From these two groups she extracted 'identical pairs' (according to the same age, sex, father's occupation, etc.) and in this way she eliminated 'intruding factors' (constant errors). Individuals who did not have partners in this sense were eliminated. The results of the experiment validated the tested hypothesis. This method of pair-comparison in ex-post experiment is elaborated in detail by H. A. David (1963). It can also be very well applied in archaeology. Using this method, the elimination of disruptive influences can be used in the application of a cross-cultural hypothesis in archaeology.

According to D. L. Clarke, who based his concepts on D. N. Chorafas' ideas (1965), we can incorporate the passive experiment into archaeology. 'The spheres of contextual and specific observation can be fully experimental if we use suitably controlled excavation and analysis of data' (Clarke 1968: 35, 642). Clarke also incorporates the testing of hypotheses into this area.

A study by three Soviet archaeologists (Kameneckij, Maršak and Šer 1975: 110) also belongs to that category which acknowledges a wider interpretation of experiment, e.g. passive experiment and controlled factors only are included.

When carrying out formalised investigation, an archaeologist must group or divide his material and determine the borderline meaning of this or that indicator according to two eventualities – that the hypothesis may be either true or

false. The skill of the experimenter (verification of a hypothesis in this way represents a typical experiment) rests in the fact that he must formulate as precisely as possible the problem pointing to the material and find such indicators as would minimise the possibility of an ambivalent answer.
(*ibid.*: 110)

One of the tasks of archaeology is also to study the experimentation of our ancestors. The simplest forms of experiment are directly connected with everyday human activity. Even the etymology of the word 'experiment' points to this fact – for example, Romance languages use the same expression for both 'experiment' and 'experience'. There is no precise dividing line between pre-scientific and scientific experimentation. They are both based on the same method of trial and error. Simple experiments connect our everyday experience with the practices of human beings in the past, and form a good base for analogy and parallels. With the help of the above-mentioned methods we can reconstruct in archaeology the old practices.

Experimentation always represents a risk to a certain extent. This is because in its early stages experimentation was so directly connected with securing necessities of daily life that it had to be treated with the greatest caution – an eventual failure could directly jeopardise the 'experimenter's' life. Consequently, most innovations in technological methods occurred only very gradually and slowly and only where this did not threaten the stability of a given society. The well-known conservatism of subsistence farmers is a case in point. Prehistoric societies were also likely to be disinclined towards experimentation which could increase the risks of failure. Any new result would be accepted only when it was fully incorporated into the ideology. Although subsistence economies appear primitive from our modern, prejudiced point of view, they were, in reality, finely tuned towards preserving a given status quo. Additional changes could have threatened this system adapted to given conditions. The reluctance of modern pre-literate societies to accept changes – and their strong preference for the norms of their own society – also played a decisive role. That such caution was justified can be seen from the many catastrophic results that were brought about by the interventions of modern society, however well intentioned, in so-called primitive societies.

Experimentation also presupposes a certain degree of development and secure background, sufficient spare time and material resources. Another prerequisite is also a sufficient degree of individualism in society and the readiness of the community to accept experimentation and its results. This means that development of experimentation, especially in the sphere of production, is conditional on the differentiation and specialisation of production. These technological experiments can best be studied by means of their results: artefacts.

With the development of such conditions, the scope for experimentation was bound to increase and to turn eventually to quantitative experiment. The earliest instances of this can be found on an Egyptian instruction for the manufacture of the hardest type of bronze, noting that an optimal ratio, presumably the result of an experiment, was of 88% copper and 12% zinc. This supposition is highly probable because the production of bronze developed over a relatively short period of time and was also relatively complex; we cannot, therefore, suppose that its optimalisation (the hardness demanded) was arrived at by a fortuitous process of 'natural selection'. This implies certain social prerequisites. On the other hand, a wide variety of changes over a single period of time or their alteration in time can serve as an indicator of experimentation, too. The statistical analysis of the Pendžikent ceramics determined that the greatest changes in the shape of ceramics corresponded with the highest level of economic stability (Kameneckij, Maršak and Šer 1975: 112–13).

Some further approaches

Ideas about prehistory are usually formulated on the basis of an analogy with a similar real-life situation, that is, the recent life style of primitive societies. This is the domain of cultural and social anthropology (Eggert 1974, 1976, Gibbon 1984, Thomas 1979, Tooker 1982, Ziegert 1964). Social and cultural anthropology provides us not only with concrete examples for partial analogies but also with the whole of its theory (Charlton 1981). We are indebted to anthropology, but this does not mean that we can abandon the responsibility of a critical approach.

Let us have a closer look at our benefactor. Cultural anthropology, social anthropology, ethnology and ethnography form a mixed entity in which individual distinctions are stipulated really only by cultural and conventional traditions. They are usually affiliated with the so-called social sciences in contrast to history, which is most frequently seen as properly belonging to the humanities. In this complex of knowledge ordinary language usage combines with an unlimited range of terms of all possible levels without any consistency. As a result, the borderline between description and interpretation is quite vague – a criticism often levelled by anthropologists at historiography.

However, anthropology concerns itself with far richer material than does archaeology, which is seen in its wider and more universal connections.

Anthropology can combine the observation of living societies with manifestations of cultures (not only the material aspects) past and present and, moreover, it can also take into consideration ideas expressed verbally by members of the ethnic group under study. Anthropology therefore combines ordinary language statements which a given society makes about itself (however, even this language includes a large number of abstract terms) with assertions uttered in the language of the social sciences and humanities. As in archaeology, the great majority of ethnographic material is seen as indicators only; however, anthropological hypotheses are based on or derive from a personal social experience and from experience of society methodically and critically processed by sociology.

Anthropological empirical material is, in principle, recent in origin. When processing it, it is therefore necessary to put a special emphasis on synchronics, that is, the functional and structural dependencies. This, however, also leads to a situation where the anthropological ideas about evolution stem precisely from the synchronics of which they are so well aware. As a result extreme conclusions are often reached, such as an overestimation of function (functionalism), a rejection of history (structuralism) or a construction of ideal history (neo-evolutionism).

Anthropology also often constructs its schemes of evolution on the basis of universal concepts inspired above all by sociology and philosophy. For example, L. A. White postulates a so-called analytical reality which is obtained by the elimination of space, time and particulars.

'Analytical reality', detached from all concrete points of reference, can only contemplate its own navel and search for the illustrations of its own reality, rather than for evidence. This is where hypothesis ends and ideology begins. Ideology is not empirically demonstrable, but equally it cannot be empirically rejected; rather, the proof of its credibility depends on its control over political power. In such conditions, it is left in peace to elaborate its internal cohesion, and to resolve problems of its own choice. It is then bound to reality only by Ptolemy's Effect. Successors to Ptolemy managed to explain all the planetary movements unforeseen by his theory thanks only to their practice of adding any number of epicycles to planetary revolutions. Ptolemy's Effect means, then, that a wrong theory can explain anything if its basic erroneous propositions are altered and modified by a plethora of qualifications. The basic beliefs can in this way remain unchanged, while at the same time appearing to explain all the facts, which are qualified in advance anyway by the flexible application of terminology within a given ideology. As a rule, such terminology is metaphorical ('a leading role', 'organic whole'), meaningless ('objective process', 'progress'), or mutually complementary ('evolution – revolution', 'base – super-structure'). Such terms can be combined to form associations at random ('forces of progress', 'organic revolution'). Such an approach has been evocatively summarised by that well-known specialist in this field, Konstantin Černenko (former Soviet premier, † 1985): 'Naturally, new facts can supplement and make more accurate existing views. There are truths, however, that do not lend themselves to any revisions: problems which were solved a long time ago. In trying to resolve scientific problems, we must not forget the basic principles of dialectical materialism' (Rudé Právo, 15 June 1983). In this way it was possible to develop, for instance, the incontrovertible theory of the succession of socio-economic formations.

Let us return, however, to mainstream anthropology. What are of interest to archaeologists in the field of anthropology are its general propositions. We hope that these can be validated by archaeological indicators, either directly or by means of specific archaeological terms. The degree of universality of such assertions can vary; they can be dependent in varying degrees on a specific time or space or, on the other hand, be unconstrained by either time or space. The existence of the latter type of proposition may be successfully doubted; if they exist at all they are only few, and so general as to be at best of a trivial nature.

In any case general terms in anthropology possess a large number of ethnographic indicators which then allows their detailed specification. Anthropology obtains indicators not only by the direct description of a far wider class of phenomena than archaeology does, but also by means of a number of methods inaccessible to archaeology. We can offer but a few examples: direct observation, opinion polls, oral traditions and historical material. These methods link anthropology with sociology and other social sciences and enable it to adopt their data and theories (and paradigms!) and carry out a constant evaluation of their respective results.

It is usually through other social sciences (although in some cases this can be done directly and independently) that anthropology and, with its help, archaeology make use of the terminology and theories of other scientific disciplines, such as systems theory (Doran 1970, Flannery 1967, Lowe 1985, Plog 1975), information theory, cybernetics, catastrophe theory (Renfrew 1978, 1979), etc.

Obviously, such adoptions are not and cannot be without problems and we can illustrate this with one of the most frequently used terms – 'system'. The term 'system' is used always as a slogan, often as a description and sometimes as an explanation. What then is a system?

(1) Something consisting of a set (finite or infinite) of entities,
(2) among which a set of relations is specified, so that:
(3) deductions are possible from some relations to others or the history of the system (Rappoport 1968: 453).

Our aim is, therefore, to find a specification of characteristics (attributes) which would correspond to the above definition. Systems theory assumes that such sets of data have something in common. But what that something is, nobody has yet managed to discover, apart from the fact that different sorts of systems exist which have only the above-mentioned definition in common. Systems theory has at its disposal a whole range of terms used to describe specific relations – from equifinality, equilibrium and feedback to function and adaptability. We do not mean to underestimate this terminology; however, the importance of these terms seems to be heuristic rather than explanatory. They allow us to pose questions but for answers we have to look to ourselves. Description of a system by means of these terms explains only a little. It is rather a certain recipe for how to look for concrete structures within a given model. Conversely, we have to agree with E. R. Leach that: 'Friedman uses expressions like model, system trajectory, social formation, structure and so on as if he was merely performing the three card trick on a race track. By such means one might quite easily demonstrate that the moon is made of green cheese' (Leach 1977: 163).

Adoption of the term 'adaptation' also presents problems. We have to find out *what* is being adapted, and *to what*, and this is not an easy task in the case of a society. Every society adapts not only to its environment but above all to its 'niche' (that is, how it defines its environment, on the basis of its cognitive map). It adapts according to its image – that is, according to its notions about itself and its goals. The term 'functional' is not only an adjective as, for example, 'red', but also a relation. We need to know what it relates to and this presents a problem, as we have seen with the term 'adaptation'.

Human activity can no longer be considered to be only a function within the limits of the system, and it cannot be reduced to an objective effect. What appears dysfunctional or non-functional in one state of the system does not have to be so in a future state of the same system or with regard to other systems.

An additional problem is the fact that deterministic systems demand precision and our data are not precise. This is not because we measure or weigh our artefacts incompetently but because they belong to a separate part of culture – e.g. material culture, which can be impaired. This is not to mention difficulties arising from precise chronology. Such systems also lead us to adopt a notion (and this is their main shortcoming, both methodological and ontological) that the main variables of the system do really exist, and, if they do not behave in the way we expect them to, that this is due to unforeseen and random partial conditions thanks to 'non-rationalisable or historical remnants' (N. Hartman). We have thus divided the world artificially into chaos and cosmos. (Further criticism of the systems approach was voiced by Berlinski 1976, Hodder 1986, Lowe 1985, Lowe and Barth 1980 and Salmon 1978, 1980, Salmon and Salmon 1982.)

The success of classical experimentation was facilitated in the first place by the fact that it was applied in areas with an exactly corresponding structure – e.g. in those sectors of science which were engaged in a study of well-organised, narrowly determined systems that could be described by means of simple mathematical functions. A simple functional dependency was then identified with a law. The form of experimentation corresponding to such systems was identified with experimentation as such, and the concept of experimental sciences was more or less identified with those sciences that investigated such well-organised systems. It was for this reason that other sciences tried – even though unsuccessfully – to adapt themselves to this demand and to strive to fashion their methodology and laws in a similar way.

It is only in the past few decades that systems other than deterministic – e.g. stochastic, diffusive or poorly organised – ones are given consideration.

It is possible to distinguish three kinds of stochasticity. The weather forecast can serve as an example of the first kind. No one would dispute that weather is a determinable system, and that the basic variables affecting weather are known to us. In spite of this, we are unable to forecast the behaviour of the weather systems accurately; the individual deviations from the ideal pattern are put down to unpredictable interference which was not incorporated into the forecasts, or to an excessively large amount of input data, some of which remained unprocessed. Consequently, our theories about the weather, however lucid they may be, lose their predictive value and we get wet. It may therefore be more practical to regard weather as a case of simple diffusion.

On the other hand we may be faced with problems which we cannot understand from the theoretical point of view, and yet they produce practical results. For instance, the basis of such a fundamental and important technological process as the Bessemer technique of making steel remains a puzzle, and yet we are able to use it. It is an advantage to regard such processes as stochastic, and hope all along that one day we may be able to work out a comprehensive theory to explain their operation.

But the truly stochastic systems are those which are capable of self-regulation and learning, those which influence their environment and change it as well as themselves. It is really from this point of view that stochasticity is a property of human society. Here it is impossible to find the classic deterministic theory in a form pure enough and on a scale large enough to provide both explanation and prediction.

If we understand culture (in its cultural and anthropological sense) to be a system, we must be aware that culture keeps on redefining its environment and, consequently, itself. With regard to culture, environment consists of things which influence culture's inputs. As long as culture influences environment it simultaneously alters environment's input to itself in a cycle of mutually influencing development. In continuously articulating with its environment, culture not only alters itself, but changes its environment as well; environment thus regulated becomes, in fact, a part of culture, except for those aspects which are independent of and incidental to cultural development.

In addition to the individual incorporated in culture (society, history), culture represents itself as the individual's environment and the individual then becomes an element subordinate to the system. The individual is therefore defined from outside, through his construction of culture. In order to explain, for example, the behaviour of a certain social group or to deduce from one of its stages its next state, we would have to carry out an analysis of all its acts and influences which are in operation. This would presuppose a super-human intelligence like the well-known demon of Laplace, and we cannot very well identify ourselves with him. In order to come to a conclusion we need to have at our disposal optimal information in any given time period, and this can be supplied only with a type of analysis which comprehends the system we are investigating as stochastic, uncertain, and 'fuzzy'. This applies, naturally, to the present, the detailed knowledge of which is impossible, and equally to the past, which can be reconstructed only partially. What is characteristic for human beings is precisely the ability to determine intuitively the degree of probability of an event without knowing fully, or at all, conditions surrounding it. Here a certain element of freedom is introduced, and this element forms the premise on which the entire system is based. Society is formed by people who act in the same way as we do – they see the others as a diffuse system – and, therefore, society is in reality a diffuse system. Human society is a self-organised system that can learn. Not only does it receive information, but it also originates it. It is for this reason that human society should be studied – just like a diffuse system – also in the past. This is supported by V. V. Nalimov who, interestingly, states:

If we imagine a civilisation existing on some other planet, which has reached approximately the same degree of development as ours, then their scientific theories may be entirely different from ours ... We can suppose that any extensive scientific theory is intrinsically bound up with the individuality of its creator just as in, for example, art. The difference lies, as we can see, in the fact that great scientific theories are conducted in time in such a way as to evolve towards a certain extreme; however, it is not clear what the speed of such progress is. (Nalimov 1971: 49–50)

P. L. Kapica recounted examples of basic discoveries in physics which changed its nature – discoveries which could not have been foreseen and which had, therefore, to be discovered by chance. Electricity was discovered in this way, as was, for instance, electromagnetism, and radioactivity. In relation to existing theories, these discoveries were fortuitous and could have occurred much earlier or much later. And this is physics, which is much more exact than archaeology and prehistory!

Hypotheses concerning prehistory

The mutual relationship between archaeology and prehistory is defined in a number of ways. The same can be said about their relation to history, anthropology and sociology (Charlton 1981, Whitley 1986). Somewhere in between we find ethnohistory, palaeohistory, and palaeoethnology. We come across differences stemming from different personal approaches, schools of thought and also entire national and cultural complexes. In addition, these approaches change with the times. This is not surprising, as the social sciences and humanities study human beings and problems they pose for themselves. Already the definition of man is a problem in itself. If you do not believe it is, read the novel *Unnatural Animals* by the French writer Vercors.

The concept of history is also understood in a variety of ways and a given meaning only transpires when we take into account the context. A distinction is made between history which is understood as something that really happened (*res gestae*), and history which is a collection of statements about what happened (*historia rerum gestarum*). A distinction is made between history which includes all the past of humanity, and history which records human past only since the existence of written sources.

Sociology is understood as a discipline 'concerned with developing systematic, reliable knowledge about human social relationships in general and about the products of such relationships' (Hoult 1977: 307).

All these are very fine definitions. However, when we begin to apply them, our enchantment with them soon disappears. Let us demonstrate this with an example. 'In practice', adds Hoult in his *Dictionary of Modern Sociology*, 'it is often difficult to distinguish between sociology and socio-cultural anthropology, since both fields are primarily concerned with the study of human social relationships in general.' If we, therefore, understand history in the sense of something that really happened, it also makes sense to talk about the prehistory of humanity but not about archaeology. As soon as we understand history as, for example, a reconstruction of the past, then we can use both terms, archaeology and prehistory, and this also applies if we intend history to be a scientific discipline.

However, as soon as we stress the sociological (or anthropological) aspect of archaeology the situation changes drastically: that is to say, each science operates with different concepts of time and space and this applies to sociology as well as to history. To overstate the matter somewhat, history studies revolutions but not revolution as such; sociology, in contrast, examines revolution but not revolutions. We may understand it better if we remind ourselves of Oscar Wilde's words that all beautiful things belong in the same age – a fact also known to lovers. The category of general statements made by a sociologist includes all events which he can describe without regard to time and space. Consequently, a sociologically orientated archaeologist can, in an extreme case, abandon prehistory as a time span (this occurs in the case when these statements exceed, as far as their generality is concerned, this period); he can also abandon prehistory as a science and, finally, also science altogether. More and more archae-ologists are setting out on such trips.

Let us, however, return to history as a scientific discipline. History in this sense does not concern itself with the whole panorama of the past; for example, the private life of the Joneses is of no interest to it. It is interested in the remaining, fairly vague portion, which it calls 'historical facts'. It is a fairly relative category – there is one set of facts from the point of view of world history and another from the point of view of a nation. Con-sequently, we can ask: what sort of 'historical' (e.g. significant for history) facts do we have in the prehistoric part of history? Firstly, we cannot trace them very well from excavations and, secondly, if they did exist at all what kind of facts were they? It would seem that in prehistory it was the 'sociological' facts which were of utmost importance, and if this is the case, prehistory does not have much in common with history itself. Past human activity then becomes a parade of sociological experiments. This statement may seem somewhat daring, but let us cite one indisputable fact in its support – that is, that historians and archaeologists do not understand each other. The same also applies to ethnohistory, the methodology of which is, according to Kroeber, the utilisation of historic data in the solution of anthropological problems (Kroeber 1915, 1952).

We have so far not mentioned another characteristic of history, namely, its function. As Claude Lévi-Strauss said, humankind distinguishes two kinds of society – cold and hot. 'Hot' societies are those which decide to interpret themselves through their own history. Soon after Lévi-Strauss, some French post-structuralists began to take this idea to its logical conclusion. They understood history as a stick by means of which the Western world rules over the rest of the world. (Some anthropologists made identical statements also about their science.) Another French graduate – the Kampuchean dictator Pol Pot – employed the same crystal-clear reasoning when he liquidated history and with it millions of human beings and strove to instal pure sociology (somewhat utopian in character, of course).

Our situation is now so complicated that we can do nothing but resort to a solution along the lines of Columbus, or Alexander with the Gordian knot. The solution is, of course, at hand – we shall put all the pigeon-holes with archaeology, prehistory, anthropology and sociology aside and strive to investigate what and how we can relate about the past of humankind before the birth of history (in its narrower sense).

We shall approach this task from top to bottom – that is, we shall first ask what we can say and how about the object of archaeology or prehistory and only then what the properties of prehistory as such are.

Let us then return to something which we already know – that is, archaeography and the various specific archaeological theoretical concepts. Using various indices of similarity we can follow generic (for example, categories, classes), typological (type, variant) and settlement relationships. The units resulting therefrom can be arranged according to time (degree, phase, sequence, stage, stadium), space (region, area, horizon) and time and space (cultures, complexes). However, we do not know in principle what a certain time and space range of distribution of a specific kind of artefact means and what kind of substrata we can assume. This stage, too, is extremely hypothetical because it originates gradually and unnoticed as a result of the great time-and-space anthropological hypotheses. Archaeography is preceded genetically by archaeology and it, in turn, is preceded by anthropological statements. However, these links are two-directional; it is sufficient to modify slightly one basic unit in archaeography and suddenly the whole theory alters. This was recently illustrated very well by L. R. Binford and J. A. Sabloff (1982).

Thomsen's scheme of three periods, coupled with individual finds of archaeological material, placed the great story of Lucretius into concrete space and enabled its further development. Gradually, as finds accumulated, the description and comparison also grew wider and it was necessary to constitute further and further periods, cultures and sub-cultures in order to render their development in a narrative. The story of prehistory was expanding. This was at the same time accompanied by the disintegration of the evolutionist paradigm. Temporal and spatial specifications came to the fore more and more, and, in place of the outlines of a general evolution, contacts, migration and communications were studied. Such description, although derived from anthropology, is termed historico-narrative description and it also serves as an explanation of a kind. However, it is narrative and historic in the sense used in palaeontology or geology rather than that used in history itself and for this reason it was not influenced by historiography to any great extent.

The historico-narrative tradition is seen by our contemporaries (especially the Anglo-American circle) as solely descriptive and not explanatory. However, when doubts are cast on the existence of cultures and the research emphasis is shifted to the inner core of individual entities, we meet with scepticism regarding both the possibility of a holistic picture of prehistory in general, and the possibilities of a historical description in particular. For example, New Archaeology defines history as a discipline where scientific method cannot be used and it even denies that history has any meaning at all.

Recently, attention has focused on the investigation of hypotheses regarding functional and systematic dependencies which are supposed to represent further levels of explanation. Functional dependencies are studied when investigating mutual relations of individual artefacts and their attributes within a certain temporal and spatial range from the point of view of a selected system (production, ecological, sign, etc.). It is usual in this case for interpretation – in the form of a hypothesis – to come first. This is for the simple reason that we have to select both the investigated unit and the theoretical perspective. This selection then plays a decisive role. We can pose a question: 'What hypotheses about prehistoric functional and systemic dependencies can we formulate, or better still, how can such hypotheses be tested on archaeological material?'

We can also ask the same question in reverse. What are the rules for translating statements formed in an internal archaeological language (Frerichs 1981) into a language which is the property of other sciences, or into an everyday language? It is precisely through the 'archaeologist/non-archaeologist' language and non-archaeological terminology that archaeology becomes a part of science, culture, society, tradition and ordinary life and this gives it a meaning in the end.

Archaeology searches in the language of 'non-archaeology' for its hypotheses and explanations. However, if we take, for example, a simple archaeographic description, we can see that it has very little in common with other languages, and that it cannot be directly translated into them. The situation improves somewhat when we look at specific archaeological categories and the description of spatio-temporal chronology and dependencies. But, on the whole, these are not much better, as contemporary criticism points out. There are not many hypotheses which can be tested with their help.

However, let us not be one-sided in our criticism. If archaeological material serves only for testing anthropological hypotheses, then it can lead (and this has often been the case up till now) to a situation where the partial statements connected by some trivial 'Mickey Mouse' laws or by some artificial evolutionary scheme are shattered.

What is really needed in this situation is some common framework which would allow us to pose our own questions. What archaeology or prehistory (or whatever you want) needs is a systematic examination of its suppositions – in fact very much the same kind of thing as history found in the theory of history, metahistory or, in German, *Historik*. J. Rüsen (1983: 21) defines it in this way: 'The theory of history is a reflection of historical thought which has thrown light on the position of historical thinking as a science.'

What does such a meta-prehistory look like? It is best to demonstrate this by way of an example which will form the subject of our next chapter, and also by our further remarks.

On communication and organisation

Let us begin with an analysis of the basic condition for the existence of human history – communication: communication as a process of establishing the social unity of individuals with the help of signs (Cherry 1968: 305). We could argue that human behaviour cannot be limited to communication only. Nevertheless, the fact remains that that which is not communicable and that which it is not necessary to communicate – e.g. the basic vital functions and needs – are more or less constant. What are decisive from the point of view of communication are the modifications and variation of the behaviour that lies in between.

Natural selection itself, in the sense of suitable changes from a random variability, represents a simple form of communication. In the case of heterosexual organisms this mechanism is supplemented by communication between organisms. They have already put between themselves and the environment a more or less conscious selection. A human being begins with the organisation and communication of his/her sexual relations and in accordance with these builds – especially in the beginning – his/her social organisation and culture (Friedrich Engels 1884). The culture itself is built on learning – that is, communication.

A human being is formed by his culture and society. These form, at the same time, his environment, which he in turn shapes. Culture is nothing more than some kind of a stockpiled evolution. In culture, a human being formulates in advance answers to environmental demands. This is done by constantly rearranging, adding, combining and withdrawing his artefacts and mentefacts – i.e. his activity. It is for this reason that culture must be an organic entity in which information, communication and organisation are interconnected. Let us illustrate this with the example of tools.

Physical anthropologists can tell us which artefacts were fashioned by the hand of specific hominids. That is to say, tools are only as good or as bad as the hands which made them. Let us also add that they are as good or as bad as the language and thought of their makers. Man is defined by his tools – not only by his material implements such as stone axes, or ploughing equipment, but also by his domestic animals and, above all, words and language. Like the chicken and the egg, the types of tool – material and linguistic – cannot be separated.

The primary function of the first chipper was the modification of nature for the procurement of food and raw materials. The number of implements and operations gradually grew; things transformed into raw material were processed, and their characteristics became more discernible. The environment could now be perceived as divisible into functions, operations, something which could be manipulated and constructed, something which was composed of attributes. Consequently, it could be replicated, reassembled and, therefore, communicated.

The first tools imitated and extended some of the capabilities of human organs, above all hands. Using tools, a range of basic tasks could be performed, such as grasping, handling, scraping, cutting, piercing, delivering blows, etc. Human physical activity represented a small complex of basic mechanical operations (pulling, lifting, grinding, etc.). All physical activity could be reduced to these operations and they represented the basic parts of this activity.

Individual tools, above all the most primitive ones, were connected with these basic operations – implements and operations are inseparable. Implements were therefore common to everybody, just as the operations carried out with their help were common to everybody. It was only later that tools, operations and activities became specialised (trades) and each sector created its own tools and operational universals. The situation is the same in language – there is a basic vocabulary set and there are specialist dictionaries.

Gradually, implements became specialised and their individual functions became independent. A chopper, a universal tool for performing all the basic operations, gradually became differentiated into various implements with special functions – for cutting (knife), stabbing (pointed edge, dagger), chopping (axe), striking (bludgeon, hammer) and other functions.

Marx wrote that even the most insignificant human creature surpasses the most complex work of, for example, bees, because man first thinks out what he is going to do. As the pioneering research of J. Piaget and L. S. Vygotskij showed, and as subsequent experiments have repeatedly demonstrated, thinking is initially linked with sensory-motor activity, and is also inseparable from it.

Similarly, words become more specific and effective as they become specialised. It is a long journey from simple tools and pictures – notions derived from unco-ordinated activity and syncretic thinking – to specialised technology and discursive thought. Vocabulary was, originally, common to all, just as the implements were; today everybody participates in the total vocabulary of a language only to a certain, often quite small, degree. Every discipline has its own vocabulary. As a rule, we control only the simplest of the implements and machinery; the rest is the domain of a specialist. Along with specialisation, co-ordination of different technological functions emerged. Technological operations have become more and more complex, forming long sequences of separate activities which have to follow each other with precise timing. Man is able to perform activities such as crushing, knocking, scraping, grating, soaking, whetting, grinding, sawing, polishing, and pounding, but above all, he is capable of co-ordinating these simple basic activities into one long sequence producing a final result planned in advance. And this is not all. Man is capable of dedicating specific tools to specific tasks in anticipation of results and, in turn, of employing machines composed from them. The manuscript *Mechanical Problems*, ascribed to Aristotle, enumerates the basic mechanical tools of his time: lever, lever with counterweight, balance scales, beam scales, pincers, wedge, axe, crank, roller, wheel, pulley, block, potter's wheel, sling, oar, and cog wheel. These simple tools served man for over fifteen centuries and what wonderful things he managed to create with their help: even cathedrals.

The structure of tools, the organisation of technological operations and of social relations, necessarily require the organisation of society as well. Society represents an embodiment of fixed relationships between people, a certain communicative and organisational scheme.

The ability to establish connections, mutual bonds, inflexion and syntax gradually comes to the foreground. This happens not only in language but also in other sign systems, in production and in society itself. According to W. James man does not consist of only one social persona – there are as many such personae connected with each human being as there are people who form their picture of the individual. Thanks to their number, these social 'I-pictures' make up a system entirely dependent on the communication media. On the basis of this system it is possible to reconstruct – although only in general outlines – not only society, but also individuals, and this can be done precisely thanks to the communication media. Cliché, motifs, and other basic units of folk epics with their ability to be built up, interchanged and linked, gradually form the edifice of the mythological duplication of the world, constructed on the basic oppositions according to the picture of human society. This represents at the same time evidence about the basically parallel evolution of technology, language, psychology, knowledge and society as mutually invariable communication media.

C. Lévi-Strauss characterises the system of knowledge in pre-literate societies as a 'science of the concrete' and compares it with do-it-yourself activity (*bricolage*). A do-it-yourself enthusiast can manage a number of things but always only with the help of the tools he has in his workshop. He constructs only what he can manufacture with his tools and with the materials he has at hand.

A simple list of primitive technology, tools and materials, picture-notions of primitive thoughts rather than defined concepts, a limited number of basic units of myths, fairy tales and other folklore forms – all these are materials good enough for do-it-yourself activity.

Only later, with occupational/craft specialisation, did the difference between do-it-yourself individual and technician, folklore and literature, individual pieces of knowledge and science, begin to emerge.

The life of an individual is not the subject of history and, equally, individual relationships in their totality are not the subject of sociology. Basically, as far as history (in its wider sense) is concerned, we are not interested in what was said at a given moment but how it was communicated – the method of communication and what could be expressed through its means. Prehistory, too, is not interested in individual life in prehistoric times but in culture and society and their fate. This means that the objectification of man serves as prehistory's model – that is, man's role in relation to others, his social standing and the way in which roles and status manifest themselves in his behaviour and communication.

Archaeologists who handle the most concrete objects (usually broken) are not interested in why these were destroyed, whether in an argument or through clumsiness: this is not a type of event which would concern them. On the contrary, they strive to find out connections of a supra-individual nature – in other words, basically a concrete complex of sign systems which would represent the culture in the given period; a system which itself forms an interrelated system whose internal relationships form further sub-systems. In the same way, the relationships of people within a society form a system which is different in relation to every individual.

These relationships form a complex which has to be either deciphered or accepted with its customs and objectified: tasks faced not only by the archaeologist, but also by the ethnologist who, in living societies, studies problems similar to those found in archaeology. A decision to decipher the system means, at the same time, a necessity to formulate a certain descriptive and explanatory framework, because reality is always recon-structed in relation to a certain aim. The question is, what means do we use to explain such a framework, and from what point of view? Even description alone requires a need to separate oneself from the object of description. Consequently, it is evidence of disharmony with a given state. An archaeologist is effectively relieved of such problems, thanks to the chronological distance placed between him and his data. At the same time, it is precisely because of this distance that he is all the more exposed to other problems. In a living society the system of mutual ideas, attitudes, behaviour, communications and objects is not mechanically divided into spiritual and material culture and for this reason we cannot say that one is a reflection of the other. On the contrary, they all connect and merge in the concrete activities of an individual. However, it is almost impossible to reconstruct this state and we must, therefore, base our quest on what there is available to us in archaeology – that is, material culture, defined in time – and study its relationships to other sign systems. But even those have been, in fact, constructed only artificially as hypotheses, up to the final syntheses and reconstruction: 'there is no autonomous category *economy* as a separate sphere of social life in precapitalist societies; we must insist on the historical relativity of economic categories and in fact the category *economic* itself' (Gledhill and Larsen 1982: 198). This statement can, at the same time, serve as a criticism of Binford's technomic, socio-technic and ideo-technic classes of artefacts and of Clarke's economic, ideological, social and material-culture sub-systems. Just because contemporary society is divided in this way does not imply such divisions existed in the past.

The problem rests in the fact that individual, partial sign systems can be separated and they do indeed behave as systems, but they do so at the cost of losing their correspondence to other systems. This is because they behave according to the logic of things rather than the aims of their creators and users. This is also the reason why linguists and archaeologists diverge when investigating identical models and why archaeologists observe different behaviour in the individual sub-systems of artefacts.

The only way open to us is to separate all possible subordinate systems, investigate their functioning and, above all, their mutual relations. This, of course, means hypothesis after hypothesis and an opportunity for short cuts. Fortunately, prehistory is so distant that for us it grows old only very slowly.

Every artefact can be rendered by a description without being reduced to it. The reverse is true of the products of thought and speech (mentefacts) – they cannot be reduced to artefacts. Archaeologists know of 'Homo pictor' and 'Homo faber' and we are now trying to discover 'Homo loquens'. Unfortunately, it seems that there are great discrepancies in the fates of these three gentlemen. Pictor created his masterpieces during the Magdalenian period and his previous explorations did not justify such an enormous explosion of artistic sense and art (including their spatial and numerical distribution). Equally, we canot explain the swift decline and discarding of this method of expression. From that time, Mr Pictor can only be followed through the forms of artefacts intended for everyday use and their decoration. Faber was for a long time satisfied with relatively primitive tools – until some 20,000 years ago. Then another lull set in, lasting practically until the Middle Ages – a revolution which never ceases to astonish us. And old Loquens – we know hardly anything about him!

We can suppose, on the basis of ethnographic and historical parallels, that it was precisely during those periods when Messrs Pictor and Faber enjoyed their well-deserved rest that Mr Loquens engaged in intensive activity. 'The evolution of language', Mumford said:

was incomparably more important to further human development than the chipping of a mountain of hand-axes. Besides the relatively simple coordinations required for tool-using, the delicate interplay of the many organs needed for the creation of articulated speech was a far more striking advance. This effort must have occupied a greater part of early man's time, energy, and mental activity, since the ultimate collective product, spoken language, was infinitely more

complex and sophisticated at the dawn of civilization than the Egyptian or Mesopotamian kit of tools.
(Mumford 1967: 8–9)

P. Lieberman (1975, 1984) has recently published the results of his experiments in which he suggests that it was precisely the imperfections in the anatomy of larynx and pharynx, preventing the development of articulated speech, which eliminated Neanderthal man from subsequent evolution.

Our conclusion is quite dismal for archaeology – it seems that Messrs Faber and Pictor will not tell us much about their colleague Loquens and it seems that they are not even equipped to do so. The study of relationships between sign systems leads to the revelation that though each of the systems reacts to another system, each of them is different and therefore reacts slightly differently. This is because each system is a filter that lets through and consequently records only selected information. However, what can be studied is how one component distorts another and this in itself is an important subject. This should be investigated, above all, by the archaeological critique of material, but at the same time this task is so permanent and vast that it can be identified with practically all archaeological activity.

Things conscious and unconscious

Some statements carry no significant message. It means nothing to be told that a person has two ears; but to be told that he has one ear represents a message.

The natives of Fiji, Darwin reminisced, were astonished by the English rowing boats but disregarded great vessels. This was because they themselves made boats similar to those of the English and could compare their construction. As far as the large sailing ships were concerned they had nothing to compare them with and were therefore not interested in them – they did not carry any message as far as the natives were concerned. Things too familiar or too completely unknown do not, in themselves, convey a message.

Anything new needs to be compared with the old. However, for a child everything is new and that is why he/she remembers so little later. Montaigne's father was very well aware of this fact. When he was showing his son a rare animal – a salamander – he wisely boxed his ears and said, 'Now you will remember salamander for the rest of your life!' And so he did, thanks to the sensory memory.

In a word, the new cannot exist without the old. The old is nothing more than an experience which has been gained up to the present point in time, a classified and fixed experience. The new, therefore, seems to us only a variation of the old scheme. A message is something which is unknown; it therefore means something new. It therefore requires a certain customary state of things, something to which we do not react at all, or if we do, then only subconsciously, something which is not the subject of communication. According to Claparède's psychological law we do not realise precisely what we normally experience. The message and its background form an inseparable pair and we cannot discuss communication without first analysing this basis of a message.

Let us examine these relationships using the example of artefacts. We can distinguish two types of characteristics: first, those characteristics of which their creators and users were aware; and, second, those which were not subject to conscious evaluation and did not serve the purpose of communication but which, nevertheless, formed its basis.

Let us illustrate this with an example. The year 1612 found the mathematician, astronomer and astrologer Johan Kepler in Linz in Austria, where there was an unusually productive grape harvest. At that time, however, barrels were in short supply and wood and coopering expensive. Having successfully sold several barrels of wine, it occurred to Kepler that if he developed a barrel optimal in terms of surface and capacity he could make a fortune. He spent three sleepless nights working on this problem and in the end succeeded in calculating the optimal form. How surprised he was when he found out that his shape coincided with the shape of real barrels. 'Who can deny that human nature itself, without any deep conscious deliberations, learns the basic rules of geometry?'

Since we cannot assume theoreticians of Kepler's standing amongst the coopers, we presume that the preference for more advantageous patterns of barrels occurred more or less unintentionally, by trial and error. In the case of artefacts (and similarly, technology) we can, as a rule, observe a long chain of forms leading to functional optimalisation as a variation on natural selection. This is comparable with the contemporary concept of evolution, as a change occurring at random during the reproduction of a given state.

However, functional optimalisation need not be the only criterion in the evaluation of culture patterns (Simmel's logic of cultural circuits), scientific paradigm (Kuhn's interpretation), artistic style or method of cognition (Foucault's discourse) or simply the logic of the situation. In these cases we are concerned with a certain framework which can be filled in and which, at the same time, serves as a filter.

According to Claude Lévi-Strauss, ethnological problems in general are problems of communication (unconscious changes in the communication structures also fall into this category). On the other hand, changes in unconscious characteristics – that is, characteristics which do not serve communication purposes – are the domain of archaeology and these are typical of the majority of archaeological, typological, temporal and spatial elements. This is also why they can be investigated with ease by means of archaeological indicators.

Apart from gradual changes of material culture, we can find other aspects of society which are more or less unconscious: economic dependencies, long-term social trends, customs, language development, myths, all codes of communication, etc. The universally shared patterns of behaviour and activity also belong here. What all these levels have in common is the absence of their explicit manifestation in material culture; they are not directly referred to because they are thought obvious and can, therefore, be followed only with the help of indicators.

These unconscious points of reference are something that appeared more or less as a part of the social environment to contemporary human beings, and they are, therefore, comparable to the external ecological environment. Thanks to our total overview, we observe in fact only the results of activity but not the activity itself. However, the more these unconscious and uncommunicated changes and tendencies prevail, the less important is the conscious behaviour.

The most basic level is formed by the biological nature of man. This is determined by natural selection, and the history of mankind begins precisely at the moment when this law concerning the evolution of man's physical constitution loses its validity. Man, in fact, transfers the operation of the principle of natural selection to his activity, his creations and his concepts. This is why we can talk about evolution of artefacts and, consequently, the evolution of culture.

The more human activity and its consequences become subordinated to unconscious selection, the greater influence such selection has on human beings – it exercises more or less the same influence as the environment. 'It is necessary to go into the past to discover the deep-lying forms, which, so often unconscious, are determinative of the social process', Durkheim had written in 1899 (according to Bellah 1959: 447).

When we investigate ethnological phenomena, we can see that the deeper we dig into the past the more important the framework becomes, and it is the subconscious framework which is the most important of all. All that is individual and subjective is lost in the depths of time. We can observe this phenomenon in the evolution of literature. The oldest works of literature manage by simply stating the hero's status. Only later do we have the development of the epic description of actions, which is gradually supplemented by description of expressions, character and, finally, psychology. As soon as man becomes capable of consciously forming structural relationships, and of creating his conception of the world, he is in a position to carry out conscious selection. The mythological categorisation of his actions is replaced by the stress on their uniqueness.

Within the historical framework, events take on an increasing importance. We could say that the autonomous value of human activity is only possible within the framework of history. And if individual actions have their meaning, their picture – a historical picture – must have meaning too. The autonomous development of structures is overcome by our realisation of their connectedness: evolution gives place to history.

Awareness of individual attributes (conscious attributes) serves the purpose of communication (as, for example, the manifestation of a status or kinship). If we can determine those artefactual attributes which were consciously recognised by their makers, we can, through the changing relations between such attributes, test hypotheses about communication and, consequently, also the organisation of society. This means that we can study how the present was perceived in the past by those who lived in it.

The need to approach the interpretation of archaeological materials in a way which will reflect the cognitive framework of their originators asserted itself only very gradually in archaeology. We can mention here, for example, folk taxonomy, ethno-archaeology and attempts at symbolic, structural and cognitive archaeology.

However, the relationship between conscious and unconscious attributes is changing all the time. Moreover, conscious attributes are growing in number and are also becoming more specialised. Finally, their relationships are in a process of constant and dynamic change.

Napoleon always defeated the Austrian generals, to their great surprise, because they always kept to all the rules of military art, and Napoleon was, according to them, a pure dilettante. In reality Napoleon was no amateur – he knew the rules very well and he could, therefore, forecast the Austrians' manoeuvres and then destroy their rules. By disregarding old rules he in fact created new ones. One can understand then why the Austrian army had the reputation of being always perfectly prepared for war – the previous one.

Herein lies the chief problem concerning rules of human behaviour. As soon as they are formulated, a new Napoleon appears who takes advantage of them and alters them. If this applies to characteristics which are conscious, albeit canonised in dogmas and maxims, it is even more true of unconscious characteristics. Although they operate *as* laws (and they are often identified with them) they are as far removed from laws as a kitten from a tiger – their strength equals our weakness, that is, ignorance. (Let us also add that they operate not only convergently but also divergently. A relatively inconspicuous, unintentional or fortuitous impulse can lead to immeasurable consequences. Let us put aside Cleopatra's cute nose which so influenced Caesar and instead cite the consequences of not using a wheel in pre-Columbian civilisations.)

The role of archaeology is therefore to investigate communication and organisation in prehistory in all the aspects mentioned above and, particularly, from the point of view of the variable relationship between conscious and unconscious characteristics.

Prehistory and history

For archaeologists, history is a scarecrow, a punch-bag and a sacrificial lamb. In order to perform these roles, history is identified with the history of events, a history purely narrative, linear and diachronic, a history of the unique and particular. So far only B. G. Trigger (1978b) and I. Hodder (1986, 1987a, b) have attempted to explain to archaeologists that there also exists a different concept of historiography, but without any success.

It is obvious that the attitude of most archaeologists is unjustified because contemporary historiography tends more and more towards synchronic relationships, the investigation of forms of collective life and institutions and the investigation of long-term social and economic relationships. It co-operates closely with other social sciences, using modelling, systems and structural analyses and mathematical and statistical methods (Barraclough 1979). To mention just one example, P. Chaunu established serial history, which studies repeated elements. To borrow the words of Ferdinand Braudel, history shifted from 'l'histoire événementielle' (history of events) to the history of 'longue durée'.

Now that we have overcome the feeling of fear and repulsion towards history we can treat it with a little less prejudice, although what follows might seem to betray sentiments to the contrary.

'History is all bunk', Henry Ford once said and there is no doubt that he meant historiography. Even so, let us apply this definition from the father of 'Tin Lizzy' to the subject of historiography.

We can distinguish two levels in social activity. *The first level* is events, communication during the events and reporting on those events. We cannot limit ourselves to the events only. The events are reported; in a sense they are performed so that they can be reported on: the reference is often more important than the event itself. In prehistory this level can be followed only by means of indicators and even this can be done only to a limited extent. This is because individual events do not have meaning here, only the events which have been categorised. However, historiography can count on explicitly stated verbal sources and, consequently, individual events which also have meaning within the framework of history.

As soon as we have formulated unconscious relationships (and, similarly, as soon as we recognise laws independent of man, for example, natural laws) they cease to appear as a framework of human activity but, on the contrary, they now appear within its framework. Their conceptual expression enables not only their analysis, variation and experimentation but also their incorporation within a necessarily more abstract and universally conceptual and paradigmatic framework. It facilitates conceptual and intellectual activity, which forms the precondition of historical activity and history. It is not by chance that the origin of history is usually linked with the existence of writing. It is writing that enables us to record and encompass more extensive complexes of knowledge. This conceptual expression is possible only within a common framework and with the concept of the whole in mind. This forms the *second level*. The world of man is impossible without conceptions of the universe and in this lies the difference between man and animals. Man acts and communicates within the framework of this perception and within the conceptual aids it offers. One of the basic concepts of the world is the concept about its past.

In the 'cold' (C. Lévi-Strauss), 'oral' (M. McLuhan), 'archaic' (M. Eliade) societies this conception is mythological. A myth categorises strictly every event and places it within an action and narrative scheme – individual events have meaning only within its framework.

History itself originated when the mythological model was abandoned. The origin of history is basically linked with the notion that there is a definite meaning in arranging events into temporal and causal chains and that when the connections between them are studied, the explanation will surely follow. However, the concrete concept of historical explanation differs from period to period, and the same will apply when history is explained in retrospect by historiography. This is also the reason why each historical explanation, each concept of history, chooses its own facts which it considers to be historical. However, in contrast to the mythological period, history chooses facts with an independent value, and it is precisely this value which gives them the right to be mentioned. It is a history of intentions and of their corrections – a narrative history.

Archaic structures of seriation and explanation of events exist, of course, also in the historical period and in different strata of society (varying in size but usually large), and different components of an individual's personality pay homage to such structures, even in present times.

Just as we have the poetics or syntax of events and references, we also have the unconscious structures of concepts relating to the past; that is, the structure of *how* rather than *what*, is being related. Historiography must therefore reconstruct those forms which enabled the participants to perceive events as unique, important and historical. In prehistory, of course, the perceptions of the past and the present merge and they are, therefore, placed in an immediate relation to the organisation of a society, which makes interpretation easier.

Historiography also investigates the environment which was exposed to historical events. In archaeology the investigation of such an environment is dominant if only because that which corresponds to the present-day archaeological units was not, as a rule, even realised by the original participants in the events: it was merely an unconscious environment for them.

Description and explanation in prehistory are therefore of a different nature from those in history. In prehistory we are guided by the social sciences rather than the arts, we follow evolution rather than history and in contrast to narration we make a distinction between explanation and description. The study of individual actions and conscious behaviour characteristic of historiography has no meaning in prehistory, and consequently, historical narrativity is of no importance.

On the contrary, it is because historiography began to explore more and more the unconscious aspects of life in the past that it had to learn to adopt the standpoints and methods of archaeology (or of the social sciences, usually through the means of cliometry). It is not by chance that G. Bachelard and G. Canguilhem use the term archaeology to denote the deeper, anti-positivistic research of the history of science and that M. Foucault called one of his books explicitly *L'Archéologie du savoir*. In his book Foucault draws attention to recent changes which the concept of 'document' has undergone. Whilst before it used to be interpreted as a direct source of what had happened, nowadays we strive to obtain a dehumanised picture of relationships to which people are subordinate in their activities. Whilst, in the past, historiography used to transform remains of the past into documents, now there is a tendency to transform the documents into the remains of the past. By the same token, the study of non-linear dependencies is more and more appreciated in historiography.

It was in prehistory that the basis for the historicisation of society was formed, and for this reason the events of that time cannot be expressed by the usual historiographic means. On the other hand, we can claim that historic societies, including contemporary societies, are based on unconscious structures comparable with those of prehistoric societies. They have, therefore, to be investigated by non-classical historiographic means – in other words, those which basically correspond to archaeological or, better still, archaeographic methods. It is paradoxical that archaeology can in fact learn more about its methods and objectives from their application in history. However, it is this influence that can lead to a conceptual enrichment of archaeology.

In conclusion, let us also mention some problems common to historiographical pre-historiographic interpretation (a somewhat unusual, but rather apt term). The first one is the relationship of our methods of interpretation of the past to the actual, existing interdependent relationships in the past.

To what extent is our global view of the past also an abstract view? If we take a global view of the landscape we can see it only in rough outlines. We do not see trees but a wood and this is because individual trees appear to us as indicators of a wood. If we want to describe a greater temporal or spatial range we cannot describe individual human acts but only patterns resulting from activities of whole groups of people. A global view cannot be simply identified with 'laws' or the 'march' of history, its 'process'; we cannot identify the rules of interpretation and depiction with the laws of that which is being depicted. However, this is often the case in archaeology, historiography and anthropology.

Bearing this in mind, let us borrow from L. N. Gumilev his 'historioscope' (Gumilev 1970). Let us then set it at the widest field of vision (100,000 years), in other words, the smallest enlargement. What we can now see are only demographic explosions, technological advances and the basic socioeconomic forms, such as hunting and gathering or agriculture. If we focus the instrument at the period of five thousand years we can follow the succession of individual cultures; and when we focus even closer we can study the fortunes of a single culture. The older a culture is, the less contact with other cultures there will be: its evolution will be autochthonous. If we follow the time scale leading to the present day, the cultural development will be less and less independent. And if we keep on focusing, individual relationships will eventually appear within our field of vision and, finally, we may be able to see only one person, let us say Shakespeare.

If we focus our instrument on Shakespeare, we will not gain much information concerning his person; Shakespeare can be understood only within the framework of his time (and he will reward us by telling us more about his time than any other individual). A focus on Robinson Crusoe would come sufficiently near the truth, but this is because his life was perfectly ahistorical.

This is all very annoying. When the field of vision is at its widest we can see things in their widest connections, but at the same time each concrete event in the past is isolated from the others. By contrast, the nearer we get to the present, the more interdependent each event becomes. However, let us not despair. We have, in fact, managed to catch up with a science as precise as physics – at least as far as Heisenberg's uncertainty principle is concerned.

Every picture – and this goes for the written depiction of the past as well – must have its background and foreground. Sociology summons to the centre of the stage universal relationships, and individual events are relegated to the background, to the role of the chorus line, whilst prehistory finds important the wide scenery of the background, in front of which the individual actors come and go very quickly. The background and foreground depend on the angle of vision, on the standpoint of the observer. If we observe something of a more complex nature, say a landscape, we always have to focus our attention on the individual parts while the rest serves as a neutral background. It is only later that we can perceive the landscape in its totality, but at a price: the original fine distinctions are supplanted by certain short cuts – what we see has been transformed via the apparatus in our head which deals with the processing of previous information. And our view of history or prehistory is created in a similar way.

However, the reverse can be true as well. If we stand in front of a picture, the picture itself can impose our position on us. Stendhal wrote in his diary that as an ordinary participant he saw everything there was to see in the battle of Bautzen (1813): that is, nothing. Stephen Crane described battle in the same way. True, they were artists, but in 1914 the British Admiralty thought it necessary to establish a committee, 109 years after the Battle of Trafalgar had taken place, to unify the reports of the participants in the battle. The description of a battle from the point of view of commanding generals is, of course, quite different from that according to the ordinary participants in the battle: they would have a different angle of vision – their commanding posts. If we read a description of a battle from the point of view of generals (and historians usually do so) we, the readers, find ourselves in the place of generals (at last!) and this may often be the reason why those historical texts are read and written. The identification with generals may be flattering, but J. G. Droysen called this view, practised by Rank's historiography school, the 'objectivity of a eunuch'.

The picture of prehistory also moulds its readers. The view towards the past is different from the view in the past; the view of a system is different from the views within the system. It is also for this reason that we should appreciate the present tendencies in archaeology (structural and cognitive archaeology) which strive to achieve a radical change in our angle of vision.

To the ambivalence of the views *towards* and *from*, others can be added, such as diachronics and synchronics, vertical and horizontal relations, time and space and, at another level, individual and universal, history and sociology. As Byron said, the problem with women is that we cannot live either with them or without them (more recently, women seem to have developed the same opinion about men). If we concentrate on one aspect, the other escapes us, but at the same time they cannot exist without each other.

In mythology the difference between the past and the present dwindles, there exists only eternal present, but only thanks to the fact that it is so steeped in the past. Life repeats itself constantly and practically without a change in the natural cycles of the day, the year and human life. All the events that were here already will be repeated; 'the self-same things happen to people' wrote Solomon. All our pairs, e.g. diachronics/synchronics, individual/universal, rest here as a caterpillar in a cocoon. It was only the Jewish and Christian conceptions of history with a goal at the end that unfolded these cycles into a straight line. Hence the notion of future and the problems with diachronics and synchronics. At present, synchronics – the non-personal and abstract relations between people – exercises more and more influence on us. Every day we are deluged with synchronic information from a vast space: daily news bulletins from the whole of the world.

Let us, however, return to prehistory. Relations between individual societies were rare and by their nature more often than not they represented danger. If we were to execute a narrow synchronic cut through prehistory, for example the year 10001 BC, we would obtain only a scattering of unconnected situations. Only in a younger period could we note the relations of larger and larger entities. Each such entity is a synchronic whole, full of interconnections and structural bonds, capable of being rendered perhaps by sociology or structural historiography, which concentrate precisely on the synchronic aspects of the past. The postulation of world history in historiography became possible only in the eighteenth century, when, as far as information was concerned, the world began to coalesce into one.

To study unconnected events makes hardly any sense. If we are therefore looking for interconnected complexes of events, we find that the deeper and deeper we retreat into the past, the more and more we have to concentrate on complexes defined by time: that is, complexes linked by genesis, tradition and mutual influences. The relationship of time and space becomes more and more complex, the amount of data diminishes with time and their temporal definition becomes less and less specific. It is estimated that in the Iron Age time definition can be stated with a precision of ± 100 years; in the Upper Palaeolithic ± 1,000 years; and in the Lower Palaeolithic ± 100,000 years. In addition, the number of investigated units – e.g. people – diminishes drastically. According to our estimates, fourteen billion people lived their existence in the years BC, compared with fifty-four billion who have lived since then and are still living. A non-specific temporal seriation then makes it impossible to construct a precise chronology sequence in space. In addition, there are also complications with specifying the value of individual associations of artefacts: do they indicate a spatial, functional, ethnological or evolutionary complex?

A twentieth-century Czech historian (J. Slavík) coined his own epitaph: 'Born in modern times, died in the Middle Ages.' And he was right because the inscription was not allowed to be engraved on his tombstone. Similarly, we say that some groups of people live in prehistory even today. The problem of non-contemporaneity in the present was first formulated by J. G. Herder, and it is also the problem of prehistory. As soon as we adopt a certain evolutionary scheme, time becomes schematised, and in sociology calendar time can evaporate altogether. Of Australian aborigines, with their linguistically mature and inwardly oriented culture, we can state that they lag behind us technologically by about six millennia; or that the distance between them and us, measured on the time scale of technological evolution, represents no more than about one per cent. Yet, in terms of kinship structures, they are far more evolved than our own society, and in terms of leisure, they are far better off than the most developed Western nations. Which statement shall we stress?

Evolutionary schemes enable us in archaeology to carry out a temporal classification of material which is not otherwise dated, and when a new method of absolute dating is discovered, its results can either confirm or disprove our theories. The last time this happened was with the introduction of radiocarbon dating, and our cherished theories ended up leaping out of the window, like speculators after the collapse of the Stock Exchange.

However, it does not seem probable that we could find some simple recipe suitable for all occasions, which would enable us to pacify the quarrelling relatives – synchronics/diachronics and others. Let us, however, ask George Bernard Shaw what he thinks about it all: 'I learnt long ago that though there are several places from which the tourist may enjoy a view of Primrose Hill, none of these can be called *the* view of Primrose Hill. I now perceive that the political situation is like Primrose Hill' (Shaw 1956: 128). Replace 'political' with 'prehistoric' and Shaw's observation encapsulates the dilemma faced in archaeology. Shaw continues:

Wherever I have been I have found and fervently uttered a true view of it; but as to the true view, believe me, there is no such thing. Place all the facts before me; and allow me to make an intelligent selection (always with the object of getting my man in); and the moral possibilities of the situation are exhausted. (ibid.)

This is also the solution to Byron's paradox raised earlier.

8 Epilogue

We still maintain a connection between the Romans and ourselves.
After all, we come to possess even contemporary events through
imagination.

Michel de Montaigne

After such extensive forays into the past and the present of archaeology as a
discipline, we can be forgiven if we briefly adopt a more distanced view.

If we accept a parallel with description in biology, then individual
scientific disciplines, schools of thought, theoretical and methodological
approaches, and, in the final analysis, the individual scholars, form a single
current, within which they compete for their place in the sun, for
recognition; but they also co-operate with one another. Every element
strives aggressively to occupy the largest amount of space, but it also
changes in the process. This is shown in the number of times archaeology
has altered its direction, significance, and ambitions, its field of operations,
and its approaches. How many times doubts were raised about its
autonomy and value and, conversely, how many times it exaggerated its
own importance! In actual fact, all elements share in the ecosystem,
responding to the influence of the broader social environment of other
disciplines and to the internal evolution within the subject. Perhaps this
thought can justify the 'environmentalist' approach, favoured to some
extent over others in the present volume.

Archaeology can, of course, be regarded from other perspectives, for
instance in the way Saussure regarded language. We can postulate the
existence of archaeological 'langage' (systematic structure), irrespective of
individual archaeologists, yet we also have to allow for the existence of
'parole' (the actual words used) – the practitioners of the discipline. We can
contemplate the variation in individual views and approaches, yet we have
to integrate the insights which changed the structure of the entire archaeological knowledge, as was the case with Thomsen. Further, we can
contemplate archaeological discourse in Foucault's perspective. Archaeology is, of course, influenced by its own development. Compare, for
instance, the classical, antiquarian and modern forms of archaeology. Here
we can see not only the subject changing, but also the basic units for

contemplation. Artefacts, originally invested with sacred meaning in the classical world, subsequently assumed a monetary value, on account of their rarity and age, during the Enlightenment; while the modern understanding of artefacts is only a few decades old and keeps changing.

We have found out that archaeology is not the only discipline concerned with prehistory, and at the same time we know that so far as prehistory is concerned, archaeology occupies the central position. For this reason, it is often identified with prehistory. This is why archaeology has an immutable duty to remain accessible to other disciplines. Only on the basis of such cross-fertilisation can it set its own objectives.

The history of methodology in other disciplines, and the history of archaeology itself, make it very clear that the concepts of the past – the creation of synchronic and diachronic entities – are constructed as general hypotheses. We cannot dismiss them just because most of these cannot be verified. Nevertheless, empirical observations directly depend on the theoretical framework and the methods employed in their procurement. All too often general method and theory is handed to archaeologists as a compendium of conventions and tasks, rather than as a range of concepts – such a cookbook approach breeds misapprehension, disappointment and the expectation that one can get by theory-free.

Continual specialisation gives archaeologists enough of their own problems, however: they are evaluated and they evaluate one another on the basis of the increase in the number of finds and on their external assessment. This in turn serves to evaluate the status and independence of the discipline. Archaeological training is oriented in the same direction. Far too much acknowledgement is given to the fact that the methodology of archaeology and most of its current knowledge were gained in the opening decades of the twentieth century. We also have to recognise that archaeology was essentially invented by the dilettanti, people without specialist training in archaeology, people trained in other disciplines and people with broad cultural, scientific and artistic interests. For them the disparity between facts and hypotheses did not exist. Judged from the present-day perspective, they committed ridiculous errors. Nevertheless, we all profit from their work and their ideas.

What is important now is the search for new relationships, new forms of expression, new questions. Semiology and linguistics, for instance, now search for more basic elements to contemplate than words. Semiological structural analysis is contributing decisively to the analysis of elements of folklore, which correspond to the artefacts of material culture investigated by archaeology.

Human activity has to be investigated as a process of communication, unfolding through the operation of individual symbolic systems and mediated through aspects of material culture such as clothing, diet, and so on. Palaeotechnology, palaeoeconomy, palaeoecology, palaeosociology, etc., are in the process of becoming more and more integrated, enhancing the reconstruction of prehistory with new dimensions.

Through archaeology, we are in a position to improve our understanding of other cultures, to articulate more effectively our relationship with the natural world, to discover unsuspected possibilities and to pose unanswered questions. Heraclitus considered the fate and the character of human beings as identical. *Arche* teaches us to understand ourselves, to identify ourselves in other peoples, cultures, and in the past. And this can serve as a response to the question put by Maurice Barrès, the writer, to Contenau, the orientalist, shortly before the First World War, as they came to rest before the Hittite fortress at Kadesh. 'One could carry out wonderful excavations here', said Contenau wistfully. 'I admit that such investigations would be very amusing and stimulating', Barrès replied, 'but what of the Hittites themselves? How are we to relate them to ourselves? In their struggle against the Egyptians, I feel no more kinship with them than I would with two armies of ants.' (Quoted after Vokounová-Davidová, M. 1938. Problém lidského osudu v epických básních akkadských. *Česká mysl* 34: 24–41.)

Select Bibliography

Quince. Is all our company here?
Bottom. You were best to call them generally, man by man, according
to the script.
Shakespeare, A Midsumer-night's Dream

This list of references is selective and does not purport to include all the
authorities cited in the text.

Adams, W. Y. 1988. Archaeological classification: theory versus practice. *Antiquity*
61: 40–56.

Agrawal, D. P. 1970. Archaeology and the Luddites. *Antiquity* 44: 115–29.

Aldenderfer, M. S. 1982. Methods of cluster validation for archaeology. *World
Archaeology* 14: 61–72.

Aldenderfer, M. S. and Blashfield, R. K. 1978. Cluster analysis and archaeological
classification. *American Antiquity* 43: 502–5.

Allsworth-Jones, P. and Wilcock, J. D. 1974. A computer-assisted study of
European Palaeolithic 'leafpoints'. *Science and Archaeology* 11: 25–46.

Almgren, B. 1965–6. Das Entwicklungsprinzip in der Archäologie – eine Kritik.
Tor 11: 15–38.

Ambros, C. 1978. (ed.) *Základné Metodologické Problémy a Marxistické Kategórie v
Archeologii.* Archaeological Institute of Slovak Academy of Sciences, Nitra.

Ammerman, A. J. and Cavalli-Sforza, L. L. 1973. A population model for the
diffusion of early farming in Europe. In A. C. Renfrew (ed.) *The Explanation
of Culture Change: Models in Prehistory,* 343–57. Duckworth, London.

    1979. The wave of advance models for the spread of agriculture in Europe. In
A. C. Renfrew and K. L. Cooke (eds.) *Transformations: Mathematical
Approaches to Culture Change,* 275–93. Academic Press, New York.

Angeli, W. 1958. Typologie und typologische Methode. *Archaeologia Austriaca* 23:
104–8.

Ankel, C. and Gundlach, R. 1969. Die Archäographie – eine
anwendungsorientierte archäologische Disziplin. *Archäographie* 1: 7–24.

Arkadev, A. G. and Braverman, E. M. 1971. *Obučenije Mašiny Klassifikacii Objektov.*
Nauka, Moscow.

Artamonov, M. I. 1947. Arheologičeskie teorii proischoždenija indoevropejcev v
svete učenija N. Ja. Marra. *Vestnik Leningradskogo Universiteta* 2: 79–106.

    1950. *Proishoždenie Slavjan.* Federal Society for Dissemination of Political and
Scientific Knowledge, Leningrad.

1971. Arheologičeskaja kultura i etnos. In A. L. Sapiro (ed.) *Problemy Istorii Feodalnoj Rossii*, 16–32. Leningrad University Press, Leningrad.

Artanovskij, S. N. 1973. Sovremennaja zarubežnaja filosofskaja mysl i problemy etnokulturnyh issledovanij. In Ju. V. Bromlej (ed.) *Etnologičeskie Issledovanija za Rubežom*, 77–104. Nauka, Moscow.

Ascher, R. 1961. Analogy in archaeological interpretation. *Southwestern Journal of Anthroplogy* 17: 317–25.

Avdusin, D. A. 1953. Neonormanistskie izmyslenija buržuaznyh istorikov. *Voprosy Istorii* 12: 114–20.

Baker, C. M. 1978. The size effect: an explanation of variability in surface artifact assemblage context. *American Antiquity* 43: 288–93.

Balcer, B. H. 1970. W sprawie klasyfikacji materiałów krzemiennych. *Wiadomości Archeologiczne* 35: 147–63.

Barich, B. E. 1977–82. Archeologia teoretica: il problema della teoria in archeologia preistorica e nelle scienze umane. *Origini* 11: 7–44.

Barraclough, G. 1979. *Main Trends in History*. Holmes and Meier, New York.

Barth, F. 1959–60. The land use pattern of migratory tribes of south Persia. *Norsk Geografisk Tidsskrift* 17: 1–11.

Bartra, R. 1964. *La Tipología y la Periodificación en el Método Arqueológico*, Supplement 5. Tlatoani, Mexico.

Bašilov, V. A. 1978. Konferencija po probleme istorizma arheologii. *Kratkie Soobščenija* 152: 109–11.

Bayard, D. T. 1969. Science, theory, and reality in the 'new archaeology'. *American Antiquity* 34: 376–84.

1978. 15 Jahre 'New Archaeology'. *Saeculum* 29: 69–109.

Behrens, H. 1984. *Die Ur- und Frühgeschichtswissenschaft in der DDR 1945–1980: Miterlebte und Mitverantwortete Forschungsgeschichte*. Peter Lang, Frankfurt-on-Main.

Bellah, R. 1959. Durkheim and history. *American Sociological Review* 24: 447–61.

Benfer, R. A. and Benfer, A. N. 1981. Automatic classification of inspectional categories: multivariate theories of archaeological data. *American Antiquity* 46: 381–96.

Bergmann, J. 1970. Die ältere Bronzezeit Nordwestdeutschlands: neue Methoden zur ethnischen und historischen Interpretation urgeschichtlicher Quellen. *Kasseler Beiträge zur Vor- und Frühgeschichte* 2.

Berlinski, D. 1976. *On System Analysis*. MIT Press, Cambridge, Mass.

Berry, B. J. L. 1961. A method for deriving multifactor uniform regions. *Przegląd Geograficzny* 33: 263–82.

Binford, L. R. 1962. Archaeology as anthropology. *American Antiquity* 28: 217–25.

1964. A consideration of archaeological research design. *American Antiquity* 29: 425–41.

1972. *An Archaeological Perspective*. Seminar Press, New York, London.

1977. (ed.) *For Theory Building in Archaeology: Essays on Faunal Remains*,

Aquatic Resources, Spatial Analysis and Systemic Modeling. Academic Press,
  New York.
1978. *Nunamiut Ethnoarchaeology.* Academic Press, New York.
1983a. *In Pursuit of the Past: Decoding the Archaeological Record.* Thames and
  Hudson, London.
1983b. *Working at Archaeology.* Academic Press, New York.
1986. In pursuit of the future. In D. J. Melzer, D. D. Fowler and J. A. Sabloff
  (eds.) *American Archaeology Past and Future: A Celebration of the Society for
  American Archeology 1935–1985,* 459–79. Smithsonian Institution Press,
  Washington.
Binford, L. R. and Sabloff, J. A. 1982. Paradigms, systematics and archaeology.
  Journal of Anthropological Research 38: 137–53.
Binford, S. R. and Binford, L. R. 1968. (eds.) *New Perspectives in Archaeology.*
  Aldine, Chicago.
Bloomfield, L. 1933, 1958. *Language.* Holt, Rinehart and Winston, New York.
Bočkarev, V. S. 1975. K voprosu o sisteme osnovnyh arheologičeskih ponjatij. In
  V. M. Masson and V. N. Borjaz (eds.) *Predmet i Objekt Arheologii i Voprosy
  Metodiki Arheologičeskih Issledovanij.* Department of Methodology, Soviet
  Academy of Sciences, Leningrad: Symposium of April 1975. Nauka,
  Leningrad.
Bohmers, A. 1963. A statistical analysis of flint artifacts. In D. R. Brothwell and
  E. S. Higgs (eds.) *Science and Archaeology,* 469–81. Thames and Hudson,
  London.
Bonham-Carter, G. F. and Sutherland, A. J. 1968. Mathematical model and
  FORTRAN IV program for computer simulation of deltaic sedimentation.
  Computer Contribution 24–56.
Borillo, M. 1972. (ed.) *Les Méthodes Mathématiques de l'archéologie.* CNRS,
  Marseilles.
  1975. Présentation d'un centre de recherche: l'unité de recherche, analyse
  documentaire et calcul en archéologie (URADCA). *Bulletin de Liaison de la
  Recherche en Informatique et Automatique* 16: 11–16.
Borillo, M. and Bourelly, L. 1976. (eds.) *Banques de données et méthodes formelles en
  archéologie préhistorique et protohistorique.* CNRS, Nice.
Borillo, M., Fernandez de la Vega, W. and Guenoche, A. 1977. (eds.)
  Raisonnement et méthodes mathématiques en archéologie. CNRS, Paris.
Boriskovskij, P. I. 1960. V. I. Lenin i problemy zakonomernostej razvitija
  pervobytnogo obščestva. *Vestnik Leningradskogo Universiteta* 8: 75–7.
Bouzek, J. and Buchvaldek, M. 1971. (eds.) *Nové Archeologické Metody I: Třídění
  Materiálu.* Charles University Press, Prague.
Bove, F. J. 1981. Trend surface analysis and the Lowland Classic Maya. *American
  Antiquity* 46: 93–111.
Brajčevskij, M. Ju. 1970. Avtomatičeskoe postrojenie arheologičeskih izolinij. In
  B. A. Kolčin and J. A. Šer (eds.) *Statistiko-Kombinatornye Metody v
  Arheologii,* 120–2. Nauka, Moscow.

Breeding, K. J. and Amoss, J. O. 1972. A pattern description language – PADEL. *Pattern Recognition* 4: 19–36.

Brentjes, B. 1971. Diskussionsbemerkung (zu Mohr). *Ethnographisch-Archäologische Zeitschrift* 12: 71–3.

1972. Diskussionsbemerkung (zu Guhr 1972). *Ethnographisch-Archäologische Zeitschrift* 13: 417–18.

Brew, J. O. 1946. The use and abuse of taxonomy. In Archaeology of Alkali Ridge, southwestern Utah. *Papers of the Peabody Museum of American Archaeology and Ethnology* 21. Harvard University Press, Cambridge, Mass.

Brice, C. R. and Fennema, C. L. 1970. Scene analysis using regions. *Artificial Intelligence* 1: 205–66.

Briggs, L. I. and Pollack, H. N. 1967. Digital model of evaporite sedimentation. *Science* 155(3,761): 453–6.

Brjusov, A. Ja. 1952. *Očerki po Istorii Plemen Evropejskoj Časti SSSR v Neolitičeskuju Epohu*. Soviet Academy of Sciences Press, Moscow.

1957a. Die Wanderungen der ursprünglichen Stämme und die Resultate der Archäologie: die Entstehung der Fatjanovo-Kultur. *Acta Archaeologica* 75: 309–21.

1957b. K. voprosu o teorii diffuzii. *Sovetskaja Arheologija* 1: 7–12.

1965. Le problème indoeuropéen et la civilisation des haches de combat. *Atti del VI Congresso Internazionale delle Scienze Preistoriche e Protoistoriche*, Rome (1962), vol. 2, 72–7. Sanzoni, Florence.

Bromlej, Ju. V. 1973. *Etnos i Etnografija*. Nauka, Moscow.

Bulkin, V. A., Klejn, L. S. and Lebedev, G. S. 1982. Attainments and problems of Soviet archaeology. *World Archaeology* 13: 272–95.

Bunge, W. 1962. *Theoretical Geography*. Lund Studies in Geography, Series C, 1.

Burckhardt, J. 1977. *Griechische Kulturgeschichte Bd 3*, DVT, Munich.

Butzer, K. W. 1972. *Environment and Archaeology – An Ecological Approach to Prehistory*. Methuen, London.

1982. *Archaeology as Human Ecology: Methods and Theory for a Contextual Approach*. Cambridge University Press, Cambridge.

Cafagna, A. C. 1960. A formal analysis of definitions of 'culture'. In G. E. Dole and R. L. Carneiro (eds.) *Essays in the Science of Culture: In Honor of Leslie A. White*, 111–32. Thomas Y. Crowell, New York.

Carmack, R. M. 1972. Ethnohistory: a review of its development, definitions, methods and aims. *Annual Review of Anthropology* 1: 227–46.

Carnap, R. 1959. *Induktive Logik und Wahrscheinlichkeit*. Springer, Vienna.

Carr, C. 1984. The nature of organisation of intrasite archaeological records and spatial analytic approaches to their investigation. In M. B. Schiffer (ed.) *Advances in Archeological Method and Theory*, vol. 7, 103–222. Academic Press. New York, London.

1985 (ed.) *For Concordance in Archaeological Analysis: Bridging Data Structures, Quantitative Techniques and Theory*. Westport, Kansas City.

Cavalli-Sforza, L. L. 1971. Similarities and dissimilarities of sociocultural and biological evolution. In F. R. Hodson, D. G. Kendall and P. Tautu (eds.) *Mathematics in the Archaeological and Historical Sciences*, 535–41. Edinburgh University Press, Edinburgh.

Cazzella, A. 1985. L'archeologia dopo la *new archaeology*: il rapport con l'etno-antropologia. *Dialoghi di Archeologia* 3: 11–24.

Chang, K. C. 1967. *Rethinking Archaeology*. Random House, New York.

1968. (ed.) *Settlement Archaeology*. National Press, Palo Alto.

Charlton, T. H. 1981. Archaeology, ethnohistory and ethnology: interpretative interfaces. In M. B. Schiffer (ed.) *Advances in Archaeology* 4: 129–77. Academic Press, New York, London.

Chenhall, R. G. 1975. *Museum Cataloging in the Computer Age*. The American Association for State and Local History, Nashville.

Cherry, C. 1968. *On Human Communication*. Cambridge, Mass., London.

Chomsky, N. 1957. *Syntactic Structures*. Mouton, The Hague.

Chorley, R. J. and Haggett, P. 1967. (eds.) *Models in Geography*. Methuen, London.

Chorafas, D. N. 1965. *Systems and Simulation*. Academic Press, New York, London.

Christenson, A. L. and Read, D. W. 1977. Numerical taxonomy, R-mode factor analysis and archaeological classification. *American Antiquity* 43: 505–6.

1978. Comments on cluster analysis and archaeological classification. *American Antiquity* 43: 174–83.

Civjan, T. V. 1973. *Strukturno-Tipologičeskie Issledovanija v Oblasti Gramatiki Slavjanskich Jazykov*. Nauka, Moscow.

Clark, G. A. and Stafford, C. 1982. Quantification in American archaeology: a historical perspective. *World Archaeology* 14: 98–118.

Clarke, D. L. 1962. Matrix analysis and archaeology, with particular reference to British Beaker pottery. *Atti del VI Congresso Internazionale delle Scienze Preistoriche e Protoistoriche*, Rome (1962), vol. 2, 37–42. Sanzoni, Florence.

1968. *Analytical Archaeology*. Methuen, London.

1970. Analytical archaeology: epilogue. *Norwegian Archaeological Review* 3: 25–34.

1972. (ed.) *Models in Archaeology*. Methuen, London.

1973. Archaeology: the loss of innocence. *Antiquity* 47: 6–18.

1977. (ed.) *Spatial Archaeology*. Academic Press, New York, London.

Cole, J. P. and King, C. A. M. 1968. *Quantitative Geography: Techniques and Theories in Geography*. J. Willey, London.

Coles, J. M. 1979. *Experimental Archaeology*. Academic Press, New York, San Francisco, London.

Collingwood, R. G. 1946. *The Idea of History*. Clarendon Press, Oxford.

Conkey, M. W. 1978. Context, structure and efficiency in Palaeolithic art and design. In M. L. Foster and S. Brandes (eds.) *Symbol as Sense: New Approaches to the Analysis of Meaning*, 225–48. Academic Press, New York.

Courbin, P. 1982. *Qu'est-ce que l'archéologie?: essai sur la nature de la recherche archéologique*. Payot, Paris.

Cowen, J. D. 1969. Presidential address. *Proceedings of the Prehistoric Society* 35: 1–10.

Cowgill, G. L. 1972. Models, methods and techniques for seriation. In D. L. Clarke (ed.) *Models in Archaeology*, 381–424. Methuen, London.

1982. Clusters of objects and associations between variables: two approaches to archaeological classification. In R. Whallon and J. A. Brown (eds.) *Essays on Archaeological Typology*, 30–55. Center for American Archeology Press, Evanston.

1986. Archaeological applications of mathematical and formal methods. In D. J. Melzer, D. D. Fowler and J. A. Sabloff (eds.) *American Archeology Past and Future: A Celebration of the Society for American Archeology 1935–1985*, 369–93. Smithsonian Institution Press, Washington.

Cronin, C. 1962. An analysis of pottery design elements, indicating possible relationships between three decorated types. In P. S. Martin *et al.* (eds.) *Chapters in the Prehistory of Eastern Arizona I*, 105–14. Chicago Natural History Museum, Fieldiana, Anthropology 53, Chicago.

Crüger, H. 1967. Die Bedeutung einer wissenschaftlichen Methodologie für die Archäologie. *Deutsche Zeitschrift für Philosophie* 5: 549–62.

Cullberg, C. 1968. On artifact analysis: a study in the systematics and classification of a Scandinavian early Bronze Age material with metal analysis and chronology as contributing factors. *Acta Archaeologica Ludensia* 4(7).

Cuvillier, A. 1954. *Manuel de sociologie*, vols. 1 and 2. Presses Universitaires de France, Paris.

Daniel, G. E. 1943. *The Three Ages: An Essay in Archaeological Method*. Cambridge University Press, Cambridge.

1950. *A Hundred Years of Archaeology*. Duckworth, London.

1962. *The Idea of Prehistory*. Watts, London.

1966. *Man Discovers His Past*. Duckworth, London.

1967. *The Origins and Growth of Archaeology*. Penguin, Harmondsworth.

1975. *A Hundred and Fifty Years of Archaeology*. Duckworth, London.

1981. *Towards a History of Archaeology*. Thames and Hudson, London.

(ed.) Daniels, S. G. H. 1972. Research design models. In D. L. Clarke (ed.) *Models in Archaeology*, 201–29. Methuen, London.

Danilova, L. V. 1968. Spornye problemy teorii dokapitalističeskih obščestv. In L. V. Danilova (ed.) *Problemy Istorii Dokapitalističeskih Obščestv*, 27–66. Nauka, Moscow.

David, H. A. 1963. *The Method of Paired Comparisons*. C. Griffin, London.

David, N. 1971. The Fulani compound and the archaeologist. *World Archaeology* 3: 111–31.

Davidson, D., Richer, S. and Rogers, A. 1976. A simulation program for the analysis of archaeological distributions. *Newsletter of Computer Archaeology* 11(4): 1–10.

Deetz, J. F. 1965. The dynamics of stylistic change in Arikara ceramics. *University of Illinois Series in Anthropology* 4.

1967. *Invitation to Archaeology*. The Natural History Press, Garden City.

1971. (ed.) *Man's Imprint from the Past: Readings in the Methods of Archaeology*. Little, Brown, Boston.

1977. *In Small Things Forgotten: The Archaeology of Early American Life*. Anchor Press, New York.

Dennell, R. 1983. *European Economic Prehistory*. Academic Press, New York, London.

Dethlefsen, E. S., and Deetz, J. F. 1966. Death's heads, cherubs and willow trees: experimental archaeology in colonial cemeteries. *American Antiquity* 31: 502–10.

Dibble, H. L. and Chase, P. G. 1981. A new method for describing and analysing artifact shape. *American Antiquity* 46: 178–87.

Dinçol, A. M. and Kantman, S. 1969. (eds.) *Analitik Arkeoloji – Denemeler*. University Press, Istanbul.

Djindjian, F. 1985a. Seriation and toposeriation by correspondence analysis. *Pact* 11: 119–35.

1985b. La sériation en archéologie: un état de l'art. Méthodes et applications. *Panorama des Traitements de Données en Archéologie* 1: 9–46.

Doluhanov, P. M. 1978a. Istoki migracij (modelirovanie demografičeskih processov po arheologičeskim i ekologičeskim dannym). In L. S. Klejn, G. S. Lebedev and A. D. Stoljar (eds.) *Problemy arheologii II*, 38–42. Leningrad University Press, Leningrad.

1978b. O rabote teoretičeskogo seminara Leningradskogo otdelenija instituta arheologii. *Kratkie Soobščenija* 152: 100–5.

Doluhanov, P. M., Kozłowski, S. K. 1980. *Multivariate Analysis of Upper Palaeolithic and Mesolithic Stone Assemblages: Typology and Ecology*. State Publishing House for Scientific Literature, Cracow.

Donato, G., Hensel, W. and Tabaczyński, S. 1986. (eds.) *Teoria e pratica della ricerca archeologica: premesse metodoligiche*. Il Quadrante Edizioni, s. l.

Doran, J. E. 1970. Systems theory, computer simulations and archaeology. *World Archaeology* 1: 289–98.

1972. Computer models as tools for archaeological hypothesis formation. In D. L. Clarke (ed.) *Models in Archaeology*, 425–51. Methuen, London.

1986. Formal methods and archaeological theory: a perspective. *World Archaeology* 18: 21–37.

Doran, J. E. and Hodson, F. R. 1975. *Mathematics and Computers in Archaeology*. Edinburgh University Press, Edinburgh.

Dunnell, R. C. 1970. Seriation method and its evaluation. *American Antiquity* 35: 305–19.

1971. *Systematics in Prehistory*. Macmillan, New York.

1986. Methodological issues in American artifact classification. In M. B. Schiffer (ed.) *Advances in Archaeological Method and Theory*, vol. 9, 149–207. Academic Press, New York, London.

Earle, T. K. and Christenson, A. L. 1980. *Modeling Change in Prehistoric Subsistence Economies*. Academic Press, New York.

Earle, T. K. and Ericson, J. E. 1977. (eds.) *Exchange Systems in Prehistory*. Academic Press, New York.

Eden, M. and Halle, M. 1961. The characterization of cursive writing. In C. Cherry (ed.) *Fourth London Symposium on Information Theory*, 287–99. Butterworths, London.

Edmonson, M. S. 1961. Neolithic diffusion rates. *Current Anthropology* 2: 71–102.

Eggers, H. J. 1939. Natürliche Erkenntnisgrenzen bei vorgeschichtlichen und volkskundlichen Fundkarten. In K. Kaizer (ed.) *Beiträge zur Volkskunde Pommerns*, 166–73. L. Bamberg, Greifswald.

1950. Das Problem der ethnischen Deutung in der Frühgeschichte. In H. Kirchner (ed.) *Ur- und Frühgeschichte als historische Wissenschaft: Wahle Festschrift* 49–59. Carl Winter University Press, Heidelberg.

1959. *Einführung in die Vorgeschichte*. Piper, Munich.

1974. Methodik der Prähistorie. *Enzyklopädie der Geisteswissenschaft und Arbeitsmethoden* 10. Lieferung, Oldenburg, Munich, Vienna.

Eggert, M. K. H. 1974. Zur Theoriebildung in der europäischen Ethnologie. *Zeitschrift für Volkskunde* 70: 58–63.

1976. On the interrelationship of prehistoric archaeology and cultural anthropology. *Prähistorische Zeitschrift* 51: 56–60.

1978. Prähistorische Archäologie und Ethnologie: Studien zur amerikanischen New Archaeology. *Berliner Jahrbuch für Vor- und Frühgeschichte* 4: 102–45.

Eggert, M. K. H., Kurz, S. and Wotzka, H. P. 1980. Historische Realität und archäologische Datierung: zur Aussagenkraft der Kombinationsstatistik. *Prähistorische Zeitschrift* 55: 110–45.

Eliade, M. 1952. *Images et symboles: essais sur le symbolisme magico-religieux*. Gallimard, Paris.

Fedorov-Davydov, G. A. 1970. Ponjatija 'arheologičeskij tip' i 'arheologičeskaja kultura' v 'analitičeskoj arheologii' Devida Klarka. *Sovetskaja Arheologija* 3: 258–70.

Fehon, J. R. and Scholz, S. C. 1978. A conceptual framework for the study of artifact loss. *American Antiquity* 43: 271–3.

Feleppa, R. 1986. Emic, etic and social objectivity. *American Anthropologist* 27: 243–55.

Feustel, R. 1973a. Zum Problem der Evolution und Revolution in urgeschichtlicher Zeit. *Ethnographisch-Archäologische Zeitschrift* 14: 55–80.

1973b. *Technik der Steinzeit: Archäolithikum – Mesolithikum*. Böhlaus, Weimar.

1975. *Entstehung und Entwicklung sozialer Verhältnisse in der Urgesellschaft*. Museum für Ur- und Frühgeschichte Thüringens, Weimar.

1979. *Abstammungsgeschichte des Menschen*. Fischer Verlag, Jena.

Fischer, U. 1987. Zur Ratio der prähistorischen Archäologie. *Germania* 65: 175–95.

Flanders, R. E. 1960. A re-examination of Mill Creek ceramics: the Robinson technique. *Journal of the Iowa Archaeological Society* 10: 1–35.

Flannery, K. V. 1967. Culture history v. cultural process: a debate in American archaeology. *Scientific American* 217: 119–22.

1976. (ed.) *The Early Mesoamerican Village: Archaeological Research Strategy for an Endangered Species*. Academic Press, New York.

Ford, J. A. 1954. The type concept revisited. *American Anthropologist* 56: 42–54.

Freeman, H. 1961. On the encoding of arbitrary geometric configuration. *Ire Transactions Electron. Comput.* EC-10(2): 260–8.

Frerichs, K. 1981. *Begriffsbildung und Begriffsanwendung in der Vor- und Frühgeschichte: zur logischen Analyse archäologischen Aussagen*. P. D. Lang, Frankfurt-on-Main, Bern.

Friedrich, M. H. 1970. Design structure and social interaction: archaeological implications of an ethnographic analysis. *American Antiquity* 35: 332–43.

Fritz, J. M. 1978. Palaeopsychology today: ideational systems and human adaptation in prehistory. In C. L. Redman *et al.* (eds.) *Social Archaeology: Beyond Subsistence and Dating*, 37–59. Academic Press, New York.

Gabor, D. 1965. Character recognition by holography. *Nature* 208: 442–3.

Gallay, A. 1986. *L'Archéologie demain*. Belfond, Paris.

Gardin, J.-C. 1955. Problèmes de la documentation. *Diogène* 11: 107–24.

1958a. *Centre d'Analyse Documentaire pour l'Archéologie*. CNRS, Paris.

1958b. Four codes for the description of artifacts: an essay in archaeological technique and theory. *American Anthropologist* 60: 335–57.

1970. (ed.) *Archéologie et calculateurs: problèmes sémiologiques et mathématiques*. CNRS, Paris.

1974. A propos de modèles en archéologie. *Revue Archéologique* 2: 341–8.

1978. *Code pour l'analyse des ornements*. CNRS, Paris.

1979. *Une archéologie théorique*. Hachette, Paris.

1980. *Archaeological Constructs: An Aspect of Theoretical Archaeology*. Cambridge University Press, Cambridge.

1987. Questions d'epistémologie pratique dans les perspectives de l'intelligence artificielle. *Bulletin de la Société Française de Philosophie* 81: 69–112.

Gardin, J.-C., Guillaume, O., Herman, P. O., Hesnard, A., Renaud, M. and Zadora-Rid, A. 1987. *Systèmes experts et sciences humaines: le cas de l'archéologie*. Byrolles, Paris.

Gardin, J.-C. and Jaulin, B. 1968. (eds.) *Calcul et formalisation dans les sciences de l'homme*. CNRS, Paris.

Gelfand, A. E. 1971. Rapid seriation methods with archaeological applications. In F. R. Hodson, D. G. Kendall and P. Tautu (eds.) *Mathematics in the Archaeological and Historical Sciences*, 186–201. Edinburgh University Press, Edinburgh.

Gening, V. F. 1976. Problema sootnošenija arheologičeskoj kultury i etnosa. *Voprosy Etnografii Udmurtii* 1: 3–37.

1983. *Objekt i Predmet Nauki v Arheologii.* Scientific Mind, Kiev.

Gening, V. F., Zaharuk, Ju. N., Kameneckij, I. S., Klejn, L. S., Masson, V. M. and Fedorov-Davydov, G. A. 1973. O sostojanii i zadačah teoretičeskih issledovanij po arheologii SSSR. In A. A. Askarov and Ju. F. Burjakov (eds.) *Tezisy Dokladov Sessii Posvjaščennoj Itogam Polevyh Arheologičeskih Issledovanij 1972 Goda v SSSR,* 6–10. FAN, Tashkent.

Gero, J. and Mazzullo, J. 1984. Analysis of artifact shape using Fourier series in closed form. *Journal of Field Archaeology,* 11: 315–22.

Gessinger, J. and Rahden, W. von. 1988. *Theorien vom Ursprung der Sprache.* De Gruyter, West Berlin, New York.

Gibbon, G. 1984. *Anthropological Archaeology.* Columbia University Press, New York.

Gibbs, J. P. (ed.) 1961. *Urban Research Methods.* Van Nostrand, Princeton.

Gjessing, G. 1975. Socioarcheology. *Current Anthropology* 16: 323–42.

Glassie, H. 1975. *Folk Housing in Middle Virginia: A Structural Analysis of Historical Artifacts.* University of Tennessee Press, Knoxville.

Gledhill, J. and Larsen, M. 1982. The Polanyi paradigm and a dynamic analysis of archaic states. In A. C. Renfrew, M. J. Rowlands and B. A. Segraves (eds.) *Theory and Explanation in Archaeology: The Southampton Conference,* 197–229. Academic Press, New York.

Glock, C. Y. 1965. Y a-t-il un réveil religieux aux Etats-Unis? In R. Boudon and P. Lazarsfeld (eds.) *Le Vocabulaire des sciences sociales: concepts et indices,* 49–68. Mouton, Paris.

Goldmann, K. 1974a. Die zeitliche Ordnung prähistorischer Funde durch Seriation. *Archäologische Korrespondenzblatt* 4: 89–94.

1974b. Erfahrungen mit der chronologischen Seriation. *Informationsblätter zu Nachbarwissenschaften der Ur- und Frühgeschichte* 5: 1–4.

1979. Die Seriation chronologischer Leitfunde der Bronzezeit Europas. *Berliner Beiträge zur Vor- und Frühgeschichte* N. F. 1.

Goode, W. J. 1951. *Religion among the Primitives.* The Free Press, Glencoe.

Gould, P. R. 1963. Man against his environment: a game-theoretic framework. *Annals of the Association of American Geographers* 53: 290–7.

Gould, R. A. 1978 (ed.) *Explorations in Ethnoarchaeology.* University of New Mexico Press, Albuquerque.

1979. *Living Archaeology.* Cambridge University Press, Cambridge.

Gould, R. A. and Schiffer, M. B. 1981. (eds.) *Modern Material Culture: The Archaeology of Us.* Academic Press, New York.

Gould, R. A. and Watson, P. J. 1982. A dialogue on the meaning and use of analogy in ethnoarchaeological reasoning. *Journal of Anthropological Archaeology* 1: 355–81.

Gräslund, B. 1974. Relativ datering: om kronologisk metod i nordisk arkeologi. *Tor* 16.

Green, D., Haselgrove, C. and Spriggs, M. 1978. (eds.) *Social Organisation and Settlement*. BAR International Series, Supplement 47, Oxford.

Grigorev, G. P. 1969. Soveršenstvovanie metodiki izučenija paleolita v SSSR. *Teoretičeskie Osnovy Sovetskoj Arheologii (Tezisy Dokladov na Teoretičeskom Seminare LOIA AN SSSR I–IV 1970 G.)*, 12–17. Archaeological Institute of Soviet Academy of Sciences, Leningrad.

Grišin, Ju. S. and Maslennikov, A. A. 1978. Metodologičeskij seminar Instituta Arheologii AN SSSR v 1957–1976 gg. *Kratke Soobščenija* 152: 92–9.

Grjaznov, M. P. 1969. Klassifikacija, tip, kultura. In *Teoretičeskie Osnovy Sovetskoj Arheologii (Tezisy Dokladov na Teoretičeskom Seminare LOIA AN SSSR I–IV 1970 G.)*, 18–22. Institut Arheologii Akademii Nauk SSSR, Leningrad.

Grünert, H. 1977. Unfreie bei der germanischen Stämmen zu Beginn unserer Zeitrechnung: methodische Bemerkungen zur Vereinigung der Aussagen archäologischer und schriftlicher Quellen in der Frühgeschichtsforschung. In J. Herrmann (ed.) *Archäologie als Geschichtswissenschaft: Studien und Untersuchungen*, 235–49. Akademie-Verlag, East Berlin.

Grünert, H. and Guhr, G. 1969. Herausbildung und Systemscharakter der vorkapitalistischen Gesellschaftsformationen: Bericht und Diskussionsbemerkungen zur Arbeitstagung auf dem IV. Historiker-Kongress der DDR, Leipzig, 1968. *Ethnographisch-Archäologische Zeitschrift* 10: 227–39.

Guhr, G. 1969a. Ur- und Frühgeschichte und ökonomische Gesellschaftsformationen: ein Beitrag zum Karl-Marx Jahr 1968. *Ethnographisch-Archäologische Zeitschrift* 10: 167–212.

1969b. Karl Marx und theoretische Probleme der Ethnographie. *Beiheft zum Jahrbuch des Museums für Völkerkunde zu Leipzig* 26. Akademie-Verlag, East Berlin.

1979a. Die Ethnologie in der Urgeschichtsforschung. In J. Preuss (ed.) *Von der archäologischen Quelle zur historischen Aussage*, 59–99. Akademie-Verlag, East Berlin.

1979b. Über Engels sog. 'philosophischen Dualismus': Bemerkungen zur 'doppelten Art der Produktion und Reproduktion des unmittelbaren Lebens' im Werk von Marx und Engels. *Ethnographisch-Archäologische Zeitschrift* 20: 363–77.

Gumilev, L. N. 1970. *Poiski Vymyslennogo carstva*. Nauka, Moscow.

1975. Ethnogenèse et biosphère de la Terre. *Acta Ethnographica Academiae Scientiarum Hungaricae* 24: 27–46.

Günther, R. 1965. Revolution und Evolution im Weströmischen Reich zur Zeit der Spätantike. *Zeitschrift für Geschichtswissenschaft* 13: 19–34.

Hachmann, R. 1970. *Die Goten und Skandinavien*. De Gruyter, West Berlin.

1971a. *Die Germanen*. Nagel, Munich.

1971b. *The Ancient Civilization of the Germanic Peoples.* Barrie and Jenkins, London.

Hachmann, R., Kossack, G. and Kuhn, H. 1962. *Völker zwischen Germanen und Kelten: Schriftquellen, Bodenfunde und Namengut zur Geschichte des nördlichen Westdeutschlands um Christi Geburt.* Karl Wachholtz, Neumünster.

Hägerstrand, T. 1967. *Innovation Diffusion as a Spatial Process.* Chicago University Press, Chicago.

Haggett, P. 1961. Land use and sediment yield in an old plantation tract of the Serra do Mar, Brazil. *Geographical Journal* 127: 50–62.

1965. *Locational Analysis in Human Geography.* Edward Arnold, London.

Hammond, G. and Hammond, N. 1981. Child's play: a distorting factor in archaeological distribution. *American Antiquity* 46: 634–6.

Harbaugh, J. W. and Bonham-Carter, G. 1970. *Computer Simulation in Geology.* Wiley, New York, London, Sydney, Toronto.

Harmad, S. R., Stentis, H. D. and Lancaster, J. 1976. (eds.) *Origins and Evaluation of Language and Speech.* Annual of New York Academy of Science 280.

Hassan, F. A. 1988. Prolegomena to a grammatical theory of lithic artifacts. *World Archaeology* 19: 281–96.

Hawkes, C. F. C. 1954, Archaeological theory and method: some suggestions from the Old World. *American Anthropologist* 56: 155–68.

Hawkes, J. B. 1967. God in the machine. *Antiquity* 41: 174–80.

1971. Are there really things called cultures? *Antiquity* 47: 176–8.

Hensel, W. 1964a. Z dziedziny metodyki badania kultury materialnej Prasłowian. *Slavia Antiqua* 11: 176–94.

1964b. L'archéologie et la culture matérielle dans les campagnes. *Archaeologia Polona* 6: 107–23.

1971. *Archeologia i Prahistoria: Studia i Szkice.* Ossilineum, Wrocław, Warsaw, Cracow, Gdańsk.

1977. Archäologie, Urgeschichte, Geschichte, allgemeine Geschichte. In J. Herrmann (ed.) *Archäologie als Geschichtswissenschaft: Studien und Untersuchungen,* 29–37. Akademie-Verlag, East Berlin.

Herrmann, J. 1965. Archäologische Kulturen und sozialökonomische Gebiete. *Ethnographisch-Archäologische Zeitschrift* 6: 97–128.

1974. R. Feustel: *Technik der Steinzeit,* Herrmann Böhlaus, Weimar. *Zeitschrift für Geschichtswissenschaft* 22: 571–2.

1975. Methodische Probleme der sozialökonomischen Analyse auf der Grundlage archäologischer Quellen. In K. H. Otto and H. J. Brachmann (eds.) *Moderne Probleme der Archäologie,* 29–34. Akademie-Verlag, East Berlin.

1977a. (ed.) *Archäologie als Geschichtswissenschaft: Studien und Üntersuchungen.* Akademie-Verlag, East Berlin.

1977b. Archäologie als Geschichtswissenschaft. In J. Herrmann (ed.) *Archäologie*

als *Geschichtswissenschaft: Studien und Üntersuchungen*, 2–28.
Akademie-Verlag, East Berlin.
  1986. Archäologische Quellen: Analyse historischen Strukturen und
  Rekonstruktion von Ereignisgeschichte. *Slovenská Archeologia* 34: 249–60.
Hietala, H. J. 1984. (ed.) *Intrasite Spatial Analysis*. Cambridge University Press,
  New York.
Hietala, H. J. and Stevens, D. S. 1977. Spatial analysis: multiple procedures in
  pattern recognition. *American Antiquity* 42: 539–59.
Higgs, E. S. 1972. (ed.) *Papers in Economic Prehistory*. Cambridge University Press,
  Cambridge.
Higgs, E. S. and Jarman, M. R. 1975. *Palaeoeconomy: Papers in Economic Prehistory*
  2. Cambridge University Press, Cambridge.
Hill, J. N. 1968. Broken K Pueblo: pattern of form and function. In S. R.
  Binford and L. R. Binford (eds.) *New Perspectives in Archaeology*, 103–42.
  Aldine, Chicago.
  1977. (ed.) *Explanation of Prehistoric Change*. University of New Mexico Press,
  Albuquerque.
Hill, J. N. and Evans, R. K. 1972. A model for classification and typology. In
  D. L. Clarke (ed.) *Models in Archaeology*, 231–73. Methuen, London.
Hill, J. N. and Gunn, J. 1977. (eds.) *The Individual in Prehistory: Studies of
  Variability in Style in Prehistoric Technologies*. Academic Press, New York,
  London.
Hillier, B., Leaman, A., Stansall, P. and Bedford, M. 1978. Space syntax. In D.
  Green, C. Haselgrove and M. Spriggs (eds.) *Social Organisation and
  Settlement*, 343–81. BAR International Series, Supplement 47, Oxford.
Hjelmslev, L. T. 1961. *Prolegomena to a Theory of Language*. University of
  Wisconsin, Madison.
Hockett, C. F. 1977. *The View from Language: Selected Essays*. University of
  Georgia Press, Athens.
Hodder, I. 1977. Some new directions in the spatial analysis of archaeological data
  at the regional scale (macro). In D. L. Clarke (ed.) *Spatial Archaeology*,
  223–351. Academic Press, New York, London.
  1978a. (ed.) *Simulation Studies in Archaeology*, Cambridge University Press,
  Cambridge.
  1978b. *The Spatial Organisation of Culture*. Duckworth, London.
  1982a. (ed.) *Symbolic and Structural Archaeology*. Cambridge University Press,
  Cambridge.
  1982b. *Symbols in Action*. Cambridge University Press, Cambridge.
  1982c. *The Present Past: An Introduction to Anthropology for Archaeologists*. B. T.
  Batsford, London.
  1985. Postprocessual archaeology. In M. B. Schiffer (ed.) *Advances in
  Archaeological Method and Theory*, vol. 8, 1–26. Academic Press, New York,
  London.

1986. *Reading in the Past: Current Approaches to Interpretation in Archaeology.* Cambridge University Press, Cambridge.

1987a. (ed.) *The Archaeology of Contextual Meanings.* Cambridge University Press, Cambridge.

1987b. (ed.) *Archaeology as Long-Term History.* Cambridge University Press, Cambridge.

Hodder, I., Isaac, G. and Hammon, E. 1981. (eds.) *Pattern of the Past: Studies in Honour of D. L. Clarke.* Cambridge University Press, Cambridge.

Hodder, I. and Orton, C. 1976. *Spatial Analysis in Archaeology.* Cambridge University Press, Cambridge.

Hodson, F. R. 1980. Cultures as types? Some elements of classification theory. *Information of Archaeology Bulletin* 17: 1–11.

Hodson, F. R., Kendall, D. G. and Tautu, P. 1971. (eds.) *Mathematics in the Archaeological and Historical Sciences.* Edinburgh University Press, Edinburgh.

Hole, F. and Heizer, R. F. 1966. *An Introduction to Prehistoric Archaeology.* Holt, Rinehart and Winston, New York.

Hole, F. and Shaw, M. 1967. *Computer Analysis of Chronological Seriation.* Rice University Studies, Monographs in Archaeology 53(3). Houston.

Hołubowicz, W. 1957. O metodzie wydzielania kultur archeologicznych. *Pierwsza Sesja Archeologiczna IHKM PAN,* 81–2. Warsaw, Wrocław.

Horst, F. 1975. Zur Entwicklung der Produktivkräfte in den jungbronzezeitlichen Siedlungsgebieten des Weser-Oder-Raumes. In K. H. Otto and H. J. Brachmann (eds.) *Moderne Probleme der Archäologie,* 129–40. Akademie-Verlag, East Berlin.

Hoult, T. H. 1977. *Dictionary of Modern Sociology.* Totowa, New York.

Huggett, J. and Baker, K. 1985. The computerised archaeologist: the development of expert systems. *Science and Archaeology* 27: 3–7.

Hymes, D. H. 1970. Linguistic models in archaeology. In J.-C. Gardin (ed.) *Archéologie et calculateurs: problèmes sémiologiques et mathématiques,* 91–120. CNRS, Paris.

Ihm, P. 1977a. Deux transformations pour le traitement mathématique des problèmes de sériation. In M. Borillo, W. Fernandez de la Vega and A. Guenoche (eds.) *Raisonnement et méthodes mathématiques en archéologie,* 139–44. CNRS, Paris.

1977b. Introduction à la statistique unie et multidimensionelle. In M. Borillo, W. Fernandez de la Vega and A. Guenoche (eds.) *Raisonnement et méthodes mathématiques en archéologie,* 34–71. CNRS, Paris.

1978. *Statistik in der Archäologie: Probleme der Anwendung, allgemeine Methoden, Seriation und Klassifikation.* Rheinland Verlag, Bonn.

1983. Korrespondentenanalyse und Seriation. *Archäologische Informationen* 6: 8–21.

Isaac, G. L. 1971. Whither archaeology? *Antiquity* 45: 123–9.

1981. Analytical archaeology. *Antiquity* 55: 200–5.

Ivanov, V. V. and Toporov, V. N. 1974. *Issledovanija v Oblasti Slavjanskih Drevnostej: Leksičeskie i Frazeologičeskie Voprosy Rekonstrukcii Tekstov.* Nauka, Moscow.

Jaspers, K. 1966. *Vom Ursprung und Ziel der Geschichte.* Piper, Munich.

Jażdżewski, K. 1969. O możliwościach poznawczych archeologii w kwestiach etnicznych. *Prace i Materiały Muzeum Archeologicznego i Etnograficznego w Łodzi, Seria Archeologica* 16:7–21.

1979. Badania nad poczatkami organizacji wczesnopaństwowych. *Acta Universitatis Lodziensis, Zeszyty Naukowe Uniwesytetu Łodzkiego, Nauki Humanistyczno-Społeczne, Folia Archaeologica* 1(36): 3–25.

Jičín, R., Pilous, Z. and Vašíček, Z. 1969. Grundlagen einer formalen Methode zur Zusammenstellung und Bewertung von Bestimmungsschlüsseln. *Preslia* 41: 71–85.

Jochim, M. A. 1976. *Hunter-Gatherer Settlement and Subsistence.* Academic Press, New York.

1979. Breaking down the system: recent ecological approaches in archaeology. In M. B. Schiffer (ed.) *Advances in Archaeological Method and Theory*, vol. 2, 77–119. Academic Press, New York, London.

Johnson, Jr, LeRoy. 1972. Introduction to imaginary models for archaeological scaling and clustering. In D. L. Clarke (ed.) *Models in Archaeology*, 309–79. Methuen, London.

Jope, E. M. 1973. The transmission of new ideas: archaeological evidence for implant and dispersal. *World Archaeology* 4: 368–73.

Kameneckij, I. S. 1970. Arheologičeskaja kultura – ee opredelenie i interpretacija. *Sovetskaja Arheologija* 2: 18–36.

Kameneckij, I. S., Maršak, B. I. and Šer, J. A. 1975. *Analiz Arheologičeskih Istočnikov (Vozmožnosti Formalizovannogo Podhoda).* Nauka, Moscow.

Kansky, K. J. 1963. Structure of transport networks: relationships between network geometry and regional characteristics. *University of Chicago, Department of Geography, Research Papers* 84: 128–47.

Keene, A. S. 1981. *Prehistoric Foraging in a Temperate Forest: A Linear Programming Model.* Academic Press, New York.

Kehoe, A. B. and Kehoe, T. F. 1973. Cognitive models for archaeological interpretation. *American Antiquity* 38: 150–4.

Kelley, J. and Hanen, M. P. 1985. *Archaeology and the Methodology of Science.* Academic Press, Toronto.

Kendall, D. G. 1971. Seriation from abundance matrices. In F. R. Hodson, D. G. Kendall and P. Tautu (eds.) *Mathematics in the Archaeological and Historical Sciences*, 215–52. Edinburgh University Press, Edinburgh.

Kent, S. 1984. *Analysing Activity Areas: An Ethnoarchaeological Study of the Use of Space.* University of New Mexico Press Albuquerque.

Kintigh, K. W. and Ammerman, A. J. 1982. Heuristic approaches to spatial analysis in archaeology. *American Antiquity* 47: 31–63.

Klejn, L. S. 1962. Katakombnye pamjatniki epohi bronzy i problema vydelenija arheologičeskih kultur. *Sovetskaja Arheologija* 2: 26–38.

1969. Die Donez-Katakombenkeramik, eine Schnurkeramik der Becher-Kultur. In H. Behrens and F. Schlette (eds.) *Die neolithischen Becherkulturen im Gebiet der DDR und ihre europäischen Beziehungen*, 192–200. Deutscher Verlag der Wissenschaften, East Berlin.

1971. Was ist eine archäologische Kultur? *Ethnographisch-Archäologische Zeitschrift* 12: 321–45.

1972a. Berichtigungszusatz zum Artikel 'Was ist eine archäologische Kultur?' *Ethnographisch-Archäologische Zeitschrift* 13: 367–8.

1972b. Die Konzeption des 'Neolithikums', 'Äneolithikums' und der 'Bronzezeit' in der archäologischen Wissenschaft der Gegenwart. *Neolithische Studien* 1: 7–20, Wissenschaftliche Beiträge der Martin-Luther-Universität Halle Wittenberg 1 (L7).

1973. Sally R. Binford, Lewis R. Binford (eds.) *New Perspectives in Archaeology*, Chicago, Aldine, 1968. *Sovetskaja Arheologija* 2: 303–12.

1974. Kossinna im Abstand von vierzig Jahren. *Jahresschrift für Mitelldeutsche Vorgeschichte* 58: 7–55.

1975a. K razraboke procedury arheologičeskogo issledovanija. In V. M. Masson and V. N. Borjaz (eds.) *Predmet i Objekt Arheologii i Voprosy Metodiki Arheologičeskih Issledovanij*. Department of Methodology, Soviet Academy of Sciences, Leningrad: Symposium of April 1975: 42–4. Nauka, Leningrad.

1975b. Problema smeny kultur v sovremennyh arheologičeskih teoriah. *Vestnik Leningradskogo Universiteta* 8: 95–103.

1977. A panorama of theoretical archaeology. *Current Anthropology* 18: 1–42.

1978. *Arheologičeskie Istočniki*. Leningrad University Press, Leningrad.

1979. (ed.) *Tipy v Kulture*. Leningrad University Press, Leningrad.

1981. Die Ethnogenese als Kulturgeschichte, archäologisch untersucht: neue Grundlagen. *Beiträge zur Ur- und Frühgeschichte* 1: 13–26.

1982. *Archaeological Typology*. BAR International Series, Supplement 153, Oxford.

Klejn, L. S., Lebedev, G. S. and Stoljar, A. D. 1973. (eds.) *Problemy Arheologii II*. Leningrad University Press, Leningrad.

Klejn, L. S., Minjaev, S. S., Piotrovskij, J. J. and Hejfec, O. I. 1970. Diskussija o ponjatii 'arheologičeskaja kultura' v problemnom arheologičeskom seminare leningradskogo universiteta. *Sovetskaja Arheologija* 2: 298–302.

Klindt-Jensen, O. 1975. *A History of Scandinavian Archaeology*. Thames and Hudson, London.

Kluckhohn, C. K. M. 1941. The way of life. *Kenyon Review* 3: 160–79.

1957. *Mirror for Man: A Survey of Human Behavior and Social Attitudes*. Farewell Publishers, Greenwich.

Knabe, G. S. 1959. Vopros o sootnošenii arheologičeskoj kultury i etnosa v sovremennoj zarubežnoj literature. *Sovetskaja Arheologija* 3: 243–57.

Kohl, P. L. 1981. Materialist approaches in prehistory. *Annual Review of Anthropology* 10: 89–118.

Kolčin, B. A. 1979. (ed.) *Novoe v Primenenii Fiziko-Matematičeskih Metodov*. Nauka, Moscow.

Kolčin, B. A. and Šer, J. A. 1970 (eds.) *Statistiko-Kombinatornye Metody v Arheologii*. Nauka, Moscow.

Kovalevskaja, V. B. 1970a. K izučeniju ornamentiki nabornyh pojasov VI–IX vv. kak znakovoj sistemy. In B. A. Kolčin and J. A. Šer (eds.) *Statistiko-Kombinatornye Metody v Arheologii*, 144–55. Nauka, Moscow.

1970b. Recherches sur les systèmes sémiotiques en archéologie par les méthodes de la théorie de l'information. In J.-C. Gardin (ed.) *Archéologie et calculateurs: problèmes sémiologiques et mathématiques*, 187–92. CNRS, Paris.

Kozłowski, J. K. 1975. Model postępowania badawczego w archeologii. *Historyka* 5: 25–46.

Kramer, C. 1979. (ed.) *Ethnoarchaeology: Implications of Ethnography for Archaeology*. Columbia University Press, New York.

Kroeber, A. L. 1915. Eighteen professions. *American Anthropologist* 17(2): 283–8.

1952. *The Nature of Culture*. University of Chicago Press, Chicago.

Kronenfeld, D. B. 1985. Numerical taxonomy: old techniques and new assumptions. *Current Anthropoloy* 26: 21–41.

Krumbein, W. C. 1955. Experimental design in the earth sciences. *Transactions of the American Geophysical Union* 36: 1–11.

1959. Trend-surface analysis of contour-type maps with irregular control-point spacing. *Journal of Geophysical Research* 64: 823–4.

Kruskal, J. B. 1971. Multi-dimensional scaling in archaeology: time is not the only dimension. In F. R. Hodson, D. G. Kendall and P. Tautu (eds.) *Mathematics in the Archaeological and Historical Sciences*, 119–32. Edinburgh University Press, Edinburgh.

Kunst, M. 1982. Intelektuelle Information – genetische Information: zu Fragen der Typologie und der typologischen Methode. *Acta Praehistorica et Archeologica* 13/14: 1–26.

Kushner, G. 1970. A consideration of some processual designs for archaeology as anthropology. *American Antiquity* 35: 125–32.

Lagrange, M. S. and Renaud, M. 1984. Deux expériences de simulation du raisonnement en archéologie au moyen d'un système expert: le système SNARK. *Informatique et Sciences Sociales* 14: 161–88.

Lahitte, H. B. 1977. On theory in archaeology. *Current Anthropology* 18: 748.

Langer, S. K. 1942. *Philosophy in a New Key: A Study in the Symbolism of Reason, Rite and Art*. Harvard University Press, Cambridge, Mass.

Laplace, G. L. L. P. 1957. Typologie analytique: application d'une nouvelle méthode d'étude des formes et des structures aux industries à lames et lamelles. *Quaternaria* 4: 133–64.

Laporte, G. and Taillefer, S. 1987. An efficient interchange procedure for the archaeological seriation problem. *Journal of Archaeological Science* 14: 283–9.

Leach, E. R. 1977. A view from the bridge. In M. Spriggs (ed.) *Archaeology and Anthropology: Areas of Mutual Interest*, 161–76. BAR International Series, Supplement 19, Oxford.

Leeuw, S. E. van der. 1981. (ed.) *Archaeological Approaches to the Study of Complexity*. University of Amsterdam Press, Amsterdam.

Leone, M. P. 1972a. (ed.) *Contemporary Archaeology: A Guide to Theory and Contributions*. Southern Illinois University Press, Carbondale and Edwardsville.

1972b. Issues in anthropological archaeology. In M. P. Leone (ed.) *Contemporary Archaeology: A Guide to Theory and Contributions*, 14–27. Southern Illinois University Press, Carbondale and Edwardsville.

1982. Some opinions about recovering mind. *American Antiquity* 47: 742–60.

1986. Symbolic, structural and critical archaeology. In D. J. Melzer, D. D. Fowler and J. A. Sabloff (eds.) *American Archaeology Past and Future: A Celebration of the Society for American Archaeology 1935–1985*, 415–38. Smithsonian Institution Press, Washington.

Leroi-Gourhan, A. 1965. *Le Geste et la parole II: La mémoire et les rythmes*. Albin Michel, Paris.

Lesman, Ju. M. 1979. K primeneniju metodiky raspoznavanija obrazov dlja analiza keramičeskogo kompleksa. In B. A. Kolčin, (ed.) *Novoe v Primenenii Fiziko-Matematičeskih Metodov*. Nauka, Moscow.

Lévi-Strauss, C. 1955. *Tristes tropiques*. Plon, Paris.

1962. *La Pensée sauvage*. Plon, Paris.

1964. *Mythologiques I. Le Cru et le cuit*. Plon, Paris.

1967. *Mythologiques II. Du miel aux cendriers*. Plon, Paris.

1968. *Mythologiques III. L'Origine des manières de table*. Plon, Paris.

1971. *Mythologiques IV. L'Homme nu*. Plon, Paris.

Lieberman, P. 1975. *On the Origins of Language: An Introduction to the Evolution of Human Speech*. Macmillan, New York.

1984. *The Biology and Evolution of Language*. Harvard University Press, Cambridge, Mass.

Lishka, J. J. 1975. Broken K revisited: a short discussion of factor analysis. *American Antiquity* 40: 220–7.

Longacre, W. A. 1964, Archaeology as anthropology: a case study. *Science* 144(3,625): 1,454–5.

1968. Some aspects of prehistoric society in east-central Arizona. In S. R. Binford and L. R. Binford (eds.) *New Perspectives in Archaeology*, 89–102. Aldine, Chicago.

Lord, A. B. 1960. *The Singer of Tales*. Harvard University Press, Cambridge, Mass.

Lowe, J. W. 1985. Quantitative systems theory: its utility and limitations. *Journal of Anthropological Research* 41: 42–61.

Lowe, J. W. and Barth, R. J. 1980. Systems in archaeology: a comment on Salmon. *American Antiquity* 45: 568–75.

Lu, K. H. 1965. Harmonic analysis of the human face. *Biometrics* 21: 491–505.

Lüning, J. 1972. Zum Kulturbegriff im Neolithikum. *Prähistorische Zeitschrift* 47: 145–73.

Lynd, R. S. 1945. *Knowledge for What?* Princeton University Press, Princeton.

Malik, S. C. 1971. New trends in archaeology: a review. *Proceedings of the Nagpur University Archaeological Congress*, Nagpur.

Malina, J. 1977. System of analytical archaeography. *Studie Archeologického Ústavu ČSAV v Brně* 5(2). Academia, Prague.

   1980a. Metody experimentu v archeologii. *Studie Archeologického Ústavu ČSAV v Brně* 8(1). Academia, Prague.

   1980b. *Archeologie Včera Dnes Aneb Mají Archeologové Šedé Hmoty Více za Nehty než za Ušima?* Jihočeské Museum, České Budějovice.

   1983. Archaeology and experiment. *Norwegian Archaeological Review* 16: 69–85.

Malinowski, B. 1939. The group and the individual in functional analysis. *American Journal of Sociology* 44: 938–64.

Malmer, M. P. 1962. Jungneolithische Studien. *Acta Archaeologia Lundensia*, Series in 8°, 2.

Mannheim, K. 1953. *Essays on Society and Social Psychology*. Routledge & Kegan Paul, London.

Markarjan, E. S. 1969. *Očerki Teorii Kultury*. State Publishing House for Scientific Literature, Jerevan.

Marquardt, W. H. 1978. Advances in archaeological seriation. In M. B. Schiffer (ed.) *Advances in Archaeological Method and Theory*, vol. 1, 257–314. Academic Press, New York, London.

Maršak, B. I. 1970. Kod dlja opisanija keramiki Pendžikenta V–VI vv. In B. A. Kolčin (ed.) *Arheologija i Estestvennye Nauki*, 25–52. Nauka, Moscow.

Marshack, A. 1977. The meander as a system: the analysis and recognition of iconographic units in Upper Palaeolithic compositions. In P. J. Ucko (ed.) *Form in Indigenous Art: Schematisation of Aboriginal Australia and Prehistoric Europe*, 286–317. Australian Institute of Aboriginal Studies, Canberra.

Martin, P. S. 1971. The revolution in archaeology. *American Antiquity* 36: 1–8.

Masson, V. M. 1969. Priroda i proishoždenie civilizacii. *Priroda* 3: 2–14.

   1970. Razvitie teoretičeskih osnov sovetskoj arheologii. *Teoretičeskie Osnovy Sovetskoj Arheologii (Tezisy Dokladov na Teoretičeskom Seminare LOIA AN SSR I–IV 1970 G.)*, 23–7. Institut Arheologii Akademii Nauk SSSR, Leningrad.

Masson, V. M. and Borjaz, V. N. 1975. (eds.) *Predmet i Objekt Arheologii i Voprosy Metodiki Arheologičeskih Issledovanij*. Soviet Academy of Sciences, Leningrad: Seminar of April 1975. Nauka, Leningrad.

Matthews, J. 1963. Application of matrix analysis to archaeological problems. *Nature* 198(4,884): 930–4.

McCormick, B. H. 1963. The Illinois pattern recognition computer: ILLIAC III. *Ire Transactions Electron. Comput.* EC-12(5): 791–813.

McNairn, B. 1980. *The Method and Theory of V. Gordon Childe: Economic, Social and Cultural Interpretations of Prehistory.* Edinburgh University Press, Edinburgh.

Meggers, B. J. 1968. (ed.) *Anthropological Archaeology in the Americas.* The Anthropological Society of Washington, Washington.

Meggers, B. J. and Evans, C. 1975. La 'seriación fordiana' como método para construir una cronología relativa. *Revista de la Universidad Católica* 3(10): 11–40.

Meier, C. 1973. Die Enstehung der Historie. In R. Koselleck and W. D. Stempel (eds.) *Geschichte – Ereignis und Erzählung,* 251–306. Fink, Munich.

Meletinskij, E. M. 1976. *Poetika Myfa.* Nauka, Moscow.

Melton, M. A. 1960. Intravalley variation in slope angles related to microclimate and erosional environment. *Bulletin of the Geological Society of America* 71: 133–44.

Melzer, D. J., Fowler, D. D. and Sabloff, J. A. 1986. (eds.) *American Archaeology Past and Future: A Celebration of the Society for American Archeology 1935–1985.* Smithsonian Institution Press, Washington.

Menghin, O. 1952. Urgeschichtliche Grundfragen. In V. Valjavec (ed.) *Historia Mundi,* vol. 1, 229–58. Francke, Bern, Munich.

Merriam, D. F. and Sneath, P. H. A. 1966. Quantitative comparison of contour maps. *Journal of Geophysical Research* 71: 1,105–15.

Miller, D. and Tilley, C. 1984. (eds.) *Ideology, Power and Prehistory.* Cambridge University Press, Cambridge.

Moberg, C.-A. 1969. *Introduktion till Arkeologi: Jämförande och Nordisk Fornkunskap.* Natur och Kultur, Stockholm.

1970a. Archaeograms and historical entities: comments on analytical archaeology. *Norwegian Archaeological Review* 3: 21–4.

1970b. Discussion consécutive à l'exposé par M. J. Doran de la communication de M. D. L. Clarke. In J.-C. Gardin (ed.) *Archéologie et calculateurs: problèmes sémiologiques et mathématiques,* 359–60. CNRS, Paris.

1976. *Introduction à l'archéologie.* Maspéro, Paris.

1981. (ed.) *Similar Finds? Similar Interpretations?* University of Gothenburg Press, Gothenburg.

Mohapatra, G. C. 1974. Lithic industries in Himachal Pradesh. In A. K. Ghosh (ed.) *Perspectives in Palaeoanthropology,* 199–212. K. L. Mukhopadhyaya, Calcutta.

Mongajt, A. L. 1967. Arheologičeskie kultury i etničeskie obščnosti (K voprosu o metodike istoriko-arheologičeskih issledovanij). *Narody Azii i Afriki* 1: 53–65.

Moore, J. A. and Keene, A. S. 1983. *Archaeological Hammers and Theories.* Academic Press, New York.

Moscati, P. 1987. *Archeologia e calcolatori.* Giunti, Rome.

Moszyński, K. 1962. *O Sposobach Badania Kultury Materialnej Prasłowian.* Ossolineum, Wrocław.

Muller, J. 1968. The generative analysis of art styles. Paper read at the 67th

Annual Meeting of the American Anthropological Association, Seattle, Washington.

Mumford, L. 1967. *The Myth of the Machine: Technics and Human Development.* Harcourt, Brace and World, New York.

Nalimov, V. V. 1966. *Novye Idei v Planirovanii Eksperimenta.* Nauka, Moscow.

1971. *Teoria Eksperimenta.* Nauka, Moscow.

Narasimhan, R. 1966. Syntax-directed interpretation of classes of pictures. *Communication Association Comput. Mach.* 9: 166–73.

Narr, K. J. 1978a. Typologie und Seriation. *Bonner Jahrbücher* 178: 21–30.

1978b. *Zeitmasse in der Urgeschichte.* Westdeutscher Verlag, Opladen.

Neustupný, E. 1971. Whither archaeology? *Antiquity* 45: 34–9.

1973a. Jednoduchá metoda archeologické analýzy. *Památky Archeologické* 64: 169–234.

1973b. Sekvenční metoda vedení archeologických výzkumů. *Archeologické Rozhledy* 25: 300–28.

1983. *Demografie Pravěkých Pohřebišť.* Archaeological Institute of the Czech Academy of Sciences, Prague.

1986. Nástin archeologické metody. *Archeologické Rozhledy* 38: 525–49.

Nikiforov, V. N. 1971. K. Marks i F. Engels ob asiatskom sposobe proizvodstva. In G. F. Kim (ed.) *Problemy dokapitalistieskih Obšestv v Stranah Vostoka,* 3–44. Nauka, Moscow.

Okladnikov, A. P. 1959. 'Proischožděnie semji, častnoj sobstvenosti i gosudarstva' F. Engelsa i sovremennost. *Sovetskaja Arheologija* 4: 5–9.

Orme, B. J. 1974. Twentieth-century prehistorians and the idea of ethnographic parallels. *Man* 9: 199–212.

1981. *Anthropology for Archaeologists: An Introduction.* Duckworth, London, Cornell University Press, Ithaca.

Orton, C. 1982. *Mathematics in Archaeology.* Cambridge University Press, Cambridge.

Otto, K. H. 1953. Archäologische Kulturen und die Erforschung der konkreten Geschichte von Stämmen und Völkerschaften. *Ethnographisch-Archäologische Zeitschrift* 1: 1–27.

Otto, K. H. and Brachmann, H. J. 1975. (eds.) *Moderne Probleme der Archäologie.* Akademie-Verlag, East Berlin.

Parry, M. 1930. *Studies in the Epic Technique of Oral Verse-Making.* Harvard University Press, Cambridge, Mass.

Patrick, L. E. 1985. Is there an archaeological record? In M. B. Schiffer (ed.) *Advances in Archaeological Method and Theory,* vol. 8, 27–62. Academic Press, New York, London.

Permjakov, G. L. 1970. *Ot Pogovorki do Skazki: Zametki po Obščej Teorii Kliše.* Nauka, Moscow.

Piggott, S. 1960. *Approach to Archaeology.* A. & C. Black, London.

Pike, K. L. 1967. *Language in Relation to a Unified Theory of the Structure of Human Behavior.* Mouton, The Hague, Paris.

Pleiner, R. and Rybová, A. 1978. (eds.) *Pravěké Dějiny Čech.* Academia, Prague.

Plog, F. T. 1974. *The Study of Prehistoric Change.* Academic Press, New York, London.

1975. Systems theory in archaeological research. *Annual Review of Anthropology* 4: 207–24.

1978. Cultural resource management and the 'New Archaeology'. In C. L. Redman, *et al.* (eds.) *Social Archaeology: Beyond Subsistence and Dating,* 421–9. Academic Press, New York.

Podborský, V., Kazdová, E., Košťuřík, P. and Weber, Z. 1977. *Numerický Kód Moravské Malované Keramiky: Problémy Deskripce v Archeologii.* Brno University Press, Brno.

Poršnev, B. F. 1974. *O Načale Čelovečeskoj Istorii.* Mysl, Moscow.

Price, B. 1982. Culture materialism: a theoretical review. *American Antiquity* 47: 709–41.

Propp, V. J. 1928. *Morfologija Skazki.* Nauka, Leningrad.

1946. *Istoričeskie Korni Volšebnoj Skazki.* Nauka, Leningrad.

1968. *Morphology of the Folktale.* University of Texas Press, Austin.

1976. *Folklor i Dejstvitelnost.* Nauka, Moscow.

Quimby, G. L. 1960. Habitat, culture, and archaeology. In G. E. Dole and R. L. Carneiro (eds.) *Essays on the Science of Culture: In Honor of Leslie A. White,* 380–9. Thomas Y. Crowell, New York.

Raab, L. M. and Klinger, T. C. 1980. (eds.) *The Design of Archaeological Research.* Aldine, Chicago.

Rakitov, A. I. 1969. K voprosu o strukture istoričeskogo issledovanija. In A. V. Gulyga and J. A. Levada (eds.) *Filosofskie Problemy Istoričeskoj Nauki,* 161–85. Nauka, Moscow.

Rappoport, A. 1968. General system theory. *International Encyclopedia of the Social Sciences* 15: 452–8.

Rathje, W. L. 1974. The Garbage project: a new way of looking at the problems of archaeology. *Archaeology* 27: 236–41.

Read, D. W. 1982. Toward a theory of archaeological classification. In R. Whallon and J. A. Brown (eds.) *Essays on Archaeological Typology,* 56–92. Center for American Archaeology Press, Evanston.

Redman, C. L. 1973. (ed.) *Research and Theory in Current Archaeology.* Wiley, New York.

1978. Multivariate artifact analysis: a basis for multidimensional interpretations. In C. L. Redman *et al.* (eds.) *Social Archaeology: Beyond Subsistence and Dating,* 159–92. Academic Press, New York.

Redman, C. L., Berman, M. J., Curtin, E. V., Langhorne Jr, W. T., Versaggi, N. M. and Wanser, J. C. 1978. (eds.) *Social Archaeology: Beyond Subsistence and Dating.* Academic Press, New York.

Regnier, S. 1977. Sériation des niveaux de plusieurs tranches de fouille dans une zone archéologique homogène. In M. Borillo, W. Fernandez de la Vega and

A. Guenoche (eds.) *Raisonnement et méthodes mathématiques en archéologie*, 146–55. CNRS, Paris.

Renfrew, A. C. 1969a. David L. Clarke: *Analytical Archaeology*, London, Methuen, 1968, and Sally R. Binford, Lewis R. Binford (eds.) *New Perspectives in Archaeology*, Chicago, Aldine, 1968. *Antiquity* 43: 241–4.

1969b. Peter Haggett: *Locational Analysis in Human Geography*, London, Edward Arnold, 1965, and Richard J. Chorley and Peter Haggett (eds.) *Models in Geography*, London, Methuen, 1967. *Antiquity* 43: 74–5.

1973a. *Social Archaeology: An Inaugural Lecture*. University of Southampton Press, Southampton.

1973b. (ed.) *The Explanation of Culture Change: Models in Prehistory*. Duckworth, London.

1978. Trajectory discontinuity and morphogenesis: the implications of catastrophe theory for archaeology. *American Antiquity* 43: 203–22.

1979. (ed.) *Transformations: Mathematical Approaches to Culture Change*. Academic Press, New York.

1982. *Towards an Archaeology of Mind: An Inaugural Lecture*. Cambridge University Press, Cambridge.

1983. Divided we stand: aspect of archaeology and information. *American Antiquity* 48: 3–16.

1984. *Approaches to Social Archaeology*. Edinburgh University Press, Edinburgh.

Renfrew, A. C., Rowlands, M. J. and Segraves, B. A. 1982. (eds.) *Theory and Explanation in Archaeology: The Southampton Conference*. Academic Press, New York.

Richards, J. D. and Ryan, N. S. 1985. *Data Processing in Archaeology*. Cambridge University Press, Cambridge.

Rivera, M. A. 1979. *Panorama de las Investigaciónes Arquelógicas en Chile: Revista Documentos de Trabajo*. Chile University Press, Antofagasta.

Rivkina, R. V. and Vinokur, A. V. 1968. *Socialnyj Eksperiment*. Naukam Moskva.

Rohlf, F. J. and Sokal, R. R. 1967. Taxonomic structure from randomly and systematically scanned biological images. *Systematic Zoology* 16: 246–60.

Roper, D. C. 1976. A trend-surface analysis of Central Plains radiocarbon dates. *American Antiquity* 41: 181–9.

Rosen, R. 1967. *Optimality Principles in Biology*. Butterworths, London.

Rouse, I. 1970. Comments on analytical archaeology: classification for what? *Norwegian Archaeological Review* 3: 4–12.

1972. *Introduction to Prehistory: A Systematic Approach*. McGraw-Hill, New York.

1973. Analytic, synthetic, and comparative archaeology. In C. L. Redman (ed.) *Research and Theory in Current Archaeology*, 21–31. Wiley, New York.

Rowlands, M. J. 1982. Processual archaeology as historical social science. In A. C.

Renfrew, M. J. Rowlands and B. A. Segraves (eds.) *Theory and Explanation in Archaeology: The Southampton Conference*, 155–74. Academic Press, New York.

Rowlett, R. M. and Pollnac, R. B. 1971. Multivariate analysis of Marnian La Tène cultural groups. In F. R. Hodson, D. G. Kendall and P. Tautu (eds.) *Mathematics in the Archaeological and Historical Sciences*, 46–58. Edinburgh University Press, Edinburgh.

Rüsen, J. 1983. *Historische Vernunft*. Vandenhoek-Ruprecht, Göttingen.

Rybakov, B. A. 1978. Istorizm arheologii. *Kratkie Soobščenija* 152: 5–7.

Sabloff, J. A. 1981. (ed.) *Simulations in Archaeology*. University of New Mexico Press, Albuquerque.

Sackett, J. R. 1969. Factor analysis and artifact typology. *American Anthropologist* 71: 1,125–30.

Salmon, M. H. 1978. What can systems theory do for archaeology? *American Antiquity* 43: 174–83.

1980. Reply to Lowe and Barth. *American Antiquity* 45: 575–9.

Salmon, M. H. and Salmon, W. 1982. *Philosophy and Archaeology*. Academic Press, New York, London.

Sanders, W. T. and Price, B. J. 1968. *Mesoamerica: The Evolution of a Civilization*. Random House, New York.

Sangmeister, E. 1967. Methoden der Urgeschichtswissenschaft. *Saeculum* 18: 199–244.

Santley, R. S. and Turner, E. R. 1977. On theory in archaeology. *Current Anthropology* 18: 747–9.

Sapir, E. 1949. The emergence of the concept of personality in a study of cultures. In *Selected Writings of Edward Sapir*, 590–7. University of California Press, Berkeley and Los Angeles.

Schiffer, M. B. 1972. Archaeological context and systemic context. *American Antiquity* 37: 156–65.

1976. *Behavioural Archaeology*. Academic Press, New York, London.

1978 (ed.). *Advances in Archaeology*, vol. 1. Academic Press, New York – London, continued every year.

1981. A synthetic model of archaeological inference. In P. Grebinger (ed.) *Discovering Past Behaviour*, 123–39. Gordon and Breach, New York.

1983. Toward the identification of formation processes. *American Antiquity* 48: 675–706.

1987. *Formation Processes of the Archaeological Record*. University of New Mexico Press, Albuquerque.

Schild, R. 1980. (ed.) *Unconventional Archaeology: New Approaches and Goals in Polish Archaeology*. Ossolineum, Wrocław, Warsaw.

Schnapp, A. 1980. (ed.) *L'archéologie aujourd'hui*. Hachette, Paris.

Schröder, K. 1969. Geometrische Probleme im System ARDOC. *Archäographie* 1: 93–105.

Schulz, W. 1970. *Kausalität und Experiment in der Sozialwissenschaften: Methodologie und Forschungstechnik.* Hase und Koehler, Mainz.

Schweitzer, B. 1938. Strukturforschung in Archäologie und Vorgeschichte. *Neue Jahrbücher für das kalssische Altertum, Geschichte und deutsche Literatur und für Pädagogik* 13 (N. F. 1): 162–79.

Schweizer, B. 1969. Das Problem der Form in der Kunst des Alterstums. In U. Hausmann (ed.) *Allgemeine Grundlagen der Archäologie*, 163–203. C. H. Beck, Munich.

Sellnow, I. 1961. *Grundprinzipien einer Periodisierung der Urgeschichte: ein Beitrag auf Grundlage ethnographischen Materials*, 15–38. Akademie-Verlag, East Berlin.

Semenov, J. I. 1967. Über die Periodisierung der Urgeschichte. *Ethnographisch-Archäologische Zeitschrift* 8(1).

Semenov, S. A. 1964. *Prehistoric Technology.* Adams and Dart, Bath; Cory, Adams and MacKay, London; Barnes and Noble, New York.

1968. *Razvitie Tehniki v Kamennom Veke.* Nauka, Leningrad.

1974. *Proischoždenie Zemledelija.* Nauka, Leningrad.

1978. Sistemnyj podchod i 'analitičeskaja arheologija' D. Klarka. *Kratkie Soobščenija* 152: 43–8.

Shanks, M. and Tilley, C. 1987a. *Re-Constructing Archaeology.* Cambridge University Press, Cambridge.

1978b. *Social Theory and Archaeology.* Polity Press, Cambridge.

Shaw, G. B. 1956. *Music in London*, vol. 3. Constable, London.

Shennan, S. J. and Wilcock, J. D. 1975. Shape and style variation in central German Bell Beakers: a computer-assisted study. *Science and Archaeology* 15: 17–31.

Sheridan, A. and Bailey, G. 1981. (eds.) *Economic Archaeology: Toward an Integration of Ecological and Social Approaches.* BAR International Series, Supplement 96, Oxford.

Sibson, R. 1977. Multidimensional scaling in theory and practice. In M. Borillo, W. Fernandez de la Vega and A. Guenoche (eds.) *Raisonnement et méthodes mathématiques en archéologie*, 73–97. CRNS, Paris.

Sieveking, G. de, Longworth, I. H. and Wilson, K. E. 1976. (eds.) *Problems in Economic and Social Archaeology.* Duckworth, London.

Simek, J. F. 1987. Integrating pattern and context in spatial archaeology. *Journal of Archaeological Science* 11: 405–20.

Sklenář, K. 1983. *Archaeology in Central Europe: The First 500 Years.* Leicester University Press, Leicester.

Smirnov, E. S. 1928. Mathematische Studien über individuelle und Kongregationenvariabilität. Verhandlungen des V. internationalen Kongresses für Vererbungswissenschaft (Berlin 1927), 2: 1,373–92. Bornträger, Leipzig.

1969. *Taksonomičeskij Analiz.* Moscow University Press, Moscow.

Smith, B. D. 1977. Archaeological inference and inductive confirmation. *American Anthropologist* 79: 598–617.

Sneath, P. H. A. 1967. Trend-surface analysis of transformation grids. *Journal of Zoology* 151: 65–122.

Sneath, P. H. A. and Sokal, R. R. 1973 (eds.) *Numerical Taxonomy: The Principle and Practice of Numerical Classification.* W. H. Freeman, San Francisco.

Sokal, R. R. and Rohlf, F. J. 1966. Random scanning of taxonomic characters. *Nature* 210: 461–2.

Solberg, B. 1986. Automatic versus intuitive and impressionistic classification of Norwegian spearheads from A.D. 550–1100. *Norwegian Archaeological Review* 19: 77–89.

Sorokin, P. A. 1958. *Fads and Foibles in Modern Sociology and Related Sciences.* Vision Press, London.

Soudský, B. 1967. *Principles of Automatic Data Treatment Applied on Neolithic Pottery.* Archaeological Institute of Czechoslovak Academy of Sciences. Prague.

Spaulding, A. C. 1953. Statistical techniques for the discovery of artifact types. *American Antiquity* 18: 305–13.

1978. Artifact classes, associations, and seriation. In R. C. Dunnell and E. S. Hall (eds.) *Archaeological Essays in Honour of Irving B. Rouse,* 27–40. Mouton, The Hague.

Spriggs, M. 1977. (ed.) *Archaeology and Anthropology: Areas of Mutual Interest.* BAR International Series, Supplement 19, Oxford.

Spriggs, M. 1984. (ed.) *Marxist Perspectives in Archaeology.* Cambridge University Press, Cambridge.

Šprincová, S. 1972. K některým problémům vymezování regionů. *Acta Universitatis Palackinae Olomoucensis, Facultas Philosophica, Supplementum* 20: 80–2.

Steiger, W. L. 1971. Analytical archaeology? *Mankind* 8: 67–70.

Stiles, D. 1977. Ethnoarchaeology: a discussion of methods and applications. *Man* 12: 87–103.

Stjernquist, B. 1966. Models of commercial diffusion in prehistoric times. *Scripta Minora Regiae Societatis Humaniorum Litterarum Lundensis* (1965–6) 2. C. W. K. Gleerup, Lund.

Stoetzel, J. and Lazarsfeld, P. 1965. Définition d'intention et espace d'attributs. In R. Boudon and P. Lazarsfeld (eds.) *Le Vocabulaire des sciences sociales: concepts et indices,* 183–93. Mouton, Paris.

Stoljar, A. D. 1978a. Arheologičeskie gipotezy proischoždenija izobrazitelnogo iskusstva v svete faktov i teorii (uroki istoriografii). *Problemy Istoriografii i Istočnikovedenija Otečestvennoj i Všeobščej Istorii,* 186–201. Leningrad University Press, Leningrad.

1978b. Evoljucija formy 'naturalnogo maketa' v genezise verhnepaleolitičeskogo animalizma. In R. S. Vasilevskij (ed.) *Pervobytno Iskusstvo,* 86–105. Nauka, Novosibirsk.

Swadesh, M. 1952. Lexico-statistic dating of prehistoric ethnic contacts, with special reference to North American Indians and Eskimos. *Proceedings of the American Philosophical Society* 96: 452–63.

1959. Linguistics as an instrument of prehistory. *South-western Journal of Anthropology* 15: 20–35.

1972. *The Origin and Diversification of Language*. Routledge & Kegan Paul, London.

Swain, P. H. and Fu, K. S. 1972. Stochastic programmed grammars for syntactic pattern recognition. *Pattern Recognition* 4: 83–100.

Tabaczyński, S. 1971. Kultura: znaczenie pojęcia i problemy interpretacyjne w badaniach archeologicznych. *Archeologia Polski* 16: 19–36.

Tabaczyński, S. and Pleszczyńska, E. 1974. O teoretycznych podstawach archeologii: prezentacja i próba analizy poglądów D. L. Clarke's. *Archeologia Polski* 19: 7–94.

Taylor, W. W. 1948. A study of archaeology. *American Anthropological Association Memoir* 69. Menasha.

1967. *A Study of Archaeology*. Arcturus Books, Southern Illinois University Press, Carbondale and Edwardsville.

1972. Old wine and new skins: a contemporary parable. In M. P. Leone (ed.) *Contemporary Archaeology: A Guide to Theory and Contributions*, 28–33. Southern Illinois University Press, Carbondale and Edwardsville.

Teoretičeskie Osnovy Sovetskoj Arheologii (Tezisy Dokladov na Teoretičeskom Seminare LOIA AN SSSR I–IV 1970 G.). 1970. Archaeological Institute of Soviet Academy of Sciences, Leningrad.

Teoria i Metody Archeologičeskih Issledovanij. 1980. Nauka, Kiev.

Thomas, D. H. 1972. A computer simulation model of Great Basin Shoshonean subsistence and settlement patterns. In D. L. Clarke (ed.) *Models in Archaeology*, 671–704. Methuen, London.

1973. An empirical test for Steward's model of Great Basin settlement patterns. *American Antiquity* 38: 155–76.

1978. The awful truth about statistics in archaeology. *American Antiquity* 43: 231–44.

1979. *Predicting the Past: An Introduction to Anthropological Archaeology*. Holt, Rinehart and Winston, New York.

Thompson D'Arcy, W. 1917, 1952. *On Growth and Form*. Cambridge University Press, Cambridge.

Tooker, E. 1982. Ethnography by archaeologists. *1978 Proceedings of the American Ethnological Society*, American Ethnological Society, Washington.

Topolski, J. 1976. *Methodology of History*. PWN, Warsaw, D. Reidel, Dordrecht.

Tran Duc Thao. 1984. *Investigations into the Origin of Language and Consciousness*. D. Reidel, Boston.

Tretjakov, P. N. 1948. *Vostočnoslavjanskie Plema*. Soviet Academy of Sciences Press, Moscow.

1950. Proizvedenija J. V. Stalina o jazyke i jazykoznanii i voprosy proischoždenija narodov. *Voprosy Istorii* 10: 3–18.

1970. Arheologičeskie kultury i etničeskie obščnosti. *Teoretičeskie Osnovy Sovetskoj Arheologii (Tezisy Dokladov na Teoretičeskom Seminare LOIA AN SSR I–IV 1970 G.)*, 29–33. Archaeological Institute of Soviet Academy of Sciences, Leningrad.

Trigger, B. G. 1968. *Beyond History: The Methods of Prehistory*. Holt, Rinehart and Winston, New York.

1970. Aims in prehistoric archaeology. *Antiquity* 44: 26–37.

1978a. No longer another planet. *Antiquity* 52: 193–8.

1978b. *Time and Traditions: Essays in Archaeological Interpretation*. Edinburgh University Press, Edinburgh.

1980. *Gordon Childe: Revolutions in Archaeology*. Thames and Hudson, London.

1984a. Archaeology at the cross-roads: what's new? *Annual Report of Anthropology* 13: 275–300.

1984b. Alternative archaeologies: nationalist, colonialist, imperialist. *Man* 19: 355–70.

1986. Prospects for a world archaeology. *World Archaeology* 18: 1–20.

Trudzik, Z. 1965. Żrodła archeologiczne na tle problematyki kultury. *Archaeologia Polski* 10: 42–74.

1971. O przedmiocie archeologii i jej procesie badawczym. *Studia Archeologiczne* 4: 5–69.

True, D. L. and Matson, R. G. 1970. Cluster analysis and multidimensional scaling of archaeological sites in northern Chile. *Science* 169(3,951): 1,201–3.

Tugby, D. J. 1958. A typological analysis of axes and choppers from southeast Australia. *American Antiquity* 24: 24–33.

1965. Archaeological objectives and statistical methods: A frontier in archaeology. *American Antiquity* 31: 1–16.

Tuggle, H. D., Townsend, A. H., Riley, T. J. and Morgan, C. J. 1972. Laws, systems, and research designs: a discussion of explanation in archaeology. *American Antiquity* 37: 3–12.

Turnbaugh, W. A. 1978. Floods and archaeology. *American Antiquity* 43: 593–607.

Tyldesley, J. A., Johnson, J. S. and Snape, S. R. 1985. 'Shape' in archaeological artifacts: two case studies using a new analytical method. *Oxford Journal of Archaeology* 4: 19–30.

Tyler, S. 1969. (ed.) *Cognitive Anthropology*. Holt, Rinehart and Winston, New York.

Ucko, P. J., Tringham, R. and Dimbleby, G. W. 1972. (eds.) *Man, Settlement and Urbanism*. Duckworth, London.

Udalcov, A. D. 1953. (ed.) *Protiv Vulgarizacii Marksizma v Arheologii*. Soviet Academy of Sciences Press, Moscow.

Uhr, L. 1973. *Pattern Recognition, Learning, and Thought: Computer-Programmed Models of Higher Mental Processes*. Prentice-Hall, Englewood Cliffs.

Urbańczyk, P. 1983. O mozliwosciach poznawczych archeologii. *Przegląd Archeologiczny* 29: 5–49.

Vašíček, Z. and Jičín, R. 1971. The problem of similarity of shape. *Systematic Zoology* 21: 91–6.

Vértes, L. 1968. Rates of evolution in Palaeolithic technology. *Acta Archaeologica Academiae Scientiarum Hungaricae* 20: 3–17.

Vierra, R. K. and Carlson, D. L. 1981. Factor analysis, random data and patterned results. *American Antiquity* 46: 272–83.

Voorrips, A. 1985. (ed.) *To Pattern the Past: Mathematical Methods in Archaeology. Pact* 11.

Voprosy teorii i metodologii arheologičeskoj nauki. 1978. *Kratkie Soobščenija* 152.

Vossen, R. 1970. Klassifikationsprobleme und Klassifikationssysteme in der amerikanischen Archäologie. *Acta Praehistorica et Archaeologica* 1: 29–79.

Wahle, E. 1941. Zur ethnischen Deutung frühgeschichtlicher Kulturprovinzen: Grenze der frühgeschichtlichen Erkenntnis, 1. *Sitzungsberichte der Heidelberger Akademie der Wissenschaften phil.-hist. Klasse* (1940–1), 2.

1964. *Tradition und Auftrag prähistorischer Forschung: Ausgewählte Abhandlungen*. Duncker, Humbolt, Berlin.

Wartołowska, Z. 1964. Metoda dialektyczna w badaniach archeologicznych. *Światowit* 25: 213–36.

Washburn, D. K. 1977. A symmetry analysis of Upper Gila area ceramic design. *Papers of the Peabody Museum of Art and Ethnology* 68. Harvard University Press, Cambridge, Mass.

1983. (ed.) *Structure and Cognition in Art*. Cambridge University Press, Cambridge.

Waterhouse, V. G. 1974. *The History and Developments of Tagmemics*. Mouton, The Hague, Paris.

Watson, P. J., LeBlanc, S. A. and Redman, C. L. 1971. *Explanation in Archaeology: An Explicitly Scientific Approach*. Columbia University Press, New York.

1974. The covering law model in archaeology: practical uses and formal interpretations. *World Archaeology* 6: 125–32.

1984. *Archaeological Explanation: The Scientific Method in Archaeology*. Columbia University Press, New York.

Watson, R. A. 1972. 'The 'new archaeology' of the 1960s. *Antiquity* 46: 210–15.

Weawer, W. 1948. Science and complexity. *American Scientist* 36: 536–44.

West, F. H. 1983–4. Typologie und Interpretation. *Jahrbuch des Bernischen Historischen Museums* 63/4: 283–91.

Whallon, Jr, R. 1968. Investigations of late prehistoric social organization in New York State. In S. R. Binford and L. R. Binford (eds.) *New Perspectives in Archaeology*, 223–44. Aldine, Chicago.

1972. A new approach to pottery typology. *American Antiquity* 37: 13–33.

1977. The application of formal methods of typology in archaeological analysis. In M. Borillo, W. Fernandez de la Vega and A. Guenoche (eds.)

Raisonnement et méthodes mathématiques en archéologie, 201–13. CNRS, Paris.

Whallon, R. and Brown, J. A. 1982. (eds.) *Essays on Archaeological Typology*. Center for American Archaeology Press, Evanston.

White, J. P. and Thomas, D. H. 1972. What mean these stones? Ethno-taxonomic models and archaeological interpretations in the New Guinea Highlands. In D. L. Clarke (ed.) *Models in Archaeology*, 275–308. Methuen, London.

White, L. A. 1959. *The Evolution of Culture: The Development of Civilization to the Fall of Rome*. McGraw-Hill, New York.

Whitley, A. J. M. 1986. Archaeology and the social sciences: why they should not be integrated. *Archaeological Review Cambridge* 5: 206–14.

Wilcock, J. D. 1971. Non-statistical applications of the computer in archaeology. In F. R. Hodson, D. G. Kendall and P. Tautu (eds.) *Mathematics in the Archaeological and Historical Sciences*, 470–81. Edinburgh University Press, Edinburgh.

Wilcock, J. D. and Laflin, S. 1974. (eds.) *Computer Application in Archaeology. Proceedings of the annual conference of the University of Birmingham Computer Centre*. University of Birmingham Press, Birmingham.

Willey, G. R. 1973. Peter J. Ucko, Ruth Tringham, G. W. Dimbleby (eds.) *Man, Settlement and Urbanism*, London, Duckworth, 1972. *Antiquity* 47: 269–79.

Willey, G. R. and Phillips, P. 1965. *Method and Theory in American Archaeology*. University of Chicago Press, Chicago.

Wolf, E. R. 1984. Culture: panacea or problem? *American Antiquity* 49: 393–400.

Wolfram, S. 1986. *Zur Theoriediskussion in der prähistorischen Archäologie Grossbritanniens: ein forschungsgeschichtlicher Überlick über die Jahre 1968–1982*. BAR International Series, Supplement 306, Oxford.

Wylie, A. 1985. The reaction against analogy. In M. B. Schiffer (ed.) *Advances in Archaeological Method and Theory*, vol. 8, 63–111. Academic Press, New York, London.

Yellen, J. E. 1977. *Archaeological Approaches to the Present: Models for Reconstructing the Past*. Academic Press, New York.

Zaharuk, Ju. N. 1976. Arheologičeskaja kultura: kategorija ontologičeskaja ili gnoseologičeskaja. *Vostočnaja Evropa v Epohe Kamnja i Bronzy*, 3–10. Nauka, Moscow.

Żak, J. 1975. Teoretyczne uwagi o refleksji prahistorycznej. *Archeologia Polski* 14: 28–59.

Ziegert, H. 1964. Archäologie und Ethnologie: zur Zusammenarbeit zweier Wissenschaften. *Berliner Jahrbuch für Vor- und Frühgeschichte* 4: 102–49.

General index

abstraction, 17, 124
'Achsenzeit', 1
adaptation, 73–4, 222, 244
ages, systems of; evolutionists', 42;
  geological, 69; Nilsson's, 42; 19th
  century, 51–2, Renaissance, 19, 20, 21;
  Soviet bloc, 139, 141–2; three age system,
  26, 30; *see also*: Thomsen, C. J. (Index of
  names)
agrobiology, 227
Altamira, Spain, 48
America, South, 125
analogy, 223–4; ethnographic, 215
analysis, internal, 107, 113
analytical archaeology, 116
analytical reality, 120, 242
analytical–synchronic studies, 123
anatomy of speech, 257
ancient world, 9–12, 25, 270; *see also*: Greece;
  Mesopotamia; Rome
Anglo-Saxons: /Continental differences,
  ix-x, 82, 87; empiricism, 71, 105, 109–13,
  134; *see also*: Britain; United States
animal remains, 151
animism, 42, 89
Annalistes, French, x, 86
anomalous evidence, 52–3, 122
anthropogeography, 55–6
anthropological school, 42, 58
anthropology: and evolutionism, 42, 53, 58;
  functionalism, 242; and history, 241;
  hypotheses, 7, 241–3; indicators, 243;
  language of, 241, 242; migrationism and,
  62; and neo-evolutionism, 91, 242; New
  Archaeology and, 123, 126; relationship to
  archaeology and prehistory, 48, 109, 129,
  247; and social archaeology, 129; as social
  science, 241; and sociology, 243, 248;
  spatial concepts, 55–6; structural, 131, 242;
  terminology, 218, 219, 241, 242
anthropometry, 183, 195
antiquarianism, 11–12, 19–20, 24–32, 36,
  149–50; *see also* collecting

archaeography, 34, 249, 251
archaeology: classical, 27, 46, 48, 87;
  prehistoric, *see individual aspects*
arche, 1–7, 271
archetypes, Jungian, 84
architecture, 131
arithmetics, political, 16
art: artefacts as works of, 27, 30–1, 157–8;
  aesthetic sense of, 2, 13, 84, 149; history
  of, (binary opposition), 87–8,
  (comparative method), 56,
  (Enlightenment), 23, 24, (and prehistoric
  art), 89, (Renaissance), 15, 18–19, (spatial
  concepts), 56–7, (terminology), 219, (20th
  century), 56–7, 87–8, (typological
  method), 46; prehistoric, 48, 87, 88–90,
  131, 145–6, 256
artefacts, 270; as art, 27, 30–1, 157–8;
  attributes, 160, 260; concept, 150–1;
  conscious/unconscious characteristics,
  258; description, 156, 256, 160; 18th
  century, 27–8, 29; experiments, 241;
  historical view, 154; loss of superiority as
  source, 151–3; makers' attitudes to,
  160, 201–3, 260;
  mediaeval interpretations, 14; methods of
  deposit, 158; modern conceptions, 112–13,
  117, 155; New Archaeology and, 126–7;
  19th century analysis, 50; origins, theories
  of, 14, 28, 149; semiology, 130; settlement
  archaeology, 132; structure, 130–2;
  terminology, 221; transformation of, 157;
  trial and error, 258; *see also*: collecting;
  tools
artificial intelligence, 137
assemblages, 38, 47, 106–7, 111, 117, 150
association techniques, 193, 206, 207, 209
astronomy, 71
attributes: of artefacts, 160, 260; concept of,
  117, 221, 252; and description, 162, 194; in
  research process, 156; as indicators, 155;
  selection, 194, 201; weighting, 161
Australian aborigines, 267

Index of names